The Unknown Europe
—— *How Eastern Europe Got That Way* ——

James R. Payton Jr.

CASCADE *Books* • Eugene, Oregon

THE UNKNOWN EUROPE
How Eastern Europe Got That Way

Copyright © 2021 James R. Payton Jr.. All rights reserved. Except for brief quotations in critical publications or reviews, no part of this book may be reproduced in any manner without prior written permission from the publisher. Write: Permissions, Wipf and Stock Publishers, 199 W. 8th Ave., Suite 3, Eugene, OR 97401.

Cascade Books
An Imprint of Wipf and Stock Publishers
199 W. 8th Ave., Suite 3
Eugene, OR 97401

www.wipfandstock.com

PAPERBACK ISBN: 978-1-6667-0475-4
HARDCOVER ISBN: 978-1-6667-0476-1
EBOOK ISBN: 978-1-6667-0477-8

Cataloguing-in-Publication data:

Names: Payton, James R. Jr., 1947–, author.

Title: The unknown Europe : how Eastern Europe got that way / by James R. Payton Jr.

Description: Eugene, OR: Cascade Books, 2021 | Includes bibliographical references.

Identifiers: ISBN 978-1-6667-0475-4 (paperback) | ISBN 978-1-6667-0476-1 (hardcover) | ISBN 978-1-6667-0477-8 (ebook)

Subjects: LCSH: Europe, Eastern | Europe, Eastern—History | Europe, Eastern—Civilization | Europe, Central | Balkan Peninsula

Classification: DJK38 P39 2021 (print) | DJK38 (ebook)

10/21/21

for Lisa Elliott
loving sister, faithful friend

Contents

List of Maps and Pictures | ix
Preface | xi
Acknowledgments | xv
Notes on Pronunciation | xvii
Explanation about Names | xix
Note on Maps | xxi
    Map 1: Political map of Eastern Europe (2021) | xxii
    Map 2: Relief map of Eastern Europe | xxiii

Chapter 1. Introduction | 1

Part One: Getting Our Bearings

Chapter 2. Prehistoric Eastern Europe | 9
Chapter 3. A Bird's Eye View, from Byzantium to Bosnia | 27
Chapter 4. A Question of Terminology | 41
Chapter 5. Problems in the Historiography of Eastern Europe | 46

Part Two: Turning Points in Eastern European History

Chapter 6. The Evangelization of the Slavs (860s) | 65
Chapter 7. The Conversion of Vladimir and Kievan Rus' (988) | 82
Chapter 8. The Development of States (Tenth–Twelfth Centuries) | 100
Chapter 9. The Fourth Crusade (1204) | 130
Chapter 10. The Invasion of the Mongols (1240s) | 150
Chapter 11. The Battle of Kosovo (1389) | 167

Chapter 12. The Battle of White Mountain (1620) | 183
Chapter 13. The Dismemberment of Poland (1772, 1793, 1795) | 200
Chapter 14. The Aftermath of World War I (1918–22) | 214
Chapter 15. The Coming of Communism (1945–48) | 234
Chapter 16. The Overthrow of Communism (1989) | 248

Part Three: Epilogue

Since 1989 | 271

Bibliography of Works Cited | 277
For Further Reading | 282

Maps and Pictures

Map 1: Political map of Eastern Europe (2021) | xxii

Map 2: Relief map of Eastern Europe | xxiii

Picture 1: Wooden statue of Cyril at Fortress Devin (near Bratislava, Slovakia) | 76

Picture 2: Close-up of Cyril's hands, with Glagolitic letters carved into them | 77

Picture 3: Foundation of ninth-century church at Fortress Devin (near Bratislava, Slovakia) | 77

Picture 4: Wooden statues of Rastislav and Cyril at Fortress Devin (near Bratislava, Slovakia) | 78

Picture 5: Statue of Cyril and Methodius (Ohrid, North Macedonia) | 80

Picture 6: St. George the Great Martyr Church (Sophia [ancient Serdika], Bulgaria) | 89

Picture 7: The Hagia Sophia (Istanbul [Constantinople], Turkey) | 90

Picture 8: The Dome of the Hagia Sophia (Istanbul [Constantinople], Turkey) | 91

Picture 9: Mosaic of Christ with the Virgin Mary and John the Baptist/Forerunner (Istanbul [Constantinople], Turkey) | 92

Picture 10: Statue of Jaroslav dedicating his building of St. Sophia to God (Kiev, Ukraine) | 95

Picture 11: Fresco of Jaroslav's family on wall of St. Sophia (Kiev, Ukraine) | 96

Picture 12: Sarcophagus of Jaroslav within St. Sophia
(Kiev, Ukraine) | 97

Picture 13: View of Samuil's fortress of in Ohrid (formerly Bulgarian Empire, now North Macedonia) | 115

Picture 14: Another view of Samuil's fortress
(Ohrid, North Macedonia) | 115

Picture 15: Church in the village of Vidocha ("Poked-eye"),
North Macedonia | 117

Picture 16: Icon of the Forty Martyrs of Sebaste in the church in Vidocha, reimagined to point to the blinding of Samuil's army (Vidocha, North Macedonia) | 117

Picture 17: Equestrian statue of King (Kralj) Tomislav
(Zagreb, Croatia) | 120

Picture 18: Statue of Bishop Grgur (Split, Croatia) | 121

Picture 19: Glagolitic inscription, back wall of St. Stephen's Cathedral
(Zagreb, Croatia) | 122

Picture 20: Copies of the four horse statues, taken from the Hippodrome in Constantinople during the Fourth Crusade (St. Mark's Square, Venice, Italy) | 148

Picture 21: Reliquary with the remains of Prince Lazar
(Belgrade, Serbia) | 178

Picture 22: Hradčany Castle, from across the Vltava River
(Prague, Czech Republic) | 186

Picture 23: Statue of King Charles I/IV (Prague, Czech Republic) | 187

Picture 24: Church of our Lady before Týn (Prague, Czech
Republic) | 192

Picture 25 Site of the Defenestration of Prague (Hradčany Castle) | 196

Picture 26: Statue of Tomáš Masaryk near Hradčany Castle
(Prague, Czech Republic) | 229

Picture 27: Statue of Pope John Paul II, commemorating his papal visit
(Djakovo, Croatia) | 252

Preface

EASTERN EUROPE HAS BEEN unfamiliar territory to most of us in the western world. Of course, we know some countries there: Poland, Hungary, Serbia, and the Czech Republic are nations we recognize, even if many of us could not immediately point them out on a map. In addition, we know some of the main cities in Eastern Europe: we have all heard of Prague, Warsaw, Budapest, and Belgrade, even if we might not immediately remember in which countries they are found.

But we can hardly claim to know much about Eastern Europe. There is reason—or, as we will see, at least excuse—for this. Beyond that, for several hundred years, all the countries of Eastern Europe were subsumed within huge empires that were not interested in promoting knowledge of or sympathy with their various subject peoples, their respective histories, or their plights within the empires. After a brief window of less than two decades of independence between the two world wars of the twentieth century, all of Eastern Europe was swallowed up again—this time into the Communist bloc, under the control of one dominating power, the Union of Soviet Socialist Republics [USSR]. The Communist bloc looked upon the West as the enemy to be feared and the foe to be conquered. Given that, the Soviets were no more willing than their imperial predecessors in Eastern Europe had been to encourage familiarity with the peoples or states of the region. As with the former empires, the USSR squelched anything among the peoples of Eastern Europe that would encourage a sense of national identity or distinctiveness vis-à-vis either their Russian overlords or the other peoples and nations within the Communist bloc. The Iron Curtain had descended, and the peoples and countries of Eastern Europe were behind it.

With 1989, this dramatically changed. In that year, the Communist bloc imploded. With that collapse, the various countries of Eastern Europe all cast off their former overlords and embarked on the path of establishing themselves as independent states—some for the first time in many years, one (Slovenia) for the first time ever. The last decade of the twentieth century witnessed a remarkable opening up of Eastern Europe to the rest of the world. Travel to and throughout Eastern Europe became welcome and, for the most part, unhindered. Some of those reading this may already have traveled to and in the region. Business interactions proceeded in ways and at a pace inconceivable during the period of Communist dominance. Service organizations of various kinds mounted numerous efforts to assist the peoples and states of the region.

A great deal of interaction between Eastern Europe and the western world has taken place since 1989. These years also witnessed numerous tensions within the region, some of which exploded into horrific brutalities. Intervention by the western world brought ceasefire, although not peace. It became increasingly obvious that few people in the West—including the news media, western governments, and their policy advisors—had much understanding of the background to the tensions among the peoples of the region, on the one hand, or the history of Eastern Europe, on the other. Living now in the aftermath of escaping from the USSR's Communist domination, Eastern Europe's peoples and nations welcome us, as I have repeatedly found in my own experience, to become better acquainted with them.

Developing such familiarity is not an onerous task: Eastern Europe and its history are intriguing. While it is part of the continent of *Europe*, it is a segment of Europe very different from the one we have studied in our schooling. The Europe we learned about is *Western* Europe; we know a fair amount about its history. While we may not keep it all sorted out well, we recognize names like Charlemagne, Bismarck, and Napoleon; battles like Hastings and Waterloo; and events like the Protestant Reformation and the French Revolution. By contrast, we know very little about the other half of the continent, *Eastern* Europe, and its history. Few people in the West would recognize the leading dynasties—Piast, Árpád, Trpimirović, Přemyslid, Nemanjić—that once ruled over the powerful states of Eastern Europe's past (not to mention identifying which state they governed). Almost no one in the West knows who Khan Boris, Prince Rastislav, St. Sava, or Prince Mieszko were, or why they were important for the history of Eastern Europe. Not many would know much about the Battle of White Mountain or that of Kosovo-Polje, or why the dates 1772, 1793, and 1795 were significant—or which state they affected. All these dynasties, leaders, battles, and dates—with many others, in each category—had profound influence on various states within Eastern Europe and the history of the region, with effects reaching to the present day. Without familiarity with all these (and many others), one cannot hope to understand what has transpired in Eastern Europe, either in the past or in more recent events.

The stories and the collective history of the region are fascinating; they open up a world in many ways similar to our own, and yet one profoundly different. Getting to know the history of Eastern Europe offers the opportunity to become familiar with what has happened in the region and how its peoples view themselves and others—and with that, the opportunity to learn something about ourselves and consider the ways we view ourselves and others. There is much to commend the study of the history of Eastern Europe. I have found that study fascinating over the past three decades and still do today. Let me indicate briefly why.

Although I took my graduate studies in Western European history, in my teaching career my academic interests increasingly turned eastward. For one thing, fascination with Eastern Orthodoxy as (to Western Christian tastes) an exotic but deliciously different approach to Christianity compelled my respect for the faith embraced by so many in Eastern Europe. In addition, the humbling recognition that, not medieval Western Europe, but the Byzantine Empire constituted the pinnacle of Christian civilization at the time beckoned me to consider the eastern half of the continent, on which Byzantium had tremendous influence. Exploring how the various nations of the region flourished and related to their neighbors, as well as how Eastern European peoples later endured under oppressive imperial regimes, intrigued me. Further, the gloriously unforeseen collapse of Communist domination in the region in 1989, all without a single shot being fired by those who threw off their former overlords, constrained me to turn my attention to this wondrously new but very old portion of the world, in which nations have been reborn while we in the West looked on.

The study of the history of Eastern Europe is fascinating in its own right. I am delighted to invite you to come along on this historical journey into the unknown Europe.

As we get set to embark on that journey, some of you may already have noticed some unusual capitalization in what you have just read. What is treated in this volume requires frequent use of the contrasts "eastern" and "western" (or "east" and "west"). These words will be capitalized when referring to regions of the world (so, "the East" or "the West") or the European continent ("Eastern Europe" and "Western Europe"), as well as to the relevant major traditions of Christianity ("Eastern Christianity" or "Eastern churches" and "Western Christianity" or "Western churches"). Further in this regard, "church" will only be capitalized if it is identifying a particular congregation or building (e.g., "St. George the Great Martyr Church" [in Sophia, Bulgaria]). In all other instances, when "church" appears ("the church," "the Roman church," "the Roman Catholic church," "the Western church," "the Eastern churches," "the Orthodox churches"), it will not be capitalized.

Acknowledgments

As THIS PROJECT COMES to completion, I wish to express gratitude to many people who have encouraged and stimulated me in the captivating journey that has brought me to this point. My colleagues in the History department at Redeemer University over the years—Harry Van Dyke, Jacob Ellens, Norman Sennema, Darren Provost, David Zietsma, Kevin Flatt, and Helen Vreugdenhil—were unfailingly supportive as I increasingly devoted my attention to teaching a variety of courses on the history of Eastern Europe over the last twenty-five years of my career. I am indebted to the students who took these courses—from the first-year general overview and a second-year course on Islam in Europe, through upper-level courses on Byzantium, the Balkans, and Ukraine, topped off by a senior seminar on Kosovo—for their interest and engagement with the material. I am grateful to Redeemer University's administration for financial support, which allowed me to travel to and participate in conferences in several Eastern European countries. This enabled me to engage with scholars and others from these nations, immeasurably enriching my insights into the peoples of the region and the ways they perceive themselves, their places in history, and their neighbors—fundamental considerations for understanding that history.

I cannot begin to express how much I owe to my friends and colleagues in the executive committee of "Christians Associated for Relationships with Eastern Europe" [CAREE], a non-government organization that has worked for peace, justice, and reconciliation in and for the region since the most frigid depths of the Cold War. Joining with them in study, collaboration, and conferences in North America, and in interfaith dialogues in post-conflict situations in Eastern Europe, afforded me the opportunity to learn from their expertise and to engage with them in these peace-making pursuits. This project owes much to them all: Paul Mojzes, Priscilla Felisky-Whitehead, Joseph Loya, Leonid Kishkovsky, Paul Crego, Ines Murzaku, and Walter Sawatsky. That they afforded me the privilege to serve CAREE as executive secretary (1998–2006) and then as president (2006–11) will always remain cherished honors.

I am grateful to Dean Ratomir Grozdanoski of St. Clement of Ohrid Orthodox Theological Seminary (Skopje, North Macedonia) for the privilege of giving an invited lecture to the seminary community and guests in October 2004; to Peter Kuzmić, president of Evangelical Theological Seminary (Osijek, Croatia), for the privilege of teaching summer courses in 2007 and 2009; and to Boris Gunjević for arranging for me to teach at Matthias Flacius Illyricus Faculty of Theology (Zagreb, Croatia) in the summer of 2008. All this allowed me to interact with faculty and students at these institutions and, beyond that, to travel in their beautiful countries and become more familiar with their rich histories. Additional opportunities in May 1999 to give history lectures in the liberal arts program of Crimean Medical University (Simferopol, Crimea) and to bring the English keynote address at a conference at the Academy of Sciences (St. Petersburg, Russia) led to beneficial collaboration with fellow scholars and deepened insights into the history and culture to be experienced in these places. Finally in these regards, I was honored by invitations from the prime minister of Macedonia (2007) and the minister of culture of Macedonia (2010) to attend international conferences on dialogue among religions and civilizations (both held in Ohrid, North Macedonia).

For preparing both the maps used in this volume, I thank Daniel Feher. The pictures used in this volume are all photographs I have taken on trips into Eastern Europe between 1999 and 2013. I express gratitude for permissions granted to use material from articles I have previously published: "Religion and the Historiography of Eastern Europe," *Religion in Eastern Europe* 21.2 (2001) 1–16; "Bypassing the History of Eastern Europe: A Failure of Twentieth Century Christian Scholarship," *Christian Scholar's Review* 29 (2000) 713–30; and "Revisioning the Historiography of Eastern Europe," *Fides & Historia* 31 (1999) 77–89.

Last, but certainly not least, I am grateful to my wife Sharon, who has encouraged me while I have focused so much time and attention on this post-retirement project. Life with her energizes me to enjoy each day—and with the completion of this project, I'll have fewer distractions in those days.

This volume is dedicated to my sister, Lisa Elliott. She has always supported and encouraged me over the years. Growing up with her and being her big brother has been my joy.

Notes on Pronunciation

IN THE LANGUAGES USED in Eastern Europe, some letters of the alphabet either carry diacritical marks or have distinctive pronunciations or both. For readers who may not be familiar with these differences from English usage, note the following:

In Czech:

"á" is pronounced "ah" (as in f<u>a</u>ther)

"c" is pronounced as "ts" (as in ca<u>ts</u>)

"č" is pronounced as "ch" (as in ri<u>ch</u>)

"í" is pronounced as "ee" (as in b<u>ee</u>t)

"ř" is a *rolled* "r"

In Magyar:

"á" is pronounced as "ah" (as in f<u>a</u>ther)

"cs" is pronounced as "ch" (as in <u>ch</u>eese)

"gy" is pronounced as "dg" (as in ba<u>dg</u>er)

In Polish:

"ie" is pronounced as "ye" (as in <u>ye</u>s)

"sz" is pronounced as "sh" (as in <u>sh</u>ow)

"ł" is pronounced as "w" (as in <u>w</u>all)

"w" is pronounced as "v" (as in <u>v</u>eal)

"w" (at the end of a word) is pronounced as "ff" (as in sta<u>ff</u>)

In Romanian:

"Ceau" is pronounced as "chow"

"ş" is pronounced as "ch" (as in ri<u>ch</u>)

In Serbo-Croatian:

"č" is pronounced as "ch" (as the first *ch* in <u>ch</u>urch)

"ć" is pronounced as "ch" (as the second *ch* in chur<u>ch</u>)

"j" is pronounced as "y" (as in <u>y</u>et)

Explanation about Names

In dealing with Eastern European history, it is important to recognize that some names of rulers and other significant persons have appeared in two ways in the literature, in the original language (possibly with diacritical marks) or in a Latinized form. In this book, we will give the original name first, followed in square brackets by its Latinized version. To avoid possible confusion, we will use the original form of the name in subsequently referring to the person. The reason for doing so should be clear from the following examples:

> Stjepan [Stephen]—Stjepan is the Serbo-Croatian form of the name.
>
> István [Stephen]—István is the Magyar (Hungarian) form of the name.
>
> Vladislav [Vladislas]—Vladislav is the Bohemian (Czech) form of the name.
>
> Władysław [Vladislas]—Władysław is the Polish form of the name.
>
> Boleslav [Boleslas]—Boleslav is the Bohemian (Czech) form of the name.
>
> Bolesław [Boleslas]—Bolesław is the Polish form of the name.

As can readily be seen, using the Latinized (and perhaps more commonly recognized) form of the name could be—and has often been—confusing as one tries to learn about the history of the various Eastern European peoples. To avoid this, we will use the original form of each of these names (and others that may appear) in this book.

Note on Maps

THE TWO MAPS THAT follow offer basic familiarity with the geography of Eastern Europe. This note explains what each map offers and its limitations.

Map 1 is a political map of the region as of January 1, 2021. It offers readers a basic familiarity with the region in the present day. However, the borders of even present-day states have changed considerably over the course of the centuries covered in this volume: this is true for Bulgaria, Hungary, Poland, Croatia, Serbia, and Bosnia-Herzegovina. Further, some states that arose earlier in Eastern European history no longer exist: this is true for Moravia and Kievan Rus'. For maps indicating earlier borders of contemporary Eastern European states and for maps of earlier states no longer in existence, readers should consult historical atlases of the region.[1]

Map 2 offers a relief map of the region, pointing out the mountain ranges and rivers that have influenced Eastern European history as it unfolded. (Borders of contemporary states are faintly indicated in broken lines, so readers can correlate this map with Map 1.)

---

1. Two excellent resources in this regard are Magocsi, *Historical Atlas,* and Hupchick and Cox, *A Concise Historical Atlas.*

Map 1: Political map of Eastern Europe (2021)

Map 2: Relief map of Eastern Europe

— CHAPTER 1 —

Introduction

"We are what history has made us.... Our history has formed our experience of the world."[1]

When we who live in the West—Western Europe and North America—speak of "Europe," we almost always actually refer to *Western* Europe. It is really the only "Europe" we know. We picked up this pattern in school: textbooks and teachers in primary and secondary schools, and even in universities, commonly use "Europe" as if *Western* Europe is all there is to the continent.

But Europe extends far beyond the German-speaking nations of Germany and Austria, which are the outmost edges of how we typically use the term. The nations to their east—Poland, Slovakia, and Bulgaria, among others—are also European. They are the "other" Europe, *Eastern* Europe—the Europe *unknown* to us in most regards. Geographically, the European continent extends all the way to the Ural Mountains in Russia. Actually, then, Western Europe constitutes less than half of the total land mass of Europe: most of the continent falls outside our common use of the term. This book deal with this other, unknown, Europe.

The paths of historical development have not been the same for the two parts of the continent. The history of Western Europe—dealing with England, France, Germany, the Netherlands, Belgium, Spain, Portugal, Italy, Norway, Sweden, Scotland, and the rest—has taken a different trajectory than its eastern counterpart has. This volume will guide readers into the historical development of the unknown Europe.

To be sure, the two Europes shared similar backgrounds and some influences. Both built on the heritage of the ancient world. Additionally, for centuries, the Christian faith took root in and significantly shaped the history of both segments of Europe.

---

1. Havel, *Summer Meditations*, 125–26.

In the midst of those similarities, though, pronounced differences also emerged. While both Eastern and Western Europe took up the Greco-Roman heritage, they did so from different centers: Rome shaped Western European experience, but Byzantium exercised the greatest influence in Eastern Europe. While we in the West probably have at least vague notions of how Rome shaped Western Europe, we have come to know little about Byzantium and even less about the profound ways it influenced numerous people groups, including many in Eastern Europe. Rome and Byzantium focused on different elements of the Greco-Roman heritage, making for significant dissimilarities in what unfolded over the course of centuries. With that, Christianity as it developed in the two segments of Europe moved in discordant directions,[2] affecting and shaping the cultures developing in the two parts of the continent. With these differences even in what Eastern Europe and Western Europe shared, readers can begin to sense why Eastern European history and culture are sometimes only subtly different from, but often dramatically other than, the Western Europe they have learned about in their schooling.

What This Volume Will Do

This volume asks and answers why we have not known more about Eastern Europe, even though much of the schooling offered in North America and the English-speaking world has focused on Europe. It will point to the situation in prehistory that set the stage for it, the historical significance of the geographical limitations of Greek and Roman civilization during antiquity, and the impact that had for subsequent developments of Western European schooling. It will also indicate how the dramatic development of Eastern European states during what we call the Middle Ages came to be forgotten, and why that all remained unknown to us in the West.

The subtitle—"How Eastern Europe Got That Way"—is both cheeky and precise. The cheeky element recognizes an attitude too often found in the West as it views other areas of the world. For the past five centuries, the West has been in the vanguard of the privileged, in many ways dominating what has happened in much of the rest of the globe.[3] In this situation, it has become almost a default position for many to look down on or disregard what has transpired in other geographical regions—even among our closest neighbors,

---

2. For an examination of this divergence, see Payton, *Light from the Christian East*, 13–42; the remainder of the volume focuses on teachings and practices within Orthodoxy, comparing them with Western Christian approaches.

3. For a recent scholarly reflection on this phenomenon, see Ferguson, *Civilization*.

such as Eastern Europe. As the privileged, we in the West have readily thought of our culture, status, or accomplishments as the harbingers of progress and endorsed what is among us as a sort of norm for advanced society and culture. Others, then, need to "catch up" with the way the West has developed. For Eastern Europe to be "that way"—different from, other than, us—would then imply deficiency in what has developed in the region.

But by presenting the history of Eastern Europe this book will challenge and correct that attitude. It will show how the remarkable and resilient civilizations in Eastern Europe developed over the centuries. This volume will lay out, in condensed form, what happened to shape Eastern Europe—to make it, indeed, different from, other than, us.

What We Will Find

The assumption of the superiority of the West noted above actually runs aground on what transpired in the long period after the collapse of the Roman Empire.[4] As the centuries from antiquity unfolded, the developments in Eastern Europe advanced far beyond anything going on in Western Europe. To be sure, the western half of the continent would catch up and, in the wake of devastating invasions that overwhelmed Eastern Europe in the thirteenth century and subsequently, surpass its eastern sibling. But for several centuries, the advanced peoples of Eastern Europe lived in and developed significant civilizations more accomplished and sophisticated than anything that had arisen in Western Europe. This book will lay out how and why Eastern Europe attained such pre-eminence, and how that pre-eminence came to an end.

For centuries after that, the West paid scant attention to Eastern Europe, until, in the aftermath of World War II, the tensions of the Cold War reversed that pattern dramatically. The need to know as much as possible about the nations that ended up constituting the Communist bloc led to the establishment in major universities of study centers focused on Eastern Europe. The last half of the twentieth century finally saw the West develop a keen interest in the region. Myriad books and scholarly articles focusing on Eastern Europe were published, as the West sought to learn about that part of Europe that had become communist by Russian intervention.

---

4. On this, note the discussion below about when the Roman Empire came to an end, in chapter 6.

INTRODUCTION

How We Will Approach It

While I am a "baby boomer" who grew up during the Cold War, and so might well have developed interest in Eastern Europe because of its role in that tense period, I was not attracted to Eastern European history until after the 1989 collapse of Communism throughout the region. My interest in that history focused not on the aberration occasioned by the Soviet domination for the last half of the twentieth century; rather, it was on the actual histories of the various peoples and nations themselves, seeking to understand them on their own terms. It has been an engrossing journey, which I want to share with readers in this book.

Studying and teaching Eastern European history for nearly three decades at university level entailed becoming conversant with the scholarly literature about that history. This led me to identify some significant problems in how the vast bulk of post-World War II studies examined the area.[5] While these studies provided much information about the various countries of the Communist bloc, they did little to help understand the peoples and nations of the region on their own terms—which is what I was primarily interested in (and what, from my perspective as a historian, is what history *should* be especially concerned to discover and present). It surely does not need much argument to point out that focusing on peoples while they are under foreign domination is hardly the way to learn about them for who they are themselves. However helpful these numerous studies were in the exigencies of the Cold War, they proffered little assistance in better understanding the peoples and nations of the regions themselves. If one desires to learn about the history of Eastern Europe, it will not do just to study the Communist period—which is what most of the histories of Eastern Europe produced in the West have done.[6]

This volume will look at the long-term, broad sweep of Eastern European history by examining significant watershed events in it. A full treatment of that history is, of course, far beyond the scope of a book of this size. But years of studying and teaching Eastern European history have convinced me that we can get a good sense of the region's history by focusing on these eleven significant turning points.

---

5. We consider them below, in chapter 5.

6. To be sure, since the collapse of Communism in Eastern Europe in 1989, a few books have expanded that treatment somewhat, to cover the whole twentieth century. While this is undeniably an improvement, it still leaves out multiple centuries that shaped and influenced the history of Eastern Europe; for a fuller discussion of this concern, see Payton, "Revisioning the Historiography."

All peoples' histories have such epochal events that end up exercising extraordinary impact on what happens among them. Western readers can probably name a few—e.g., the signing of the Magna Carta in 1215, and the American and French revolutions of 1776 and 1789. Each of these, to be understood and appreciated, requires familiarity with what led up to it and eventuated from it. The same is true of Eastern Europe: several turning points can be identified that grew out of prior developments and exercised significant impact on a people or on the region more widely. This volume will consider eleven such events, as a way of developing a basic familiarity with Eastern European history.

But why focus on these eleven? They stand out, in my estimation, as pivotal for the unfolding and development of that history. Someone else might offer a sound argument that other episodes should be added or might want to substitute another event for one included here. However, as I have taught and reflected on the history of Eastern Europe, these eleven have struck me as key to the way that history unfolded. Conversations over the last two decades with Eastern Europeans themselves, both recent immigrants to North America and in various Eastern European countries, have confirmed the significance of the events treated. Familiarity with them will give a good vantage-point from which to make sense of the rest of Eastern European history, and to understand what is going on in the region in the present.

In each case, the treatment will not just focus on the particular event itself; it is necessary to consider the prior history that led up to it, then the event, and finally its consequences or impact. This will require painting, at times, with a broad brush as we treat the respective histories. Each of the treatments would need to receive more nuanced consideration if it was the focus of a lengthier study or a book on its own. But my purpose here is not to respond to every question that could be raised or to consider all other possibilities for interpretation; rather, I intend, building on solid familiarity with the respective histories covered in each presentation, to offer readers treatments that will enable them to imbibe a general sense of Eastern European history, both in itself and in its distinctiveness from the Western European history with which they are more familiar. I am bold to hope that this volume may stimulate some of them toward further interest in the history of Eastern Europe; if so, the "For Further Reading" section at the end of the book offers numerous options to consider from volumes I have found informative.

An Alternative Embrace of History

As we get into this, readers should be advised that this will push us into a different historical sensibility than we usually manifest when thinking about the past. As the privileged in the contemporary world situation, we are often rather blissfully unaware of our own history—and whatever familiarity we have is often limited to the last couple of centuries.

This is not the way history functions among Eastern Europeans. All the nations in the region have long memories, which still respond profoundly to what happened to their ancestors centuries ago. As later chapters will show, Eastern European awareness of history almost always includes a strong dose of nostalgia for long-gone glory days and a painful awareness of what happened to their nation in the sometimes distant past. This kind of sensibility is virtually unknown among us in the West. But if western readers are to make sense of Eastern Europe, they must open themselves to that long history.

Structure

To get ready for this exploration, we must get well oriented: Part 1 helps us do that. Chapter 2 presents basic information about prehistoric Eastern Europe, which is foundational to understanding what unfolded in the region during historical times. Chapter 3 will then offer an overview of how Eastern European history unfolded, to serve as a backdrop for the subsequent, more detailed treatment of the particular turning points. Before that, though, chapter 4 addresses a question about the terminology used to describe the region in the historiography produced about it, and chapter 5 draws on this to consider the historiography on the region, identifying three main problems that have gotten in the way of understanding Eastern European history. This sets us up, in Part 2, to plunge into the eleven turning points in that history.

Part One
Getting Our Bearings

──────── CHAPTER 2 ────────

Prehistoric Eastern Europe

"Two worlds, next to each other
at an unbridgeable distance."[1]

As we turn to an overview of prehistoric Eastern Europe, it is important to be reminded what is meant by the term "prehistoric." As usually employed when considering the roots of western civilization, the term refers to the period before the development of the first civilizations (in Sumer and Egypt); thus, the "prehistoric" period ends around 3000 BC. While this serves as a valid periodization for the roots of western civilization in the broad sense, it does not work for other civilizations or areas of the world; e.g., the prehistoric period in Western Europe, specifically, would extend to the first century BC, when the Romans began to keep records of their campaigns in Gaul and Germany.

"Prehistoric" as a designation is not bounded by dates, but by *written records*. If used appropriately with regard to the many geographic and cultural regions of the world, "prehistoric" refers to the period before written records began to be kept in or about that region. Accordingly, "prehistoric," when applied to Eastern Europe, covers the period up to the sixth century AD—i.e., about the time the Slavic peoples began to migrate into the "known" world and others began to write down information about them. (The Slavic peoples were not then literate and so were not keeping records about themselves.)

The study of prehistoric Eastern Europe is, obviously, not the province of historians. Other kinds of scholars—among them, archaeologists, paleontological geographers, linguists, and physical anthropologists—have used their expertise and specific tools to learn a considerable amount about Eastern Europe in its prehistoric period. In what follows, we will draw from what they have discovered in order to lay the foundation for

---

1. Krleza, *Return of Philip Latinovicz*, 63.

our study of the history of the region. It is important to do so: some basic information about the prehistory of the area is essential for understanding that history. Our concern will not be to survey all that has been discovered about prehistoric Eastern Europe; rather, we will focus on what has been learned about the various peoples who inhabited the area during the period. During subsequent history, the Slavic peoples eventually became the dominant ethnic group, numerically, in Eastern Europe; consequently, we will give special attention to what has been learned about them and their relationships to neighboring peoples.

In the following treatment, we will situate the various peoples who lived in the region chronologically and geographically and consider some of what took place during the region's prehistoric period. To make this material easier to assimilate, we will make connections to information we have about other areas of the ancient world and to what we know of the map of Eastern Europe today.

The Peoples of Prehistoric Eastern Europe

Scholars of Eastern Europe's prehistoric period have been able to identify most of the peoples who lived in the region before the migrations (or, invasions)[2] of the Slavic peoples, where those peoples lived, and where the Slavic peoples themselves lived.

Since most early peoples lived a semi-nomadic existence, they often left little evidence of their presence in regions through which they passed. Consequently, we do not know, with any certainty, when people began to reside in Eastern Europe. However, archaeological investigations, together with careful analysis of what ancient authors understood to have been true in bygone eras, as well as what those authors knew from the events of their own times, have provided a considerable amount of evidence about Eastern Europe's prehistoric inhabitants. With this evidence, scholars have been able to identify several early peoples who lived in the region and the general geographical areas where they lived.

---

2. Historians have come to recognize that, in the case of both the Germanic peoples' movement into Western Europe and that of the Slavic peoples into Eastern Europe, the designation "invasion" reflects the perspective of the settled civilizations of the Mediterranean basin into whose territory the "barbarian" peoples of the north were coming; from the perspective of those northern peoples, however, the movement was a "migration." In contemporary parlance, historians use the terms interchangeably; this arises, in part, from a recognition that the prior preference for the term "invasion" saw the movement almost exclusively from the standpoint of the settled civilizations of classical antiquity and was, thus, historically slanted.

The Peoples of the Northern Tier

Celts: These peoples dominated the earliest prehistory of both Western and Eastern Europe. While they did not have a coordinated empire under the rule of a single ruler or run by some form of bureaucracy, the Celts controlled most of the European continent, at one time or another, over a span of nearly 2,000 years. They left archaeological evidence of the form of their settlements, their industry (especially mining), and their burial practices.

Ancient Roman sources described the Celts as fearsome warriors. Indeed, the Celts inflicted one of the worst defeats on the armies of Rome in her history: in 390 BC, they routed Roman forces, marched on to Rome, and sacked it. (This was the last time Rome endured this humiliation until it happened under the Vandals in 410 AD.) The Celts also spread into Asia Minor (contemporary Turkey), especially its northeastern area. They lived in the area of Galatia; St. Paul's letter to the Galatians in the New Testament of the Bible was sent to churches that almost certainly included people of Celtic stock.

Without a coordinated empire, the Celts' vast holdings were exposed to the onslaughts of other peoples, and eventually they lost their control of Eastern Europe. In due course, their area of influence shrank considerably further. Today, the remnants of the Celts survive in parts of Scotland and in Ireland.[3]

Balts: These people lived along the southeastern shore of the Baltic Sea—on a contemporary map, in parts of Poland, Lithuania, and Belarus. Unlike most of the rest of the peoples of Eastern Europe, they did not migrate to other areas. Their descendants continue in this area to the present day. They include the Lithuanians and some of the ethnic stock in both Estonia and Latvia.

Germans: Prior to their division into the several Germanic tribes better known from subsequent history, these people lived in the area of contemporary Denmark, eastern Germany, southern Scandinavia, and northern Poland. Long before the time of the Slavic invasions, they had developed into a variety of distinct Germanic tribes. While many of them made incursions into Eastern Europe, none of the Germanic tribes remained permanently there; they eventually found their way into various areas of Western Europe.

Scythians: These were a Central Asian people who swarmed into Eastern Europe and significantly impacted the region. They burst into what is now southern Ukraine by the seventh century BC at the latest and around 500 BC swept through much of Eastern Europe in a wave of conquest and

---

3. A good treatment of the history of the Celts is Herm, *The Celts*; Berresford, *Celtic Inheritance*, examines the traces of Celtic influence, especially in the British Isles.

destruction that earned them a terrifying reputation in the ancient world.[4] Although they did not build a lasting empire, they destroyed much of what had preceded them before returning to what is now southern Ukraine, creating a vacuum in Eastern Europe into which other peoples subsequently could move—including Celtic, Germanic, and Slavic peoples.

Sarmatians: About 200 BC, the Sarmatians invaded the territory of the Scythians and subjugated them. This was the prelude to the Sarmatians' further conquest of the whole of what is today southern Ukraine. This conquest brought a substantial portion of the early Slavic peoples under their control. The Sarmatians were eventually overrun by various invaders (including the Goths), with the Huns finally obliterating the last vestiges of the Sarmatians' power in the fourth century AD.

Goths: These were a Germanic people whose original homeland had been in southeastern Sweden. They are mentioned here separately from other Germanic tribes because the Goths invaded and, for a considerable period of time, resided in Eastern Europe; during that period, they subjugated several Slavic peoples. In the first century AD, the Goths crossed the Baltic Sea and brought the northern area of present-day Poland under their control. From there, they pressed on toward the Black Sea, taking control over the Slavic peoples who inhabited the areas on their path. At the Black Sea, this large people split in two. One segment headed eastwards and became known as Ostrogoths (the prefix "Ostro-" meaning "east"); they subjugated what is today southern Ukraine. The other segment turned westwards and came to be referred to as Visigoths (with "Visi-" meaning "west"); they moved toward the Danube River and the Roman province of Dacia (roughly, contemporary Romania). The Ostrogoths and Visigoths ruled over these areas until the incursions of the Huns in the late fourth and early fifth centuries AD. Under Hunnic pressure, both Ostrogoths and Visigoths pushed into the eastern half of the Roman Empire and subsequently migrated into Western Europe.[5]

The Peoples of the Southern Tier

During the prehistoric period, three people groups lived in the southern tier of Eastern Europe—the Thracians, the Illyrians, and the people inhabiting what later became the Roman imperial province of Dacia. Of these, two managed a modicum of continued residence there after the Slavic

---

4. St. Paul used the Scythians' notorious reputation to make his argument in Colossians 3:11.

5. For more on the Goths, see Wolfram, *History of the Goths*.

invasions—a remnant of the ancient Illyrians and a portion of the people of the Roman province of Dacia, the Vlachs.

Thracians and *Illyrians*: The ancient Greeks knew that these two peoples lived to their north: the Thracians held the territory to the east, the Illyrians the lands to the west. The Thracians' lands were bounded by the Prut River, the Carpathian Mountains, and the southern drop of the Danube River; thus, their territory included most of contemporary Romania, Slovakia, and the eastern half of Hungary. The Illyrians' lands began at the Danube River, arched to the north and west through the foothills of the Sudeten mountain range and cut back through the Italian Alps to the Gulf of Venice; consequently, their territory included, on a contemporary map, the western half of Hungary, part of the Czech Republic, most of Austria, and Slovenia. In the south, both the Thracians and the Illyrians were bordered by Macedonia (which lay north of mainland Greece, but was inhabited by people of Greek stock).

Over the course of centuries, with the lands of Eastern Europe an inviting target, both the Thracians and the Illyrians were attacked by invaders who preceded the entrance of the Slavic peoples; eventually, both the Thracians and the Illyrians were overrun and destroyed by the Roman armies. These two peoples left no written evidence of their civilizations; indeed, they even left little archaeological evidence of their presence in the area. As far as scholars have been able to discover, the ancient Thracians seem to have disappeared without a trace (although it is possible that some of the people who later inhabited the Roman province of Dacia may have been, in part, of Thracian stock). While the ancient Illyrians left no unquestioned remains of their civilization, it is generally agreed that a remnant of them retreated into the rugged and virtually inaccessible Sar and Pindus mountain ranges of present-day Albania (to the south of their ancient homeland). There they continued to live over the centuries. Their isolation assured a maintenance of their early ethnic stock, for the most part. However, other peoples eventually moved into the lowland areas of present-day Albania, and some of the descendants of the ancient Illyrians intermarried with the newcomers. Contemporary Albanians are descended, probably in large part, from the ancient Illyrians. Their distinctive language argues for this: the Albanian language gives evidence of being of great antiquity and is, in all likelihood, a variation of ancient Illyrian (which remains otherwise unknown, since it left no literary remains).

Vlachs: During the early second century AD, the Roman Emperor Trajan conquered the region of Dacia (which included virtually the whole of present-day Romania). Although the Romans captured the area and brought the inhabitants there into the orbit of Roman civilization, imperial forces were unable to retain control of it. By the middle of the third century, Roman legions withdrew from the territory. In the intervening period, the people who inhabited the area had been considerably Romanized. They referred to themselves as Vlachs.

In the three centuries following the Roman withdrawal, the territory was overrun by various invading peoples—among them, Goths, Huns, Avars, and Slavs. For self-preservation, the Vlachs who survived found safety in the Transylvanian Alps and the lower region of the Carpathian Mountains, living a semi-nomadic life in remote areas. They remained in their mountain refuges until around 1300, when the invasions finally came to an end. Then they came down from their mountain strongholds and peopled the plains of Wallachia and Moldavia—much of present-day Romania and Moldova. Their language is a variant of ancient Latin. It had probably already taken on some regional peculiarities during the Vlachs' seclusion in the mountains. Through intermingling with the Slavic peoples in Wallachia and Moldavia after the thirteenth century, the Romanian language received a strong admixture of Slavic forms and endings. However, the Romanians are not of Slavic stock.

The Slavic Peoples

The dominant people group in *Western* Europe came to be the *Germanic*: most of the nations of Western Europe, wherever they live and whatever language they speak, are of Germanic extraction. By contrast, the people group that eventually filled that role for *Eastern* Europe was the *Slavic*. The Slavs eventually became the predominant inhabitants of both the northern and the southern tiers of the region: the various Slavic peoples of contemporary Eastern Europe constitute some two-thirds of the total inhabitants of the area, and their political and cultural influence has been preponderant. Consequently, it is not surprising that the question of the original habitat of the Slavic peoples has been the subject of serious investigation and considerable argument, especially among scholars of Slavic heritage; nor is it surprising that the respective claims have often betrayed a certain nationalistic bias.[6] Nevertheless, a general scholarly consensus on the answer to the question exists at present.

---

6. The Russian scholar Dolukhanov has noted that this has become a significant point of contention among Polish, Ukrainian, and Russian scholars—who commonly claim pride of original place for lands mostly within their current national borders (*The Early Slavs*, 145); after making this observation, it is at least mildly ironic that Dolukhanov goes on to argue that the original Slavic homeland must have been in Ukraine and Belarus (146–70)—countries that Russia has claimed as part of its historical patrimony.

According to this consensus, the early Slavic peoples inhabited an oblong area northeast of the Carpathian Mountains: its westernmost boundary seems to have been the middle basin of the Vistula River, with the eastern reaches extending to the Dnieper River (near Kiev); it reached, in the north, to the Pripet River; on the south, it extended to the headwaters of the Prut, the Dniester, and the Bug Rivers. Thus, the original residence of the Slavic peoples was bounded on the north by that of the Balts, and to the west by that of the Germanic tribes; its southern boundary was comprised of the Carpathian Mountains; to the east, it did not quite extend to the Black Sea. On a present-day map, the Slavic peoples' original habitat would have included southeastern Poland, southern Belarus, the western half of Ukraine, and the northern part of Moldova.

The Slavs may have inhabited much of this region before 500 BC, but that is not certain. However, if they did not already live there, then the Scythian invasion of Eastern Europe about that time, which so devastated and depopulated that region, would have allowed Slavic peoples who had not been attacked to expand into the area. During the prehistoric period, the Slavic peoples remained a collection of ethnically related but not politically integrated tribes: they neither created a unified governmental structure over their large territory nor attempted to expand it by conquest into some form of an empire.

In this location, the early Slavic peoples were beyond the range of intimate contact with the cultures of classical antiquity. For this reason, the Slavic peoples remained, for a long period, unknown to the Greeks or the Romans. Greek merchants had established trading outposts along the shores of the Black Sea by the eighth century BC and had subsequently probed into the interior of what is today southern Ukraine, but this did not bring them into significant or extensive contact with the early Slavic peoples. As regards ancient Roman civilization, the foothills of the Carpathians were the furthest extent of the Roman empire. Thus, the early Slavs were just beyond the reach of the classical cultures of Greece and Rome.

The peoples of the Mediterranean world had some awareness of a vast group of peoples beyond the Carpathian Mountains. However, the Slavic peoples had no significant exposure to those civilizations prior to their migrations/invasions into the area south of the Carpathians. This had significant ramifications for the subsequent development of Slavic civilization, on the one hand, and, on the other, for interest in and knowledge about the Slavic peoples in later periods.

Earliest Evidence about the Slavs

The earliest evidence about the Slavic peoples comes from two quite different fields of scholarly investigation. The first offers what has been learned by a comparison of the vocabulary of early Slavic language with other known early languages; the second considers the earliest written records in which the Slavic peoples are mentioned. What initially appears, in both instances, to be rather unpromising shards of information turns out to be quite revealing about the Slavic peoples themselves and about what others knew about them, down to the recent past.

Information from Early Slavic Vocabulary

Historians of Eastern Europe are greatly indebted to linguistic scholars who have examined early languages. What those scholars have learned reveals quite a bit about the early Slavic peoples and how they compared and related to their immediate neighbors.

The Slavic Language's Family Group: Careful analysis of languages throughout the known world has enabled linguistic scholars to speak of a few "families" of languages—e.g., Semitic, Turkic, and Indo-European. Within these families, the various languages that comprise them, for all their differences from each other, nevertheless manifest a common background in basic terminology that distinguishes the languages in that family from languages in other such families. Among those families that have been identified, the one significant for our purposes is *Indo-European*; it is so designated because linguistic scholarship has established that there is a common root to all the languages that were spoken by the earliest peoples who lived in a broad geographic expanse stretching from present-day India through Western Europe. (Migrations and invasions by members from other linguistic family groups have led to some languages now being spoken in these geographic areas that do not belong to the Indo-European language family.)

Linguistic scholars usually do not hypothesize how long ago the original language of each of the various language families may have been still one language. However, for Indo-European, it could have been no later than 3000 BC, to allow enough time for the developments and differentiations to have taken place that are manifest in the languages throughout that broad geographic area by the time we begin to have written records. One of the early languages into which the original Indo-European language developed was what is called "proto-Slavic" (the "first" or "original" Slavic language), out of which all the Slavic languages developed. Another is designated "proto-

Germanic" (the original Germanic language), out of which the various Germanic languages subsequently developed (including Gothic).[7]

Comparison of Vocabulary: Since both the language of the early Slavic peoples and that of the Goths (who are Germanic) are members of the Indo-European family of languages, the two languages are distantly related to each other. That has allowed linguistic scholars to compare the respective vocabularies. Historians have profited from what these scholars have been able to discover about the relationships between the two languages in the matter of "loan words" (i.e., words borrowed from one language and incorporated into another). Linguistic discoveries in this area of investigation have shown, with striking clarity, how the early Goths and Slavs were different and what their original relationship to each other must have been.

Through analyzing the respective vocabularies of early Gothic and early Slavic, linguistic scholarship has discovered that the Slavs had no words for "helmet," "sword," or "armor."[8] The words they came to use for these, and for an extensive list of other martial implements, were all loan words from Gothic. In at least two regards, this is revealing. In the first place, it shows that the early Slavs were not particularly militaristic, but that the Goths were. If the Slavs had no words for these items, then such items must have been unknown to the Slavs until they encountered the Goths, from whom the Slavs borrowed the words. The fact that the terms eventually adopted by the Slavs for these implements of warfare were Gothic shows that these items played a pronounced role in the Goths' relationship to the Slavs: the items made a significant enough impression on the Slavs that they appropriated the Gothic designations for them. Secondly, this cluster of information reveals what the relationship of the two groups of peoples to each other must have been. If the Slavs ended up adopting the Goths' designations for these martial implements, then the Slavs' exposure to the Goths needed to last long enough to make it important for the Slavs to have terms for these items. Further, these implements would have been a significant enough element of what the Slavs were exposed to with the Goths that the Slavs adopted the Gothic designations for the items. This makes it highly likely that the Goths conquered the Slavs and subjugated them to Gothic rule.

It is significant that the early Slavic language already had its own words for agriculture and cattle-raising. This indicates that the early Slavic peoples were engaged in both of these activities well before contact with the Goths.

---

7. For a wide-ranging treatment on this large topic, see Mallory, *In Search of the Indo-Europeans*.

8. For this and related issues, see Cross, *Slavic Civilization*.

In addition, it demonstrates that the early Slavic peoples were not simply nomads, but that they settled into an area to cultivate its farmland.[9]

Two further points arise from what we have just considered. First, the early Slavic peoples would have recognized themselves as involved in a quite different kind of life than that of their Gothic neighbors and masters. Secondly, the early Slavs and the Goths (of Germanic stock) knew each other as opponents, with the Slavs being the ones enduring Gothic/Germanic subjugation. The tension between Germans and Slavs that marks so much of the history of Eastern Europe has deep roots, indeed.

Early References to the Slavs

In this category, it is important—for reasons that will become clear below—to distinguish between references from classical antiquity (i.e., ancient Greece, the Hellenistic period, and ancient Rome) and those from the Byzantine era.

References from Classical Antiquity: In the fifth century BC, the Greek historian Herodotus mentioned that a group of peoples lived between what are today known as the Dnieper and the Dniester Rivers, in the area near contemporary Kiev. He referred to them as the "Neuri." While the reason he used that designation remains unknown, scholars are fairly certain that the people he spoke of were early Slavs. At the very least, these "Neuri" lived in the area that has been identified as the original home of the Slavic peoples; further, the Scythian invasion a few decades earlier (around 500 BC) had decimated the prior inhabitants and would have allowed Slavic peoples to settle in that area. If the Neuri were not Slavic, then the Neuri must have been displaced from the area and Slavic peoples must have moved into it very soon after Herodotus's time. On the whole, it is more likely that the Neuri were Slavic.

The fact that this information comes from none other than Herodotus himself is significant. Historians look upon him as the first great historian; indeed, he is often called "the father of historiography." He wrote with considerable care and precision, based on reliable witnesses or first-hand evidence; in this regard, Herodotus may have had first-hand experience of these Neuri himself, since he had lived in one of the Greek trading colonies on the northern shore of the Black Sea, not far from the area he described when he wrote about them. His reference to the Neuri is viewed, consequently, as

---

9. For wide-ranging treatments of these and related issues, see Gojda, *The Ancient Slavs*; Dolukhanov, *The Early Slavs*; and, more expansively, Barford, *The Early Slavs*.

reliable evidence of the existence by that time of what were probably Slavic people in the area described.

The next known references to the Slavic peoples come about five centuries later, in the first century AD. One is found in the works of Pliny the Elder (23-79 AD), who noted that a people whom he called the "Venedi" lived in the vicinity of the Vistula River. Another first-century AD reference comes from the Roman historian Tacitus. In his book *Germania* (98 AD), he states that the "Venedi" lived to the east of one of the confederations of Germanic tribes. This is a fairly indefinite description of the Venedi's locale, but it accords with the data about the early residence of the Slavic peoples.

Near the end of the second century AD, the Egyptian geographer Claudius Ptolemy noted that the Venedi lived beyond the Carpathian Mountains—which he referred to as the "Mountains of the Venedi." He further stated that they lived in the vicinity of the Vistula (in agreement with what Pliny the Elder had noted) and that their lands extended up to what we know as the Baltic Sea—which he called "the Venedic Gulf."

By way of explanation, it should be noted that the designation "Venedi" sometimes appears as "Veneti" or "Venedae" in the ancient sources. Whichever spelling is used, it is clear that the terms refer to the same peoples. From references that appeared among authors subsequently (to be considered below), it is certain that the peoples referred to by these designations were Slavic peoples. Scholars have puzzled over various possibilities for the etymology of this Venedi/Veneti/Venedae term; the explanation that seems most probable to them now is that it comes from the Celtic *uindo*, which means "white." According to this understanding, the designation was one probably originally given to the Slavic peoples by the Celts. As a dark-haired (or, at times, red-haired) people themselves, the Celts may well have been struck by the light blonde hair color of these Slavic peoples, and the term by which the Celts referred to them must have become known to the Romans (who, as we noted above, had had more contact with the Celts than they would have preferred!).

References from the Byzantine Era: As far as is known today, there were no written references to the Slavic peoples after the time of Claudius Ptolemy until the sixth century AD. By then, the western half of the Roman Empire had succumbed to the onslaughts of various Germanic invaders; Western Europe had entered into the Middle Ages. The center of European scholarship had long since shifted to the east: Byzantium was now the place that offered intellectual leadership. Among the scholars of the Byzantine Empire, there were some who made reference to the Slavic peoples.

One of the greatest of the Byzantine historians, Procopius, in a work of 512, wrote about the "Sclavini" who lived in northern Europe. In a work written about four decades later, he further noted that the "Sclavini" had already migrated into the Byzantine Empire. The significance of these references for our question becomes clear from the comments of Jordanes, a Gothic historian of the era. In a work of 551, he wrote about the Slavic peoples. He noted that the "Venedae" lived over an immense area, having spread from the Vistula River. In this identification of their original geographic home, he agrees with all the references back to the first century AD. Jordanes noted that the Venedae existed in a number of distinct tribes, and he stated that their name for themselves was not "Venedi," but "Sclaveni."

In the seventh century, the "Ravenna cosmographer"—an otherwise unknown author of a study of geography, written in Ravenna, Italy—wrote that the "Sclavini" lived in "Scythia." Scythia was his generic term for all of northeastern Europe. (Ravenna was an outpost of Byzantine imperial authority in Western Europe at that time.)

By way of explanation, it should be noted that the term "Sclaveni"/"Sclavini" is the Greek form for "Slav." After the mid-sixth century, following the usage of Procopius and Jordanes, the term "Slav" (Sclavini) becomes more and more frequent, with the prior term "Venedi" passing out of use.

Significance of the Distinction between Classical and Byzantine Era References: Scholars of Eastern European history have often noted that we would know more about the early movements and developments of the Slavic peoples if they had been better known to the writers of ancient Greece or Rome. However, since they were just beyond the furthest extent of either of the great civilizations of classical antiquity, the early Slavic peoples remained unfamiliar to those civilizations (and were themselves not exposed to those civilizations).

The Byzantines had more intimate familiarity with the Slavic peoples, who migrated into most of Eastern Europe—and, particularly, into territories of the Byzantine Empire. As a consequence, Byzantine authors knew and wrote more about the Slavs than had their predecessors in ancient Greece and Rome. While scholars today might well desire to have even more than is now available from the Byzantine writers, we can be grateful for what they provided during the early periods of Byzantine interaction with the Slavic peoples.

The reason to point to this is not just an antiquarian interest in "who knew what when about whom" in the ancient world: this distinction between the classical era and the Byzantine one is of greater significance than merely isolating when peoples of the Mediterranean basin began to become knowledgeable about and interested in the Slavs. If one keeps in mind when and how historical study developed in Western Europe, this distinction helps to account for the lack of knowledge among the people of Western Europe (and North America) about Eastern Europe and its Slavic inhabitants.

The West has historically looked to the writings of the ancient Greeks and Romans as the treasury of information about antiquity. This was true already in the medieval period in Western European history. In emerging from the isolation of the early Middle Ages, Western European scholars ended up developing an interest in the history and geography of the world. That scholarship turned to the works of ancient Greece and Rome as offering the best and most complete information; the Byzantine scholars' works were at that time not at all well-known in the West. All the historical and geographical knowledge during the Middle Ages was based on the writings of the authors of the classical era. Since none of these writers had any appreciable information about the Slavs, western scholars showed and developed little interest in the Slavs' history or their cultural evolution.

It was not until the late Renaissance—about the middle of the fifteenth century—that the works of scholars of the Byzantine era began to become known in the West. By then, however, Western Europe was preoccupied with other fields of investigation and scholarly development that more directly related to its own civilization. Indeed, the great era of Western European accomplishments had begun: since the early fourteenth century, nations had been coalescing into distinct entities in Western Europe (and they continued to do so); in the late fifteenth century, Columbus discovered the Americas; the sixteenth-century Reformation rent the fabric of medieval Western Christendom; and during the sixteenth and seventeenth centuries, western civilization was engaged in those imperialistic ventures that would lead it to dominate the world, well into the twentieth century. That said, during the late seventeenth century, some western scholars finally started doing geographical and historical research beyond what was available in ancient literature, resulting in some interest in and better awareness of Eastern Europe.[10]

However, well before then, by the mid-fifteenth century, the southern tier of Eastern Europe had entered upon a period of foreign dominance. Both Byzantium itself and a substantial portion of the Slavic peoples of the region either had been incorporated into the Ottoman Empire or were under its influence and control. By 1530, all the nations of the northern tier except Poland had been swallowed up by the Habsburg Empire or the Russian Empire, and Poland disappeared from the map in 1795. Western scholars showed little interest in learning about the history and cultural

---

10. See the interesting discussion of this phenomenon in Wolff, *Inventing Eastern Europe*.

development of subject peoples; thus, they did not study or write about the history of Eastern Europe. That pattern continued, virtually without interruption, almost as long as the Ottoman Empire stood—i.e., nearly until the end of World War I. Thus, the distinction between information available through authors of the classical era, on the one hand, and of the Byzantine era, on the other, has turned out to be a highly significant one for the western world's knowledge about (and interest in) the Slavs and Eastern Europe, down into the past century.

What that has meant is that the West has known virtually nothing about the peoples of Eastern Europe until the last half-century—even though they were living right next door, as it were. Aside from a few intrepid scholars who explored the history of Eastern Europe, the region attracted little attention, and its various peoples even less. The fact that the Greeks and Romans did not get beyond the Carpathian Mountains, and thus did not themselves interact with the Slavs who lived just north of them, has significantly influenced how much—or, rather, how little—became known in the West about Eastern Europe and its inhabitants.[11]

The Dispersion of the Early Slavic Peoples

From their original homeland, the early Slavs spread out to the east, west, and south. Precisely when this migration began cannot be said with certainty. It seems likely that there had been numerous "small-scale" migrations, with families or groups of limited size moving into uninhabited territories in all these directions, for quite a while before the larger movements began. For example, scholars are fairly certain that some Slavs had already started migrating through the Carpathian Mountains, into contemporary Hungary, and on toward the Danube River and the Roman Empire's frontiers in the early first century AD. However, their numbers were not large enough to establish them as the dominant people in any area into which they entered. By the third century, this limited migration gave way to more systematic movement; we know that by this time, the Slavic peoples were "on the move." By the late eighth century, these larger migrations/invasions had come to an end.

As we have seen, the early Slavic peoples had never amalgamated into a single state, but they had shared a common language and a similar lifestyle. As a result of their dispersion to the east, west, and south, the original

---

11. See below, chapter 14, for a discussion of the impact this had after World War I, when western rulers attempted to draw up a new map for Eastern Europe's liberated peoples.

Slavic language diverged into "sub-families" of Slavic languages. In addition, the dispersion to these three points of the compass led the various Slavic peoples into differing historical experiences and has shaped the history of the several Slavic peoples down to this day.

In what follows, we will consider the divisions of the Slavic peoples that resulted from their dispersion: first, noting how the languages diverged from proto-Slavic into "sub-families" as the various Slavic peoples migrated in different directions; and, secondly, identifying where the respective groups settled. With this, we will indicate the various contemporary Slavic languages into which each of the respective "sub-families" of Slavic languages developed.

The Divergence of the Original Slavic Language

Proto-Slavic, belonging to so many peoples who were not otherwise coordinated into some organizational whole, doubtless had a variety of minor dialectical differences, depending on where one was in the large original Slavic homeland.[12] As the respective groups of Slavs began to migrate and to set further distances between themselves and other Slavs who had originally lived at some distance away already, these dialectical differences must have become more pronounced.

In due course, as the three groups of Slavs lived through the long period of migration and settlement, proto-Slavic must have diverged into Eastern, Western, and Southern Slavic languages. Each of these would have been understood by those within its own group but would have been somewhat harder to understand for peoples in the other two groups. Even so, in the ninth century, when the first Slavic literature was produced by missionaries from Byzantium, the language in which that literature was written was readily understood by Slavs in all three of the language groups. Over the subsequent course of time, East Slavic, West Slavic, and South Slavic each continued to diverge from the other two.

The various groupings of East Slavs, West Slavs, and South Slavs, having settled down, lived in considerable independence from other Slavic peoples, even in their own sub-group. In that situation, the East, West, and South Slavic languages developed further, into the distinctive languages known to us today (e.g., as Russian, Polish, or Serbo-Croatian). Linguistic

---

12. This is easier to understand if we consider the differences in spoken English across North America, with numerous regional linguistic peculiarities, in spite of the fact that we have both a written language and mass media, which exercise some control over possible developments. The early Slavic peoples had neither of these.

scholars point out that the various Slavic languages in each of the three distinct groups are closely related to each other; this argues for original "East Slavic," "West Slavic," and "South Slavic" languages out of which the distinct languages known today developed. Those scholars also note that the various languages of each of the groups are almost always closer to each other than they are to languages in either of the other two Slavic language groups. Even so, all the Slavic languages are obviously related to each other: they all developed out of the "proto-Slavic" language.

The East Slavs

Among the three groups, the "East Slav" group is, numerically, the largest, comprising some two-thirds of the total number of Slavs. The East Slavs spread out beyond the earlier boundaries of the original Slavic homeland to include the rest of contemporary Ukraine, Belarus, and Russia. With the vast extent of the Russian lands—all the way through Siberia to the Pacific Ocean, the Aleutian Islands, and North America—there is no definitive eastern boundary to this movement. However, as this group of Slavs came to have control over this vast territory, they did not eliminate or even outnumber its prior inhabitants. The descendants of many of those earlier inhabitants still live within contemporary Russia, holding on to their own distinctive cultures and languages.

As the East Slavs migrated, groups of them settled down at various points while others pushed on farther. One significant result of this, over the course of time, was that the "East Slavic" language that they came to share as their migrations began gradually diverged into three distinct Slavic languages—Russian, Ukrainian, and Belarusian. The contemporary borders of these distinct nations today approximate closely the original territories in which these languages came to be spoken.

Because of their geographical distance from both the ancient Mediterranean basin and from Western Europe as it developed during the Middle Ages, the East Slavs remained outside the orbit of influence of either Byzantium or of Western European civilization longer than either the West or the South Slavs. In due course, the East Slavs were also drawn into those orbits, but they remained outside the direct influence or control of either Byzantium or Western Europe.

The West Slavs

The West Slavs migrated the least geographical distance. Already inhabiting the eastern half of Poland, groups among the West Slavs migrated westward, all the way to the Elbe River (in contemporary Germany). Thus, they came to inhabit all of Poland and a considerable portion of eastern Germany. Some West Slavs migrated in a more south-westerly direction and settled in the contemporary Czech Republic and Slovakia. The dominant Slavic peoples in this area were the Poles, Czechs (or "Bohemians"), Moravians, and Slovaks. The "West Slavic" language that they had come to share diverged, over the course of time, into the three contemporary West Slav languages of Polish, Czech (spoken by the descendants of both the Bohemians and Moravians), and Slovak.

The direction of the West Slavs' migrations led them further away from possible Byzantine influence and more into the future orbit of Western European civilization, as it developed during the Middle Ages. The West Slavs regularly came into contact and conflict with the Germans. The West Slavs also came under the influence of Rome more than they did of Byzantium, with all the differences in culture and in the practice of the Christian faith involved in that contrast.

The South Slavs

The South Slavs migrated through and beyond the Carpathian Mountains that had been, in earlier times, the southernmost boundary of Slavic territory. They thus entered upon lands that had been (or, at least, had been claimed as) part of the old Roman Empire. As the successor of "old" Rome, Byzantium—which called itself "new" Rome—looked on those lands as belonging to her. Thus, the South Slavs almost immediately encountered the most sophisticated and, militarily, most powerful empire of that time. Some of them came, in the estimation of Byzantines, as invaders; others of them were invited to enter by Byzantine emperors, who wanted the Slavs to fight with and drive out other peoples whom the Byzantines wished removed from imperial territory. In either event, whatever the Byzantines may have hoped would ultimately happen, these South Slavs stayed in the territory that they entered.

Given the mountainous geography of much of the territory into which they migrated, it is not surprising that the respective Slavic peoples developed several distinct languages out of the South Slavic tongue. The contemporary South Slav languages are Slovene, Serbo-Croatian (with Serbs,

Croats, and the residents of Bosnia-Herzegovina speaking this language), Macedonian, and Bulgarian. While all these peoples initially came under the influence of Byzantium, the Slovenes and the Croats were ultimately drawn into the sphere of Roman influence. The rest of the South Slav peoples remained in the orbit of Byzantium.

As a final point with regard to the South Slavs, it is important to note that they came to be separated from both the West Slavs and the East Slavs by a band of peoples of other ethnic stocks—by Germans (in contemporary Austria), by Magyars (in contemporary Hungary [from the ninth century onwards]), and by Vlachs/Romanians (in contemporary Romania [from the fourteenth century onwards]). This limited the South Slavs' direct contact with other Slavic peoples, on the one hand; on the other, it meant that most of the South Slavs later fell under the control of the Turks as the Ottoman Empire swept into and over southeastern Europe. Thus, the South Slavs' history was influenced by their experience of Ottoman rule, something that neither the East Slavs nor the West Slavs experienced to any significant degree.

———— CHAPTER 3 ————

A Bird's Eye View, from Byzantium to Bosnia

"In this region of the world,
we have too much history."[1]

THIS CHAPTER OFFERS AN overview of the history of Eastern Europe,[2] to serve as a foundation for more detailed treatments in following chapters on specific events that have significantly shaped that history. Along the way here, we will connect elements in this overview with those from the history of Western Europe with which readers are more familiar, to show similarities and differences in how the histories of the two segments of Europe unfolded. This will invite reflection on some questions about us who live in the West and about the study of history as we have focused and practiced it—all as a way to prepare for learning about the history of Eastern Europe.

The Byzantine Foundation

In considering the history of Eastern Europe, we must begin with Byzantium, since it had enormous impact on the development of the nations and cultures of so much of the region—especially among the East and the South Slavs, but also (initially and despite interruption) among the West Slavs.[3] Typically, we in the West pay almost no attention in our schooling to Byzantium, its empire, or its civilization.[4] The historical focus in

---

1. The Croatian intellectual Boris Gunjević offered this assessment during a conversation with the author in a coffee shop in Zagreb, Croatia, in May 2008.

2. Some of the material in this chapter previously appeared in Payton, "Bypassing the History"; used here with permission.

3. See the treatment in chapter 6.

4. This situation, lamented by John Julius Norwich, led him to produce a three-volume history of Byzantium, which he condensed into a single volume, *Short History*

western education for the period when the Byzantine Empire existed (from 330 to 1453) has been on the collapse of the Roman Empire in the west and the ensuing chaos in Western Europe, and then on what we call the "medieval" period—the "middle" ages, between the ancient Greco-Roman civilization and the advent of the Renaissance and Reformation. This is understandable: what took place in Western Europe during this lengthy period has profoundly shaped that western civilization that Western Europe and North America share. In studying medieval Western Europe, we in the West are studying our own roots.

However, this virtually exclusive preoccupation with medieval Western Europe may skew our perceptions of relative significance. While what took place in the millennial period between the destruction of the Roman Empire in the west and the dawning of early modern Europe significantly molded the civilization in which we live, if we infer that what was going on in Western Europe was the pinnacle of human accomplishment in that timespan, we are profoundly mistaken. For almost the whole of the Middle Ages, Western Europe was "small potatoes," its accomplishments dwarfed by the much more sophisticated achievements of Byzantium.[5]

Byzantium's Distinctive Path

While Western Europe experienced a devastating cultural collapse and governmental chaos as the Middle Ages began, and could only rebuild slowly and arduously over the following centuries, Byzantium never knew such a collapse: no barbarian-induced chaos befell Byzantium and forced her to start anew. Under Constantine the Great and his successors in Byzantium, the new capital of the Roman Empire built on the achievements of Greco-Roman civilization.[6] More, the leaders of Byzantium self-consciously and deliberately sought to redirect that civilization in specifically and distinctively Christian directions: the Byzantines took up the best of the ancient world and transformed it into the world's longest-lasting and widest-spread Christian civilization. Learning flourished in the various centers of the Byzantine Empire, and especially in the capital city; her leading churchmen

---

of Byzantium; he intended his volumes to offer "some small amends" for the glaring omission of Byzantium in western educational curricula (xli [see also xxxix]). While Norwich's volumes are well-written and entertaining, as treatments of Byzantium they are flawed in some serious regards. For the best available studies of Byzantium's history, see Ostrogorsky, *History of the Byzantine State*; Browning, *The Byzantine Empire*; and Treadgold, *Concise History of Byzantium*.

5. For a winsome presentation of this, see Herrin, *Byzantium*.
6. See the discussions in Runciman, *Byzantine Civilization*.

were well-versed in the literatures of ancient Greece and Rome, in the Scriptures, and in the works of the church fathers; and Byzantium diligently sought to bring her neighbors throughout Eastern Europe into the Christian fold and bestow on them the benefits of Christian civilization. A few examples of Byzantine efforts in these regards point to the impact Byzantine accomplishments had for and in Eastern Europe.

Byzantium's Distinctive Thought

While the Byzantines drew on the ancient Hellenic and Hellenistic philosophical and literary heritage, already by the mid-fourth century they were quite alert to the dangers of that intellectual culture. Among the Greek-speaking Byzantines, the awareness of the corrupting influence of ancient philosophy reached such an intensity that the term they came to use for "pagan" was "hellene"—the Greek term for "Greek." Byzantine intellectuals sought to articulate faithfully Christian perspectives as over against the accepted postulates and assumptions of ancient pagan philosophical thought—especially Platonism in its various forms. Byzantine Christian thought and church life developed a distinctive approach to the faith and practice of Christianity; we in the West know this tradition of Christianity as Eastern Orthodoxy, the faith embraced in Byzantium long ago and today in much of Eastern Europe.

That so many western scholars have assessed Byzantine Christian thought (and its contemporary manifestation, Eastern Orthodoxy) as only a baptized form of Greek philosophy surely did not come from a close reading of the primary sources. I have studied Eastern Orthodoxy, off and on, for forty-five years, and Byzantium for more than thirty-five. The evidence is "all over the place" in Byzantine (and Eastern Orthodox) thought. No one would reasonably claim that the Byzantines were absolutely successful in eradicating from the patterns of their thought all traces of Platonic or other Greek philosophical influences, to be sure; however, making due allowances for such traces is a far cry from what long has been the common western scholarly assessment of Byzantine Christian (and Eastern Orthodox) thought. Indeed, throughout the whole of their more than millennial existence, the Byzantines showed a finely attuned sensitivity to even slight traces of Aristotelianism and the various shades of Platonism; by contrast, the influence of Plato and Aristotle went virtually unchallenged in Western Christian thought until well past the end of the Byzantine Empire. For anyone who affirms the importance of developing a distinctively Christian mind, the Byzantine intellectual tradition offers much to consider.

Byzantium's Distinctive Religious Art

Moreover, under the Byzantines a recognizably Christian art emerged. For this, they turned away from both the idealized art of the ancient Greeks and the more realistic art of the ancient Romans. What Byzantine artists sought to develop was an art that reflected, not the present world, but the coming one.[7]

Anyone who has looked closely at a Byzantine icon has encountered the striking results of their endeavors. In an Orthodox icon, we are not really dealing with a work of art so much as a work of contemplation. Rather than we as viewers being the ones who "see" the artwork, we are seen by it: no matter where you go in the room, the icon is looking at you; the central person or persons—Christ and/or the saints—is summoning you to enter into the experience represented in the icon. None of this is either incidental or fortuitous; it was the intended purpose of Byzantine religious art.

Further, the figures presented in the icon don't look quite "normal," the way we encounter people in this world. Once more, this is intentional: those portrayed have been so transformed by grace that they live out of the coming world, not the present one; recognizably human, they are nonetheless other than what we might meet on the street. The icon invites us, too, to live out of the new creation, rather than remaining rooted in the old one—out of the age that is coming but is not yet, rather than the one that is wasting away and will soon be no more. All this, and more, was consciously sought in the religious art developed by the Byzantines; their achievement remains captivating and, in a striking sense, spiritually compelling for all those who have eyes to see.[8]

Byzantium's Distinctive Contributions

In other ways, as well, Byzantium went its own distinctive way. She developed the political arts of diplomacy to a pitch such as the world had never before seen.[9] She explored, through often brutal difficulties, the tensions between ruler and ruled; she developed codes of laws that have been the foundation of legal and governmental systems in Europe, both East and West; and she developed ways of taking care of the disadvantaged in society

---

7. See the wide-ranging discussion in Runciman, *Byzantine Style and Civilization*.

8. For a penetrating presentation about iconography, see Ouspensky and Lossky, *The Meaning of Icons*, 9–55; for a profound metaphysical reflection on the significance and role of icons, see Evdokimov, *Art of the Icon*.

9. See the treatment in Obolensky, *Byzantium and the Slavs*, 1–22.

that were more than just the bread and circuses of Roman antiquity.[10] Byzantine experience dealt with the perennial problems of human existence in a flawed world. She bequeathed her endeavors in all these areas to the East and South Slavs of Eastern Europe.

Western Neglect of Byzantium

However, we in the West have given little attention in our education—at the primary level, in secondary school, or in university—to Byzantium. That invites some questions about that schooling. Given what we have just surveyed, the neglect of Byzantium seems curious: while education appropriately prepares us to live within the culture in which we find ourselves, such education is an exercise in parochialism if it focuses only on itself. For the education within a civilization to examine nothing but its own roots is historical narcissism. To be sure, what has developed in Western Europe and North America in the centuries since the medieval period warrants careful attention, since western civilization has profoundly impacted the entire world. But western civilization is certainly not the whole story; indeed, for much of the story, it is a relatively insignificant "bit" player in the development of civilization.

Unquestionably, scholars interested in the development of Christendom, on the one hand, and Christian scholars interested in discerning how to develop and articulate a Christian approach to civilization in the contemporary world, on the other, should be attracted by Byzantium. The undeniable fact that the first, the most accomplished, and the longest-lasting such civilization was Byzantium should not be ignored. Where else can one find a determinedly Christian civilization that exercised so much influence in the world? Where else can one encounter a Christian civilization that experimented with the implications of the Christian faith in so many areas of life? Where else, indeed, can anyone find a Christian state that lasted for more than 1,100 years, and which knew only Christian rulers for all but nineteen months of that period?

Byzantine history should certainly be an inviting field for those intrigued by Christendom and its influence on life, society, and culture. Those who seek to articulate such an approach in the present day would do well to pay attention to Byzantium. Scholars focused on the development of Christendom have risen to the occasion and produced numerous studies on Byzantium and its influence—even if those studies have not yet

---

10. See the seminal studies by Constantelos, *Byzantine Philanthropy,* and *Poverty, Society and Philanthropy.*

worked their way into the regular curricular offerings in western educational circles. It is disappointing that scholars in institutions concerned to articulate and inculcate a Christian approach to scholarship and culture have not turned to the study of Byzantium as a significant historical resource for their concerns.[11]

Shaping Eastern Europe

Byzantium did not hoard the riches of her Christian culture to herself. Rather, she sought to impart her Christian civilization, its insights, and its benefits to her neighbors. In that way, Byzantium had a lasting effect on the world in general, and on Eastern Europe particularly, down to the present day.

Imparting the Christian Faith

In mission endeavors conducted over the course of several centuries, Byzantium brought the message of the Christian faith to her various neighbors. While she was successful in this outreach with many nearby peoples,[12] the culmination of Byzantium's evangelistic efforts came in Eastern Europe, with the conversion of the Slavs in the ninth and tenth centuries. Christianity and civilization came together to the Slavs; and both came in Byzantine flavor.

Byzantium's work in these regards set a distinctive stamp on these peoples. Where her mission endeavors were given free reign,[13] she passed

---

11. The 2002 edition (the last one I received) of *Directory of American Byzantinists* listed scholars from both Canada and the U.S.A. involved in Byzantine studies. This directory included only four faculty from the 105 institutions in the Coalition of Christian Colleges and Universities (CCCU), an organization that prioritizes a Christian approach to scholarship and culture. Only three of those faculty (including me) had research interests in Byzantium, and only two (one of them me) taught any courses in Byzantium or Byzantine studies.

12. The following peoples were converted to Christianity via Byzantine mission endeavors: the Zichi and the Abasgi on the eastern shore of the Black Sea; the Lazi and the Tzani on the southeast coast of the Black Sea; the Georgians and the Alans in the Caucasus region; and the Romanians and some of the Albanians (using the names anachronistically, but to indicate the peoples who were converted and the places they eventually settled) in the Balkans.

13. Among the West Slavs, the state of Moravia requested Byzantine missionaries in 862; Cyril and Methodius were sent in response. The ruler of Moravia, Rastislav, and his people responded eagerly to the Byzantine mission endeavors. However, palace intrigues led to Rastislav being displaced from the throne and the Christian mission

on the Byzantine Christian heritage and its concern for distinctively Christian civilization to the peoples of Eastern Europe—to Bulgaria, Serbia, and Kievan Rus' (the state out of which Russia, Ukraine, and Belarus all eventually developed). Byzantine efforts resulted, not only in the conversion of these Slavic peoples, but in their imbibing the Byzantine approach to both Christianity and civilization; the Slavs who were evangelized and instructed by the Byzantines came to flourish under their tutelage, as can be demonstrated in a variety of ways.

Developing Christian Cultures

Among these, one that stands out is the development of Slavic literature. After the Byzantine missionaries, Cyril and Methodius, prepared an alphabet with which they reduced the Slavonic language to written form (in the ninth century), they translated the Scriptures, liturgies, and other Christian literature into the Slavonic tongue. Literacy among the Slavic peoples thus began with and built on Christian literature; since they were learning to read and write their own native tongue, the Slavic peoples could and did go on to develop their own vernacular literatures.

The Byzantine influence was significant for the development of Slavic cultures, consequently, in two regards: in the first place, the translations offered the Slavic peoples some of the richest contributions of the most advanced Christian civilization that had ever existed; secondly, in providing a way to write in the Slavic language, Byzantine efforts made for the development of vernacular literatures that, drawing on and building from the Christian literature made available by Byzantine translations into Slavonic, assured that those Slavic vernacular literatures would be steeped in the Christian faith. In this way, Byzantium's Christian civilization molded the beginnings of the literatures and cultures of the Slavic peoples in most of Eastern Europe, with effects still perceived in these languages and cultures to the present day. At the time, nothing remotely comparable was taking place among the peoples of Western Europe.

Byzantine efforts in these regards bore remarkable fruit among the Slavic peoples, substantially more than Rome was achieving at the time in Western Europe. We can get a sense of the considerable difference in sophistication between the Western Europe, which is our background, and

---

work turned over to German missionaries, who insisted on Western Christian practices. In this way, the initial Byzantine mission efforts were stanched among the West Slavs, all of whom ended up being drawn into Western Christianity rather than Eastern Orthodoxy. For more detail on this, see chapter 6.

Eastern Europe, under Byzantine influence, by comparing the attainments in literacy in royal courts. In 1215, King John of England signed the *Magna Carta* with an "X," because he could neither read nor write. Already 150 years earlier, in Kievan Rus', the children of the nobility were taught to read and write three languages.[14] The difference is undeniable and dramatic; other examples to the same effect could be adduced.

The point to appreciate is that, as argued above, during what we in the West call the medieval period, the center of historical gravity for European culture, sophistication, and civilization was not found in Western Europe; it was in Eastern Europe, in the "Byzantine Commonwealth."[15] And the European countries that could legitimately be called advanced were the ones in Eastern Europe, which had been molded by Byzantine influences.

The Eclipse of Eastern Europe

However, these noteworthy developments of Christian culture within Eastern Europe were brought to a screeching halt by outside forces—forces from which Western Europe escaped, in large part, because they spent their strength on Eastern Europe. Due to its geography, Eastern Europe had always been exposed to assault from Central Asian peoples, who could pass without notable hindrance across the broad expanses of the Russian steppes and then come swarming north of the Black Sea, bursting into Eastern Europe in waves of destruction. This had frequently happened over the centuries: Scythians had thus inundated Eastern Europe about 500 BC, Huns in the fourth and fifth centuries AD, Avars in the sixth and seventh centuries, Bulgars in the seventh, and Magyars in the ninth. After that, a period of almost 350 years passed—to the mid-1200s—in which Eastern Europe was spared such ravages.

Devastated by Invasions

During that period, Byzantine mission and civilizing efforts had borne remarkable fruit; however, the resultant Christian civilizations that had developed among the Slavic peoples were all devastated by the rampages

---

14. According to accounts from the period, in mid-eleventh-century Kievan Rus', Prince Vsevolod could read and write three and could speak at least five languages.

15. This designation for Byzantium and the nations she influenced in Eastern Europe has won acceptance among scholars via the insightful treatment found in a work so entitled by Obolensky, *The Byzantine Commonwealth*.

of the Mongols in the 1240s.[16] The state of Kievan Rus', with almost all of its glorious achievements, was demolished by forces under the leadership of Batu Khan, whose successors ruthlessly dominated much of the former Kievan Rus' territories for the next two centuries. While the rest of Eastern Europe escaped prolonged repression by the Mongols, all the states in Eastern Europe except Bohemia were laid waste by these invaders; for quite a while, anything more than mere survival was a luxury.

It took most of the rest of the 1200s for Eastern Europe to recover from the devastations wrought by the Mongols. Kievan Rus' did not recover; Bulgaria and Serbia did, though, and each managed to rebuild a strong Christian state, molded by Byzantine cultural influences. However, the Ottoman Turks gained a foothold in Europe in the mid-1300s. Before the end of that century, both Bulgaria and Serbia had been overwhelmed by this Muslim powerhouse, and with the conquest of Byzantium by Ottoman forces in 1453, the southern tier of Eastern Europe passed into a period of repression in which Christian culture and civilization suffered grievously. This night lasted for five centuries.

Swallowed by Empires

In the northern tier of Eastern Europe, Turkish invasions provoked havoc and resulted in some loss of territory, but the Turkish advance was eventually halted. Even so, the rest of the nations of Eastern Europe at the time—Poland, Bohemia, and Hungary—were all swallowed up by surrounding empires. By the late 1300s, most of the states of Eastern Europe had lost their independence; by 1530, all of them except Poland had; and as of 1795, Poland had also succumbed. By the late eighteenth century, there were no independent Eastern European states. During the nineteenth century, two states (Romania and Serbia) broke free from Ottoman control; the rest of Eastern Europe would not again know freedom until the twentieth century.

Centuries of Repression

During the period of their subjugation, the various peoples of Eastern Europe endured oppression of various kinds and differing degrees. While the northern nations in the region found themselves repressed by fellow Christians—Roman Catholic Habsburgs, Protestant Prussians, or Orthodox Russians—the nations of the southern tier of Eastern Europe suffered greatly

---

16. See the treatment below, in chapter 10.

under Muslim domination by the Ottoman Turks. The repressing empires prohibited anything that would enable any of the Eastern European peoples effectively or constructively to nurture its sense of self-identity: culture clubs, vernacular literatures, and ethnic holidays were all proscribed. Nevertheless, families and villages passed down recollections of bygone national glories. These stories held out hope for deliverance; yet at the same time they made the repressions seem all the more intense. The sufferings and collective memories together shaped the respective self-understandings of the various subject peoples of Eastern Europe. Even so, this was meager fare to sustain their respective hopes for such extended periods of time.

Hope and the Church

How, though, did the peoples of Eastern Europe manage to retain their hopes for restored freedom and statehood? For virtually all of them, the story was the same: the place where that dream was protected and nurtured was the church.[17] However restrictive the oppressing empires otherwise were, each of them allowed the church, to varying degrees, to function apart from imperial control. In that way, throughout Eastern Europe, awareness of nationality and commitment to religion were fused, with consequences lasting to the present day. On the one hand, this allowed the church to serve as the cohesive bond among the people and kept the Christian message in the forefront of their consciousness; on the other, this fusion could also allow the Christian message to be co-opted for political sloganeering and xenophobic hysteria. In either case, the experience of the peoples of Eastern Europe over the last five centuries allowed the church to retain a leading role in their nations and cultures. Obviously, the experience of the church in Eastern Europe in this regard has been dramatically different from what has transpired with the church in the West during this time period.

In the half-millennium between the subjugation of much of Eastern Europe and its renewed freedoms after World War I—those centuries when western civilization came to full flower and dominated the rest of the world in so many ways—the peoples of Eastern Europe knew little more than faint hope kept alive by memory of the distant past. Among them, history flourished—but in a different way than among us in the West.

---

17. For a careful treatment of this in the case of the Bulgarians, see Hupchick, *Bulgarians in the Seventeenth Century*; Hupchick's analysis offers a pattern that, *mutatis mutandis*, would apply to virtually all the nations of Eastern Europe.

Sense of History

It has often been noted that the peoples of Eastern Europe have a different sense of history than we in the West do.[18] Theirs is undeniably a deeper, certainly a more painful, and unquestionably a more compelling sense of history. We may remember significant events from our collective past, but they rarely grip us profoundly. How different it is among Eastern Europeans! The mention of the Battle of White Mountain in 1620 may cause a Czech to clench his teeth; a reference to the Battle of Kosovo-Polje in 1389 will likely bring a tear to the eye of a Serb; and an allusion to the Zaporozhian Sich of the Cossacks might provoke a far-away look on the visage of a Ukrainian. History lives more powerfully among Eastern Europeans than it does among us.

We in the West have been advantaged to be in the vanguard of the victorious for the last several centuries, but we hardly live in any profound awareness of our history. As we consider the peoples of Eastern Europe, however, we are confronted by the historical awareness of others—others who have been sharers in European civilization and in its Christian heritage, indeed, but who have been, for half a millennium, the victims of the march of time. The self-understanding of the various peoples of Eastern Europe challenges what has been (at least, until recently) our common western assumption of progress. What the peoples of Eastern Europe have known over the last several centuries has forced them to ask penetrating questions about the course of history, especially about the alleged progress of which their various repressors were supposedly the embodiments. As the Polish philosopher Stanisław Jerzy Lec poignantly put it, "Is it progress if a cannibal eats with knife and fork?"[19]

Studying Eastern Europe opens up the possibility of learning from much deeper, richer senses of history than have developed among us in western civilization. And as we see our western dreams of progress vanish in the contemporary world, we might do well to reconsider how we view the past; this might set us up better, both to live in the present and to prepare for the future. The historical awareness of the peoples of Eastern Europe might offer us insights in those regards.

---

18. This is emphasized, *inter alia*, by Heymann, *Poland and Czechoslovakia*, vi; Mojzes, *Yugoslavian Inferno*, 50; and Hoffman, *Exit into History*, xiv, xvi, 293.

19. Cited from *Oxford Dictionary of Quotations*, 415:10.

The Re-Emergence of Eastern Europe

Since 1989, Eastern Europe has emerged from the Communist domination that had kept it in thrall since the end of World War II. The states of the region have taken their first steps—all painful, some brutal—into the freedom to govern themselves. The world witnessed nations being born or reborn and stepping into an uncertain future: this in itself invites close interest, for it does not happen often. The three decades since the collapse of the Communist bloc have also shown western organizations and nations intervening in a multitude of ways in the region, with widely varying results.

The Collapse of Communism

The whirlwind of revolution in 1989 showed that Communism had claimed neither the allegiance nor the hearts of the peoples of Eastern Europe. Even so, no one in the West foresaw the collapse: the most knowledgeable commentators on world affairs did not see it coming, no history or political science professors predicted it, and, despite intensive espionage activities, no western government anticipated it. The repudiation of Soviet domination rendered most western military plans pointless and much confident prophetic literature obsolete. And yet the most powerful and imposing menace the world had known since the end of Nazism came to an end in Eastern Europe without a single gunshot fired by those throwing off the Communist yoke. The collective will of the long-repressed and misused peoples of Eastern Europe simply shrugged off what western nuclear arsenals could not budge. If these people have that kind of inner strength, after so long suffering, then surely we in the effete West have something we can learn from them. An excellent way to begin to do that is to study the history of Eastern Europe.

The Difficulties of Independence

The joyful beginnings of the new states of Eastern Europe soon foundered, though, on the shoals of harsh reality. In the years since 1989, each of the countries has wrestled with imposing difficulties in trying to rid itself of the unwanted legacies of long subjugation under oppressive empires of past and, with Communism, of recent memory. The deep sense of history considered above has contributed, both negatively and positively, to these struggles.

On the one hand, it has led to tension and provoked hostility. Almost always in Eastern Europe, history dresses itself up in ethnic costume; often, that costume includes concealed weapons. The years since 1989 have witnessed old animosities and resentments finding contemporary expression throughout the region; this can be seen in the relationships between Romanians and Hungarians, between Czechs and Slovaks—and in the Orange Revolution of 2004 and again, since 2014, between Ukrainians and Russians. The evidence was at its most graphic, though, in the warfare that broke out in the former Yugoslavia. There, the collective memories of Croats, of Serbs, and of Boshniaks all harked back to the days when their respective nations had flourished in the region. Those same memories compelled each of these peoples to demand for their states in the present the full territory ever held by their respective ancestor states. However, those earlier states of Croatia, Serbia, and Bosnia of these collective memories had all flourished at different times, and their various borders had overlapped significantly. Given the tensions among Croats, Serbs, and Boshniaks that had simmered and occasionally burst into flame in preceding centuries, and with the fuel of new hopes and expectations after Communism's collapse, it is not surprising that Yugoslavia was engulfed in the conflagration of war. Anyone familiar with the region knows that Kosovo has been a flash point for tensions between Serbs and Albanians for centuries: virtually holy land to the Serbs, but populated in overwhelming numbers by Albanians, Kosovo is claimed by each side as its own. In post-Communist Yugoslavia, each side engaged in hostilities against the other which eventually led to intervention by outside forces in 1999. Subsequent involvement by the North Atlantic Treaty Organization [NATO] and the United Nations in Kosovo has quieted the tensions, but not resolved them.

On the other hand, the same deep sense of history that has borne such bitter fruit has also contributed positively to developments within the nations of Eastern Europe since 1989. The sense of commonality fostered by the collective histories has encouraged a unity for these peoples that has allowed them to forge a shared commitment to their now independent states. With this, they have shown themselves ready, for the most part, to endure the pains necessary to enable their states to flourish. The resilience they manifested over the course of many centuries of repression as they nourished their hopes collectively has served them well, for the most part, in the generation since 1989, as they have been learning to shape their own national destinies.

Conclusion

It is important for the West to become familiar with the history of Eastern Europe. For one thing, it would help us in the future deal more wisely with whatever problems may occur in the region, which might necessitate further vigorous involvements by western nations. The warfare in the former Yugoslavia in the early 1990s and the conflicts about Kosovo at the end of that decade offered compelling evidence of the importance of such understanding and appreciation. The decisions taken and actions endorsed by countries from the West that tried to intervene in the conflicts showed little understanding of the self-perceptions of the Croats, Serbs, and Boshniaks, in the earlier conflict, or the Serbs and Albanians, in the latter one, or of these peoples' respective views of and actual histories with each other. Many of these decisions and actions, well-meant as they unquestionably were, actually served to prolong the conflicts and even worsen them. Greater familiarity with the history of these peoples and of their views of self and others would not have made dealing with the warfare simple, but it might have helped find ways to avoid exacerbating the conflicts—which some western decisions and actions did. There are other tense relationships within Eastern Europe that might yet invite outside intervention, in order to forestall conflict. In today's global village, we cannot afford not to become familiar with the histories and self-perceptions of the peoples of Eastern Europe.

The same necessity arises, utterly apart from questions of conflict. In the years since the collapse of Communism, western organizations of several kinds—from the realms of business, education, service, and missions—have reached into the various countries of Eastern Europe. What became evident and has been repeatedly stressed in advice given in books, magazine and trade articles, and in comment by a wide variety of people, is that western organizations need to understand and appreciate the heritage, background, and history of the state in which they are trying to operate. Failure to do so has resulted far too often in the failure of the project. Only as we in the West sympathetically and appreciative learn the history of Eastern Europe can we hope to reach out to the various nations in it.

If the West becomes familiar with the history of Eastern Europe, we will be better able both to contribute significantly to peace in the present world and also to work far more effectively within the region. Beyond these considerations, the history of Eastern Europe offers fascinating intellectual challenges; not least among them is the opportunity for those interested in history to explore the deep sense of history that pervades the region.

CHAPTER 4

A Question of Terminology

"The idea of Eastern Europe... is much
older than the Cold War."[1]

IN PREPARATION FOR PLUNGING into this study of Eastern Europe's history, it may be helpful to become aware of a scholarly disagreement about the way to refer to the region.[2] Because of that argument, readers may encounter differing designations for the area. Being at least acquainted with the terminologies used and the rationales for them will help readers avoid possible confusion when they encounter alternative designations.

This brief presentation will not try to settle the scholarly question. What I intend to do here is indicate the contours of the disagreement. Then I will comment on and respond to some of the argument and indicate why this book will refer to the region as "Eastern Europe."

"Eastern Europe" or "East Central Europe"?

The conflict over the best designation to use for the region is not a new problem. Francis Dvornik, a respected specialist in the area from a previous generation, wrote about this question almost sixty years ago: "In the last decades the problem of the division of European history into Eastern and Western spheres and the limits of these spheres have been the object of numerous scholarly discussions.... The concept of 'eastern Europe' changed through different periods, and its definition varies according to the convictions or prejudices of the historian dealing with this problem."[3] The argument about how to refer to the region is, consequently, one of long standing.

---

1. Wolff, *Inventing Eastern Europe*, 3.
2. Some of the material in this chapter appeared previously in Payton, "Bypassing the History," and Payton, "Revisioning the Historiography"; used here with permission.
3. Dvornik, *Slavs in European History*, xxii–xxiii.

The commonly used designation "Eastern Europe" seems straightforward enough, but it is not without its problems. Although the obvious differentiation from "Western Europe" seems to be nothing more than a geographical designation, for many scholars the signification of the adjective has had less to do with geography than with politics. The *political* connotation of *Eastern* Europe was certainly not beclouded with ambiguity:[4] during the last half of the twentieth century, when the vast bulk of publications dealing with the region were published in the West, "Eastern Europe" included the countries outside the former Union of Soviet Socialist Republics [USSR] that comprised the Soviet bloc—including the mavericks Yugoslavia, Albania, and Romania. However, this usage has come under fire among some scholars because it describes the geographic area in terms of political structures externally imposed after World War II and maintained for most of the last half of the past century. The label "Eastern Europe," thus, forced a designation onto the area that had nothing to do with the area in itself. According to this argument, the designation suffers under the disability that it lent only an artificial and external unity to the area—a unity that, furthermore, no longer exists.

Several scholars argued that it would be better to opt for a *geographical* designation for the area. The one most frequently proposed is "East Central Europe." These scholars have argued that, as over against the politically-charged designation noted above, "East Central Europe" offers the advantage of referring to unchanging geographic characteristics: it would include that segment of the European continent between 10°E and 30°E longitude. (From this perspective, "Eastern Europe" would then refer to the area beyond the edge of East Central Europe to the Ural Mountains, at 60°E longitude; thus, it would include eastern Belarus, eastern Ukraine, and European Russia.)

One can appreciate the desire to adopt a designation that avoids the unwelcome connection to the period of the USSR's hegemony over the area. While one must recognize the significance of Communist Russian domination of the region for most of the last half of the twentieth century, it is even more necessary to recognize that the region has had its own distinctive history for centuries, during most of which neither tsarist Russia nor the Communist USSR exercised any appreciable influence. As a result of these

---

4. In the estimation of one scholar in the field, "Eastern Europe is far more of a political expression than a geographical one" (Walters, *The Other Europe*, xi); this political sense of the designation was assumed in the approach found in Swain and Swain, *Eastern Europe since 1945*, and in Augustinos, *National Idea in Eastern Europe*.

(and other related) considerations, the designation "East Central Europe" initially won some significant support in scholarly circles.[5]

It turned out, though, that while this geographic term offered a designation that might avoid the vagaries of political affiliation, it could not escape those that—to appropriate Dvornik's assessment above—arose from "the convictions or prejudices" of the historians who use it. For some who appropriated the term, "East Central Europe" includes all the nations within the indicated longitudinal limits—which is precisely what one would expect in such a geographical usage.[6] However, for others, East Central Europe includes only the northern tier of the geographic area,[7] with the southern tier being designated "the Balkans" or "Southeastern Europe."[8]

The reasons offered for this distinction have nothing to do with that geographical focus that proponents of "East Central Europe" emphasized in preferring it to "Eastern Europe"; those reasons are either historical or cultural, or an amalgam of the two. The general *historical* justification is that the two tiers encountered quite different outside influences during the past half-millennium and, consequently, warrant being kept distinct. The *cultural* defense of this distinction is that, in the lengthy period before the last five hundred years, the two tiers were shaped by the contrasting emphases of Rome and Western Christianity in the northern area, and of Byzantium and Eastern Christianity (with subsequent influences from the Ottoman Empire and Islam) in the southern region. In any event, these differences are seen as weighty enough to legitimize separating the two parts of what is, geographically, unquestionably a single area.[9]

Observations

Whatever one thinks of these considerations, it is clear that "East Central Europe" has turned out to be considerably less than an innocuous geographical designation. Given the way this terminology has ended up being appropriated by various scholars, the designation has lost some of its luster.

5. The designation was adopted for the ground-breaking ten-volume series, *History of East Central Europe*, eds. Sugar and Treadgold.

6. Rothschild used the designation in this fashion in *Return to Diversity*; it is also used thus in Drachkovitch, ed., *East Central Europe*.

7. This is the way the term was used by Wandycz in *The Price of Freedom*; Wandycz's book dealt only with Poland, the Czech Republic, Slovakia, and Hungary. In *Poland and Czechoslovakia*, Heymann used "East Central Europe" with the same delimitation (21).

8. Crampton identified this coalition of terms as distinctive to American scholarship on Eastern Europe (*Eastern Europe*, xi).

9. See the discussion in Wandycz, *The Price of Freedom*, 1–11.

Actual usage ended up offering considerably less clarity than it was expected to provide: it came to be used in two quite divergent, even opposed, senses. With this, the alleged preferability of the designation on the basis of its pristine geographical reference was compromised.

Beyond that, one of those senses makes it difficult to present what is undeniably a fundamental consideration regarding the history of the region—namely, the commonalities in the experience of the peoples throughout the entire area. While the historical and cultural divergences between the northern and southern tiers noted above need to be acknowledged and given their due weight, the common experience throughout the region is even more basic in my estimation to understanding what has transpired in its history. A further disability for the designation "East Central Europe" is that it is not the way scholars usually referred to the region in the past.

The argument in favor of "Eastern Europe" is not actually limited, as one might surmise from the comments of its opponents noted above, to the political distinctions of the post-World War II period. A good case can be made in favor of the designation "Eastern Europe," a case that has nothing to do with the period of Communist domination.

For one thing, it is clear that most of those who ultimately settled in Western Europe were of Germanic stock; by contrast, the predominance of those who came to reside permanently in the eastern half of the continent were of Slavic stock. In this sense, Europe can be distinguished into *Western* and *Eastern*. In addition to the commonality in ethnic heritage throughout the eastern portion of Europe, the various peoples of the region faced similar pressures from outside forces during much of their history. Moreover, all the peoples of the region passed through similar socio-economic and political experiences as peoples, experiences different from what became the basic pattern for the peoples of Western Europe. This legitimizes referring to the region as *Eastern* Europe, in simple contrast to *Western* Europe. Finally, the designation "Eastern Europe" has the sanction of regular historiographical usage: for a considerable period of time, "Eastern Europe" served as the preferred designation.

A good case can be made, then, for "Eastern Europe" as a legitimate historical designation for the region, quite apart from the political divergence of the last half of the twentieth century. The obvious contrast to *Western* Europe comports with most of the history of the region. Beyond that, "Eastern Europe" has the undeniable advantage of being the term most commonly encountered in the literature, both in the past and still in the present. Because of these (and other) considerations, in this book we will refer to the region as "Eastern Europe."[10]

---

10. The case for this perspective is capably argued in Bideleux and Jeffries, *History of Eastern Europe*, 8–30; although Walters views "Eastern Europe" primarily as a political designation (*The Other Europe*, xi), at a later point in his treatment he nevertheless indicates other considerations that lend a unity to the whole area and would legitimize denominating it "Eastern Europe" (*The Other Europe*, 110–31); Simons, *Eastern Europe*, also recognized a basic similarity in background throughout the region that would allow it to be considered as distinct from Western Europe, apart from and preceding the imposition of Soviet control (1–14); see also Wolff, *Inventing Eastern Europe*, who argued that Western Europeans have viewed Eastern Europe as an identifiable geographical and cultural unit distinct from Western Europe since at least the time of the Enlightenment (3–8); significantly, Drakulić—an Eastern European writer (from Croatia)—has poignantly argued that there remains, and for a considerable time to come will almost certainly continue to remain, significant differences between the peoples and cultures of Eastern and Western Europe: see her discussions at *Café Europa*, 1–51.

CHAPTER 5

Problems in the Historiography of Eastern Europe

"Today's Eastern Europe is a living lesson in how much
it [a collective past] does matter."[1]

READING, RESEARCH, AND CAREFUL reflection led me to recognize three significant problems in the historiography of Eastern Europe (i.e., the way that history has been written).[2] Pointing them out and elaborating on them will help readers see the need for a quite different approach to the study of Eastern European history—the approach taken in the rest of this book.

Introduction

The 1989 collapse of Soviet domination over Eastern Europe put the historiography of the region in considerable upheaval. Communist hegemony over Eastern Europe from soon after World War II through the end of the 1980s profoundly shaped, not only the history of Eastern Europe, but also the way that history was studied and taught. With the collapse of the Communist bloc, historiography on Eastern Europe has had to add assessments of the Communist impact and legacy. Furthermore, that historiography also now needs to incorporate the post-Soviet state of affairs throughout the region. However, the historiography of Eastern Europe needs to change more than just its treatment of the Soviet Union's relationship to and effects on Eastern Europe.

---

1. Hoffman, *Exit into History*, 293.
2. Some of the material in this chapter appeared previously in Payton, "Revisioning the Historiography," and in Payton, "Religion and the Historiography"; used here with permission.

Scholarly study of the history of Eastern Europe only began in earnest after the end of World War II.[3] A few intrepid scholars had been exploring that history previously, to be sure, but the history of Eastern Europe as an academic discipline dates only from shortly after the region's incorporation into the Communist bloc. The collapse of the Iron Curtain in 1989 brought an end to Soviet hegemony throughout the region and, as noted above, a considerable challenge to the historiography of Eastern Europe as it had developed to that point. Undeniably, 1989 drastically changed the character of the historiographical game; at the least, much of the previous rationale for playing it was irrevocably altered. In the years since then, the various nations of Eastern Europe, individually and collectively, entered upon wide, new, and virtually unanticipated possibilities for self-determination. Some of the steps they have taken have raised questions about the historiography of Eastern Europe. Consequently, assessing that historiography is both appropriate and timely.

We cannot attempt a thorough assessment of that historiography in all its facets and emphases here, however. While such an evaluation would be a welcome contribution to scholarship, it would be a vast undertaking,[4] far beyond the possibilities of our review here. Our focus will be more modest: we will be concerned with broad patterns found in the historiography—specifically, with three significant problems that get in the way of understanding the region and its peoples. These problems are the temporal imbalance, the lack of general treatments, and the failure to treat religion as a formative influence in the history of the region. The discussion here will describe these concerns and seek to demonstrate, from several vantage points, why they are significant.

3. Long before World War II, the peoples and rulers of Western Europe knew about Eastern Europe, of course; at the latest, by the time of Charlemagne in the late eighth century, the Germanic peoples of Western Europe knew about Slavic neighbors to their east. The awareness of the differentness of the eastern regions and their inhabitants waxed and waned over succeeding centuries. Petkov, *Infidels, Turks, and Women*, treated how the peoples of the Holy Roman Empire viewed the residents of the Balkans; Wolff has shown (*Inventing Eastern Europe*, 5–10) that the *philosophes* played a significant role in defining what became the common Western European (and, eventually, North American) view of Eastern Europe. Even so, whatever interest there was in Eastern Europe in previous centuries, and whatever writing was produced about the region during those times, western scholarship did not turn its attention to the history of Eastern Europe until shortly after the end of World War II.

4. An evaluation of this sort would require painstaking consideration of the principal themes of the historiography, the insightful contributions found in the literature, and the controversies among scholars in the field; discussion of the numerous monographs that have advanced historical understanding in the sub-fields of the history of Eastern Europe; and assessment of the various national histories that have been produced.

Temporal Imbalance

A notable problem in what have been the prevailing patterns of historiography on Eastern Europe is temporal imbalance. In comparison with the length of time that invites attention, what is actually covered in the historiography is a terribly short piece. The first unquestioned references to the inhabitants of Eastern Europe date from the sixth century AD.[5] From then onwards, written sources record what has transpired in the region. Since historical treatment depends on written records, the *history* of Eastern Europe begins from the sixth century and continues to the present. Given that, it is striking to discover how little of that history is actually covered in the historiography that has been produced.

There are scores, if not hundreds, of scholarly books dealing with the history of Eastern Europe, but almost all these volumes examine only the last fifty years or so of the twentieth century. One book stands out as an exception to this generalization: E. Garrison Walters' *The Other Europe: Eastern Europe to 1945* only anticipates, rather than focuses on, the Communist period. This volume is the only one of its kind, however. Scholars in Western Europe and North America restricted their research on and investigation of Eastern Europe to the period since World War II. The books published on this period of Eastern European history have unquestionably advanced and deepened the understanding of what has transpired in the various countries of the area during that period. Some of these studies focused on one nation; others described the Soviet bloc more generally. The bibliographies offered at the end of the respective books indicate how many such volumes were published on this brief segment of the region's history; to take one example, Joseph Rothschild's *Return to Diversity: A Political History of East Central Europe since World War II* listed ninety-four such titles.[6]

However, those same bibliographies indicate the paucity of scholarly work on preceding eras of Eastern European history. To be sure, some books on individual nations or geographic areas within Eastern Europe include helpful treatments on the period before the twentieth century,[7] but those

---

5. These are found in the works of the Gothic historian Jordanes and in the Byzantine historian Procopius. Earlier references to the peoples north of the Carpathian mountains, by Herodotus in ancient Greece and by various authors in the Roman Empire, spoke about peoples whom the authors and their respective civilizations had not actually encountered (although Herodotus himself may have met some Slavs from north of the Crimea, where he resided for a time); both Jordanes and Procopius wrote about these peoples who had moved through the Carpathians and had collided with both the Byzantine Empire and the Gothic tribes; see the treatment above, in chapter 2.

6. These are found in his "Suggested Readings," at 279–84.

7. Examples include Wandycz, *The Price of Freedom*, which spends 194 out of 273

treatments focus only on the particular nation or limited geographic area under review. Books on the broader history of Eastern Europe offered minuscule treatment, if any, of the preceding eras; even Walters' introductory overview devoted a scant sixteen pages out of 363 to the history of Eastern Europe prior to the year 1800. Other volumes manifested an even more austere penury in their attention to the preceding history: one example was R. J. Crampton's *Eastern Europe in the Twentieth Century*, which scanned the whole period up to the beginning of World War I in twenty-seven pages out of 415 in his volume; of these, less than three pages considered the period before 1800. In the main, one will search the contents, notes, and bibliographies of the abundant historiography on Eastern Europe in vain for studies of the centuries of that history prior to the twentieth. This silence is at once deafening and eloquent.

The historiographical fixation on this limited period needs to be challenged. It should be obvious that focusing on the period in which the nations of Eastern Europe were, at best, reluctant participants in the Soviet Union's theater of the absurd will hardly lead to in-depth understanding of those nations. While such scholarly studies may have been able to describe the role played by each of the respective nations in the Soviet script, those studies do not necessarily tell us much about the actors themselves. Surely it is high time to become acquainted with those actors, now that they are writing their own scripts! A comparison may help make the point: would any scholar think he or she had adequately represented the history of the Netherlands if his or her treatment focused solely on the period of its Nazi occupation in World War II? To ask the question is enough to answer it. Analogously, the serious inadequacy of the historiography on Eastern Europe in this regard is undeniable.

It should hardly seem necessary to urge historians to recognize that history is a lengthy process that shapes peoples and nations. Nevertheless, the historiography on Eastern Europe gives scant evidence of such an awareness. If the goal of historical study is to try to understand as fully as possible what has happened to peoples, nations, or areas of the world, and how this has affected them, then what has been produced on the history of Eastern Europe is seriously deficient. To assume that nothing of shaping

---

pages on the history of the nations of the northern tier of Eastern Europe before World War I; and several national histories, which often have better historical proportion: in Sugar, Hanák, and Frank, *A History of Hungary*, 266 pages out of 404 are devoted to the period before the twentieth century; Crampton, *Concise History of Bulgaria*, gives 147 pages out of 243 to Bulgarian history prior to 1918; other well-balanced national histories are Gazi, *A History of Croatia*, which devotes 169 out of 360 pages to the period before the twentieth century; and Malcolm, *Bosnia: A Short History*, which gives 136 pages out of 252 to the period before World War I.

significance for the various Eastern European peoples' self-understandings, views about neighboring peoples, emphases in culture, or development in national outlook—to name only four such possibilities—occurred between the end of the prehistoric period in Eastern Europe and the middle of the twentieth century is absurd. No one would suggest such a perspective for the history of Western Europe; nevertheless, this is what the present historiography on Eastern Europe seems to imply.

This suggestion is one that no one in Eastern Europe would begin to accept. The monolithic orientation on the last half of the preceding century indicates that the historians who have written on Eastern Europe profoundly failed to understand the peoples of Eastern Europe: it betrays a significant failure to appreciate how the peoples and nations of Eastern Europe instinctively appropriate their own history. Frederick G. Heymann urged the importance of this in the introduction to his brief volume on the West Slav nations, explaining why his treatment devoted so much attention to the history before 1900:

> The main reason for this emphasis on earlier historical roots lies in the fact that the West Slav nations are intensely history-conscious, probably more so than most other modern nations, especially in their constant relating to events and developments that go back over many centuries.... Their [Poles', Czechs', and Slovaks'] own historical perspective goes back to the Middle Ages and the times of the Reformation and the Renaissance. Without presenting, however sketchily, such phases . . . , it would not be possible even to approach the ideas that dominate the historical consciousness and with it the actions and reactions of the West Slav nations to this day.[8]

Similarly, Paul Mojzes (a Yugoslav expatriate living in the United States) urged that people in the Balkans are more intensely aware of their past, and that they reckon its relationship to the present differently,[9] than peoples in the West. As well, Eva Hoffman (a Polish immigrant to North America) argued that Eastern Europeans are shaped, both individually and collectively, by their history in ways deeper (and other) than people in the West are.[10] If

---

8. Heymann, *Poland and Czechoslovakia*, vi. In this book, Heymann devoted 122 of 162 pages to the period before World War I; his treatment does not extend into the period of Communist domination after World War II.

9. Mojzes, *Yugoslavian Inferno*, 50.

10. Hoffman, *Exit into History*, xiv, xvi; later in the book she commented further, "Why, or how, a collective past should matter in the present has always been a puzzlement to me.... And yet today's Eastern Europe is a living lesson in how much it does matter" (293).

nothing else, awareness of how the peoples and nations of Eastern Europe understand and view themselves in this regard should be enough to call the historiography on Eastern Europe to more balanced treatment of the larger sweep of that history. If such long-term historical perspective is essential to the self-understanding of the peoples of Eastern Europe, it is incumbent on historians to offer such perspective in their studies.

The events that have transpired since the collapse of the Communist bloc indicate with utter clarity how mistaken the approach of the historiography on Eastern Europe was in this regard. The historiographical neglect of the preceding centuries did not make adequate room for an understanding of the deep-seated tensions and animosities that have burst forth within Eastern Europe in the years since 1989. The tensions between Hungarians and Romanians in Transylvania stretch back long before even the 1867 restructuring of the Habsburg Empire into the Austro-Hungarian Empire, which awarded the Hungarians rule over the Romanians in the territory. The discomfort on the part of the Slovaks vis-à-vis the Czechs extends far back beyond the dismemberment of Czechoslovakia on the eve of World War II (indeed, from Slovak perspectives, it goes back for more than a millennium). The hostility between Serbs and Albanians over Kosovo, which led to and was worsened by NATO air strikes in 1999, has simmered for more than six centuries. The animosities surrounding Bosnia reach back more than a half-millennium; and the belligerence between (Roman Catholic) Croats and (Orthodox) Serbs has festered for almost eight hundred years.

Under the ideologically driven instructional demands of the USSR, the nations of Eastern Europe were expected to rewrite their histories and to play down strife among the peoples of their nations (and, indeed, among the proletariat of the Communist bloc). Evidently, these Communist lessons were not learned well by the peoples of Eastern Europe. It seems ironic that the historiography of Eastern Europe emanating from what was called the free world during the Cold War proved to be a more compliant student in this regard. The years since the end of Soviet hegemony in 1989 have shown how inadequate were the Communist orientation, on the one hand, and western historiography on Eastern Europe, on the other, for understanding either the past or the present of Eastern Europe. Unless the pattern under criticism changes drastically, that historiography will proffer little help for understanding what will likely transpire in the future, either.

The temporal imbalance becomes graphic if one considers the percentage of the history of Eastern Europe actually treated in that historiography. The geographic region has been peopled by its current inhabitants since the

Slavic invasions of the sixth through the eighth centuries.[11] Consequently, the history of these various peoples can be traced back to that period. If, to adopt a conservative point to begin, one takes 700 AD as the starting point for Eastern European history, the potential timespan for such a treatment would be a little over 1,300 years. The period of Communist domination began, at the earliest, in 1945—although for several of the countries of Eastern Europe, effective domination of government by the Communists did not occur until somewhat later.[12] Communist suzerainty ended in 1989; thus, the Communist period of Eastern European history, on which historical scholarship has focused its treatments, was only forty-four years long. This means, consequently, that these "histories" of Eastern Europe have zeroed in on 3.38 percent of the actual history of Eastern Europe.

Were one to adopt that approach with the history of the United States of America, the results would be ridiculed. If 1607 (the founding of the Jamestown colony in Virginia) can be accepted as a fair date to begin the history of what would eventually be the U.S.A., then there are (as of 2022) 415 years of that history. A history that focused on the last 3.38 percent of those four hundred years would result in a study of only the last *fourteen years*. A treatment of this sort would leave out, among other things, the Revolutionary War, the Wild West, the Viet Nam War, Watergate, and the attacks on the Twin Towers in New York—all of which have so powerfully shaped that history. However enlightening an analysis of those fourteen years might be, such a study could hardly claim to present the history of the U.S.A., or to have a good understanding of what has shaped the U.S.A. Again, analogously, no matter how insightful the studies about the last half of the twentieth century in Eastern Europe have been, the imbalance in historical treatment is a significant defect in that historiography. This deficiency must almost necessarily lead to significant misunderstandings and misrepresentations of the actual history of Eastern Europe.

Nevertheless, the concentration of historiography on Eastern Europe has been on the period of Communist domination. While there was little historical justification for that, as argued above, there was abundant political need for such information. Historical scholarship on Eastern Europe

---

11. While the Vlachs did not descend from their refuges in the Transylvania Alps and the Carpathian Mountains until around 1300, they had lived in the geographic area even before the Slavic invasions. The obvious exception to the above statement is the people of the Magyars, who only settled in the Pannonian Plain in the late ninth century. Even so, the peoples over whom they came to rule in the area had entered it no later than the sixth to eighth centuries, so the suggested period still works for our purposes.

12. The former Czechoslovakia is a case in point: the Communists did not definitively seize power there until 1948.

took its cue from the political concerns of the Cold War. Of course, the West needed to know as much as possible about the Communist bloc, so one cannot fault the provision of such information. But it should not be thought churlish to suggest that the histories of this area produced over most of the last half-century have been the handmaidens of politics and Cold War considerations—put more graphically, that history prostituted itself to political considerations. But the johns are dead; it is high time Clio[13] stopped walking the street and got back to her licit business—namely, the endeavor to understand people, nations, and areas, what has happened to them, how they view themselves and others, and the situations or outcomes that have resulted. Only as it does so will the historiography of Eastern Europe serve an understanding of the history of the area.

Lack of General Treatments

Anyone who wants to learn about the history of Western Europe or the history of western civilization can find a plethora of books, of various lengths and degrees of detail, offering general treatments of either of those histories. The contrast for the history of Eastern Europe is stark: until 1992, for more than three decades not a single volume had been available that presented a general treatment of the history of Eastern Europe. A few such books had been produced earlier, but they were long since out of print: among them were Samuel Hazzard Cross, *Slavic Civilization through the Ages*; and the two volumes by Francis Dvornik, *The Slavs: Their Early History and Civilization*, and *The Slavs in European History and Civilization*.

In 1992, a treatment with a novel approach appeared: Philip Longworth's *The Making of Eastern Europe* offered a general coverage of the region from its early history to the present, to be sure—but it did so in reverse chronological order, beginning with current events and pursuing them backwards in time to their earlier roots. This unusual approach had the advantage of allowing those unfamiliar with the region's history to trace connections back through centuries. However, welcome as the volume was, it suffered under two drawbacks: on the one hand, it did not readily allow room to treat influences or patterns that had become deeply ingrained but did not offer ready evidence of their impact in the contemporary scene; on the other—and while perhaps simplistic, nevertheless significant—this reverse chronological approach ran against the grain of almost all historiographical practice, rendering Longworth's approach quixotic and

---

13. "Clio" is the name given by the ancient Greeks to the muse who inspires the writing of history.

something less than readily assimilable by those of less inventive historical bent.[14] In 1998, another general treatment appeared, the work by Robert Bideleux and Ian Jeffries, *A History of Eastern Europe: Crisis and Change*. This volume is certainly welcome, but—at nearly 650 pages in length, with dense print (compressed into forty-seven lines per page)—it is too detailed and lengthy to serve as an introduction to the history of Eastern Europe for any but the most determined of potentially interested readers. Two atlases offered help toward a general treatment: Paul Robert Magocsi, *Historical Atlas of East Central Europe*,[15] and Dennis P. Hupchick and Harold E. Cox, *A Concise Historical Atlas of Eastern Europe*. However, these volumes were necessarily less concerned with offering a historical synthesis of Eastern Europe than with the cartographic portrayal of changes within that history and the explanations requisite to them.

It is understandable that scholars in the history of Eastern Europe did not venture into general treatments. Specialists typically prefer to remain within the areas of their close expertise, and the prospect of stepping outside that into other periods or even other regions of Eastern Europe is less than inviting. Undeniably, the history of a region as ethnically mixed, as divergent in cultural influences, and as complicated in political background and experience as Eastern Europe would stretch a scholar beyond what could feasibly be expected of any expert. Further, a historical purist might well argue that a broad survey would necessarily be somewhat superficial, would run roughshod over some important data and interpretative questions, and would end up omitting treatment of parts of the region.[16]

Both the scholarly hesitation and the purist concern are valid, of course. However, they are no less valid for the history of Western Europe or of western civilization. In both of these, the Welsh, Spaniards, Portuguese, Scots, Friesians, and Basques could complain of being omitted or inadequately treated; depending on the historian's bent of mind, he or she will necessarily give more or less weight to intellectual, social, economic, or cultural questions in a general presentation of the history of Western

---

14. Ironically, the subtitle of the second edition of Longworth's work is *From Prehistory to Postcommunism*, implying a treatment in the opposite direction from that actually taken in the volume.

15. The volume by Magocsi has appeared as volume 1 of *History of East Central Europe*, eds. Sugar and Treadgold. (Several of the volumes had already been published before Magocsi's treatment appeared. His was numbered first as offering the cartographic background to the rest of the series. The numbers assigned to the remaining volumes correspond to the historical periods treated, rather than the order of the respective volumes' publication dates.)

16. Historians of Eastern Europe frequently brought forward these arguments (and others to the same effect) against appeals for general treatments of that history.

Europe or western civilization than another historian would. Inescapably, such a general treatment will be superficial in some regards. But that is the price that must be paid to produce works that will offer an introduction to the history of any region of the world: historiographical necessity requires that scholarly niceties occasionally step aside in favor of general treatments offering readers an introduction sufficient to provide a historical context for reading and absorbing the more precise, defined treatments that specialists prefer to produce. The reluctance to venture into the writing of general treatments of the history of Eastern Europe must be overcome, if the field is to continue to attract interested readers and, ultimately, additional scholarly specialists—who typically begin as interested readers.

Undoubtedly, the difficulties involved in writing a good general treatment of the history of Eastern Europe would be considerable, but scholars have managed it—as the earlier works of Cross and Dvornik, and the more recent ones by Longworth and by Bideleux and Jeffries noted above indicate. Moreover, it has been done in related fields that are no less daunting: Dmitrij Čiževskij's *Comparative History of Slavic Literatures* offered a general treatment of that literature from its beginnings in the ninth century to the recent past, and treated the several Slavic languages' literatures in the effort. The task of producing a general history of Eastern Europe might be challenging, but it is not impossible.

There is an undeniable need for such works. Whereas those interested in learning about the history of western civilization or Western Europe can find any number of books offering general treatments of the field, anyone who desires to become familiar with the history of Eastern Europe encounters the frustration of having only two volumes currently available that could facilitate his or her preliminary investigations—and each of these has significant drawbacks. For those who teach courses in the history of Eastern Europe, the choice has been either to offer a general treatment of the material only in the lectures or to restrict the course's treatment to whatever can be accommodated with what contemporary historiography has offered. Simply put, continued interest in and growth of the academic study of the history of Eastern Europe depend on some intrepid scholars providing general treatments that could be used as viable introductions to that history. The lack of such works is a considerable lacuna in the current historiography on Eastern Europe; the sooner that gap is filled, the better.[17] This book is an attempt to do that.

17. There are some encouraging signs that both the problems presented above are beginning to be remedied. Since 1989, two books have stretched their coverage through the entire twentieth century: Crampton, *Eastern Europe,* and Held, *Columbia History of Eastern Europe.* Beyond that, the ten-volume series, *History of East Central Europe,*

The Neglect of Religion

A third shortcoming in the patterns of historiography on Eastern Europe is the failure to treat religion as a formative influence in and throughout the region. There seem to be two main reasons for this defect. One of them has to do with the recent Communist past of Eastern Europe; the other reflects contemporary scholarly approaches in the West.

As we have seen, the USSR tightly controlled Eastern Europe in the period since World War II, and this has been the period treated in most of the available studies on the region. Atheistic in ideology, Soviet Communism vigorously persecuted and in other ways sought to undermine religion, both in Russia itself and in its Eastern European satellites. Consequently, it might be argued that it is not particularly surprising that religion has not played an important role in that historiography.

However, this assessment betrays a flawed conception of what historiography on Eastern European ought to be, since it focuses on the Russian Communist overlords rather than on the peoples of Eastern Europe themselves. Historiography on Eastern Europe needs to deal with the peoples and nations of Eastern Europe as they are and have been, and not as the straitjacketed underlings of their Soviet masters. Various national histories have shown that the respective peoples of Eastern Europe have deep religious roots that have not been killed by Communism's atheistic herbicides. Indeed, the Communist rulers in several of the Eastern European nations found out, much to their surprise and chagrin, that Communist ideology and power could not get the peoples of Eastern Europe to foreswear their longstanding religious commitments. Not only did the various churches survive the period of Communist repression; as events since 1989 have shown, religion continues to be a motive force among the peoples of Eastern Europe. Thus, the failure to treat religion as an influential factor in Eastern European history indicates greater awareness of Communist predilections than of Eastern European attitudes. Historiography on Eastern Europe can no longer excuse its neglect of religion as a formative influence in the region by pointing at Communist ideology. In Eastern Europe, Communism is

---

offers coverage from earliest times to the present: these volumes offer general treatments of significant periods in Eastern European history, with the projected completed series offering coverage of the whole history. Clearly, this series goes a long way toward remedying deficiencies in the scholarly treatment of the history of Eastern Europe; however, some of the volumes have yet to be completed, and even then, there will still be need for other books that present the history of Eastern Europe in briefer compass than this series will offer. Two recent studies by Hupchick offer important contributions in this regard: *Culture and History* considers recurring themes in the history of the region, and *Conflict and Chaos* treats five perennial problems in the area.

gone, but religion remains. Historiography needs to deal with the history of Eastern Europe in ways that show why and how religion has been and continues to be a significant influence in the region.

A second reason for the neglect of religion as an influence in Eastern European historiography arises from a western habit of mind. The nations of Eastern Europe live by an attitude that the countries of the West have, to a large degree, rejected—namely, that religion can play a significant and shaping role in public life. For books on the history of Eastern Europe to proffer bona fide understanding of Eastern Europe, as opposed to projecting western attitudes upon the peoples and nations of the area, their authors must be alert to this significant cultural difference from the West.

For a variety of reasons, the cultures of Western Europe and North America have opted, for the most part, for a separation of religion from public life. Individuals are welcome to practice religion or hold religious convictions, but those individuals are expected to relegate such practices and convictions to the private sphere of life. For matters of the public square, religion is commonly looked on as an unwelcome intruder. Virtually all the nations of the West have adopted one or another form of this basic attitude, enshrining it in constitutional documents or in judicial decisions.

A fascinating evolution of this perspective has occurred in the academic world: embraced as basic assumption for society, the separation of religion from public life has, for many western scholars, been transmogrified into historiographical presupposition. That is, the *social convention* has been uncritically accepted as a *historiographical canon* by a number of western historians. In their estimation, religion not only *must not* play a public role in their own culture, but it *cannot* play such a role in another culture.[18]

One finds abundant evidence of this presupposition in many of the volumes on Eastern European history written by scholars trained in the West. However, this presupposition runs against the grain of the actual history of Eastern Europe. Throughout the region, almost everything for centuries has been, and even today continues to be, religiously driven. In Eastern Europe, faith, church, culture, and nation have been all bound up together. This can be seen from the more distant past through all the

---

18. Among the results of this have been, in the field of Reformation historiography, for example, publications that treat the theological stances and attitudes of the various reformers as matters of their private orientations. Since these matters *should not* have played significant roles in the unfolding of sixteenth-century culture, they *could not* have; with this anachronistic assumption, ostensible explanations are offered for the Reformation that have nothing to do with religion. Such volumes reveal more about contemporary scholarly myopia than they do about sixteenth-century developments. For a trenchant criticism of this approach and its results in Reformation scholarship, see Ozment, *Protestants*, 30–31.

centuries to the present. A few illustrations (out of many possible) should be enough to demonstrate this.

It has often been pointed out that the main reason why the Serbs and the Bulgarians were able to retain their distinct identities during a period of nearly five centuries of Ottoman rule was the tenacity of their respective Orthodox churches.[19] For the peoples and leaders of these nations, down to the present day, to be Serb or Bulgar has also been to be Orthodox. Separation of religion from the public sphere, as practiced in the West, is inconceivable within these nations. Among them, religion has continued to shape perception, both of self and of others—not only through the centuries of Turkish control, but even during the decades of Communist domination. This pattern has been true also for their neighbors (especially the Croats and the Romanians). Unquestionably, this needs to be taken into careful consideration in any account of the history or the present situation of these peoples. Indeed, one cannot claim to treat the history of the Balkans these peoples inhabit without explicit attention to the significance of religion and the role it has played in that long history.

Nevertheless, that significant factor is often neglected or overlooked. For all the excellence of its treatment in other regards, Lenard Cohen's *Broken Bonds: The Disintegration of Yugoslavia* was vitiated by its total omission of religious components in the breakdown of and subsequent war within the former Yugoslavia. Given his recognition that traditional religious antagonisms had played a significant role in the outbreak of conflict in 1990 and subsequently,[20] this omission was remarkable. In the second edition of this work (1995), even though he added the assessment that the ethno-religious commitments and intolerance were discernible by the late 1980s,[21] this revised edition still failed to offer any consideration of religious factors. A similar pattern is found in other works on the war within the former Yugoslavia. Alex N. Dragnich, of Yugoslavian extraction himself, but educated in the West, pointed out, in his *Serbs and Croats: The Struggle in Yugoslavia*, that religious differences have profoundly divided

---

19. Walters, *The Other Europe*, 28; Hupchick offers a detailed consideration of how this transpired in Bulgaria, despite considerable obstacles, in *The Bulgarians*.

20. Cohen cites, with approval, a sociological study that came to this conclusion (*Broken Bonds*, 269), and further notes "the Balkan region's traditional proclivity for ethnoreligiously based violence at times of regime breakdown," a situation that in his estimation made the savagery of ethnic conflict almost predictable (270). Nevertheless, his monograph offered no consideration whatsoever of religious components involved in or contributing to the breakdown of Yugoslavia or to the war that ensued in Bosnia.

21. This citation is found at 333; the second edition included a lengthy new chapter on the warfare in Bosnia and was revised extensively enough that it had a new sub-title (*Yugoslavia's Disintegration and Balkan Politics in Transition*).

the South Slavs for centuries.²² However, having acknowledged that, he never again mentioned religious division or considered its contribution to the 1990s war in his treatment.

Paul Mojzes offered a substantial corrective to this common omission with his *Yugoslavian Inferno: Ethnoreligious Warfare in the Balkans*, in which he noted, "[T]here is a great need for understanding the cause of the present great convulsion, *especially the role of the religious communities in it that most other analysts have ignored*, and to explore the approaches toward a solution."²³ One cannot do justice to an understanding of that horrendous war if the religious component so prominent in the self-understanding of the respective participants in it and in their attitudes toward their opponents is excluded.

Further, an understanding of Poland's relationship with Russia through the centuries must take into account the significance of the contrasting religious allegiances that have historically marked the two countries. The Russian conviction that Moscow was Third Rome, the successor to the Christian imperial heritage of fallen Byzantium and the only free state adhering to (Eastern) Orthodoxy, may not have been definitively articulated until the early sixteenth century,²⁴ but by the late fifteenth century the leaders of Muscovy already recognized their realm as the legitimate political and religious successor to the Byzantine Empire and acted on that conviction.²⁵ Polish advances into the lands of the former Kievan Rus' (which Muscovy considered her birthright)²⁶ were in the eyes of the Russians more than militaristic adventurism; they were also assaults by heretics and schismatics (the Poles were Roman Catholic) against a state committed to protecting and

22. Dragnich, *Serbs and Croats*, 3.

23. Mojzes, *Yugoslavian Inferno*, xv (emphasis added); at the end of his introduction, Mojzes explained that he wrote the book especially to remedy this deficiency in the treatment of the contributing factors in the war within the former Yugoslavia (xxi).

24. Although this idea had been widely expressed in the mid-fourteenth century (Toumanoff, "Moscow the Third Rome," 436–37; Dvornik, *Slavs: Their Early History*, 339), it received its classic formulation in a letter of 1510 to Basil III (r. 1505–33) from the monk Philotheus of Pskov (Dvornik, *Slavs in European History*, 374).

25. Basil II (r. 1425–62) declared himself, as ruler of Muscovy, the protector of Orthodoxy; his son, Ivan III (r. 1462–1505), manifested his understanding that he and his people had stepped into the place recently vacated by Byzantium: in 1472 he married the niece of the last Byzantine emperor, and in 1480 he adopted the title Tsar (Russian for "Caesar"), along with the Byzantine two-headed eagle for his coat of arms (Dvornik, *Slavs: Their Early History*, 339; Toumanoff, "Moscow the Third Rome," 439–41).

26. In the mid-fourteenth century, Kazimierz III [Casimir] of Poland had invaded the former territories of Kievan Rus' (Wandycz, *The Price of Freedom*, 40); subsequently, Poland took advantage of Moscow's "Time of Troubles," ultimately marching to the gates of Moscow, and besieging the city from 1610 to 1612 (Harcave, *Russia: A History*, 54–56; Dvornik, *Slavs in European History*, 466–70); see also Dvornik, *Slavs: Their Early History*, 339; see also Harcave, *Russia: A History*, 43.

advancing Orthodoxy as the true Christian faith.[27] As another manifestation of the Western Christian duplicity that had ravaged Constantinople in the name of holy war in the Fourth Crusade of 1204, Polish onslaughts required both military and spiritual opposition. In due course, Russia's participation in the dismemberment of Poland in the late eighteenth century involved not only the attempt to rid herself of a dangerous political rival, but also the elimination of the theological and ecclesiastical corruption that, to Russian perspectives, Poland embodied.

For her part, Poland's steadfast devotion to Roman Catholicism in subsequent generations embodied more than simply opposition to her tsarist rulers. It also shaped the Polish self-understanding, down to the present—as Poland's Communist leaders found out, to their consternation.[28] No less a Polish intellectual than Pope John Paul II said, during his first visit to Poland after his election as pope, "It is impossible without Christ to understand the history of the Polish nation." Western historians attempting to write about the history of Poland are hardly in a position to disagree knowledgeably.

Religious allegiances distinguished the various Eastern European peoples from each other. Behind these distinctions lurked significant disagreements in doctrine and practice. While the sharp articulation of differences between Western Christianity (whether in its Roman Catholic or Protestant forms) and Eastern Orthodoxy awaited the Slavophile declarations of the nineteenth century,[29] the differences did not wait until then to manifest themselves or to be recognized. Already in the ninth century, the Byzantine patriarch Photios denounced the Western Christian view of the Trinity and its unilateral modification of the Niceno-Constantinopolitan Creed, a creed that had been promulgated by the whole Christian church in an ecumenical council.[30] Concern with this western departure figured prominently in Eastern Christianity in the following centuries.[31] Subsequently, the Hesychast Controversy of the first half of the fourteenth century made clear to the churches of Eastern Orthodoxy just how different Western Christian approaches to devotion and theology were from those in long use among the Orthodox.[32]

27. Toumanoff, "Moscow the Third Rome," 446; Dvornik, *Slavs in European History*, 468–69; see also his *Slavs: Their Early History*, 339.

28. See Rothschild, *Return to Diversity*, 86–87, 197–98.

29. Wandycz, *The Price of Freedom*, 2.

30. Hussey, *The Orthodox Church*, 78, 84–85, 87.

31. The Council of Blachernae in 1285 repudiated the Western Christian perspective on the doctrine of the Trinity and the changes to the creed, reaffirming instead (with further explanation) the perspective of Patriarch Photios: see the treatment in Papadakis, *Crisis in Byzantium*.

32. Meyendorff, *Study of Gregory Palamas*, 237–40; for an overview of the subsequent influence of hesychasm within Orthodoxy, to the present day, see also his *St.*

While it cannot reasonably be claimed that the average person in Eastern Europe would have been familiar with the particulars of these (and other) divergences between the faith and practice of Western Christianity, on the one hand, and Eastern Orthodoxy, on the other, that should not lead to the assumption that they knew nothing of them or cared little for them. Religious exclusiveness is not necessarily predicated upon thorough understanding of disputed points. For the various peoples of Eastern Europe, with the scar of the Fourth Crusade, the lack of support from the Christian West for Orthodox Constantinople in her waning days, and the subsequent period of imperial domination by Muslim Turks, Roman Catholic Austrians, Protestant Germans, or Orthodox Russians, questions of religious distinctiveness remained of more than merely theoretical interest. They were absorbed into the thoughts and attitudes of the various peoples of Eastern Europe, whatever religious commitment was embraced by the particular nation or people group, in numerous ways. So intensely have these concerns, and the self-understandings involved with them, shaped the peoples of Eastern Europe, that it is both parochial and foolhardy of western scholars to ignore or overlook them, as has commonly been done in their historical treatments.[33] If western historiography hopes to attain and promote genuine understanding of Eastern Europe, it must treat religion as a formative influence in and throughout the region.[34]

Conclusion

The historiography of Eastern Europe is flawed by the three problems we have considered. All three need to be corrected if that historiography is to deal responsibly with the history of the region. In this book, we will offer a balanced temporal coverage, a solid general study, and a responsible treatment of the significant role religion has played in the history of Eastern Europe.

Gregory Palamas, 131–70.

33. Historians would do well to consider what Fred A. Reed, a journalist from North America who lived in the southern Balkans for nearly thirty years, had to say on this point in his *Salonica Terminus*: he distinguished between the western attitude toward faith and life and that found throughout the southern Balkans (and, more broadly, the rest of Eastern Europe) when he commented, "Faith has not yet been narrowed to a dark corridor inhabited by the old, the poor and the uneducated. Like a subterranean current it flows through public—and private—life, rising to the surface on the great festivals and saints' days, converging in seamless symbiosis with secular power" (35).

34. I have argued this pointedly in Payton, "Religion, Nationalism, and National Identities."

Part Two
Turning Points in Eastern European History

CHAPTER 6

The Evangelization of the Slavs (860s)

> "The acculturation of the Slavs . . . was probably the most important event of the ninth century. . . . This achievement was exclusively due to the two Thessalonian brothers [Cyril and Methodius], who have therefore acquired a well-deserved place in the consciousness of the Slav peoples as their apostles and teachers."[1]

THE FIRST SIGNIFICANT TURNING point in the history of Eastern Europe was the evangelization of the Slavs during the 860s. By then, they had spread out of their original homeland to inhabit almost all of Eastern Europe. Their migration had become possible because of what had earlier happened in the Roman Empire.

The Roman Empire in the Fourth and Fifth Centuries

Major events in the fourth and fifth centuries in the Roman Empire shaped the future of Eastern Europe. When Constantine the Great became the sole emperor in the early 300s, he believed he owed his status to the blessing of the Christian God. He was not yet fully committed to Christianity; indeed, he did not receive baptism until his deathbed (in 337). But he was convinced that the Christian God had granted him the imperial dignity for defending Christians against renewed persecutions visited upon them by his previous rival, Licinius.

---

1. Tachiaos, *Cyril and Methodius*, x.

The Transfer of the Capital from Rome to Byzantium

However, Constantine consequently faced a considerable problem. He did not want to offend the God of the Christians, who forbade bowing down to idols and having other gods before him—and Constantine knew that Rome, the capital city, was full of idols. Beyond that, Roman tradition required the emperor to participate in numerous rituals, including offering sacrifices to various gods. Constantine looked for a way to avoid these obligations.

Furthermore, it had become evident to him and his predecessor Diocletian that Rome was not well situated to be the empire's capital any longer. Earlier Rome had served well enough, but by the late third century, problems with the capital's location were undeniable: the Persians were attacking the eastern borders of the empire, and Germanic peoples were invading from the north. Rome was located too far away from these hot spots to deal with them quickly and effectively.

Constantine had come to appreciate the potential of another city to serve as the capital—Byzantium, the ancient Greek colony at the edge of the European continent. Surrounded by water on two sides of a triangular promontory, Byzantium would be much easier to defend from assault. Given its location at the crossroads of Europe and Asia, Byzantium could also control the trade flowing between them. Further, Byzantium was near to the danger spots: an emperor located in Byzantium could more readily deal with the Persians and the invading Germanic peoples alike. Moreover, the eastern half of the empire was far more populous and prosperous than the western half where Rome was. Finally, in Byzantium Constantine would be able to honor Christianity as his favored religion.[2]

To make a long story short, in 324 Constantine decided to transfer the capital from Rome to Byzantium. Rebuilding the city to his specifications took six years. He designated the new capital "New Rome," but it quickly became known as "Constantine's *Polis*" ("city")—contracted, "Constantinople." Of course, the inhabitants and senatorial leaders of Rome resented the transfer, but as of 330 the capital was in the eastern half of the empire. This set up a rivalry between Rome and Byzantium—two proud cities, two significant centers of civilization. Rome pained for what it had lost, and Byzantium gloried as the new upstart capital. In a variety of ways, this rivalry affected much of the subsequent history of Eastern Europe.

---

2. For about a half century, historians and political scientists have sharply criticized Constantine for a variety of supposed failures; Leithart, *Defending Constantine*, counters this effectively, through a painstaking review of the criticisms and a careful reading of the evidence.

The Collapse of the Western Half of the Empire

During the second and third centuries the empire had been weakened by invasions and civil war. Despite the best efforts of Constantine and his successors in the fourth and fifth centuries, the empire could not regain the strength it had enjoyed at the beginning of the Christian era, in the first century. Since the empire's seat was in its eastern half, the emperors inevitably spent more time dealing with problems there. With that went a neglect of the defenses of the western part of the empire. During the fifth century, Germanic peoples who had been bothering the eastern half of the empire moved westwards. Vandals, Visigoths, Ostrogoths, and others invaded, looting and sacking Rome (and other cities) and wreaking such devastation that the western half of the Roman Empire collapsed in the fifth century.

However, the Roman Empire did not come to an end then: only the western half of it did. That needs to be stressed. It is common for people in Western Europe or North America to date the collapse of the Roman Empire to sometime in the fifth century—perhaps 410 or 451 or 476 (the main dates suggested for that calamity, depending on various assessments of the importance of the particular event). However, if an Eastern European is asked when the Roman Empire came to an end, the answer is often quite precise: "May 29, 1453," the day when Constantinople was conquered by the Ottoman Turks. The Roman Empire did not end in the fifth century: it continued in the East for another thousand years. The Byzantines saw, thought, and spoke of themselves as Romans (using the Greek term for Romans, *Romaioi*, to refer to themselves) who were continuing the Roman Empire, albeit now on a Christian footing. That eastern half of the Roman Empire—commonly known now as the Byzantine Empire—did not succumb to invaders. She never experienced the chaos that followed from such conquest,[3] until 1453. The Byzantine Empire had a profound influence on the history of Eastern Europe in many ways, but especially through its evangelization of the Slavs.

The Migration of the Slavs (Sixth–Eighth Centuries)

But what does this collapse of the Roman Empire *in the West* have to do with the history of Eastern Europe, in general, and of where the Slavs lived, in particular? It all has much to say about how the Slavs ended up spreading throughout Eastern Europe. Why was it that the Slavs could move into so much territory, recognizing they were not warlike peoples, in pursuit of conquest? They could do so because the land had been vacated.

---

3. Cf., though, the treatment below of the Fourth Crusade, in chapter 9.

The people who had been living there were of Germanic stock; they had earlier fought their way across the Danube River into imperial territory. They inhabited much of this area until the fifth century, when they ended up going west because there was no way to conquer Constantinople, with its impregnable walls. But neither Rome nor other western cities had such insurmountable defenses. Many Germanic tribes headed west, in search of plunder and conquest.

They left behind a vacuum, into which Slavs spread throughout most of Eastern Europe during the sixth through eighth centuries. With the prior warlike inhabitants out of the way, the Slavs migrated south of the Carpathian Mountains, along the Danube, and settled in the vacated lands. Some other Slavs spread westwards, into territory also vacated by Germanic tribes who had headed southwards, into the Roman Empire. Other Slavs migrated eastward into what we know today as Ukraine, Belarus, and Russia.

This migration of the Slavs throughout Eastern Europe set the stage for their evangelization. As they came into territory that had belonged to (or at least been claimed by) the old Roman Empire or its continuation, the Byzantine Empire, the Slavs came within the orbits of the two centers of Christian civilization—Rome and Byzantium. The rivalry between the two capitals was played out, in part, in the evangelization efforts undertaken by the two great cities.

Slavic Nations

The Slavic peoples' spread throughout Eastern Europe was not at the point of a sword. In the first aftermath of their migrations, they built up no nations. Consequently, while both Rome and Byzantium soon initiated evangelistic efforts among various Slavic tribes, little is known about these endeavors until the ninth century. By then, two Slavic peoples had erected nations. One was Bulgaria, led by Khan Boris; the other was Moravia, led by Prince Rastislav.

Bulgaria

Bulgaria prides itself on being the oldest continuously existing state in Europe: it was established by treaty with Byzantium in 681. By then, the Bulgarians had become a major power, able to hold their own against Byzantine armies. This sounds strangely un-Slavic and requires some explanation.

Actually, the Bulgars had migrated westward from Central Asia and in the mid-seventh century invaded the regions known today as Romania and Bulgaria. There they became a ruling caste over the Slavs who had already settled in the region. Over the course of the next century, the Bulgars intermarried with their subjects, came to speak their Slavic language, and were assimilated to their subjects; by the ninth century, their neighbors thought of them all as Slavs. The Bulgarians proved to be a formidable fighting force: under her khans, Bulgaria set up a considerable empire, able to withstand and even flourish against both the Byzantine Empire and the Frankish Empire under Charlemagne.

The Bulgarian ruler, Khan Boris, wanted to protect and expand his empire. By the 860s, he also had decided to abandon the paganism of his ancestors and have his people embrace Christianity; however, he had a problem. Should he turn in the direction of Rome or of Byzantium? The latter was not particularly attractive to him, given his nation's regular warfare with the Byzantine Empire; while he wanted to have his people convert to Christianity, he did not want to open a door to unwelcome Byzantine influences that might undermine Bulgarian independence. So, in 864, Boris invited Rome to send missionaries to his nation.

Moravia

Similarly, to Bulgaria's northwest, during the early 860s the ruler of Moravia wanted to have his nation convert to Christianity. Earlier in the century, the Moravians had found themselves the targets of expansionist tendencies of the rising German state (the strongest survivor of Charlemagne's empire).[4] The German ruler, Louis, had brought the Bohemians under his rule; the Moravians, to the east of the Bohemians, managed to set up a national structure in time to avoid a similar fate. Even so, the powerful German state forced the Moravians into a vassal relationship, in which they had to follow Louis' lead. When the Moravian ruler, Mojmir, died in 845, Louis exercised the rights over his vassal state and decided who Mojmir's successor would be: Louis adjudged Mojmir's nephew, Rastislav, as neither too bright nor too strong, and so Louis appointed Rastislav to the throne of Moravia, hoping thereby to control the young Slavic nation by dominating its ruler.

However, Louis badly misread the Moravian prince. Within a few years, Rastislav won enough support among his people to stand up to the

---

4. At his death in 814, Charlemagne had passed the Frankish Empire to his son, who turned out to be an ineffectual ruler. At his death, that son parcelled out the empire among his three sons. Rather than working together for the sake of the empire, though, they ended up becoming rivals; in due course, the easternmost one became the most powerful kingdom.

German forces and expel them from his country. Then he expanded Moravia's borders southeastwards—which brought him close to the borders of the Bulgarian Empire. In this situation, with two strong states, the Germans and the Bulgarians, on either side of Moravia, the fledgling nation was dangerously exposed, and Rastislav shrewdly tried to counteract that danger. Since he also wanted to turn from the paganism of his ancestors and convert to Christianity, the two needs came together in contacts he made with Rome and Byzantium. To understand his approach, it is necessary to consider what he knew about the ways Rome and Byzantium conducted their evangelistic endeavors, for their divergence influenced Rastislav's initiatives—and the subsequent history of Eastern Europe, outside of and quite apart from Moravia.

Evangelism: From Rome, From Byzantium

As noted above, evangelism had already been going on among Slavic tribes in Eastern Europe. Both Rome and Byzantium had sent out missionaries to bring them the Christian message. What had become clear—and it was clear to both Rastislav of Moravia and Boris of Bulgaria—was that the two Christian centers approached that evangelism in significantly divergent fashions.

Different Expectations

When Rome evangelized the peoples, in both Western and Eastern Europe, she did so with the expectation they would become and remain subject to the papacy. Thus, the pope would be the universal pastor for all the church. That was how Western Christian understandings had developed after the collapse of the Roman Empire in the West, a perspective shared by western missionaries and their leaders in Rome. This served the needs of the western situation well: it enabled Rome, as the major Christian center in Western Europe, to keep watchful jurisdiction over the church. After the collapse of the Roman Empire in the West, the Roman church alone offered any stable order—and one way of keeping order is to keep things tightly under control. Rome had come to the conclusion that maintaining close supervision over teaching and practice would keep at bay the various heresies that had bedevilled the church through earlier centuries and would guarantee faithfulness to the Christian message.

Byzantium approached the process of evangelizing its neighbors differently. She had evangelized peoples to the east of the Black Sea, and to the north and west of her imperial holdings. She had not passed through the agonies of a collapse of her empire; as a result, perhaps, she was somewhat less suspicious, a little more open-handed, and less concerned with tight control than her western counterpart. When Byzantium evangelized surrounding peoples, she expected that they would defer to the wisdom of the leading clergyman, the patriarch[5] of Constantinople. But Constantinople was more pliable about precisely how things were done. Byzantium left the churches in other nations largely to govern themselves, expecting that churches would work cooperatively in relationship as almost equals—even if the first among equals would be the patriarch of Constantinople. So, the Byzantines were careful about faithful Christian teaching, but they allowed variations in practice, depending on the backgrounds, customs, and language of the peoples being evangelized.

Thus, Rome and Byzantium manifested two quite different sets of expectations as they evangelized their neighbors. Rome's determination to control contrasted sharply with Byzantium's flexibility. This offered wide opportunities for differences to develop between the two great European centers of Christian teaching in evangelistic practice.

Different Ways

How did the two centers actually engage in evangelization? Pursuant to what she wanted to achieve, Rome insisted that the language used in worship had to be one of the three holy languages—Hebrew, Greek, and Latin. Hebrew was holy because it was the language of the Old Testament. Greek was holy because the New Testament was written in it. Latin was considered holy because it was the language used in the Roman Empire, which had turned to Christianity. Only those three were acceptable languages for communicating God's truth and conducting his worship. On this, Rome insisted firmly. In actual practice, however, Roman evangelization used Latin.

The result of this approach was that Western Christian missionaries who went out to the pagan peoples of either Western or Eastern Europe used a language that no one but the speaker understood. This brought with it obvious difficulties; however, if people could be attracted by the beauties of worship, they would eventually come to recognize what the Latin words intended. Education would instruct converted peoples in Latin, and eventually that would trickle down, to some degree, to all the people.

---

5. The title "patriarch" was reserved for the church leaders of the five major centers of ancient Christianity—Jerusalem, Antioch, Rome, Alexandria, and Constantinople. The pope in Rome was the only patriarch in the western half of the old Roman Empire.

This fit with Rome's concern to keep close supervision of the developing church. It entailed early frustration, but it had the promise of long-term benefit. With this approach, those instructed in Latin could go anywhere within Western Christendom and make themselves understood; from an administrative perspective, even more important was the fact that all clergy in Western Christendom could understand the directives emanating from the Roman papacy. Good control would result, as well as conversions to Christianity.

By contrast, the Byzantines looked on no language as inherently and unalterably pagan. While they themselves used Greek, they expected their missionaries usually to work in the language of the peoples whom they sought to evangelize. They recognized that this would likely result in the establishment of churches over which Constantinople did not herself directly rule. The churches need not, from a Byzantine standpoint, be as tightly governed as an empire needed to be.

This offered the Byzantine missionary endeavors the undeniable advantage that those who heard the missionaries could understand what was being said. It thus allowed for a much readier grasp of Christian proclamation and liturgy, and for more rapid and deeper appropriation of the message, by the peoples being evangelized.

Boris of Bulgaria and Rastislav of Moravia both knew about these differences in evangelistic approach on the part of Rome and Byzantium. So, in the early 860s, as the two rulers considered converting to Christianity with their nations, both of them tried to use this divergence in a way that would be advantageous—or at least not dangerous—to their respective states.

National Conversions?

If either Boris or Rastislav were to convert to Christianity, then their people were expected to follow suit and convert to Christianity with their leaders. Both leaders expected—and the practices of both Rome and Byzantium in evangelism intended—a *national* conversion. In much contemporary historical scholarship, and in the estimation of many Christians today, such national conversions seem suspect. For many historians, they smack of little more than political decisions intended to serve some temporal ends, rather than genuine religious movements concerned with both this life and the next.[6] For many contemporary Christians, such mass conversions seem

---

6. This is the perspective presented, e.g., by Crampton in *Concise History of Bulgaria*, 12–15.

suspect, since they expect people to make individual decisions themselves whether or not to embrace Christianity.

Both Rastislav and Boris would have been profoundly surprised at the historians' assessment. To be sure, the intended conversions would unquestionably have political repercussions, but the subsequent lives of the two rulers indicate that their conversions were genuine religious decisions. That is undeniable with Boris of Bulgaria: a few years after the Bulgarians' conversion, he demitted his khanship and became a monk—hardly the choice of someone insincere in his religious convictions! As for Rastislav, he did not get the chance: he was deposed in a palace revolution, but he lost his throne for his religious commitments (as will be seen below). Both were serious about their faith. The data will not allow dismissing the conversions of Bulgaria and of Moravia as nothing more than political manipulations.

Still, the idea of a *national* conversion strikes some Christians today as odd. Many Christians in North America and Western Europe assume that people are supposed to be brought one by one into the faith. However, these Christians may not realize that they are assuming a perspective common in the contemporary West but not itself inscribed in the natural order, and unknown in much of history; that perspective is *individualism*.

Many in the West simply accept individualism as *the way things are*—and *the way things should be*. We assume individualism, talk about the individual and individual rights, and approach life and history as if individualism holds an inalienable right of place in human society. Many people in the West are unaware that the individualism we almost take for granted developed at a given point in the history of our culture: it has not been a "given," an assumption, or even a practice for most of human history. Our contemporary western emphasis on individualism was not the way society worked in the ninth century.

The assumption of individualism has shaped the way many Christians in the West think about evangelization, too. Many Christians today assert that people ought themselves, each of them, to have a personal relationship with God by faith. Fixation on such individual, personal decisions makes the idea of a national conversion appear religiously suspect.

Yet those same Christians readily recognize that individualism is not triumphant or foundational to other aspects of life. If a national leader or a parliament declares war on another nation, they recognize that the decision bears not only on the leader or the parliament, but on all the people—and certainly upon those who will be called to do the fighting. The people of the nation will hardly get the chance to vote on the decision; they are affected by it and have to deal with it. Individualism, however valuable it may be in other regards, is not foundational here. Another example may help. Almost all the inhabitants of North America came as immigrants from somewhere else in the world. The decision to emigrate was made by an adult or by parents, but the children—already living or yet unborn—were affected by this decision, even though they had no voice in or vote on the decision. That decision had wide-ranging effects, not only on those who made the decision, but also on their children. Individualism hardly obtained in that situation.

The point to make here is that individualism is not inscribed in the natural order as the only legitimate way in which decisions are made. Parents and national leaders make them all the time without seeking the approval of all those affected by the decision. A leader's decision does not just affect that leader: it impacts all the people under his or her oversight. That was understood in antiquity and the medieval period. People then expected to follow the lead of their rulers: their decisions usually entailed acceptance by the people. During the medieval period, when both Boris and Rastislav were considering converting to Christianity, national conversions were the normal pattern. It had been that way long before either Boris or Rastislav, and it would remain so long after them.

Such national conversions would be preceded by evangelization of the leader, his court, and the nobles close in rank to him. The national conversion would be sealed by their baptism and that of their people and followed up by extensive catechizing, building churches, conducting liturgies—whatever was necessary to allow that conversion to seep down into and claim the people who comprised the nation. Both rulers and missionaries recognized that much needed to be done to cause this conversion to take root and bear fruit among the people of the nation.

Cyril and Methodius, "The Apostles of the Slavs"

In 862, Rastislav sent a letter to Rome asking for missionaries. Rome was only too happy to receive this invitation, of course: she wanted to spread the Christian faith to the unevangelized. But Rastislav made a specific request, which Rome inevitably refused. He asked that the missionaries conduct their evangelistic work in the language of his people. For the reasons noted above, Rome declined the invitation.

This approach showed shrewd calculation on Rastislav's part. Moravia was situated on the edge of the German state, and her ruler Louis wanted to add Moravia to his territories. The German state was within the Roman church. By asking Rome for missionaries who would work in the Moravians' native language, Rastislav managed both to appear open to the Christian West and yet assure that he would not be taken up within it. Rome responded as Rastislav had expected. This allowed him to contact Byzantium with the same request, knowing already that his request was the Byzantine pattern. Thus, he expected to obtain missionaries who would be able to work effectively among his people; he also expected that Byzantium would take Moravia under its protective wing. This would afford him some guarantees against further German encroachments, securing both the independence of his state and the promise of good results of the missionizing efforts.[7]

Byzantium responded positively to Rastislav's request. The Byzantines already had familiarity with Slavs, owing to the many Slavic tribes that had settled within her borders. Some Byzantines could speak the Slavic language. This was true of the two figures appointed to undertake the Moravian mission, the brothers Cyril and Methodius—who, for their significant impact, have come to be known as "the Apostles of the Slavs."

Cyril and Methodius had grown up in Thessaloniki, a leading commercial city. Like many of their fellow citizens, Cyril and Methodius had learned the language of the Slavs, who lived in great numbers in the environs of Thessaloniki and carried on much trade with it. That language had not yet been reduced to writing, however. Both Cyril and his brother, the monk Methodius, were respected representatives of the Byzantine Empire: they had previously been entrusted with important, delicate *diplomatic* missions with neighboring peoples on behalf of the Byzantine Empire and the church. Now they were entrusted with a significant *evangelistic* mission—one that would profoundly influence the subsequent history of Eastern Europe.

---

7. Fortress Devin (near Bratislava, Slovakia), situated advantageously at the confluence of the Danube and Morava rivers, was probably the center of the Moravian state. (Fortress Devin is now a protected site; it includes remains of several structures, some of which date back to Rastislav's time.)

Wooden statue of Cyril at Fortress Devin.

Before Cyril and Methodius departed for Moravia, they did something never done before: they started writing in the Slavonic language. The Slavs' language had no alphabet, but Cyril—a gifted linguist—invented one (known as Glagolitic) for it. That alphabet was later simplified somewhat and given the designation "Cyrillic," in honor of the one who first devised it. The Cyrillic alphabet is still used today by most of the South Slavs and the East Slavs. The alphabet Cyril devised shows his sense of humor and of mission. Recognizing the Western Christian insistence that the only three languages appropriate for worship of and talking about God were Hebrew, Greek, and Latin, Cyril composed his Slavonic alphabet out of modified Hebrew, Greek, and Latin characters. Thus, he could claim that even Rome's demands were being met as he and Methodius evangelized the Moravians, while using the Slavs' language!

With this alphabet, plus the grammatical structure and syntax the two brothers already knew in Slavonic, Cyril translated the Gospels, liturgy, and some other materials necessary for their efforts. With these, he and

Methodius, plus a number of assistants, embarked for Moravia. Once there, the translation work continued, while the evangelization itself was going on.

Close-up of Cyril's hands, with letters of the alphabet he created carved into them.

Rastislav welcomed the brothers warmly, Cyril and Methodius began their work with their colleagues, and the Moravians responded eagerly. Instructed in their own language, they understood what was being said and soon embraced the faith. Rastislav was baptized, and his people were, as well.

At Fortress Devin, ruins of the foundation of a church built during Rastislav's reign. It is likely that Cyril and Methodius themselves presided over the liturgy here.

The Byzantine missionaries began training Moravians for the priesthood, and the task of catechizing the Moravians was proceeding well.

Wooden statues of Rastislav and Cyril at Fortress Devin.

All this was not welcome news among the Germans, for their leader recognized that if Moravia continued in this path, all his hopes of conquering Moravia would be shattered (since Byzantium would stand by her spiritual protégé). Beyond that concern, German clergy denigrated the whole process as blasphemous: how could any genuine Christian use a pagan term (the Slavic "Bog") to refer to God? With Rastislav's permission, Cyril and Methodius headed for Rome, to place their work before the pope and seek his approval. The long journey was successful: the pope recognized divine blessing on their unusual approach and, by way of exception, authorized it for Moravia.

However, back in Moravia, events were proceeding on their own. The German leaders and clergy intrigued with Svatopluk, a nephew of Rastislav, to engage in a palace revolution. He did, it was successful, and he displaced Rastislav from the throne. Then he expelled the Byzantine missionaries and turned the Moravian churches over to the German clergy—who promptly changed the language used in evangelization and the rest of church life to Latin. Did the Byzantine evangelistic mission to Moravia fail? At first glance, one might think so. However, if the concern is with evangelism, not only with influence, the question must be answered in the negative. The Moravians embraced Christianity and, although their beginnings in Slavonic worship were stifled, they continued in the Christian faith. Thus, Cyril and Methodius' labors bore significant fruit in Moravia.

Meanwhile, other doors were opening for the Byzantine missionaries. They ended up laboring successfully in Bulgaria. Khan Boris had asked for Roman missionaries, in part, because he had wanted to avoid possible political influence from Byzantium. However, the Roman missionaries had conducted their work in Latin—which none of the Bulgarians could understand. The work had proceeded slowly, at best. Further, when Boris had asked for an independent church, governed from within his own nation—the pattern set up through Byzantine missions—he had been flatly refused by the papacy, which had insisted on ultimate control from Rome. Frustrated, in 870 Boris expelled the Roman missionaries.

Meanwhile, he had heard what had taken place in Moravia. So, he contacted Byzantium, making much the same request as Rastislav had, but stipulating that the missionaries must engage in no political manipulations within his state. Assured on both counts by the Byzantine emperor and the patriarch of Constantinople, Boris welcomed the Byzantine missionaries. The Byzantine emperor sent Methodius and his assistants to Bulgaria. (By this time, Cyril had died.) In Bulgaria, the Byzantine missionaries conducted their work in Slavonic. As had been the case in Moravia, so also in Bulgaria the people understood what was declared to them and soon embraced the faith. Boris was baptized, and the Bulgarians received baptism, as well.

This was no merely political decision on Boris' part: he turned a significant portion of his funds to support the church. Among these ventures, he set up a considerable center of learning and translation at Ohrid (today in the state of North Macedonia), where Clement of Ohrid and Naum trained some 3,500 students.[8] Over the next century, Bulgaria became home to a flourishing Christian culture because of the work that was undertaken in this evangelization, a culture that would profoundly impact most of the other South and East Slav peoples.

---

8. Clement and Naum are revered as the patron saints of the state of North Macedonia: one can view Clement of Ohrid's sarcophagus (in the St. Panteleimon Church in Ohrid) and Naum's sarcophagus (in the monastery named after him on the shore of Lake Prespa).

Cyril and Methodius are recognized by all Slavs as the ones who brought the gospel to them.⁹ While the two brothers' work among the West Slavs was cut short, Cyril and Methodius nonetheless were the initiators of the West Slavs' evangelization. More directly, the South Slavs and the East Slavs owe their Christianization to the foundational efforts of the two brothers.

But why are they called "the Apostles of the Slavs"? The reason is Cyril and Methodius were the "sent ones" (the original meaning of "apostle") to the Slavs. They are revered as the initiators of the evangelistic efforts that led to the Slavs' conversion and of all that has flowed from it in shaping Slavic culture down through subsequent centuries. Across the spectrum of Slavic nations, Cyril and Methodius are remembered with devotion.

Statue of Cyril and Methodius in Ohrid, North Macedonia.

9. In the Slavic nations, one finds many memorials to Cyril and Methodius: numerous churches and several universities are named after them (indeed, in Skopje, North Macedonia, I found a pharmacy so named). I have also seen statues honoring them among the West Slavs (e.g., the wooden statue of Cyril at Fortress Devin [see figure 1]); among the East Slavs (along with one of Princess Olga, the first Rus' leader to embrace Christianity) on the main city square in Kiev, near St. Michael's Cathedral; and (among the South Slavs) a modern statue of Cyril and Methodius stands near the shoreline of Lake Ohrid, in the main business center of Ohrid, North Macedonia (see figure 5).

As a major tool for their evangelistic endeavors, Cyril and Methodius had developed an alphabet to reduce the Slavonic language to written form. Converted, the Slavic peoples soon learned to read and write. They read the Bible and the other literature translated from Christian Byzantium, and they learned to write in their own language. With this, by the late 800s, vernacular literature began to develop among the Slavs, first among the Bulgarians and subsequently among other South and East Slavic peoples. The spawn of evangelistic endeavors, vernacular literatures steeped in the Christian faith appeared among the Slavic peoples—long before anything of the sort developed among the Germanic peoples of Western Europe. To this day, Slavic languages have more theologically and ecclesiastically related terms than do any of the languages in the West.

Unquestionably, the evangelization of the Slavs in the 860s became a significant turning point in the history of Eastern Europe.

CHAPTER 7

The Conversion of Vladimir and Kievan Rus' (988)

"The Greeks led us to the edifice where they worship their God, and we knew not whether we were in heaven or on earth. For on earth there is no such splendor or beauty, and we are at a loss how to describe it. We only know that God dwells there among humans, and their service is more beautiful than the ceremonies of other nations...."[1]

TURNING TO THE SIGNIFICANCE of the conversion of Vladimir and Kievan Rus' in 988 requires facing a prior question: "What was *Kievan Rus'*"? Many people in the West have never even heard of it, although it was a major state in medieval Europe. Indeed, for a time, Kievan Rus' was the largest and most sophisticated state in all of Europe and boasted the largest city (apart from Constantinople).

Kievan Rus'

Kievan Rus' took its name from its main city, Kiev—the capital of contemporary Ukraine. The state of Kievan Rus', though, was considerably larger than Ukraine is today. Kievan Rus' encompassed all of Ukraine, almost all of Belarus, and a considerable portion of European Russia.[2] Its inhabitants were almost all Slavs; it incorporated virtually all the East Slavs into one nation.

   1. This offers the culmination of the report of Prince Vladimir's emissaries after they had visited and evaluated the religious faiths and practices of Islam, Judaism, Western Christianity, and Eastern Christianity, as reported in *The Russian Primary Chronicle*.

   2. Russian historiography readily subsumes Kievan Rus' into its history as *medieval Russia*. Ukrainian scholarship challenges this, arguing that Russia as it has developed is both culturally and geographically distant from Kievan Rus'—which Ukrainian

The Importance of Kievan Rus'

Kievan Rus' was the first state to develop among the East Slavs. Subsequently, it would be looked upon as the foundation of the nations of Ukraine, Belarus, and Russia. However, Kievan Rus' was itself important in medieval Europe for several reasons.

In the first place, Kievan Rus' was the leading state in Europe during the eleventh and twelfth centuries. With a total territory of some 800,000 square kilometers, she was Europe's largest body politic—making Kievan Rus' a good deal larger than either France or Germany today. Secondly, by comparison with all the other European states (apart from Byzantium), Kievan Rus' had the most sophisticated culture of the time, boasting a significant school system which produced considerable scholars. In the third place, Kiev (the capital city) was Europe's largest city (again, apart from Byzantium), with some 40,000 inhabitants. By today's standards, that is not large, to be sure. During the eleventh and twelfth centuries, though, Paris had only about 10,000 residents; London required another two centuries to get as many inhabitants as Kiev.

The point of all this is that Kievan Rus' was a significant state in medieval Europe. That importance was enhanced, both for that day and for subsequent history, by its conversion to Christianity under Prince Vladimir in 988. That event has had virtually immeasurable influence for the East Slavs and for the subsequent course of Europe's history.

Religious Options for Kievan Rus'

When Vladimir, the prince of the state, turned from paganism to Christianity, his choice had a huge impact for his people, but also for Europe—east and west alike. What if he had become Muslim? That was one of the options he considered. He also considered converting to Judaism (as his neighbors, the Khazars, had done). However, he went in neither of those directions; he turned to Christianity. But even there, he faced two options—the Christianity emanating from Rome and that from Byzantium. The choice he made for Byzantium and the Eastern Christianity it led has had a profound influence on what transpired in the histories of Russia, Ukraine, and Belarus to this day.

By the time Vladimir made his choice, Western Christianity and Eastern Christianity had long been moving in substantially different directions. They both professed the Christian faith, but their approaches to it varied.

---

historiography, however, claims unhesitatingly as its own medieval heritage.

Related to that, some important differences in teaching and practice had arisen to separate the two segments of Christendom and engender suspicions on the part of each against the other. The result was an increasingly vigorous, sometimes hostile tension between the two sides.

Had Vladimir opted for Western Christianity, rather than the Eastern Christianity that he chose, he and his state would have been affiliated with the Roman church and the papacy. In that situation, the subsequent course of European and of Russian history would have been considerably different than they turned out. But since he chose for Eastern Christianity, he was affiliated with Byzantium and its empire and, consequently, considerably estranged from Western Christianity. This helped to fuel the isolation that the East Slavs subsequently felt toward the rest of Europe after the Byzantine Empire was overrun by the Ottoman Turks, leaving the successors of Kievan Rus' in Muscovy as the only self-governing state committed to Eastern Christianity. This, combined with the heritage of Kievan Rus' faithfulness to Eastern Orthodoxy, contributed significantly to the sense of standing alone that has long marked Russia and has shaped its relationship to the rest of Europe. The conversion of Vladimir and Kievan Rus' has proven to be an epochal event in the history of Eastern Europe, of Western Europe, and of the rest of the world.

The Coming of the Varangians

To understand this momentous conversion, it is important first to become acquainted with the Varangians, who played a leading role in Kievan Rus'. The East Slavs living in the geographic area had not yet in the early 800s developed into a self-governing nation. They were engaged in the agricultural and herding lifestyle common among Slavic peoples, but without a ruling class. However, their neighbors had originally come west from Central Asia: the Khazars had developed a sophisticated enough state that they were able to bring many East Slavs under their rule. The Khazars dominated their Slavic subjects, demanding taxes and sometimes simply expropriating their subjects' goods. The Slavs wanted to be out from under the repression they felt from the Khazars, but the Slavs themselves did not have a leader upon whom they could rely to deliver them.

So, in the early ninth century, they asked the Varangians, whom they had periodically encountered, to come and rule over them—and deliver them from the power of the Khazars. What the Slavs received more than met their hopes; indeed, it led to the establishment of a powerful and influential state, Kievan Rus'. But who were these Varangians?

Who Were the Varangians?

The designation "Varangian" is foreign to readers in the West, but the people thus designated are not: in the West, they are known as "Vikings" or "Norsemen." Our western perception of the Vikings is colored differently than that of the East Slavs in the ninth century. In the West, the Vikings were marauding hordes who came without warning in their dragon ships, attacking and plundering villages, monasteries, and cities; killing, plunder, rape, and looting marked their incursions. The Vikings attacked England, the Netherlands, Germany, France, and much of northwestern Europe in repeated raids. Their incursions were not limited to the immediate coastal areas: their sailing abilities allowed them to venture upriver and attack far inland. Many inhabitants of Western Europe suffered the depredations of the Vikings and came to fear them.[3]

Later on, though, these marauders ended up settling into northwestern France—into the area known, after them, as "Normandy." They established a considerable medieval civilization there. In 1066, William the Conqueror and his Norman armies invaded England and set themselves up as the ruling class over the Saxon inhabitants. (Thus, much of the English noble class has its roots deep in Viking soil.) Eventually some of the Normans also ended up ruling Sicily and Naples. Thus, the Vikings became—for all their earlier fearsome pedigree—a considerable element in Western European history. There was more to them than simply the dragon ships, the looting, and the fear they engendered; the East Slavs had seen this other side.

The Varangians in Eastern Europe

In Eastern Europe, the Vikings had periodically shown they could be fearsome warriors. But they had also made a name for themselves as sophisticated merchants and traders—quite ready to protect their wares if challenged, but able to acquire wealth in other ways than plunder. These Varangians crossed the Baltic Sea and headed upstream on the rivers that emptied into it, all in search of financial gain. In due course, they established trade routes down the Volga River to the Caspian Sea and down the Dnieper River to the Black Sea. These routes opened up commerce with the Arab world (through the Middle East and into the Far East) and with the Byzantine Empire. These widespread trade endeavors required

---

3. In the liturgy used during the 800s and 900s by the Friesians, in the northern parts of the low countries, the congregation prayed, "From the wrath of the Norsemen, good Lord, deliver us."

considerable organization and control, by medieval standards. All this had impressed the East Slavs enough that they felt it wise to ask the Varangians to become the Slavs' rulers.

Not long after 830, the Varangians accepted the invitation and settled in the area around Kiev as rulers over the East Slavs. In short order, Kiev—long since established as a city for its prime location on the Dnieper River—became the capital of the emerging polity. The state led by the Varangians took its name from the city and from the term used for the Varangians who became the ruling class—"the Rus."[4] As they lived among the East Slavs, they eventually intermarried with their subjects and became Slavicized, adopting the Slavonic tongue and taking Slavic names. But the Varangians gave their name to the state and, in due course, to its people, both known as "Kievan Rus.'"

The Rule of the Varangians

The Varangians readily defeated the Khazars, liberating the Slavs. The Varangians' relationships with the Slavs were good: the rulers protected their subjects and brought unified rule and law to them. The taxes instituted by the rulers were unwelcome, of course, but the Varangian rulers recognized that they were going to be dealing with the Slavs on an ongoing basis and did not engage in the arbitrary impositions the Slavs had previously endured from the Khazars. Assimilation of rulers to ruled took place in short course, and the Slavs came to think of their rulers as fellow Slavs.

As a last point about the Varangians, it is worth mentioning "the House of Rurik." Early in the 850s, a ruler named Rurik played a central role among the Varangians. His descendants ended up becoming the ruling family for Kievan Rus'—and eventually for the Muscovite one that succeeded it as the preeminent power among the East Slavs. The House of Rurik survived as the royal family for more than seven hundred years, until the early 1600s, ruling first in Kiev and later in Moscow.

---

4. The designation "Rus'" has generated discussion among scholars of East Slavic history. The most widely accepted perspective is that the term comes from the Finnish "Ruotsi," used to refer to the inhabitants of Sweden: see the concise presentation in Subtelny, *Ukraine: A History*, 23; for somewhat more detail, see Magocsi, *A History of Ukraine*, 56–59.

Seeking a New Faith

The early Slavs practiced the pagan religion of their ancestors. It had neither priests nor temples. The Norse religion of the Varangians was also polytheistic, but with a more elaborate mythology: among the Norse gods were Odin as the chief god, Freja his wife, Thor as the god of thunder (and war), and Loki (as a sort of cosmic jokester). By comparison with Greek and Roman mythologies, Norse mythology was quite "rough-and-tumble," with the gods engaged in the same sort of pursuits as the Vikings, only on a much larger scale. Until the conversion of Vladimir and Kievan Rus' to Christianity in 988, the religion of Kievan Rus' was polytheistic; indeed, early in his reign Vladimir set up idols of several gods worshipped in Kievan Rus'.[5]

Over the course of its first century of existence, Kievan Rus' attracted increasing attention in Europe for its size, wealth, and power. It traded with the Arabs and engaged in both commerce and war with Byzantium. Through these extended contacts, the House of Rurik came to recognize that these other nations had more sophisticated religious views and practices than either the Slavs or their Norse ancestors. In due course, the Kievan Rus' rulers, and most significantly Vladimir, became convinced that they and their people needed to embrace a better religion.

The general religious disquiet evidently affected some of Vladimir's predecessors. His grandmother, Princess Olga, served as regent (945-62) after the death of her husband Igor (r. 912-45) and during the time her son Sviatoslav was a minor. In 957, while on an embassy to Byzantium, Princess Olga embraced Christianity and was baptized. Upon her return to Kiev, Christian missionaries accompanied her. No significant change followed for the religious status of Kievan Rus', though. While Olga had become a Christian, Sviatoslav (r. 962-72) did not. The ultimate change awaited the conversion of Sviatoslav's son, Vladimir (r. 978-1015).

Vladimir's Lifestyle

However impressed Vladimir may have been by the religion of his grandmother, he did not soon or without question embrace Christianity. Indeed, his lifestyle reflected little concern for whatever Christian virtues he may have encountered in her: Vladimir enjoyed feasting and heavy drinking,

---

5. The religion practiced in the time of Vladimir included elements of both Norse and East Slavic mythologies; the chief god was Perun (significantly, related to Thor rather than Odin). Other deities included Dazhbog, the Slavic sun god; Veles (or Volos), the god of cattle (or of death); and Svarog. For a concise presentation, see Cross, *Slavic Civilization*, 24-26.

had sexual liaisons with a wide number of females of varying ages and marital status,[6] and was brutal—both in warfare and in punishing malefactors in his realm. By the mid-980s, however, he had become convinced that both he and his state needed a new religious orientation.

How had he become aware of other religious possibilities? One way was doubtlessly the various diplomatic connections Kievan Rus' by then had with numerous states. Another was that Kiev was frequented by merchants from other peoples who brought their own religious views and practices with them. The Arab traders and some Bulgars living near the Volga River practiced Islam. The Khazars—by now associates of Kievan Rus' rather than enemies—had embraced Judaism, and there may have been Jewish merchants in Kiev. Frankish traders brought their Western Christian teachings and practices with them. Finally, he knew about Eastern Christianity because of contacts with and merchants from Byzantium. These last two, although both Christian, were by that time in regular tension with each other; they thus presented different options within Christianity.

The Path to Conversion

How did Vladimir decide among these options? According to the story recounted about a century later in Nestor's *Primary Chronicle* (sometimes translated under the title, *The Chronicle of Bygone Years*), Vladimir sent out representatives to attend the services of worship offered by Judaism, Western Christianity, and Eastern Christianity, and to report to him what they encountered. From those reports, he would make the decision. (As Nestor reports the results, Vladimir had already consulted with the Muslim Bulgars. Attracted by their fondness for women and indulgence, he was nonetheless disaffected by their rejection of alcoholic beverages and decided this would suit neither him nor his people.)

The emissaries' report on Judaism pointed out that it seemed to consist of rules, laws, and requirements; Vladimir opined that such a religion was hardly suited to his people. Given the rejection of Islam and Judaism, the choice would fall to either Western or Eastern Christianity. Vladimir's representatives attended worship among the Germans, who were Western Christians: the report indicated that they found the worship unintelligible (it was conducted in Latin) and said that it seemed aloof and cold. Vladimir

---

6. According to *The Primary Chronicle* (which offers the earliest records about Kievan Rus'), Vladimir had three hundred concubines at Vyshorod, another three hundred at Belhorod, and two hundred more at Berestrovo; beyond that, it was noted that he regularly seduced married women and violated young girls.

was not drawn to this. Then they attended a service in the Hagia Sophia in Constantinople; when they returned to Kiev, they were glowing in their assessment of Eastern Christianity (commonly referred to as Eastern Orthodoxy). Within the Hagia Sophia, they urged, they were swept away by the splendor of worship.

What was it that so impressed Vladimir's emissaries? Undeniably, the Hagia Sophia was an inspiring edifice. It had been built at the direction of Emperor Justinian the Great (r. 527–65), who wanted to design a style of architecture distinctive to Christianity. Earlier generations of Christians had sometimes re-consecrated as church edifices Roman pagan temples built in the round; others had accepted the basilica style of architecture used for official Roman state buildings.[7]

A pagan temple built in the round, subsequently consecrated as a Christian church, now known as the Church of St. George the Great Martyr (Sophia [ancient Serdika], Bulgaria) where Emperor Constantine the Great himself worshipped while on holidays from imperial duties.

But to Justinian, these styles were tainted by their pagan background. He desired to fashion a distinctively Christian form of architecture, never utilized before and designed to be a worthy embodiment of Christian faith and worship. So, he directed that the resultant structure should be a square

---

7. An example of this style of architecture can be seen in St. Sophia Church, also built during Emperor Justinian's reign; this church gave its name also to the city, which had to then been known as Serdika.

(representing the four corners of the earth) surmounted by a hemispherical vault (symbolizing the heavens above). The Hagia Sofia is the remarkable result of these determinations.

Completed in 537, the Hagia Sophia ("the Church of the Holy Wisdom") was known throughout Europe, both East and West, simply as "the Great Church" for more than four centuries. It was by far the largest church edifice in all Christendom.

The Hagia Sophia.

More than mere size made the Hagia Sophia special, however. Within it, one encountered a wonder of architectural engineering, designed to awe all who saw it. The nave was a cube surmounted by four huge vaults that supported a hemispherical dome. The sheer size, though, was enough to dumbfound an observer: the cube was twenty-five meters on a side, the vaults soared above the cube another thirteen meters, and above them rested the dome—also twenty-five meters in diameter. The total effect was staggering: the top of the dome towered more than fifty meters above the floor on which one stood. Beyond all this architectural magnificence, the base of the dome consisted of forty round-headed windows (between which were the slenderest of supports possible).

The Dome of the Hagia Sophia.

Because of the sunlight pouring through the windows, the dome appeared to hover above the rest of the church. As an edifice, the Hagia Sophia was a wonder—both architecturally and in initial religious impression.[8]

Beyond all that, Eastern Orthodox worship involves the whole person in a straightforward way—namely, via all five senses. Clouds of incense to smell, icons and mosaics to see, chanting and singing and preaching to hear, icons and crosses to touch and kiss, and the Eucharist to taste—in every Orthodox service, the whole person is thus involved. The emissaries from Kievan Rus' experienced this worship.

---

8. Constructing this remarkable edifice had faced the builders, Anthemius of Tralles and Isidorus of Miletus, with a plethora of architectural difficulties, especially arising from challenges of handling the thrust of the building's weight. After several failed efforts, though, they succeeded in building the remarkable edifice. One evidence of the mastery of their achievement is that the building has survived war and earthquake and, with various minor repairs over the centuries, still stands and is in use today.

Mosaic of Christ with the Virgin Mary and John the Baptist/Forerunner.

Further, they may well have learned enough Greek because of prior interaction with Byzantine representatives in Kiev to follow the liturgy: if so, they would also have been profoundly impressed. The Liturgy of St. John Chrysostom—used on most Sundays of the church year in Orthodoxy—offers a rich Christian worship experience itself. That liturgy comes in a repeated ebb and flow of acknowledgment of divine greatness and praise to God, of confession of human failure and unworthiness, of pleas for mercy, and assurance of divine love to the unworthy, all interspersed with prayers for the needs of society and the world; altogether, it is a most compelling form of worship, which, if the representatives of Kievan Rus' experienced it with any modicum of understanding, would also have been winsomely attractive. With and undergirding all the above, the beauty of the clerical vestments, the solemnity of worship, and the rhythmical chanting all contributed to a sense of wonder and beauty in the presence of God. The representatives of Kievan Rus' were impressed and attracted to what they had experienced. Their report on Eastern Christianity was glowing; Vladimir declared for Eastern Christianity.

In this regard, it is worth noting something evident already in Nestor's account, for this element becomes an abiding trait of Christianity as practiced in Kievan Rus' and its successor states among the East Slavs. Nestor's chronicle indicates that *beauty itself* played an important role for Vladimir and his people in discerning where God is genuinely worshipped. To this day, Christianity among the East Slavs lays heavy stress on beauty: whether in church architecture, in clerical vestments, in choral music, in icons, or whatever else, beauty is essential. This has been accounted for in various ways, including reference to the wide landscapes of the Russian steppes and the stark contrasts in natural colors found there.[9] However that may be, it is undeniable that beauty is for the East Slavs probably more essential to proper worship of God than it is to any other group within Christendom. Indeed, among the East Slavs, it is more important that worship and praise be beautiful than intelligible. Optimally, worship should be both, for people need to learn and understand the faith. However, if choice must be made, then beauty is more important,[10] for it reflects the splendor of God, the wonder of his love, and the unfathomable ways in which he deals with humanity.[11]

A Genuine Conversion?

In 988, Vladimir was baptized, and with him the people of Kievan Rus', who embraced Eastern Orthodoxy in a national conversion. As with the earlier cases of Rastislav of Moravia and Boris of Bulgaria,[12] so again with Vladimir and Kievan Rus', some scholars have dismissed the conversion as simply a political expedient. However, considering all the relevant data presents quite a different picture. While the conversion to Eastern Christianity undoubtedly had political implications—connections to Byzantium, Vladimir's marriage to the Byzantine princess Anna, etc.—it unquestionably marked a dramatic change in Vladimir himself, such as Christian teaching indicates attends a genuine conversion.

Almost immediately after Vladimir was baptized, he showed clear opposition to the prior paganism of Kievan Rus': he had the idols that had been set up to pagan gods on the hills of Kiev toppled and rolled down into the Dnieper River. As well, virtually as soon as Vladimir was converted, he cut back on how much he ate and drank, became faithful to his wife (the Byzantine princess Anna), and curtailed his brutality in warfare and the punishments of criminals. In the latter regard, he showed a remarkable openness to reconsider the accepted practices of his people: he came to the conclusion that capital punishment was wrong, since it cut off any

9. This is argued, *inter alia*, by Arseniev, *Russian Piety*, and by Pascal, *Religion of the Russian People*.

10. This can be recognized, e.g., in the continued preference in Russian Orthodoxy for using Old Church Slavonic (the ancient Slavic language used in the translation works of Cyril and Methodius), rather than contemporary Russian.

11. For a discussion of the importance of beauty in Orthodoxy, see Evdokimov, *Art of the Icon*.

12. See above, chapter 6.

hope of a criminal's repentance and amendment. His Byzantine instructors were astonished at this suggestion; Byzantium, while Christian, had few compunctions about imposing capital punishment as an appropriate penalty for a wide variety of infractions. In due course, the Byzantine advisors prevailed upon Vladimir not to eliminate capital punishment; the fact that he considered what was at the time such a remarkable position shows the genuineness of change in Vladimir attendant upon his conversion to Christianity. He was clearly pondering the implications of his newfound Christian commitment for his rule.

In other ways, too, this conversion manifested itself: subsequent to his conversion, Vladimir turned a considerable portion of his revenues to support the needy and the aged, built homes for the destitute, established orphanages, and erected hospitals. As ruler of a converted Kievan Rus', Vladimir was clearly working out the implications of the dominical command to love God and neighbor. By the prince's insistence, monasteries within the state of Kievan Rus' engaged not only in prayers and pursuit of holiness for the monks but also served the spiritual and material needs of the people: he directed that hospitality for travellers, spiritual counsel for anyone seeking it, and provision of needs for the destitute mark monastic practice in his realm. As a final argument for the genuineness of his conversion, it can be noted that after his baptism Vladimir devoted 10 percent of the entire income of the wealthiest state in all of Europe to the support of the church (including the building of churches and supporting missionaries in their catechetical endeavors). With him, and because of him, Kievan Rus' was transformed.

The transformation continued under his successors, especially during the rule of his son, Jaroslav the Wise (r. 1019–54). The reign of Jaroslav was the high point of Kievan Rus' history. He supported monasteries, which continued the sort of service to God and society inaugurated by his father. In addition, Jaroslav funded translation centers, which built on and carried further the scholarly accomplishments ongoing since the preceding century in Bulgaria, thus offering still more of Byzantium's rich Christian heritage in Slavonic translation to the increasingly literate upper classes of Kievan Rus'. During his reign, schools served the court of Kievan Rus', offering sophisticated education to the children of the royal and noble families. (Some schools had been established earlier, under Vladimir, but their successes became notable during Jaroslav's reign.)

Further, Jaroslav had many churches built throughout Kiev. Under him, Kiev ended up with four hundred churches for its 40,000 inhabitants—a ratio of one church for every hundred residents. An enduring legacy from Jaroslav is the magnificent Church of the Holy Wisdom (commonly known as "St. Sophia").

Near the rebuilt Golden Gate (in Kiev, Ukraine),
a statue of Jaroslav dedicating St. Sophia to God.

The inspiration for it was the Hagia Sophia in Byzantium. This church served as a place of Christian worship for some nine hundred years, until it was turned into a museum by the Communists in the twentieth century.

On one of the walls of that church, a fresco of Jaroslav and his family still can be seen.

Badly worn, but still visible: Jaroslav and his family pictured on a wall in St. Sophia.

This is worth noting because Jaroslav and his family enjoyed great respect, not only in Kievan Rus', but throughout contemporary Europe. He was the leader of a large, powerful, wealthy, and unquestionably Christian state. Other states sought contacts with him and his family; indeed, this was so common that Jaroslav came, with good reason, to be called "the father-in-law of Europe." During the Middle Ages, nations regularly sealed relationships with other states by dynastic marriages; Jaroslav was in this respect exceedingly well-connected. One daughter was married to the King of Hungary, another to the King of Norway, a third to the King of France; one son to the daughter of the King of Poland, another to a Byzantine princess, and a third to the sister of the bishop of Trier in Germany.

THE CONVERSION OF VLADIMIR AND KIEVAN RUS' (988)

Jaroslav's sarcophagus is found in a small enclave within St. Sophia. Special x-ray techniques have confirmed (via broken bones and lasting skeletal effects from injuries sustained in battles) that the remains inside it are those of Jaroslav.

In Jaroslav's schools, Kievan Rus' developed a sophisticated culture, with much emphasis on linguistic facility, far in advance of any other European nation at that time. Education was offered, not only for the clergy, but also for the sons (and some of the daughters) of the royal court. In those schools, students learned to read and write three languages. At the time in Western Europe, almost nobody in the royal courts was even literate. A comparison may help make the point: when King John signed the Magna Carta in 1215, he did so with an "X" because he couldn't read or write; at that time, students in Kievan Rus' in the noble court could read and write three languages. (Indeed, one of Jaroslav's sons, Vsevolod [1030–93], mastered five languages.)

Kievan Rus' had by far the most sophisticated court in all of Europe. At one point, the French King ended up sending some nobles to confer with Jaroslav. In due course, negotiations led to an agreement, which needed to be signed by the respective parties. The French nobles all made an "X" as their signature; they were astonished when the princess Anna signed her name in Cyrillic, with a flourish. As a final point, it is worth noting that in governmental policy, under Vladimir Monomakh (r. 1113–25), the original intuition of Vladimir became law: capital punishment was abolished, despite its precedent in the Christian empire of Byzantium. Kievan Rus' was a major European power, committed to the Christianity it had embraced in 988 under Vladimir, and to the implications and opportunities that conversion entailed.

The Significance of the Conversion

From all of this, it is clear that the conversion of Vladimir and Kievan Rus' in 988 was a genuine, profound, and far-reaching conversion. This had long-lasting impact for Kievan Rus', of course, but also for Eastern Europe, more generally, and for East Slavs, particularly. With this conversion, Kievan Rus'—at the time the largest, most powerful, and wealthiest state in Europe—entered into the large commonwealth of Christian states of Europe. This allowed Kievan Rus' to play a significant role within that commonwealth—as witnessed, among other things, by the dynastic marriages that related Kievan Rus' to other European states.

In wider and longer sweep, the conversion had ramifications for subsequent Eastern European history. Much of that history has been shaped by the determination of Muscovy—as the main successor state to Kievan Rus'—to protect and advance the cause of Eastern Orthodoxy as the true faith.[13] With regard to the East Slavs themselves, the embrace of Eastern Orthodoxy rather than Western Christianity assured their isolation after the mid-1400s, when Muscovy was left, after Byzantium's conquest by the Ottoman Turks, as the only remaining self-governing Orthodox nation. By then, the tensions between Western Christianity and Eastern Orthodoxy had long since erupted in schism, so Muscovy (and, in due course, the Russian Empire that grew out of it) saw itself as the only bulwark against the hordes of Western Christian apostasy. Orthodoxy in the Russian Empire saw resolute unwillingness to modify its rich Eastern Christian heritage as an inescapable implication of its isolated status; this perspective has continued to mark attitudes in the Russian nation and the Russian Orthodox church to the present day.

13. This becomes one of the main reasons for Russian opposition to Poland; see the treatments below, in chapter 10 and chapter 13.

In all this, Orthodoxy among the East Slavs took on distinctive hues in the way in which it was embraced and developed in Kievan Rus' and bequeathed to subsequent generations of East Slavs in Ukraine, Belarus, and Russia. Indebted to Byzantine Christianity, Orthodoxy among the East Slavs did not slavishly follow Byzantium. As noted above, the East Slavs have placed even more emphasis on beauty in their tradition than their Byzantine predecessors in Eastern Christianity had done. In that regard, the East Slavs also elaborated on something they had inherited from Byzantium—namely, a serious reservation about the abilities of the human mind to articulate the Christian faith adequately. By 988, Vladimir recognized that the four religions he had considered could argue with each other extensively, but that none of that resulted in changed positions. Beginning in Kievan Rus' and subsequently, the Orthodoxy of the East Slavs has been suspicious of human rationality when it comes to talking about God; they recognize that teaching must be done, but they do not place much confidence in theologians to lay out "the truth, the whole truth, and nothing but the truth," because they are talking about *God*. For the Orthodoxy of the East Slavs, it is better to be quiet and worship than to open one's mouth and speak error; they have greater confidence in iconographers who portray in painted beauty the wonder of what it means to belong to God. This is a distinct approach, a significant one. The conversion of Vladimir and Kievan Rus' in 988 offered Christianity "in a new key"; that conversion was a significant transitional event in Eastern European history.

CHAPTER 8

The Development of States (Tenth–Twelfth Centuries)

"There can be no objection to taking the Slavic nations as the central basis for the study of the medieval and the early modern period of Eastern Europe and to treating them as an organic unity. Not only do they form the dominating ethnic elements in these parts, but although divided geographically and culturally, all of them have many common traits in their political history, their civilization, their national character, and language."[1]

THE NINTH-CENTURY EMERGENCE OF the states of Moravia (among the West Slavs), Bulgaria (among the South Slavs), and Kievan Rus' (among the East Slavs) was followed by the development of other Eastern European states in the tenth to twelfth centuries. The early history of each of these states during this time is fascinating in its own right, but we cannot here pursue those separate histories in detail. The treatment in this chapter will offer an overview of the states that arose in these three centuries, seeking a broad familiarity with their development. This will indicate why this period is a significant turning point in the history of Eastern Europe.

States among the West Slavs

During the tenth to the twelfth centuries, two states arose among the West Slavs. Their fortunes during the period were significantly affected by what was then taking place in their neighbor to the west, Germany. The German influence was so imposing that the way states developed among the West

---

1. Dvornik, *Slavs in European History*, xxi.

Slavs and the tensions they faced in this period cannot be appreciated without some basic information about Germany at the time.

Context: German Influences

During the ninth century, the German domain had emerged as the most powerful of the three kingdoms into which the empire of Charlemagne (d. 814) was divided among his grandsons. The powerful German kingdom became a force to be reckoned with throughout Europe, both west and east. What Germany did (or tried to do) during the tenth to twelfth centuries had considerable impact on the West Slavs. In this regard, two of the lines of action pursued by the German rulers were especially significant for the development of the West Slav states in the period: on the one hand, the German kings endeavored to control the church in their realm; on the other, they were determined to expand their domain to the east. Each of these requires some elucidation to enable us to understand how they influenced the West Slavs.

Trying to Control the Church

By the middle of the 800s, German rulers were irrevocably committed to building a strong state. Essential to this, as they saw it, was the ability to control who would be appointed as bishops[2] within the German realm. This was not a new idea among rulers in Western Europe: it had been the desire of Frankish kings for several generations; nor was the idea restricted to German monarchs alone: kings in other states of Western Europe had the same intention in subsequent generations. In the period under consideration, however, the German kings were Western Europe's powerhouses, and their endeavors to control episcopal appointments—as well as the church's response to German pressures in this matter—established a pattern that not

---

2. A *bishop* served as the overseer for many priests and their parishes; this group of parishes was referred to as the bishop's *diocese* or *bishopric*, which would find its center in a major city where the bishop resided. From the Greek term for "bishop," *episkopos*, came the designation "episcopal"—referring to the office and responsibilities of the bishop. Above the bishop in the church's hierarchy was an *archbishop*, responsible for a group of bishops and their dioceses; his group of dioceses was called an *archdiocese*, and his office and responsibilities were called *archiepiscopal*. While there were other designations and offices in the church's hierarchy, they need not concern us here, except to note that in the church in Western Europe the highest position in the church's hierarchy was that of *pope*, whereas in the church in Eastern Europe the most exalted position was that of *patriarch*.

only shaped the situation subsequently for Western Europe, but also considerably influenced the development of the West Slav states.

There were several reasons why the German rulers wanted to have authority over who would be appointed to episcopal positions within the German realm. Since bishops were the leading clergymen in the main cities of the state, they held great influence: as the highest-ranking church official most people in Western Europe would ever be likely to see or hear, a bishop held considerable religious authority; and since by this time everyone in Western Europe professed commitment to Christianity, everyone would be inclined to listen carefully to whatever the bishop said.

However, the bishops' influence extended far beyond the religious and ecclesiastical roles they filled, and as a consequence they exerted considerable sway over the people who lived within the state. Well before the time of Charlemagne, Frankish rulers had been using clergymen as main figures within their bureaucracies. A major reason for this was that the clergy could read and write, and governments needed to keep records and engage in correspondence. While such clerical[3] tasks fell to the lower levels of the church hierarchy, bishops had come to play a much larger role. They usually had received more training than those lower in the church's hierarchy, for one thing; for another, with their role in ecclesiastical government, the bishops had considerable influence and administrative expertise upon which the Frankish rulers wanted to draw for the purposes of civil government. As a result, bishops had often been asked to serve as advisors to Frankish monarchs;[4] bishops had usually served the Frankish rulers well.

The benefit to civil rulers of having bishops fill such roles extended beyond the considerations so far described, though. Frankish kings had regularly dealt with nobles in their service who wanted to insure that their own sons would succeed them in whatever offices those nobles filled in the government; not infrequently, some of those nobles or their sons even sought to displace the king. Consequently, to have nobles play key roles in civil government was courting incompetence or rebellion. However, since clergy were supposed to be celibate, civil rulers who utilized bishops in their government did not have to worry about that problem in any post filled by a bishop.

---

3. In contemporary North American society, the people who do the foundational work needed in offices, banks, and other organizations are referred to as *clerks*, and the work they do is designated *clerical*. Both these terms are derived from *clericus*, the Latin term for *clergy*; contemporary parlance thus reflects the medieval historical situation described above.

4. The role a bishop fulfilled in civil government was, thus, much like that of a cabinet minister in civil governments in contemporary North America.

In view of these considerations, rulers in the Frankish kingdom had tried to assure that men they knew as reliable or were sure they could control ended up being appointed bishops in their realm. Since the German kings in the tenth through the twelfth centuries knew this Frankish pattern and were themselves working diligently to build a powerful state and a stable government, it is hardly surprising that they tried to control episcopal appointments within their realm, as their Frankish forebears had sought to do.

Given the church's dependence on Frankish military protection since the mid-eighth century,[5] and eager as the church was to assist in building Christian society in the West, the papacy had sought to work with the Frankish rulers and their descendants in the three segments into which the Carolingian Empire had been divided. Nothing of this changed with the rise of German dominance in the remains of the former empire: collaboration between church and civil government served the interests of both the church and the rising German state.

However, by the mid-eleventh century, several concerned churchmen saw the need to extricate the church from this relationship, since it had sullied the spiritual purity of the church, in their estimation. The efforts of these church leaders led to a vigorous movement for reform within the church. This movement sought, above all, to re-establish the independence of the church as over against the powerful German emperor; many of the popes thought that such independence required finding ways to limit the growth of the German empire.[6] The resultant emperor/pope conflict (known as "The Investiture Controversy")[7] had significant influence on Western Europe, indeed, but also on much of what happened among the emerging states of the West Slavs.

---

5. In 754, the Frankish ruler Pepin had come to Rome's aid when it was endangered by the pagan Lombards; in 800, Charlemagne again defended Rome against the Lombard threat.

6. The German emperor was crowned as the "Roman" emperor, and the empire he ruled was referred to as the "Holy Roman Empire"; in this study, we will use the designations "German empire" and "Holy Roman Empire" interchangeably.

7. The controversy took its name from the question of who—the pope or the emperor—had the significant privilege of "investing" the episcopal appointee with the symbols of his office (the bishop's ring and the crozier [shepherd's staff]); the one who had that privilege was understood to be the one with the final word in making the episcopal appointment.

Pushing to the East

As the tenth century unfolded, Germany was embarking on a long campaign, lasting over the next four centuries, to extend her frontiers. In the ninth century, Louis the German had tried but had been unable fully to live up to the imperial ideal of his Frankish forebears; not long after him, the eastern branch of the Carolingian[8] dynasty died out. Germany continued, however: in the early tenth century, the Duke of Saxony became King of Germany, and, even though he had no dynastic connection with the Carolingians, he and his successors laid claim to the imperial privileges of the Carolingians. Under the duke's son, Otto I (r. 936–73), Germany began to live up to those ideals.

The only direction in which Germany could expand was to the east.[9] This meant encountering and either subjugating or displacing the Slavs who lived east of the Elbe River. During the tenth century, German onslaughts forced the Slavs who lived between the Elbe and the Oder Rivers eastwards; German peoples settled into the area thus vacated. In addition, the German kingdom swallowed up all the rest of contemporary Germany, most of the territories that today belong to the Czech Republic and to Austria, and a substantial portion of western Poland. Large numbers of German settlers moved into these areas, without entirely displacing the prior Slavic inhabitants. To the east of the Oder River lived various Slavic peoples, among whom substantial numbers of Germans also settled.

Thus, Germany expanded considerably, at the cost of the various Slavic peoples who had previously lived in these areas. While this was transpiring, two states arose among the West Slavs. Both subsequently developed into strong states later, during the thirteenth through the fifteenth centuries. One of these states was within the borders of the "Holy Roman Empire" (as the expanded German realm came to be known): that state was Bohemia. The other was the state of Poland, which developed to the east of the Holy Roman Empire.

---

8. The designation "Carolingian" derives from the name of the dynasty's most significant member—"Charlemagne" (from the French), "Charles the Great" (in English), "Karl der Große" (in German), "Karel de Groote" (in Dutch).

9. This eastward orientation of Germany became so constant over the centuries that a phrase, *Drang nach Osten* ("drive toward the east"), was coined to describe it. The phrase often appears, without translation, in the work of historians and political scientists dealing with German expansionism.

Bohemia

During the ninth century, while Moravia became an independent state, Bohemia was a vassal[10] territory to Germany. This status continued for Bohemia through the tenth century. With the destruction of the state of Moravia in the early tenth century (in 906), Bohemia was left as the only group among the West Slavs with a modicum of self-government.

Early in the tenth century, the various Bohemian territories coalesced into a unified state under the able leadership of Václav [Wenceslas] (r. 921–29), a member of the Přemysl family; the Přemyslid dynasty ruled Bohemia for more than four hundred years. Václav's reign was cut short when he was assassinated by his brother, Boleslav I [Boleslas] (r. 929–67), who wanted the throne for himself. Among the Czechs, Václav has come to be looked on as a martyr. (At some unknown point during the ninth century, the Bohemians had embraced Christianity of the Western/Latin stripe.) Václav is revered as Bohemia's national saint (and has been immortalized as "Good King Wenceslas" in a Christmas carol).

Despite the unsavory beginning of his reign, Boleslav turned out to be an excellent ruler for the Bohemians. In 955, his armies fought alongside those of the German emperor, Otto I, against the Magyars at Lechfeld; at this battle, the Magyars' wide-ranging attacks throughout Western Europe were brought to an end.[11] Boleslav thus showed himself to be both a faithful vassal of the German emperor and also a defender of Bohemia (since the Magyars had been a serious threat to Bohemia). In addition, the efforts of Boleslav contributed to the conversion of the Poles to Christianity. Seeking to initiate close cooperation with them, he agreed to marry his daughter to the Polish prince, Mieszko I—provided Mieszko embraced Christianity. Mieszko did so in 966, and the Poles followed their prince in this commitment.[12]

A succession of tyrannical but less able Bohemian rulers followed Boleslav I for the rest of the tenth century and the first third of the eleventh. Then a Bohemian prince arose who was a gifted ruler, Břetislav I (r. 1034–55), "the Restorer": he managed to restore good government in Bohemia and to assert her independence from German control. Further, he expanded

---

10. In the medieval socio-economic and political system of *feudalism*, a *vassal* received certain benefits from a *lord* for pledging loyalty and submission to him; minimally, the lord promised to protect the vassal, and the vassal was expected to follow the directives of the lord. A vassal could be a person or, through the person of a ruler, the area or state over which he (or, occasionally, she) ruled.

11. This is treated below in this chapter, under our consideration of the Magyars.

12. This is treated below in this chapter, under the consideration of Poland.

the Bohemian realm: he brought all of Silesia and the territories as far as Cracow (in contemporary Poland) under Bohemian control.

Although Germany managed to regain control of Bohemia after Břetislav's death and reduce it again to vassal status, Bohemia nevertheless soon managed to attain special status within the German empire: with the emperor's approval, Vratislav II (r. 1061–92), Břetislav's son and (second) successor, was crowned king of Bohemia in 1085. He was granted this extraordinary honor for two reasons: firstly, for several years he had supported the Holy Roman Emperor, Henry IV (r. 1056–1106), during the emperor's struggle with the papacy; secondly, he had fought faithfully alongside the German emperor against a claimant to the imperial throne. In subsequent centuries, Bohemia remained part of the Holy Roman Empire, but it enjoyed an unusual privilege because of this coronation: it was the only part of the empire which could boast its own crowned king. This dignity ranked Bohemia ahead of all the other more than three hundred territories within the Holy Roman Empire. Since he was a crowned king, the ruler of Bohemia ranked second in prestige only to the emperor himself.

During the twelfth century, the Bohemian kings invited numerous German colonists into Bohemian territory, where they served as merchants or built up substantial agricultural enterprises.[13] Their contributions to the economy of Bohemia further strengthened the country. Both economically and politically, by the early thirteenth century, Bohemia had developed into one of the leading powers within the loose federation called the Holy Roman Empire.

Poland

By the middle of the tenth century, the Slavic peoples living around the Vistula River had coalesced into a nation. Under Prince Mieszko I (r. 960–92), Poland developed into a distinct state; Mieszko founded the Piast dynasty, which ruled Poland for the next four centuries. Mieszko married the daughter of Boleslav I of Bohemia and accepted Christianity in 966. In doing so, he

---

13. In this way, large numbers of Germans were attracted to Bohemia. In due course, as their agricultural and entrepreneurial enterprises prospered, they came to play a predominant role in Bohemia's economy; with that went a distinct socio-economic status within Bohemia, as well. Over the next three centuries, resentment against Germans developed among the Bohemians, who believed that they and their country were being exploited by the German residents; this resentment exploded in the Hussite wars of the 1400s (see the fuller treatment below, in chapter 12). Thus, this twelfth-century invitation from the Bohemian kings ended up having profound, though unforeseen and unintended, consequences for the history of Bohemia.

embraced Christianity of the western variety, as the Bohemians (and Moravians) had before him. While the desire behind this dynastic marriage was to establish close cooperation between the two West Slav states, the actual relationship between Bohemia and Poland over the following centuries wavered between support and hostility (even though the ruling houses continued to be closely related to each other through subsequent marriages). Rather than face invading forces from Germany, Mieszko found it wise to acknowledge German suzerainty in 973. However, neither he nor any subsequent Polish ruler ever accepted a permanent vassal status to Germany.

The pope authorized Mieszko's son, Bolesław I [Boleslas] (r. 992-1025), "the Brave," to be crowned king. The rationale for this was the papal determination to limit the German empire. To achieve that, the pope was willing to grant a royal crown to the leader of the state to the east of the Holy Roman Empire, as a barrier to further German expansion. Bolesław served the young nation well as its king, and Poland served the purpose of the papacy effectively: although the German emperor sought to subdue Bolesław and remove the obstacle he posed to the German desires to expand eastward, the emperor's efforts were unsuccessful.

Under Bolesław's successor, Mieszko II (r. 1025-34), dynastic intrigues weakened the central government. These struggles, complicated by a pagan reaction led by some nobles against Christianity, swept over Poland for a few years; the accession of Kazimierz I [Casimir], "the Restorer" (r. 1038-58) brought these struggles to an end. The German emperor had tried to make the most of the period of strife, and Kazimierz thought it wise to avoid even the appearance of challenging German power, so that he could devote himself to the Polish state's internal problems. Consequently, Kazimierz stopped using the royal title, which had irritated the German emperor. Kazimierz managed not to provoke further German encroachments, and he restored good government to Poland. The state flourished under his rule, and he was able to hand on a stable government to his son and successor, Bolesław II (r. 1058-79), "the Bold."

Bolesław proved himself an able leader in his own right, but he followed some different paths than his father had pursued. The most significant of these was that he accepted coronation as king of the Polish state in 1076, again under papal authorization. This came about in an intriguing fashion—one that indicates why he was accorded the epithet, "the Bold."

The controversy between Pope Gregory VII and Henry IV, the Holy Roman Emperor, exercised the Holy Roman Empire, its vassal states, and those that recognized German suzerainty. It was an intense struggle for the leadership of Christian Europe. Throughout that controversy, the Polish ruler Bolesław supported the pope against the German emperor. In so doing, he shifted from the approach of his father in one sense, but continued it in another: in contrast to his father, Bolesław thus stood boldly against the German empire; in keeping with his father, though, Bolesław defended Christianity in standing by the western church's leader, the pope. At the point where it seemed the pope was to achieve victory—on his way to Germany at the end of 1076, to preside over the election of a replacement for Henry IV—the pope endorsed the coronation of Bolesław. He was bold indeed in accepting it, given the German emperor's power and his determined opposition to both Poland and the pope. The German emperor manifested his displeasure in no uncertain terms.

As it turned out, Henry outmaneuvered Pope Gregory and managed to remain Holy Roman Emperor. By the time that situation had been resolved, however, Bolesław's coronation had taken place. Poland had a king: the coronation was not only a notable event in the history of the Piasts and of the nation of Poland; it was also an early manifestation of that especially close relationship between Poland and the papacy that has marked Polish history.

That Polish devotion to the cause of the pope and of Western Christianity was further evident in Bolesław's attempt to force upon Kievan Rus' (to Poland's east) a ruler willing to accept Western Christianity. By the time this transpired, Kievan Rus' had been a Christian state for nearly a century: Prince Vladimir had converted to Christianity in 988. However, Vladimir and his people had embraced Christianity of the Eastern/Byzantine stripe. Subsequently, a serious rift had opened in 1054 between Western Christianity and Eastern Christianity. Succession problems in the 1070s had made it uncertain who should sit on the throne of the Kievan Rus' state; through intrigues, Bolesław involved himself and his state in the troubles, in the hope of advancing a claimant who had expressed readiness to submit to the church leadership of Rome.

In this endeavor, Bolesław was unsuccessful: Kievan Rus' repudiated both the Polish intrigues and the man they supported. Kieven Rus' also chose deliberately to remain within the Eastern Christian orbit, unreconciled with the pope. Bolesław's endeavor was also especially unfortunate, since it impressed upon the leaders of Kievan Rus'—and, in due course, upon the leaders of the state of Muscovy that succeeded her (after the period of the Mongol invasions and rule), and then upon the Russian state, which grew out of Muscovy—that Poland was, while Slav, a danger, both to the Muscovite/Russian state and to that Eastern Christianity that Muscovy/Russia wholeheartedly defended. The Poland/Russia tension that marks so much of subsequent Polish history had its beginnings in the reign of Bolesław II.

The 1076 coronation, under papal auspices, made Bolesław a king; nine years later, in 1085, Vratislav II was crowned King of Bohemia at the behest of the German emperor, Henry IV. As noted above, Vratislav received that honor for his faithful support of the German emperor; by contrast, Bolesław received the royal dignity for his faithful support of the pope. Both the Bohemian and the Polish rulers played the parts that would be expected, given their political situation: Bohemia was a permanent vassal state within the German empire, but Poland wanted to assert her independence from the powerful German empire to her west. Similarly, both played the role that their faith demanded of them: Vratislav managed to placate the pope while supporting the emperor in the controversy, and Bolesław stood firmly in support of the pope.

The two coronations were, unquestionably, related: Henry IV made that clear when he had Vratislav crowned in 1085 as "King of Bohemia *and Poland.*" Never before had Germany accepted the coronation of any of her vassals. However, with Poland again boasting a king (with papal blessing) since 1076, it seemed prudent to the German emperor to honor his faithful vassal similarly. Beyond that, the title he bestowed was an open invitation to Vratislav to claim his full realm by attacking and trying to subjugate the Polish nation. However, Vratislav wisely never used the last portion of his title and made no attempts to establish his rule over Poland. Even so, Henry IV's action was a challenge to both Poland and the pope, and the German emperor managed to assure continued tension between Bohemia and Poland in the future.

The German emperor was thus playing on tensions already evident within Poland. The nobles of Poland resented the superiority that one family among them (the Piasts) had attained. By the time of Bolesław II's successor, they were already working at cross purposes to those of the king.[14]

Bolesław's successor ceased using the royal title, given the tensions it aroused among the nobles and the difficulty he encountered with them, and the title was not renewed in Poland for two centuries. The strife between the king and the nobility continued for the rest of the eleventh and the twelfth centuries; by the late 1100s, indeed, it had so weakened the Polish state that the Germans were able to bring Poland under their control. Emperor Frederick Barbarossa (r. 1152–90) forced Bolesław IV (r. 1146–73) to acknowledge that he held Poland as a fief of the empire, but neither Bolesław IV nor

---

14. The tension between the nobles and the kings of Poland became a continuing pattern in Poland's subsequent history. That royal/noble tension is well presented, along with many other facets of Poland's history, in the novel by Michener, *Poland*; reading this novel is a good way to develop an appreciation for the Polish experience.

his successors accepted the vassal status implied in that acknowledgement as a permanent status for their nation.

The Magyars: The Kingdom of Hungary

A fierce warrior people, the Magyars (of Finno-Ugric stock), had headed westwards from their original homelands in Siberia and, by around 860, had invaded contemporary Moldova. From there Byzantium solicited their aid in fighting against the Bulgarian Empire. But Bulgaria soon returned the favor, and with its allies drove the Magyars westward. Invited by the Germans to assist in the attack upon Moravia in the early tenth century, the Magyars contributed to the 906 destruction of that earliest of the West Slavic nations.

One of the main leaders of the Magyars in this attack was Árpád (d. 907). In due course, his descendants rose to become the sole rulers of Hungary. The Árpád dynasty dominated Hungarian/Magyar politics until the beginning of the fourteenth century (1301). The path to their control was not a straight one, however.

After the destruction of the Moravian Empire in 906, the Magyars took over the Pannonian plain (most of contemporary Hungary). However, they did not appropriate much of the former Moravian domain; almost all of it was subsumed by Germany. The Magyars received only the eastern segment of the Moravian state's former territories, the area inhabited by the Slovaks.[15] For the next half-century after the destruction of Moravia, the Magyars ravaged various parts of Western and Eastern Europe; prior to their overwhelming defeat at Lechfeld in 955, they did not coalesce into a well-organized state.

The Magyars had previously been and continued through most of the tenth century to be under the loose organization of three chieftains; these three led the Magyar forces from their respective headquarters in three different geographic areas. Árpád had been one of these chieftains, and his immediate descendants managed to retain his area of leadership and to obtain one of the others. However, the third geographic area, the easternmost of them, continued under the control of another line of leaders. Rivalry between that leader and the line of Árpád manifested itself in contrasting foreign policies. The Árpád dynasty, in due course, sought to achieve good

---

15. The Slovaks thus entered upon a millennium in which they were ruled by the Magyars. After World War I, the Slovak territories, with the ones inhabited by the Czechs and Moravians, became the state of Czechoslovakia; on January 1, 1993, that state split into two, the Czech Republic and Slovakia. Thus, in 1993, the Slovaks for the first time in their long history became self-governing.

relationships with Germany and the rest of the West; a major stimulus for this was the opposing stance taken by the rival line of leaders.

The other Magyar chieftain's line sought contact with Byzantium; he expected that such an alliance would help protect him against both Bulgaria and Germany. To seal this arrangement, Bulcsú went to Constantinople in 948 and accepted Christianity there. However, he must not have looked upon his conversion as something that ought necessarily to influence his people's religious orientation, for he made no attempts to spread among them the faith he had embraced. It seems clear that his main concern was to assure himself a free hand for further assaults upon the West; from his vantage-point, his embrace of Eastern Christianity would probably keep Byzantium from coming to the defense of Western Christianity as he continued his raids throughout Germany and the rest of Western Europe.

Bulcsú's forays into Western Europe were, indeed, wide-ranging: his forces swept through Germany all the way to the mouth of the Loire River, returning through the Rhone valley and the area we know as the French and Italian rivieras; subsequently, he attacked Lombardy (northern Italy), Andalusia (northeastern Spain), Italy (as far south as Rome), Burgundy, the Rhine valley as far north as the Scheldt river, and contemporary Switzerland. His forces were the ones finally defeated in 955 at Lechfeld.[16] Bulcsú himself was captured there, and Emperor Otto I had him hanged as a criminal. By that time, however, Bulcsú's leadership in the easternmost segment of Magyar territory had been assumed by Zombor, who had also gone to Constantinople and accepted Eastern Christianity there (in 953). His policy also looked to Byzantium rather than Germany or the West.

In contrast, the descendants of Árpád turned toward the West. In 961, Árpád's grandson asked for Christian missionaries from Rome. However, Emperor Otto I intervened with the pope to prohibit this. Given the difficulties the Holy Roman Empire and the rest of Western Europe had endured for more than half a century from the Magyars, Otto did not look with favor on mission undertakings that might get in the way of his attacking and possibly subjugating the recently defeated Magyars. He did not trust them to abandon their former marauding practices.

Over the next twelve years, however, the Árpád rulers presented a different face toward Western Europe: they brought the rampages for which they had become well known and widely feared to an end. Moreover, the Árpád ruler, Géza (r. 972–97), made obvious efforts to cement good relationships with his German neighbors; not the least of these endeavors was the marriage of his son to a Bavarian princess in 966. Given the change of

---

16. See above.

style on the part of the Magyars, the German emperor endorsed the request for missionaries when Géza renewed it in 973. Shortly after the imperial approval, missionaries from Rome arrived among the Magyars. However, the missionaries' efforts did not initially bear much fruit; services and instruction conducted in Latin were no more successful among the Magyars than they had been among the Slavs in Moravia in the preceding century. Even so, the desire to turn the Magyar state toward Western Christianity served to bring Géza and his domain closer to the West.

Géza's son and successor, István I [Stephen] (r. 997–1038), became the founder of the united Magyar monarchy. István not only fought off a relative who wanted to usurp his throne; he was also able to defeat the Magyar chieftain to the east and bring that eastern segment of the Magyar territories under his own rule. Under István, the Magyar domain finally coalesced into a well-organized state; he organized his government and Magyar society along the lines of Western European states.

During his reign, István (and the Magyars with him) embraced Christianity. As was the case with other nations and their rulers we have considered, István's choice between Western/Latin and Eastern/Byzantine Christianity was a concern of state. Given the pro-western orientation that had already marked Árpád policy, it is not surprising that István chose for Western Christianity. Even so, a contributing factor in this decision may also have been that the Magyars ruled over numerous people of Slavic stock who had lived in the area before the Magyars had taken control there. Eastern Christian missionaries had already been working among the Slavic peoples in these territories, and their use of the Slavic language had allowed them to make significant headway among the people. However, if István had embraced the Eastern/Byzantine Christianity presented by these missionaries, the Magyars' Slavic subject peoples would have better understood the teaching offered by missionaries than the Magyars could have. Such a situation could hardly work in favor of continued Magyar political and cultural domination. In view of these and other considerations, István suppressed the work of the Eastern Christian missionaries, in favor of those from the West. In due course, István's embrace of and support for Western Christianity led to his being crowned King of Hungary in 1000 under papal auspices. His importance, both as a ruler and as the one who established Christianity among the Magyars, has led to his being honored by Hungary as her patron saint.

István's successors in the Árpád dynasty continued to be strong proponents of Western Christianity and vigorous opponents of both the Byzantine Empire and the Eastern Christianity that it embraced. Much of Hungary's foreign policy during the eleventh and twelfth centuries involved opposition to Byzantium; it led, in due course, to armed clashes over control of the western half of the Balkans. Hungary saw Croatia as her protectorate there, but Byzantium had the same attitude toward Serbia and Bosnia—and still claimed Croatia as rightly hers. Elsewhere, Hungary managed to incorporate Transylvania and lands in the Carpathian Mountains that had previously belonged to Kievan Rus'. In both of these, the Magyars favored Western Christianity over Eastern Christianity (which the peoples of these South Slavic and East Slavic regions had embraced). In addition, by an agreement of union with the Kingdom of Croatia[17] at the beginning of the twelfth century (in 1102), Hungary and Croatia became one state.

Near the end of the twelfth century, under Béla III (r. 1172–96), Hungary expanded considerably, at the expense of a weakened Byzantium. By the end of Béla's reign, Hungary had come to control a large portion of the middle of Eastern Europe, down to the Adriatic Sea. There she found herself in opposition to Venice, which had emerged as a significant maritime power in the Adriatic.

States among the South Slavs

The revival of the Byzantine Empire under the Macedonian dynasty (867–1058) played a major role in the history of the southern tier of Eastern Europe during the tenth through the twelfth centuries. The Macedonian period was one of the highest points in the whole history of Byzantine culture, and Byzantine control over the various South Slavic peoples attained its zenith under them. The most notable segment of the dynasty, and the one with the most impact on the South Slavs, was the extended reign of Basil II (r. 963–1025), "the Bulgar-Slayer."

We will treat the relevant Byzantine history under our consideration of Bulgaria, Byzantium's main nemesis for so long in the southern tier of Eastern Europe. After that, we turn to the related histories of the Croats and the Serbs. Our treatment of the states among the South Slavs will conclude by looking at an area that begins to assume importance by the end of this period, Bosnia (and Hum).

Bulgaria

As the tenth century opened, Symeon (r. 893–927) was on the Bulgarian throne. He had received an education in Byzantium, since his father (Khan

---

17. This is treated below.

Boris I) had originally intended him for the priesthood. However, Symeon's elder brother had led an unsuccessful pagan rebellion against Bulgaria's conversion to Christianity; he was defeated by Boris and mutilated (a common practice at the time, to assure that this person could never again hold public office). With that, Boris revised his plans for Symeon: he now had to become khan. Well-trained as Symeon had been in Byzantium itself, he understood Byzantine perspectives from the inside. He put that knowledge to good use, both in his military adventures against Byzantium and in his determination to secure independence for the church in Bulgaria—symbolized by attaining the title of "patriarch" for the leading clergyman in Bulgaria. In view of all his accomplishments, Symeon's reign has been looked on by Bulgarians as the golden age of their nation.

During Symeon's reign, the Bulgarian Empire swallowed up a good deal more of the western half of the Balkans, removing much of what had remained in Byzantine control in the region; thereafter, he marched on Constantinople itself. While the Byzantines were confident that Symeon could not successfully storm the walls of the capital, they did not want to endure a siege. He offered to lift the siege if the Byzantine church would grant his demand for a Bulgarian patriarch; Symeon hoped that having a patriarch for the church in his state would help secure the continued independence of his country. Whatever theological and ecclesiastical misgivings the Byzantine patriarch may have had about this request, the Byzantine leaders felt compelled to acquiesce to it, and the leading clergyman in Symeon's realm was duly consecrated as patriarch of the Bulgarian church in 925.

The lifting of the siege did not end the matter, however. Byzantium wanted to weaken the Bulgarian khanate. Through diplomatic intrigues, they incited the Serbs to rebel against Symeon.[18] The Serb rebellion forced him to turn to the western Balkans; to the great surprise of Symeon, the Bulgarians, and the Byzantines, the Serbs defeated the Bulgarian forces. With this victory, the Serbs proceeded to proclaim themselves independent from Bulgaria. Soon afterwards, Symeon died (927).

His successors were not as competent as he had been, and the Bulgarian state suffered a period of weakness for the next half-century. So greatly did Bulgarian fortunes decline that, by 963, the western segment of the Bulgarian Empire became independent. It appeared that Bulgaria might wither away to an insignificant state, until the khanate fell to a gifted leader who dramatically turned the situation around again.

---

18. See the treatment below.

THE DEVELOPMENT OF STATES (TENTH–TWELFTH CENTURIES) 115

Samuil [Samuel] (r. 976–1014) came to power in Bulgaria and, with the vigor of his leadership and the excellence of his generalship, restored the fortunes of the Bulgarian Empire.

View of Samuil's fortress in Ohrid (then, in the Bulgarian Empire, but now in North Macedonia).

Another view of Samuil's fortress (Ohrid, North Macedonia).

He reclaimed all the lands previously included in Symeon's empire, again bringing the western Balkans under Bulgarian domination and subjugating the Serbs.[19] In fact, he extended the borders somewhat beyond those of Symeon's time; this was happening at about the same time Basil II was expanding Byzantine imperial territory again.

Two such neighboring empires could not, obviously, continue to grow stronger and expand without coming to a clash. Byzantium and Bulgaria finally broke into open hostilities, and nearly two decades of fighting ensued, from 996 to 1014. At first, Bulgaria did well, especially when Basil II had to turn to Asia Minor to deal with a civil war there. The Bulgarians made the most of Basil's absence, but they began suffering repeated defeats once he returned in 1009. By 1014, Basil brought the war—and the first Bulgarian Empire—to an end.

At the same time, Basil finally obtained Byzantium's revenge for the humiliation suffered two centuries earlier. (In 811, Khan Krum [who had erected the Bulgarian Empire] defeated a Byzantine army and toasted his nobles [*boyars*] with a goblet made from the skull of the Byzantine emperor, Nicephorus I.) Through a blunder by one of Samuil's generals, the Byzantines were able to surround the main Bulgarian army. (Khan Samuil was not in the field with the army; he was at his capital at the time.) After intense fighting near the village of Vidocha, in which the Bulgarians suffered extensive casualties, the Bulgarian army of some 14,000 surrendered. Basil was ruthless: he had the captives divided up into groups of one hundred; of each group of a hundred, ninety-nine were blinded, and the last was left with one eye. Then Basil had them take hands and march back to Samuil's headquarters. When they arrived and Samuil saw what had been done to his army, the shock was so severe that he collapsed and died.

---

19. See the treatment below.

THE DEVELOPMENT OF STATES (TENTH–TWELFTH CENTURIES) 117

Church in the village of Vidocha ("Poked-eye").

Icon of the Forty Martyrs of Sebaste in the church in Vidocha, modified to point to the blinding of Samuil's army.

The Bulgarian Empire fell into disarray. The Byzantines quickly took advantage of the situation and absorbed Bulgarian territories into the Byzantine Empire again. In dealing with the recently conquered lands of Byzantium's long-time enemy, Basil was surprisingly gentle. Bulgars were allowed to continue to pay their taxes "in kind,"[20] as they had under their own khans, rather than in the coinage that Byzantine citizens were required to use. Further, while Byzantium stripped the Bulgarian church of its patriarchate and demoted the former patriarch to the status of archbishop, the church in Bulgaria was allowed to remain free from control by the Byzantine patriarch.

Bulgaria ceased to exist as a state, but it lingered in the memories of its people. In due course, after the Macedonian dynasty passed from the Byzantine scene, Bulgaria was revived: near the end of the twelfth century, the brothers Ivan and Peter Asen led a revolt against Byzantium (1185–86). Successful, they established the second Bulgarian Empire. Against the common foe of Byzantium, Bulgaria then allied itself with another South Slavic state that had come to prominence in the intervening period, the state of Serbia. However, before turning to Serbia and its rise to power during this period, it is appropriate to consider what had transpired among the Serbs' northern neighbors, the Croats, since the state of Croatia developed into a significant influence in the Balkans earlier than Serbia did.

Croatia

The Croats had desired, through the first half of the ninth century, to break free of German control, but they had been unable to establish any lasting independence. German missionaries had been at work among the Croats, who as a people were converted to Christianity under their influence. Since the Croats had not coalesced into an organized nation, there was no single ruler whose conversion marked that of his people, so there is no precise year assigned to their ninth-century conversion.

By the mid-ninth century, an able Croat ruler had arisen in the person of Trpimir (r. 845–64). He had become the leader of the Croats; his descendants, the Trpimirović dynasty, became the ruling house of Croatia. Trpimir had found it necessary to fight the Byzantine Empire over some territory in the western Balkans, and his able generalship had led to the defeat of the Byzantine forces. In most of the rest of his endeavors, he also found it necessary to oppose Byzantium. One significant evidence of this was that he faithfully stood with the pope, against the Byzantine emperor

---

20. Payment "in kind" is payment rendered by giving a portion of whatever one produces (grain, fruits, animals, etc.), rather than in money of some form.

and patriarch, in the controversy that had broken out between the two segments of Christianity in the ninth century. In doing so, Trpimir set a pattern that the ruling house of Croatia subsequently followed—taking the side of the pope and Western Christianity.

However, while Trpimir and the Croats had kept Byzantium at bay, they had not managed to escape the domination of the German state. Even after Charlemagne's death and the dismantling of his empire among his grandsons, Germany—the easternmost segment of the former Frankish Empire—had been able to keep the Croats under its influence.

That changed with Branimir (r. 870–902), who sought independence for Croatia. By his time, the German state had fallen into a short period of disarray and was unable to retain control over Croatia. Branimir took advantage of the situation: contacts with the Byzantine emperor and with the pope led them both to recognize Croatia as an independent country. Branimir was astute and knowledgeable enough to recognize that, on the one hand, the Byzantine emperor, although otherwise an opponent of Croatian independence, was even more deeply opposed to the upstart Western Christian empire; and, on the other, that the pope saw the emerging German power as a threat to the church's leadership in Western Christianity. Playing on these Byzantine and papal concerns, Branimir obtained recognition for an independent state of Croatia.

Subsequently, Tomislav (r. 910–28) more forcefully repudiated German power and rallied not only the Croats themselves but also some small groups of nearby people with them, and enlarged the Croatian state. The common danger that drove these peoples together was the Magyars to the near north; for the duration of Tomislav's reign, Croatian forces were able to defeat the Magyars and hold them at bay. In 925, Tomislav accepted coronation by a representative of the pope, and the Kingdom of Croatia came into being.

Equestrian statue of King (Kralj) Tomislav (Zagreb, Croatia).

In thus crowning a ruler of Croatia as king, the pope deliberately put an obstacle in the way of further German imperial expansion in the west Balkans.

Influences from both Western and Eastern Christianity had led to some ecclesiastical confusion in Croatia. During Branimir's reign, Methodius had passed through Croatia with his colleagues (in 882). Methodius's presence there had encouraged the Croatian clergy to utilize the Slavonic liturgy (which had recently been approved by the pope for labors among the Slavic peoples). Many of the Croatian clergy—including Bishop Grgur [Gregory], the major ecclesiastical figure in early Croatian history—turned to it in preference to the Latin liturgy received from the German missionaries.

Statue of Bishop Grgur (Split, Croatia).

Subsequently, tensions flared among the Croats over the language to be used in church services. In 925, the year of his coronation, Tomislav summoned a synod to regularize church practice: not surprisingly, the German clergy insisted on uniformity in practice and the exclusive use of Latin; many of the Croatian clergy preferred to continue using the Slavonic liturgy. To many Croatian nobles, the Eastern Christian approach on the question was preferable: not only did it promote better understanding of the liturgy, but it also would help to establish Croatian independence from outside control. However, King Tomislav, recently crowned under papal auspices, supported the Western clergy (as did most of the rest of the leaders of the royal court). In due course, the synod decided to ban the Slavonic liturgy, and Croatian clergy were required to learn Latin or face removal from the priesthood.

Even so, the problem persisted, despite the synodical decision: 150 years later, Western Christian clergy were still denouncing the prevalence of the Slavonic liturgy in the church in Croatia. Indeed, the Latin/Slavonic conflict became a major element in Croatia's internal struggles. The Trpimirović dynasty regularly sided with the Western Christian clergy, always seeking to maintain good relationships with the pope and to keep Eastern Christianity at bay—not least because Byzantium was a continuing threat to Croatia's independence. Many nobles continued to support the use of the Slavonic liturgy, however; the result of this conflict between the nobles and the royal court was internal instability for Croatia.

Glagolitic inscription on the back wall of St. Stephen's Cathedral in Zagreb, Croatia, pointing to the language tensions within the church in Croatia.

The power of Croatia waxed and waned over the rest of the tenth and throughout the eleventh centuries, as influenced by the relative power of Byzantium and of Venice (which had become a maritime power and coveted the Adriatic seacoast of Croatia). By the end of the eleventh century, the Kingdom of Croatia faced significant enough danger from both Byzantium and Venice that it turned to the Magyar state for protection. Already by then, Hungary had involved itself in Croatia's internal affairs: both as a fervent champion of things western and as allied to the Trpimirović dynasty through marriage, Hungary supported the Trpimirović dynasty in the Latin/Slavonic conflict.

The last ruler from the Trpimirović dynasty died in 1089, leaving no heir. Rather than have the rule fall into the hands of those nobles who would prefer a pro-Eastern Christian stance, a court faction offered the crown of Croatia to the queen's brother, László [Ladislas] (r. 1077–95), the King of Hungary.[21] He accepted, but he was unable to establish his rule over Croatia, due to ongoing opposition from some of the nobility. Eventually, a solemn request from the Croatian court was accepted by Kálmán I [Koloman] (r. 1095–1114), King of Hungary—who thereby became King of Croatia in 1102.

Croatia thus joined Hungary by inviting its king to assume the kingship of Croatia, as well. In subsequent centuries, this arrangement was not understood by the two peoples in the same way. The Croats thought that, since they had voluntarily joined Hungary, they should remain equal partners in the resultant state (and be able to opt out of it at any point they so chose). The Hungarians had quite a different view: they believed that the Croats had freely chosen to become part of Hungary, and that this choice entailed neither special privileges nor any subsequent right of secession. Problems later arose from this difference in understanding.

Serbia

Ever since entering the western Balkans, the Serbs had usually been under the control of either the Byzantines or the Bulgarians; however, that control was often little more than nominal. Prior to their coalescing into a distinct state, the Serbs were evangelized by Eastern Christian missionaries—sometimes under Byzantine auspices, but at other times as sponsored by Bulgarian khans. Both empires professed Eastern Christianity, and the Serbs' conversion to Christianity was, thus, an embrace of Eastern Christianity, as well. Since that conversion took place prior to their becoming a coordinated state, and not under the leadership of one of their own rulers, the Serbs' conversion (like that of their neighbors, the Croats) cannot be dated with any certainty. However, it was accomplished by the end of the ninth century, at the latest.

A small Serbian state had arisen in the mid-ninth century; after a brief period of flourishing, it had soon fallen under Bulgarian control. About half a century later, in 926, the Serbs were instigated by the Byzantines to rebel against their Bulgarian lords; this led to Symeon lifting the Bulgarian siege against Constantinople and facing the Serbs in the western Balkans. The Serbs defeated the Bulgarians and managed to establish another short-lived

21. This is the first instance of a pattern that would become common throughout Eastern Europe when a nation's ruling dynasty died out: rather than another noble family of that nation assuming or being granted the privilege of monarchy, the throne would be offered to someone of "blue blood" from one of the royal families of Europe.

Serbian state; by the late tenth century, however, they were again subjugated by the Bulgarians, under Khan Samuil.[22] When Samuil's empire was brought to an end by the Byzantine Emperor Basil II, Serbia fell under Byzantine control. With the end of the Macedonian dynasty in 1058, Byzantium began to lose effective control of the outer reaches of its empire; one of the territories in which that control began to slip was Serbia. Even so, the Serbs did not then break free and establish an independent Serbian state.

About a century later, in the last third of the twelfth century, a significant state arose in Serbia under the leadership of Stjepan [Stephen] Nemanja (r. 1168–96). Serbia became a Balkan power; ruled by the Nemanjić dynasty, it lasted for two centuries, until the invasions of the Ottoman Turks brought the Serbian state to an end.

A local Serbian leader, Stjepan was able to capitalize on the weakness of the Byzantine Empire at the time (a weakness also exploited by the Asen brothers in Bulgaria).[23] Stjepan considerably expanded the area that he governed. He made alliances with the resurgent (second) Bulgarian Empire, with the German emperor (Frederick Barbarossa), and with the Byzantine emperor—the last by the marriage of Stjepan's son to the emperor's daughter. Furthermore, through his generous support for Christian building and restoration projects, both near and far, Stjepan kept good relationships with both the Byzantine patriarch and the Roman pope—no small feat, given the considerable tensions by that time between the rival ecclesiastical camps.

Nevertheless, Stjepan—and Serbia with him—did not waver in their commitment to Eastern Christianity. So fervent was Stjepan's devotion to Christianity that he abdicated the throne in 1196, in order to follow his youngest son, Sava, into monastic life. During the fifty years after his abdication, Stjepan's successors managed to add to the size of the Serbian state significantly.

Upon Stjepan's 1196 abdication, he was succeeded by another of his sons. This son has come to be known as "Stjepan 'the First-Crowned,'" (r. 1196–1228), since he was the first ruler to be crowned King of Serbia. Due to extraordinary circumstances, Stjepan was crowned by a papal representative.[24] In the early thirteenth century, this Serbian king appointed his younger brother, the monk Sava, as the first archbishop of the Serbian church—thus claiming independence for the Orthodox church in Serbia.

22. See the treatment of these conflicts between the Serbs and Bulgars above.

23. See above.

24. By the time this could transpire, the Fourth Crusade had taken place, forcing Stjepan to seek the crown from the papacy. Soon thereafter, he managed to obtain royal consecration from an Orthodox churchman—his brother!

While the appointment was thus kept within the Nemanjić family, no one thought of this as nepotism: Sava was so noted for his sanctity that no objections were raised to this appointment. He is recognized as the patron saint of Serbia.

Bosnia (and Hum)

Neither Bosnia nor Hum[25] had become significant factors in Eastern European history until just before the end of the period we are now considering. But by the end of the twelfth century, Bosnia had developed into a state of its own, and Hum was beginning to do so. While Bosnia and Hum were (and remained) distinct from each other, their respective histories were so similar that, for this period, we can treat them together.

The areas of Bosnia and Hum had been populated by Slavs during the migrations of the sixth through eighth centuries. The territories that came to be known as "Bosnia" and "Hum" lay between the two areas settled and dominated by the Croats, on the one hand, and the Serbs, on the other. Bosnia and Hum are extremely mountainous regions; this was a major obstacle, both to control of and to communication within them. Many Croats and Serbs had moved into them, but neither the Croats nor the Serbs were able to establish dominance in either area. There were earlier Slavic groups who had already settled in these areas, as well; through intermarriage, these earlier Slavic inhabitants were assimilated, over the centuries, to either Croat or Serb stock, and the language that came to be used throughout the area was Serbo-Croatian. Bosnia and Hum were, thus, from their earliest history, neither Serb nor Croat, but an area where the Serbs, Croats, and earlier Slavic inhabitants were intermingled.

Owing to the mountainous terrain, localism had marked Bosnia's and Hum's histories for virtually the whole period after the Slavic invasions. Numerous attempts by Frankish (later, German), Byzantine, and Bulgarian leaders to control Bosnia and Hum had always ended in frustration. In the tenth century, this pattern was finally broken: the Croats managed to establish, briefly, a modicum of control over Bosnia when King Tomislav took a large portion of Bosnia into his realm. With his death in 928, however, Croatia lost that control. The vigorous young Serbian state that defeated Khan Symeon's forces in the late 920s went on to incorporate most of Bosnia; Serbian rule came to an end in the 960s, though, with the collapse of

---

25. "Hum" is known today as "Herzegovina" (Serbo-Croatian for "dukedom").

that Serbian state.[26] Shortly thereafter, the Croatian state reclaimed power over Bosnia and retained it until the end of the tenth century.

During the eleventh century, rule over Bosnia shifted back and forth regularly between Croatia and nearby Serbian rulers. (Serbia was not then a state in its own right; these rulers were leaders of their respective segments of what had been the earlier Serbian state.) As for the history of Hum during these centuries, its proximity to Serbian territories assured that it was dominated—to the degree that such a mountainous region could be dominated—by Serbian rulers.

The effectiveness of Croatian and Serbian control over Bosnia and Hum must not be exaggerated, however. In both Bosnia and Hum, the local rulers almost always managed to resist anything resembling domination by any centralized government, whether from Croatia or Serbia or from gifted rulers in their own territories. While various nations regularly laid claim to Bosnia or Hum, those powers rarely had anything resembling good control of either area.

By the late twelfth century, this pattern began to be overcome by able rulers from within Bosnia and Hum. By 1180, Bosnia had broken free of external control and coalesced into a distinct state under the rule of Ban[27] Kulin (r. 1180–1204). He is remembered by Bosnians with special fondness, as the first Bosnian ruler over a Bosnian state, and as the one who was able to bring peace to it for the whole period of his rule. He achieved significant economic improvement for Bosnia; his diplomatic accomplishments included effecting good relations with the ruler of Hum (who married Kulin's sister) and with Stjepan Nemanja, the powerful ruler of Serbia.

Kulin was less successful with his neighbor to the north. By his time, Croatia had long been joined to Hungary (since 1102), and the Kingdom of Hungary laid claim to Croatian interests over Bosnia. Champion for things western as Hungary was, her monarch challenged Kulin over the orientation of the Bosnian church. What resulted from this challenge led to further developments within the Bosnian church, indeed. These belong to the next period of Eastern European history, however.

At this point, though, we should indicate the background and stimuli for the religious distinctiveness that the Hungarian king challenged. The localism noted above in regard to government in both Bosnia and Hum was reflected, as well, in the religious commitments found in them: over the centuries, the various local rulers had responded to either Western or Eastern

---

26. From about this time comes the first written reference to Bosnia: it appears in a politico-geographical handbook produced in 958 by the Byzantine emperor, Constantine VII Porphyrogenitus.

27. "Ban" is the title that had become common for a ruler in Bosnia.

Christianity, depending on whether their particular area was closer to the Croats (in which case they had adopted Western Christianity) or to the Serbs (and, so, for Eastern Christianity). Thus, Bosnia was predominantly in the Western Christian camp, but Hum was in the Eastern Christian one. However, these commitments could be and regularly were swayed, depending on the influence being wielded at different times by either the Germans or the Croats (for Western Christianity) or the Byzantines, the Bulgarians, or the Serbs (for Eastern Christianity). The result of all this was that neither Bosnia nor Hum were fully unified in Christian commitment. In the thirteenth through the fifteenth centuries, this would lead to significant developments within Bosnia. With regard to Hum, both Western and Eastern churches were present by the end of the twelfth century. When a Serbian ruler (from the Nemanjić family) came to a vigorous disagreement with the Western Christian bishop of the major city in Hum, the Serbian ruler expelled that bishop from the country. The pope reacted by excommunicating the Serbian ruler—who responded by handing over control of the churches formerly under Western Christians to the priests of Eastern Christianity who were already in the vicinity. Affairs of state from outside rulers were dictating religious policies in both Bosnia and Hum.

Given that situation, were either of them (or the two of them together) to become a centralized state, that state would face serious tension with regard to religion. If she decided for either Western Christianity or Eastern Christianity, no matter which she favored, that choice would entail her being thought of by one of her neighbors (the Kingdom of Serbia or the Kingdom of Hungary/Croatia) as committed to the wrong side and as a region that should be conquered and brought into the correct religious line. Bosnia found another option: in the early thirteenth century, Bosnia's leaders declared their own national church, affiliated with neither Western Christianity nor Eastern Orthodoxy, as a way to escape the claims of both; however, rather than avoiding the antagonism of one or the other of her neighbors by doing so, as she hoped, she gained that of both.

Concluding Observations

The period of the tenth through the twelfth centuries was significant in several ways for the development of Eastern Europe. In addition to what has already been presented, the following should be noted:

Kievan Rus'/Eastern Christianity: As seen in the preceding chapter, Kievan Rus' embraced Eastern Christianity and developed a significant Christian culture. Mongol invasions in the mid-thirteenth century destroyed this East Slav state; Mongol dominance ensued and lasted for the next two hundred years. By the end of that period, the northernmost segments of the former Kievan Rus' were able to throw off the Mongol yoke and coalesced into a distinct state, centered no longer in Kiev, but in Moscow. That state (Muscovy) was also unabashedly Christian, and distinctively committed to Eastern Christianity.

When Byzantium subsequently fell in 1453, Muscovy was the only Eastern Orthodox state left in freedom; it saw itself, not only as the protector of Eastern Christianity, but also as the protector of all Slavs—East, West, and South alike. From the Muscovite (later, Russian) perspective, all Slavs ought to be Eastern Orthodox. Much of subsequent Eastern European history has been shaped by Russian attempts to live up to these twin responsibilities.

Western Slavs/Western Christianity: With the conversion of Mieszko I of Poland, the last of the West Slavic peoples was brought into Christianity. Significantly, although the work of the Byzantine missionaries Cyril and Methodius had begun among the West Slavs of Moravia, the West Slavs were all drawn into the orbit of Western Christianity. With the embrace of Western Christianity by the Magyars, whose location separated the West Slavs from the South Slavs, there was little opportunity for interaction on the part of West Slavic peoples with South Slavic peoples who had embraced Eastern Christianity.

Since the East Slavs, led by Kievan Rus', all embraced Eastern Christianity—as did most of the South Slavs—this meant that there was a significant religious distinction between the West Slavs (together with the Slovenes and the Croats), who were Western Christians, and the South and East Slavs, who were Eastern Orthodox. In subsequent centuries, this divergence led to—or, at least, was the excuse for—profound tensions among the various Slavic peoples.

Hungary/Croatia: When the Kingdom of Croatia joined the Kingdom of Hungary, the Croatian leaders firmly and irrevocably set Croatia within the orbit of Western Christianity. Croatia had periodically known influence from Byzantium and Eastern Christianity, and many of her churches had used the Slavonic liturgy, but the Trpimirović dynasty had faithfully favored Western Christianity. Even so, the Latin/Slavonic liturgy question had shown that Croatia had not yet been definitively drawn within the Western orbit. In joining with Hungary—a vigorous champion of Western Christianity, as over against its Eastern counterpart—Croatia became, decisively, part of Western Christianity.

This would come to bear considerable historical import in subsequent centuries: it assured that the Christian West would look after Croatia as "one of its own." While a substantial portion of Croatia was swallowed up by the Ottoman Turks in the sixteenth century, when they came to control much of the state of Hungary, in due course the Habsburg Empire reasserted itself against the Turks and drove them south in the late eighteenth century. As they did so, the Western Christian Habsburg forces made sure that Croatia was delivered from Turkish rule. The same concern was not extended to Serbia, Bosnia, or Hum, which were all left under the control of the Ottoman Turkish Empire.

CHAPTER 9

The Fourth Crusade (1204)

"The Crusaders' sack of Constantinople is one of the most ghastly and tragic incidents in history.... The price was the lasting enmity of Greek Christendom. The Fourth Crusade could never be forgiven nor forgotten by the Christians of the East."[1]

ON MAY 4, 2001, at a meeting with the Greek Orthodox archbishop of Athens, Pope John Paul II startled his host by asking forgiveness for the Fourth Crusade, which sacked, pillaged, and looted Constantinople, the chief city of Eastern Christianity. Few people in the West even know what happened in the Fourth Crusade: they may know a little about the crusades, but most are unaware of what happened during the fourth one.

In contrast, virtually all Eastern Europeans know about that crusade all too well. As a Pole, John Paul II was acquainted with it in a way no other pope had been since the event. As head of the church whose crusaders so long ago perpetrated its horrors, this Polish pope knew just how painful a memory the Fourth Crusade has been for centuries to many Eastern Europeans.

It is striking that the head of the Roman Catholic church asked forgiveness for what the crusaders had done so long ago. After the Fourth Crusade, 760 years elapsed before a pope and an ecumenical patriarch (from Constantinople, the leading hierarch of the Orthodox world) even met face to face, when Pope Paul VI and the Ecumenical Patriarch Athenagoras I did so in 1964. That gives some sense of the deep rift opened up by the Fourth Crusade. But the 1964 event went no further than an embrace and a polite kiss on the cheek; in 2001, the pope asked forgiveness for what had happened in 1204. For multiplied centuries, the Eastern Orthodox have lived with the pain, remembering the horror of what took place in 1204. Now,

---

1. Runciman, *The Eastern Schism*, 149–51.

though, with John Paul II's plea, the onus is on the Orthodox. The pope has asked for forgiveness. Will the Orthodox grant it?

This chapter considers the backdrop of the awful event long ago that brought on the need for this confession. Originally, the crusades were called to send Christian knights from Western Europe to the Holy Land (Palestine), to try to win it back from the followers of Islam. The Muslims had taken control of it and of all the holy places of the Christian religion there, and the fear was that Muhammad's followers might desecrate these places of Christian devotion and spiritual pilgrimage. The goal was to liberate Palestine, waging holy war on people who were called infidels because they did not look on Christ as Savior or embrace the doctrine of the Trinity—and to return those holy places to Christian control. But the fourth of the crusades did not attack the infidels; the crusaders attacked the faithful. They did not liberate holy places from Muslim control; they desecrated holy places of the Christian faith, destroyed a Christian capital, and took over its empire.

Rivalries, West/East

To understand the Fourth Crusade, it is necessary to recall the tensions that had developed over the course of centuries between the western and eastern halves of the Roman Empire, and between the western and eastern branches of Christianity.[2] The Fourth Crusade in 1204 did not happen "out of the blue": the tragedy had deep roots. Discord had sprung up long before 1204, manifesting itself in multiple ways; however, nothing had provoked a lasting schism between Eastern and Western Christianity. Those roots produced their bitterest fruit in the Fourth Crusade—which led to a definitive breach within Christendom.

Before Constantine

The West and the East had known long-standing rivalry, going back all the way into the period of the ancient Roman Empire, long before Christianity became a significant factor there. Rome, the city from which the empire had grown, was located in the western half of the empire—an empire that included not only much of Western Europe but a good portion of Eastern Europe as well and stretched past the eastern coastline of the Mediterranean Sea. By the beginning of the second century AD, the emperors of Rome recognized that the western and eastern halves of their empire were

---

2. See chapter 6 above.

significantly different; finally, one of the emperors established a line dividing the empire in two. Subsequently, this line delimited the borders of imperial provinces and in other ways influenced Roman legal decisions and governmental administration. During the fourth and fifth centuries, the empire sometimes had two rulers, one for each half. Their cooperation assured the continued unity of the empire; the size, complexity, and problems of the empire—plus the significantly different situation of its two halves—made that seem the best way to govern it.

It takes little sympathetic imagination to appreciate that the West, and especially Rome, did not care for this. That feeling was only complicated by the widely recognized fact that the eastern half of the empire was far more populous and prosperous than the western half, even including the capital city of Rome. The eastern half profited from trade to the east with the Persians, to the south with Egypt and Africa, and to the north, with various Germanic peoples; the opportunities for trade were not nearly as plentiful or as promising in the West. So, in many ways the West, although the seat of the empire, was outshone by the East; that already assured a certain rivalry. The residents of Rome were aware of all this; it bothered them that the upstart East was outshining the capital city.

Because of Constantine

This intensified because of Constantine. When he became sole emperor, he decided for a variety of reasons to move the capital from Rome to Byzantium. This finally eventuated in 330 AD. With this, the rivalry heated up even more. Now, of all things, not only was the East more populous and more prosperous; it had also usurped the capital! The Roman Empire was no longer headquartered in Rome!

Resentment, West toward East

Full-scale resentment on the part of the West towards the East developed out of all this. With the shift of the capital, the emperors and the seat of government were in the East. The emperors' primary emphasis and concern were necessarily with their near environment, and the West ended up being neglected—at least, that was the way the West saw it. The western segment felt that it was left to its own devices, bereft of the care and protection it deserved from the emperors. In the fourth century this attitude arose; in the fifth century, with the Germanic peoples invading the western half of the empire and the emperors doing little about it, the attitude seemed confirmed. In subsequent centuries, after the collapse of the empire in the West, appeals to Byzantium for protection and deliverance went largely unanswered.[3] Consequently, the West, the original seat of the Roman Empire, harbored ill will toward Constantinople and its empire—the empire originally erected by Rome and her armies!

Sometimes, Byzantine emperors were indifferent toward the West; at other times, though, they were simply stretched too far to offer it much aid. Even so, all this contributed to a western animus again the East, which mushroomed during the fifth through the eighth centuries. In fact, the western frustration became so intense that in 754, the pope sought protection elsewhere. Rome was endangered by the Lombards, a pagan Germanic tribe that had invaded northern Italy.[4] The pope asked for help from Constantinople, but received none. Desperate, he sought protection from Pepin, the leader of the Franks, a Germanic people who had become Christian. Pepin acceded to the request and managed to defeat the Lombards and protect the city of Rome. In 800, the same scenario took place: the Lombards again threatened Rome, appeals to Byzantium fell on deaf ears, and the pope looked to the Franks once more—this time to Charlemagne, Pepin's grandson. Charlemagne fought through northern Italy, defeated the Lombards, and ended up protecting the papacy and Rome.

For this, Charlemagne was unusually rewarded: on December 25, 800, the pope crowned him "Emperor of the Romans." Doing so gave eloquent testimony to the West's bitterness, given what the act implied about the Byzantine ruler. For hundreds of years, Christian teaching had asserted that there could be only one empire, just as there is only one God who rules over heaven and earth. This one God had set up a single great empire on earth—the old Roman Empire—and had appointed a Christian emperor to rule the entire world as God's representative and vice-regent on earth.

For nearly five centuries, that had been the common political understanding throughout Christianity. Consequently, the papal coronation of Charlemagne as Roman emperor entailed a stinging repudiation and rejection of the Byzantine emperor. It was a particularly striking manifestation of the West's anger towards the East.

---

3. The only significant exception had been Justinian the Great (r. 527–65), whose ongoing endeavors to recapture the West had temporarily succeeded in regaining some of that territory, but had nearly bankrupted the empire. Not long after his death, though, virtually all the regained lands were lost again.

4. The Lombards settled in this area; to this day, northern Italy is known as Lombardy.

Differences between West and East

Rivalry and resentment were compounded by actual differences which had developed between the West and the East. In the ancient church, there had been five great centers of the church, beginning in Jerusalem; then in Antioch, where the followers of Christ were first called Christians; then in Alexandria, the great intellectual hub of the world; then in Rome, as Christianity went to the West; and subsequently in Byzantium, the capital of the empire. By the 650s, Jerusalem, Antioch, and Alexandria had all fallen to the followers of Mohammed. This left only Byzantium in the East and Rome in the West. These became the two great centers of the Christian church during the Middle Ages; each erected Christian civilizations, but they did so in different ways.

Experience

What the two halves of the old Roman Empire experienced in the early medieval period led them in dramatically different directions. Chaos ensued with the destruction of the western half of the empire under the Germanic peoples: in contrast to former imperial practice, roads went unmaintained, no universal system of law was recognized, and a common language no longer prevailed in the West. The Germanic peoples dominating the West had embraced Arianism and so did not acknowledge Jesus Christ as Son of God; thus, the former religious unity between people and rulers was severed. Governance by local Germanic lords could be whimsical; borders of influence shifted with further migrations, invasions, or warfare. The structures of society collapsed; schooling outside home or monastery became an impossibility; everything in civilization was in shambles.

From the fifth century onwards for more than five hundred years, the papacy sought to find the way out of the chaos and re-establish civilization, on Christian bases, in the West. Sending missionaries, establishing schools, coordinating contacts with her own representatives and with the emerging civil authorities alike, directing the development of appropriate law and government for the emerging Christian nations, overseeing the spiritual welfare of Western Europe—all this fell to the popes, in addition to their regular pastoral duties. With this, the papacy developed a certain sense of ownership and overall responsibility for all of Christian civilization in the West.

In sharp contrast, Byzantium knew no such chaos: she had never been conquered by Germanic tribes or any other invaders. From 330 onwards, the continuing Roman Empire in the East sought to become ever more fully a Christian civilization, building on the rich resources of the ancient Greco-Roman heritage, as purified by careful Christian evaluation. Byzantine society and government developed, without collapse or chaos. Constantinople maintained its schooling system, advancing it further with the establishment of universities; Byzantium continued to produce and support scholars; the ancient Roman legal system was enhanced by careful codification under several emperors; roads, bridges, and aqueducts were maintained; and Byzantium sought to develop a distinctively Christian outlook on how things ought to be done to the glory of God in this world. The result of all this was two very different kinds of experiences in Western Europe and in Eastern Europe.

Cultural Divergence

This also led to cultural divergence. As Rome and Byzantium developed their respective Christian civilizations, the two cultures, although both Christian, developed in different fashions. These cultural divergences contributed to what happened in 1204 in the Fourth Crusade.

One obvious divergence was in the relationship between church leaders and civil rulers in the respective Christian civilizations. The church was the only significant institution to survive the collapse of the empire in the West. Mission endeavors led to national conversions, which needed to be strengthened by establishing appropriate structures for society and government. In this, the papacy served as guide for Western Europe. There was thus one church in the West, but a number of states; no empire united civil government throughout the West. The one church was led by the bishop of Rome. So, Western European civilization knew only one overarching loyalty—to the church. Her head, the pope, exercised authority over all of Western Christendom; no civil ruler had anything remotely resembling that sweep of influence. Thus, in Western Christian civilization, the leader of the church was the *only* universal leader; his relationships with the respective princes of Western Europe were usually respectful, but never with equals. Thus, the papacy played an unrivalled role in directing the development of Western European civilization. This was simply accepted as the way things were—and the way they ought to be.

In Byzantium, church and state related in a different fashion. The Byzantine Empire had an ultimate civil ruler (the emperor) and an ultimate ecclesiastical leader (the patriarch of Constantinople). Neither was superior to the other; their roles of responsibility differed. The emperor was understood to be God's representative on earth for government; the patriarch was understood to be God's representative on earth for the church. The goal was a thoroughly articulated Christian civilization, with both components (church and state) playing their respective roles in harmony with each other.[5]

This West/East divergence in the relationships and roles of civil and church leaders may not strike people in the early twenty-first century as worthy of much consideration, since it is not a significant question in the contemporary world. However, in the Middle Ages, the two kinds of leaders were looked to as the powers of civilization; indeed, it is not too much to say that the relationship of church and state was *the* fundamental question of the medieval structure of society. Consequently, while the divergence between the western and the eastern patterns may not seem particularly significant, to medieval attitudes that divergence was striking. Of course, each side viewed its own as the only appropriate pattern; that of the other side was simply defective.

A second element in the cultural divergence was language. In the reconstituted West, the language of the old Roman Empire and of Western Christianity reasserted itself: Latin became the *lingua franca*. In the East, even during the heights of the old Roman Empire, Latin had never displaced Greek. People there had spoken both languages—Greek because that was what they had grown up with (as the common language prior to Rome's invasions), and Latin because it was the language of government and the courts. But after the capital was transferred to the East and the West was overrun by Germanic tribes, there was less and less reason for people in the East to keep learning Latin. This led to the eventual decision under Emperor Heraclius in the early 600s to adopt Greek as the official language of the empire instead of Latin. The imperial court saw scant value in continuing to use a language that no longer had any relevance to the territory it actually ruled and was not spoken by any of its subjects. With that, most people in the East, including the learned and the members of government, saw little benefit in learning Latin; most of what they might want to know from the Latin heritage had already been translated into Greek.

Similarly, in the West, with the breakdown of civilization and the consequent collapse of schooling, it was a difficult enough task just to learn Latin; Greek was largely forgotten. With these linguistic changes, communication between what had been the two segments of the old Roman Empire became

---

5. In his legislation, Emperor Justinian the Great had directed in *Novella* 6 that church and state work together in *simfonia*—a harmony that respected the role of each. It is historically and politically inaccurate to state, as has often been done by scholarship in the West, that the Byzantine empire practiced "caesaropapism" (rule of the church by the civil leader).

increasingly difficult. A few intrepid scholars in the West tried to master Greek, but it was not a common or always a successful endeavor.

In the first centuries of the Middle Ages, consequently, the two Christian civilizations lost the ability to communicate readily with each other. This led almost ineluctably to misunderstandings. A particularly striking example of the problems in this regard underlines the significance of this linguistic divergence.

A series of ecumenical councils had been held in the church. (They were called "ecumenical" because they included representatives of the church from throughout the entire known world.) These councils dealt with issues, especially doctrinal ones, that affected the whole church. The first ecumenical council was held in Nicea in 325, the second in Constantinople in 381, the third in Ephesus in 431, the fourth in Chalcedon in 451, the fifth in Constantinople in 553, the sixth in Constantinople in 680–81, and the seventh met in Nicea in 787. At the last of these, the doctrinal issue was whether icons—two-dimensional religious representations—were acceptable. The controversy had gone on for several decades, and the resultant arguments were sophisticated in several regards—much more so than the arguments on religious imagery known in the West (even down to the present day).[6] The result of the council's deliberations was the decision that, with certain qualifications, it was legitimate for Christians to have two-dimensional pictures of Christ or the Virgin Mary or other saints as aids to worship.

The minutes of the council were taken, of course, in Greek. A copy was sent to the papacy, as the leader of Christianity in the West. The pope deposited them in his archives, but a papal secretary later decided to translate them into Latin, so that the insights of the council could become known in the West. He doubtlessly put his best effort into the endeavor. However, his knowledge of Greek was limited; two significant flaws marred his translation—and produced considerable misunderstanding.

In the first place, he did not recognize two small Greek words that appeared with considerable frequency in the minutes; so, he simply omitted them as probably inconsequential. However, these two words were οὐ and μή—both of which meant "not"! Obviously, leaving those words out dramatically changed what was stated in the minutes! Secondly, beyond that egregious gaffe, he could not discern the distinctions among the three Greek words used carefully in the minutes to distinguish the *worship* that must only be offered to God, the *veneration* that can be given to icons of Christ or Mary

---

6. For a concise presentation of the arguments, see Payton, *Light from the Christian East*, 181–92.

or the saints, and the *respect* that can be accorded to kings and priests. So, the translator rendered them all with the Latin term for *worship*—thus presenting the council as teaching exactly what the council fathers had so carefully and assiduously repudiated![7] With this kind of well-meant fumbling, misunderstandings were bound to happen—and they did, frequently.

Perspectives on Faith and Practice

This all only compounded the concerns that developed between the divergent Christianities about the teaching and practice of the other. To err elsewhere might be overlooked; however, to do so in basic matters of faith and practice was a failure to be faithful to Christianity itself. The capstone of the differences considered so far came with differences in this regard between West and East.

The Role of the Papacy

The first was the role of the papacy. In its long process of digging out from under the rubble of the collapse in the West and developing a Christian civilization, the papacy played a central role (as noted above). Western Christianity acknowledged the supremacy of the pope. In the Western Christian perspective, though, this supremacy included not only the West, but the *universal* church, for the pope was the successor of Peter, the chief of the apostles. Thus, from the Western Christian perspective, the pope had the right to oversee the church *everywhere*—including the church in the Byzantine Empire. This view had long been held, but Pope Nicholas I began to act on it in the mid-ninth century, telling the church in Byzantium how to resolve its problems.[8]

However, the Byzantines were resolutely unwilling to accept what they saw as non-traditional and high-handed interference from the pope. The Byzantines knew that in the ancient church there had been five main leaders of Christianity—the bishops of Jerusalem, Antioch, Alexandria, Rome, and

---

7. In the following century, Theophylact of Ohrid, a significant Byzantine scholar, urged his fellow Greeks not to be harsh in their dealings with the Latins, since they had to work with so impoverished a language, citing the fact that the Greek language had seven different words to describe various kinds of love, whereas the Latins had only one to use for them all.

8. Specifically, he intervened to adjudicate a controverted election to the office of patriarch; however, he did not just offer his opinion and advice, but he claimed to settle the issue for the Byzantines.

Byzantium. There was only one in the West, Rome; there had been four in the East. All five, though, were equal; none of them had the right to dictate to any of the others. By the mid-ninth century, the first three were gone: Jerusalem, Antioch, and Alexandria were in the hands of Muslims. That left Rome and Byzantium; from the Eastern Christian understanding, they were *equals*. Photios, the patriarch of Constantinople, lost no time in advising Pope Nicholas to mind his own business and cease the presumption.

It is important to appreciate how each side ended up viewing the other in this regard. To the pope and the Christian West, the Byzantine response was rebellion against the legitimate authority of the chief pastor of the church. To the patriarch and the Christian East, the papal position was arrogant, attempting to dictate to others rather than dialogue with them. None of this would lead to better understanding, trust, or respect.

The Doctrine of the Trinity

More important than the issue of church government was the dissonance over the treatment of the doctrine of the Trinity. That doctrine was universally recognized as a basic, fundamental affirmation of the early Christian church. The first ecumenical council had collectively confessed that Jesus Christ is fully the Son of God. That affirmation was further elaborated at the second council with explicit reference to the divinity of the Holy Spirit. The resultant Niceno-Constantinopolitan Creed (commonly referred to as "the Nicene Creed") affirms that Father, Son, and Holy Spirit are all God, and that God is one. The Nicene Creed reads as follows:

> We believe in one God, the Father Almighty, Maker of heaven and all earth, and of all things visible and invisible.
>
> And in one Lord Jesus Christ, the only-begotten Son of God, begotten of the Father before all worlds; God of God, Light of Light, true God of true God; begotten, not made, being of one substance with the Father; by whom all things were made; who, for us and for our salvation, came down from heaven, and was incarnate by the Holy Spirit of the Virgin Mary, and was made human; he was crucified also for us under Pontius Pilate, and suffered, and was buried; and the third day he rose again, according to the Scriptures, and ascended into heaven, and is seated at the right hand of the Father; from there he shall come again, with glory, to judge the living and the dead; whose kingdom shall have no end.
>
> And in the Holy Spirit, the Lord and Giver of life; who proceeds from the Father *(and from the Son [filioque])*; who with

the Father and the Son together is worshipped and glorified; who spoke by the prophets.

And in one holy catholic and apostolic church; we acknowledge one baptism for the remission of sins; and we look for the resurrection of the dead, and the life of the world to come.

This creed offered a statement of Christian faith collectively embraced by the entire church, West and East alike. It has stood as one of the emblems and evidences of the unity of the church, from antiquity: all Christians embrace the doctrine of the Trinity. For the purposes of this chapter, two points about this creed should be stressed.

In the first place, the early church recognized, and the early church fathers always emphasized, that there is no way mere human beings can comprehend the doctrine of the Trinity. That doctrine speaks of God *as God*, and human minds are not up to the task of understanding who and what God is as God. How can one God be three persons, all three of them fully God, and yet not have three Gods? "Trinity" was a term coined to hold together the oneness and the three-ness of God at the same time, a term that embraces what is taught in the Christian scriptures, but not a term that invites or enables human comprehension. The church fathers all urged people not to try to comprehend it. The Nicene Creed was affirmed not as an *explanation* but as a *confession* of who and what God is: it was not meant as a road map for the divine interior but as a "No Trespassing" sign warning against error. This approach to the creed and to the doctrine was universally embraced throughout the ancient church, West and East alike.

Even so, the doctrine had to be catechized and preached: i.e., it had to be *taught* so as to assure faithful confession and avoid error. How was that to be done? Significantly, as patterns for doing so developed, two contrasting ways of dealing with the doctrine of the Trinity became common—one in the West, the other typical of the East. The one in the West followed Augustine; the other, which became the pattern in the East, followed the Cappadocian fathers—Gregory Nazianzen, Basil the Great, and Gregory of Nyssa. (The first two, Gregory Nazianzen and Basil the Great, were friends; Basil the Great and Gregory of Nyssa were brothers.)

Augustine of Hippo was a brilliant church father, the most influential one for Western Christianity. He put his stamp on its thought in many regards, including the doctrine of the Trinity. Augustine's approach was to begin talking about the one God, as over against the polytheism that had been common in the West. Having dealt with that, he would then talk about the three persons of the Godhead—Father, Son, and Holy Spirit—by teaching about each person in relationship to the other two. His emphasis was on the oneness of God—which consequently focused on the divine being of God, shared equally by the three persons of the Trinity.

In the East, the Cappadocian fathers approached the doctrine "from the other end," as it were. They focused on the three persons of the Trinity—Father, Son, and Holy Spirit. The Cappadocian fathers stressed that the Father is fully God, the Son is fully God, and that the Holy Spirit is fully God. Having discussed their distinctness as three divine persons who interact with humans in creation, providence, salvation, and divine self-revelation, the Cappadocian fathers then proceeded to talk about the oneness of God (i.e., the divine being, shared equally by the three persons). This approach offers a different approach to the doctrine of the Trinity—and consequently to God—from what was accepted in the West.

What difference, though, does this end up making, in the final analysis? Dealing with imponderables as the doctrine does, can differences in human approach—provided they both cover the relevant emphases—be particularly significant? From the Eastern Christian perspective, the answer must be "yes." According to the Christian East, the divergence was not only a matter of different starting points, but of relating to God. The Cappadocian approach coalesced with the Eastern Christian understanding that prayer is always communion between persons; in the question at issue, prayer by human persons reaches out to the three persons of the Trinity. From the Eastern Christian perspective, what Augustine had taught the West to do was to pray to the oneness of God—i.e., to the *being* of God. From early in the history of the teaching of the church, though, the church fathers had denied that mere creatures can have access to or approach the being of God. The divine being, they emphasized, is utterly beyond human beings. They can never have contact with the being of God; they can only have contact with God in the way God graciously deals with humankind as persons. The Greek church fathers had stressed that, while the being of God is inaccessible to humans, they nonetheless genuinely commune with the three persons of the Trinity in grace.

From the Eastern Christian perspective, Augustine's approach would make prayer impossible. It would render worship and the communion with God it fostered a self-delusion and would thus undermine Christianity itself. The divergence could only heighten the tension between West and East.

The Question of the *Filioque*

All this was intensified by the *filioque*, a Latin phrase meaning "and from the Son" added to the Nicene Creed in the Latin version used in Western

Christianity. At some point in the sixth or seventh centuries, the creed as used in the West generally came to include "and from the Son." Why had it been added?

Augustine had talked about each person of the Trinity by relating it to the other two. While the original Nicene Creed confessed that "the Holy Spirit proceeds from the Father," the pattern of teaching stemming from Augustine and prevailing in the West seemed to make it appropriate doctrinally to add "and from the Son." Furthermore, this addition helped address a doctrinal issue that had developed in the Christian West.[9] Eventually, the widespread practice of including the *filioque* received official endorsement. This took place under the instigation of Charlemagne,[10] but without consultation with the Christian East.

For Eastern Christianity, this was totally unacceptable for two basic reasons. Firstly, *filioque* could not be squared with the Eastern Christian approach to the doctrine of the Trinity; to the Christian East, consequently, the teaching enshrined in the Latin phrase was simply wrong. In the second place, the Christian East repudiated such a unilateral insertion into the text of the creed. If a creed of the universal church needs to be changed, they argued, that change must be adopted by the universal church. It dare not be decided unilaterally. Consequently, in the assessment of Eastern Christianity, the Christian West had acted precipitously and irresponsibly by adding the *filioque* to the Nicene Creed.

All the above, plus other lesser aggravations, led to considerable tension and laid the foundations for widespread misunderstanding and mistrust between Western and Eastern Christianity. The results were pride and criticism on both sides. Neither was quite willing to condemn the other outright as false Christians, but they were both profoundly suspicious of the other. This helped to open the door to what happened in the Fourth Crusade.

The Crusades

Given the longstanding rivalry, resentment, and suspicion between Western and Eastern Christianity, the stage was set for significant problems if

9. A species of "adoptionism" (a christological heresy that taught Jesus was a mere man adopted by God to play a special role in the divine plans) had arisen in Spain; western theologians found the *filioque* clause helpful in asserting that the Son of God was fully God with the Father, since it affirmed that the Holy Spirit proceeded from both the Father and the Son.

10. The pope at the time opposed the unilateral insertion of the *filioque* into the creed; however, Emperor Charlemagne exercised his influence to secure the insertion.

and when the two long-separated sides actually encountered each other. Such an encounter opened up at least two possibilities. They might interact in such a way that each would see its own limitations, be challenged by the concerns of the other, develop some appreciation and understanding of them, and learn to respect them. Conversely, the two sides might interact in a way that each would insist on its own perspectives as the only acceptable ones, underline suspicion, and heighten the tensions. With the crusades, the long-separated Christian West and Christian East finally encountered each other closely.

Purpose

The purpose of the crusades was to drive the infidels (the Muslims) from the Holy Land and reclaim control over the holy places of the Christian religion there. The popes, who called the crusades, evidently feared that the Muslims might desecrate these places of devotion and pilgrimage. In 1095, Pope Urban II issued a call for what turned out to be the First Crusade. But why did the summons to holy war suddenly arise? The Muslim Arabs had been in control of Palestine since the 640s; almost half a millennium had passed without any such crusading venture.

However, in 1071, a significant military battle had taken place: at the Battle of Manzikert, the Byzantine forces were defeated by a new Muslim power, the Turks, who had already defeated the Arabs. The Turks had come from deep in Central Asia, not far from Siberia. They came in conquest—a conquest that four hundred years later would sweep the Byzantine Empire before them, as well. The Turks had converted to Islam and now held the Holy Land. Thus, the situation had changed enough to warrant concern for the Christian holy places.

More was involved than just concern with Palestine, however. Pope Urban also wanted to bring an end to the warfare that raged in Western Europe among Christian nations. He hoped to curtail the shedding of Christian blood by Christians. He reasoned that, if leaders seemed bent on warfare, then it should at least be for more worthy purposes: if there must be fighting, let Christians fight to free the Holy Land from infidels.

The First Crusade followed in 1096. The second eventuated about half a century later, in 1147. The third came four decades afterwards, in 1189. The Fourth Crusade took place in 1204. There were a few subsequent crusades, but eventually the ideal waned and the crusades came to an end.

Problems

In the first three crusades, problems arose between the West and the East as they finally encountered each other. The face-to-face meetings did not lead to rapprochement and better understanding. Instead, tensions were underlined and suspicions were heightened. The ways this transpired are not difficult to discern.

The Western Crusaders came with the noble purpose of freeing the Holy Land from Muslim infidels. From the Western Christian perspective, any right-thinking Christian would gladly support the crusaders' worthy venture, for the sake of Christianity. When the Byzantines turned out to be fairly cool toward the idea, the Western crusaders looked on the Byzantines as renegades to the faith.

However, the Byzantines had been dealing with Muslims ruling the Holy Land for centuries: for the Byzantines, it was neither a new situation nor an invitation to holy war. In Byzantine estimation, the Western Christian crusade venture smacked of fanaticism. For some 450 years, the Byzantines had dealt with the Muslim powers with diplomacy and, only when absolutely necessary, with warfare. Not during the whole period of Muslim dominance of Palestine had there been desecration of Christian holy places. The Byzantines feared that the Western Christian crusading venture might provoke in retaliation the sort of desecration that the crusade supposedly was meant to forestall. So, to the Byzantines—who were accustomed to view this as a political reality, not a matter of religious idealism—Western Christianity's crusading perspective seemed dangerously extremist.

A second major problem was that when the crusaders appeared in the Christian East not only the knights wore armor. Of all things—from an Eastern Christian perspective—priests and monks also bore swords and shields, as fellow-soldiers in the name of Christ. These western clergy and monks saw their involvement in the crusade as a holy calling. However, from an Eastern Christian perspective, this was utterly incomprehensible and reprehensible. In Eastern Christianity, a priest or monk cannot engage in warfare as a combatant in any circumstances. A priest or monk must never engage in human bloodshed; if he does, he must be expelled from the priesthood.[11] Consequently, for Western Christian monks and priests to bear arms was, from an Eastern Christian perspective, a manifestation of a woefully flawed, defective understanding of Christianity.

---

11. The dean of a Serbian Orthodox Cathedral advised me that to this day, within most of Orthodoxy, if a priest or monk causes the death of someone, even by accident, he must demit the priesthood or leave the monastery.

Finally, this was the first time some of these western people had been out of the county in which they had been born; for many of them, it was the first time out of their own nation; for virtually all of them, it was the first time they had ever been to Constantinople. Anyone who has lived most of his life in a small town or village, or on a farm, who has also visited a major city such as New York or Toronto will almost certainly have had a similar reaction. Mouths agape, the crusaders were stunned by the size and magnificence of the buildings that pierced the sky; they could not believe what Constantinople was like. Many of them were agog at what they saw. Constantinople was, in almost all regards, overwhelming for the crusaders—and attractive, as well. Their leaders saw that the imperial court dined with gold and silver utensils and drank from crystal. Churches were awash in gold and precious stones. Byzantine nobles wore fine clothing and stunning jewelry. A major lord among the western crusaders commented, "Half the world's wealth must be in this city." That observation had an ominous ring to it: the West had noted the splendor and magnificence—and taken special note of Constantinople's wealth.

The Fourth Crusade

The first three crusades had not gone particularly well. For their part, the Byzantines were hardly surprised by the lack of overwhelming success. On the other hand, the Western Christians were suspicious about the Byzantine lack of enthusiasm and wondered whether the Byzantines might have had something to do with the failures in the crusades. None of this contributed to mutual understanding or appreciation. This was the backdrop for the Fourth Crusade.

Immediate Background

At the time of the crusade, the pope was Innocent III (r. 1198–1216), one of the most powerful, influential popes of the entire Middle Ages. Another major player was the city of Venice, at the time a significant maritime power that had made a contract with the crusaders to build some five hundred ships of various sizes to transport the crusaders to Palestine and serve their crusade. For more than a year leading up to the crusade, Venice had devoted most of its building enterprise to producing these ships. The leader of Venice, the Doge Enrico Dandolo, was responsible for this decision. However, the numbers of crusaders who showed up in Venice fell considerably short of what had been promised by those who had planned the crusade and had contracted with Venice. The city stood to lose a huge investment, and the Doge his leadership of the city, if this were not rectified.

But who would make up the financial shortfall? The papacy could not; at that point, the papacy was anything but wealthy. (It would not attain that kind of wealth until the Avignon Papacy in the next century.) The crusaders did not themselves have the resources to pay the difference. The Doge had a real problem: Venice could go bankrupt unless payment were made. So, he insisted on full payment.

Then an answer fell into their laps in the person of Alexius, the son of the previous emperor of Byzantium. His father had been displaced from the throne, but Alexius had escaped. He desperately wanted to become the Byzantine emperor, and he met with the Doge and other crusade leaders to seek their help. Aware of the financial stress, Alexius promised an exorbitant payment from the imperial coffers in Constantinople if the crusaders would help him gain the throne there. The answer had been given, so the crusade could proceed.

Events

The crusaders headed for Constantinople. The idea was, of course, to go on to the Holy Land, but they could only do that after Venice had been paid. The plan they had agreed on was to pressure the Byzantines to restore Alexius to his father's throne, that Alexius would pay them the agreed amount, and that the crusaders would then depart for the Holy Land.

In keeping with the Byzantines' prior practice with the crusaders, the Venetian ships were allowed to anchor in the Golden Horn, the marvelous seven-mile channel on the north side of Constantinople, a channel otherwise closed to foreign vessels. From there, the crusaders demanded that Alexius be put back on the throne. After a few weeks, the Byzantines—who by then were already quite dissatisfied with the man who had displaced Alexius' father—accepted the demand. Alexius was put on the throne; the crusaders then expected to be paid.

However, Alexius soon found that the imperial treasury had been depleted enough that he could not hope to pay the crusaders the amount he had promised. When he offered a partial payment in lieu of the whole, the crusaders demurred, demanding instead full payment. The Byzantines soon learned of the financial demands. Already irritated with the interference of the crusaders in their internal affairs, the Byzantines refused to allow their funds to be used to pay the crusaders. The conflict increased over the course of a few weeks.

In short order, Alexius proved inept as emperor. When someone else pressed a claim on the imperial dignity, the Byzantines were only too pleased to remove Alexius from the throne. Then the new emperor declared to the crusaders that they could forget about being paid, since that promise had been made by a predecessor whom the Byzantines had expelled from imperial office. It was no surprise to the Byzantines that the crusaders were furious with this turn of events. What the crusaders did about it was a surprise, though.

Over the preceding weeks, as the situation had deteriorated for them, the leaders of the crusade had been making plans for conquering Constantinople. They looked on this as a just response for the way they had been treated in this situation, and they could justify the planned conquest via the alleged faults of the Eastern Christians noted above. With the new emperor's abrupt dismissal of the crusaders' demand for payment, the crusade leaders let the plans they had made be known throughout their camp. Initial hesitation about attacking a Christian city was assuaged by some clergy, who assured the doubtful of various warrants for the endeavor.

Soon after the denial of their demand to be paid, the crusading armies launched their attack on Constantinople. From the crusaders' privileged positions within the Golden Horn, Constantinople was more dangerously exposed than she had even been to a hostile force. To make a long story short, the crusaders succeeded. Once they had seized a major gate and opened it to the rest of their forces, the issue had been decided.

This was the first time Constantinople's walls had ever been breached. The crusading armies broke into Constantinople, and what followed was an orgy of three days of pillage, looting, burning, killing, and rape. The crusaders destroyed much and took whatever they wanted. In due course, most of the loot and wealth found its way to Western Europe; today, much of it can be seen in the Louvre Museum in Paris or in St. Mark's Cathedral in Venice.

At St. Mark's Cathedral in Venice, copies of the statues of four bronze horses taken from the Hippodrome in Byzantium during the Fourth Crusade. (The originals are now in storage in Venice.)

The Fourth Crusade ended up being one of the sorriest blights ever on Western Christian history. Any kind of abuse of the conquered by a victorious army after a conquest ought to be repudiated; this was even more heinous, though, since the crusaders were ostensibly fighting in the cause of Christianity. The crusaders wore the cross on their tunics, their helmets, and their shields. Thus marked, they killed fellow Christians and raped nuns. They devastated and looted the most fabulous city in all of Christendom.

Effects

The Fourth Crusade had wide-ranging and long-lasting effects on the history of Eastern Europe. Scholars have noted many elements in this regard. Here, we will point out four of them.

First of all, this was shocking for Eastern Christians. That Western Christians engaged in such atrocities in the name of Christ, wearing the cross, was inconceivable and devastating. They could understand the crusaders' frustrations; they could never justify the recourse the crusaders took, and certainly not the horrors into which it led.

Secondly, the Fourth Crusade was the beginning of the end for the Byzantine Empire. The Byzantines were able to recapture Constantinople from the crusaders in 1261 and reestablish their empire, but it had been so weakened and impoverished by the Fourth Crusade that it never fully recovered. Plundered as it had been, Byzantium no longer had the funds to pay its own armies or employ mercenaries. In due course, Byzantium fell to the Turks, the very Muslim infidels against whom the crusades were supposed to fight. When Constantinople fell, the doors to Europe swung wide open to the Turkish armies. The crusades had been meant to drive the Muslims out of the Holy Land, but the Fourth Crusade ended up exposing Europe to Muslim invasion. History is sometimes tinged with bitter irony.

In the third place, the Fourth Crusade resulted in a widespread attitude within Eastern Europe that Western Christians are not to be trusted, especially if they resort to "God-talk." That has been an abiding residue of the crusade, to which an incident in the early 1990s gave eloquent if painful witness. In a major Greek Orthodox church in Thessaloniki, a Roman Catholic cardinal was addressing the congregation in one of the ecumenical contacts that had begun to take place. A woman walked in who did not recognize him, so she asked a friend who he was. She replied that he was a representative of the pope, but the questioner did not recognize the title. So her friend specified who the pope was by commenting that he was the one who had destroyed Constantinople. The questioner then spat symbolically and asked in disgust why they ought to listen to anything he might have to say. Relationships between Eastern Orthodox and Western Christians have been strained for almost eight hundred years, to the present day, by the shock and horror of what happened in the Fourth Crusade. It remains to be seen what will happen after the pope's 2001 apology.

Finally, the effects were not felt only in ecclesiastical relations or intra-Christian relationships. This distrust of the West by Eastern Europe has affected the general patterns of Eastern European attitudes toward the West in many other matters, as can be seen in the events within Yugoslavia in the 1990s. Anyone watching those events closely could recognize that the leaders in the breakaway states of the former Yugoslavia did not give serious credence to what leaders from the West said: long ago, Eastern Europeans had learned that the West cannot be trusted, even when—and, perhaps, especially when—they talk about ideals or causes.

More could be said about the results of the Fourth Crusade. Suffice it at this point to note that it is still a painful memory for many Eastern Europeans. It was certainly an epochal event in their history.

CHAPTER 10

The Invasion of the Mongols (1240s)

> "Wherever the Mongols rode they left an irretrievably ruined economy.... The campaigns of the Mongol armies were the last and the most destructive in the long line of nomad invasions from the steppes."[1]

THE MONGOLS INVADED EASTERN Europe in the early 1240s. That brief period brought almost untold devastation to the region, as it reeled before the onslaughts of their overwhelming forces. This thirteenth-century invasion was the last of many that had wreaked havoc within Eastern Europe over almost two millennia. Situating the Mongol invasion within the context of its predecessors will help to underline why the Mongol invasion had such momentous impact on the history of Eastern Europe.

A Long Series of Invasions

Eastern Europe had known a succession of invaders, all of whom had come from the Far East, in the depths of Asia. These various peoples had swept in a westward direction and had burst almost without warning into Eastern Europe. What allowed and impelled them to do so?

The Topographical Invitation

One reason had to do with topography. A broad plain stretches from Poland and Ukraine deep into Asia. This large expanse of flatland, the longest in the entire world, is commonly referred to as the Russian steppes. It was an invader's superhighway. No mountains interrupted the steppes to impede military forces; the only obstacles were a few rivers, none of which

---

1. Chambers, *The Devil's Horsemen*, 167–68.

posed insuperable difficulties for people on the move. Eastern Europe lay directly in the path of any invaders who came across those flatlands in search of loot or conquest.

A Driving Impulse

But why did these peoples head westward? However fearful they might subsequently prove to be in Eastern Europe, most of them were themselves fleeing some other power that had defeated them in their home territory. All of them had lived somewhere in Asia for centuries; some had previously moved from one area of Asia into another; many of them had become ruling powers in the territory in which they resided; all of them had developed into formidable fighting powers.[2] But the reason most of them, except the last, had headed west across the steppes was that they had been driven from their homeland by another power, which had displaced them as the dominant force there.

Fleeing in fear for their own safety, they nonetheless came with their considerable military prowess. Bursting into Eastern Europe, they had each brought conquest and destruction in their wake. No matter how fearsome any of these invasions was, however, something potentially even more dreadful always lurked in the wings: the forces that had first defeated or frightened the most recent invaders of Eastern Europe would themselves be defeated subsequently, would flee west from their powerful foes, and the pattern would repeat. This happened several times.

The pattern did not apply to the Mongols, however. When they invaded Eastern Europe, they were not running from a more formidable foe: *they themselves* were the most formidable of the foes. At the time, the Mongols were expanding their already gargantuan empire, the largest the world has ever known. It had spread from their homeland to the Pacific Ocean in the Far East and would eventually reach all the way to Hungary in the West; it incorporated China, Korea, most of contemporary Russia, what remained to Persia, most of Afghanistan, and Asia Minor (contemporary Turkey); the Mongols subjugated both Palestine and Asia Minor, defeating both crusader armies and the Seljuk Turks against whom the crusaders fought. So, the Mongols entered Eastern Europe, not in flight or fear, but in the fullness of their ferocious power and the vast resources of their huge empire. It is little

---

2. See earlier comments about the Scythians, Sarmatians, Huns, and Avars in chapter 2 and the treatment of the Magyars in chapter 8 as background for further information about them in this chapter.

wonder that Eastern Europe suffered more from the Mongols' depredations than from any of their predecessors.

The Invaders

The various peoples who had invaded Eastern Europe over the centuries were not all of the same ethnic stock or linguistic background. Nevertheless, they all came from the same general area of Asia, and they shared certain characteristics reflecting their common experience. These served in many ways to make the various invading peoples fearsome warriors; with the Mongols, these characteristics were heightened, rendering the Mongols even more terrifying than any of the preceding invaders of Eastern Europe.

Steppe Warriors

All these warrior peoples who invaded Eastern Europe had been shaped by the steppes on which they had grown up. These peoples had made their living as nomads or as herdsmen, who needed to move readily and quickly from one area to another in search of pasturage. To accommodate this, they had learned to live on horseback. Furthermore, since the land had no natural boundaries, these peoples had no natural protection; they were thus always exposed to the danger of marauders or bandits. Simply to survive and to protect their flocks and possessions, they perforce had become able warriors. Not surprisingly, they had learned to fight on horseback; all the steppe warrior forces boasted excellent cavalries.

The climate further served to harden both the warriors and their mounts. While summers and spring could provide abundant pasturage, winters were always harsh and brutal. Even mere survival required an unusual toughness on the part of both human beings and their animals. In this regard, the ponies favored by the steppe warriors were unusually hardy, by comparison with many other horses; during the winter, when pasturage in the frigid climate was unavailable, these ponies could survive by eating the branches of trees and of bushes. The steppe people themselves had to care for their flocks during the brutal winters and survive on whatever could be obtained; this also toughened them in a variety of ways. The exigencies of battle transposed that toughness into a brutality, even a callousness, which made these warriors terrifying to others.

While some of the earlier invaders had favored swords or spears, by the time of the Mongols the preferred weapons of the steppe warriors had long been bows and arrows, and the Mongol horsemen became excellent archers.

Close hand-to-hand combat with battle-axes and swords such as became common in Europe was not their pattern, although they had some weapons for this. They preferred, and their battle tactics relied on, bow and arrow.

Steppe warriors could be ruthless, even cruel. They had grown up in an unforgiving climate; their warfare was unforgiving, as well. They almost never showed mercy, and their warfare was typically brutal with their opponents. Among the Mongols, that brutality was especially noted: after battles in the Gobi Desert in Mongolia, Mongol forces would leave the wounded of the defeated force lying on the ground, where the desert rats—typically about two feet long—would finish them off. When people with such an approach to battle burst into Eastern Europe in waves of destruction, they brought a terrifying kind of warfare, marked by a startling inhumanity toward their opponents.

Because of all this, the steppe warriors frightened the peoples of Eastern Europe. They fought in a way not common in Europe and with a brutality that staggered even the most battle-hardened Europeans. In all these regards, the Mongols outstripped their predecessors among the long series of invaders.

A Series of Invaders

Eastern Europe had known a long series of such invaders from Asia. The first of whom there is record were the Scythians, who broke into Eastern Europe from somewhere in Central Asia in a wave of destruction around 500 BC. They swept through much of Eastern Europe in a terrifying swath of devastation and killing, which earned them a reputation for utter brutality among the peoples of antiquity. Their depredations were so extensive that some huge tracts of land were depopulated, owing to the multitudes killed. After this initial conquest, the Scythians pulled back to the area north of the Black Sea, in the south of contemporary Ukraine, where they set up a state that lasted for some three hundred years.

However fearsome the Scythians may once have been, they themselves were defeated by the Sarmatians around 200 BC, who overran the Scythian state. The Sarmatians did not plunge further into Eastern Europe, though. They erected their own state, which lasted until the Christian era. Their power was broken by the Ostrogoths, who took control over the region north of the Black Sea in the first century AD.

This area was soon enough exposed to the onslaughts of the next invaders from the steppes, a people whose name became a byword for brutality, the Huns. Around 370 AD, the Huns first made their appearance north of the Black Sea. There they soundly defeated the Ostrogoths, who then fled westwards before the Huns. In short order, the Huns swept through Eastern Europe, eventually plunging into Western Europe, as well. With the death of their formidable leader Attila in 455, though, the Hunnish power collapsed.

However terrifying the Huns may have been, and in the face of the legendary brutality associated with their name, they had themselves burst into Europe while fleeing from a people who had defeated them. After a respite for Eastern Europe of nearly a century after the collapse of the Huns as a power, in 550 the Avars—the people who had defeated the Huns—burst into Eastern Europe. Periodic raids in contemporary Ukraine, Poland, and Romania from their base north of the Black Sea eventually gave way to a deliberate invasion. In their incursions, the Avars swarmed through contemporary Romania, Bulgaria, and Greece, all the way to Constantinople. In due course, threatened by yet other invaders from the steppes, and facing the Byzantine armies, the Avars moved west and settled into the plains of contemporary Hungary, Slovenia, and Croatia in the early 600s. From there as their power base they continued pillaging both Eastern and Western Europe. At the end of the eighth century, the Avars were defeated and their state destroyed by Charlemagne and his Frankish armies, with their confederates.

The next invaders to plunge into Eastern Europe after the Avars were the Bulgars, who took control of contemporary Romania and much of Bulgaria around 665 AD. The Bulgars stayed and developed into a power in Eastern Europe; indeed, they fought regularly with and held their own against the Byzantine Empire's armies. The Bulgars had initially set themselves up as a ruling caste over the Slavs who had settled in those regions, but within a century the Bulgars had been assimilated to the Slavs.[3]

About two centuries later, around 860, the Magyars—originally from northern Siberia—swept across the Russian steppes, broke into Eastern Europe, and repeated the pattern of the Avars. Endangered by both the Bulgarian state and the Byzantines, the Magyars headed west and settled in the plains of Hungary. There they continued their pillaging activities until the mid-tenth century, when they were soundly defeated at the Battle of Lechfeld in 955. Soon afterwards, they developed a state and adopted Western European practices. The Magyars have remained in this location to the present day: the overwhelming preponderance of the residents of contemporary Hungary (and a considerable minority in Romania) are of Magyar heritage.

---

3. See above, chapter 6.

The next (and last) group of these invaders was the Mongols, who came after an interval of nearly four hundred years. Unlike most of the preceding invaders, the Mongols did not burst into Eastern Europe with a more fearful opponent on their heels; the Mongol invasion was a continuation of the empire-building inaugurated by their redoubtable leader, Genghis Khan. The Mongols outstripped their predecessors in the devastation they brought to Eastern Europe.

The Mongols have been known in history by other names. Sometimes they have been referred to as "Tatars," but this designation is inaccurate, since the Tatars were only one of the tribes united under the Mongol banner by Genghis Khan. The Mongols have also been called "Tartars." Some have supposed that this designation was only a variant on "Tatar," but that derivation is mistaken. The designation "Tartar" is a testimony to the fear induced by the Mongols: "Tartar" actually comes from *Tartarus* (Latin; Greek, Τάρταρος), the term for the region of Hades where the wicked are punished—"hell." The way the Mongols fought was so horrific, and the brutality they visited upon their opponents so terrifying, that "Tartar" came into use to describe them, as demons from hell. This indicates clearly the fear with which they were viewed.

Strengths of the Mongol Army

During the twelfth century, Genghis Khan united the previously rival tribes of Mongolia into a cohesive body and developed a formidable army out of their warriors. With this force, he defeated the considerably more sophisticated civilization of China, as well as Korea, the remnants of Persia, and Afghanistan; then he sent his armies further west. During the thirteenth century, the Mongol army was the best in the world.

Genghis Khan had at his disposal the tough Mongol warriors. After defeating China, he then shrewdly learned from the Chinese about more organized warfare, including strategy, tactics, deployment of forces, and intelligence-gathering. With these he honed his armies so that they could use their military prowess to even better effect. The outcome was an awkward but successful marriage between the ruthless brutality of steppe warriors and the sophisticated military science of the Chinese. The result was the Mongol army that built the largest empire the world has ever known.

Commitment of the Troops

The Mongol army was marked by commitment, both to other soldiers and to their leaders, all the way through the ranks to the khan. This characteristic had been thoroughly drilled into Genghis Khan's forces in two significant ways. Not surprisingly, the ways this was instilled reflected the harshness of the culture in which it arose.

Soldiers in the Mongol army had long since learned that they dared show no cowardice and must not tolerate it in others. The penalty for cowardice was brutal. The army was organized by units of ten warriors, with those units coordinated in further multiples of ten.[4] If anyone in a unit fled on the battlefield or otherwise showed cowardice, he and the other nine in his unit were all executed. Commitment to bravery and to one's fighting unit thus coalesced. With the Mongol armies, cowardice was not tolerated, and commitment to one's unit was unquestioned.

Furthermore, loyalty to their leaders, focused on loyalty to the khan, was absolutely demanded. Genghis Khan's father had been tricked and killed by some people who were supposedly his allies. Subsequently, someone took advantage of Genghis Khan while he was still only a young man. Once he became leader of the Mongols, he tolerated absolutely no disloyalty at any level, whether to him as khan or to any leader in the Mongol forces. Any disloyalty or treason was punished by a long, slow, brutal, and public death. It would last for days, and people were forced to watch it.[5] Few people ever showed disloyalty to Genghis Khan, and the few who did ended up serving as sobering warnings to everyone else.

---

4. A significant problem faced by earlier Mongol leaders was that consolidated forces ended up fighting in units composed of men from the same tribe. Genghis Khan ended this tribal organization of the Mongol forces: he intermingled the men of the various tribes and, with his stern demand for loyalty, managed to establish an overarching loyalty among the whole fighting force.

5. At one point, Genghis Khan uncovered a plot, hatched by his uncle, to remove Genghis from power (and, presumably, assume it himself). Genghis gathered large numbers of the Mongol army's leadership and brought his uncle, with his sons (so, Genghis's cousins—whom he adjudged were "in" on the plot), and caused them to sit in the middle of the assembled group. The crowd observed while Genghis's cousins each swallowed gravel until they all died. Genghis's uncle watched all this; then he was placed in the circle and had his joints cut off (beginning with fingers) and fed to him until he died, too.

A Steppe-Toughened Cavalry

The Mongol forces were composed of cavalry. This afforded them great mobility and speed, far in advance of any army dependent on infantry. Beyond this general advantage of any cavalry force, the Mongol cavalry had some other strengths.

For one thing, having grown up on the steppes, the Mongols were used to long days on horseback and were accomplished horsemen. Mongol armies could easily cover fifty miles a day—a considerable distance on horseback. The reason they could regularly cover so much ground was that each Mongol soldier had three or four horses. Periodically, he would change mounts so that he could continue at a steady trot. Thus, only about a quarter or a third of the time would any of his horses actually be carrying his weight; the rest of the time these sturdy ponies would just be trotting alongside.

Beyond that, the Mongol horses were tough little mounts. They were not the big plow horses ridden by European knights in the Middle Ages. The horses used by the people of the steppes were smaller, but very tough. They did not carry the heavy armor that weighed down the already massive horses of the European knights. With less weight, the Mongols' horses were much faster and could cover more distance than those of their opponents. The Mongols used all this to good advantage in their invasion of Eastern Europe.

As noted above, both the steppe warriors and their horses were used to brutal winters. A remarkable thing about the Mongol army was that it could and did fight in winter. Recognizing this as one of their strengths, they would sometimes conduct their campaigns in the winter months, resting in the summer in order to allow their horses to graze and get strong again. Europeans did not expect such tactics, and when they fought in winter, they sometimes blundered into Mongol traps: if the Europeans sent their cavalry out onto the frozen lakes, the horses would slip and slide on the ice; the Mongols had wrapped their mounts' hooves in felt to assure good footing. The results of such battles were not hard to predict.

Beyond all this, the Mongols were outstanding archers. They used two different bows, for shooting different distances; while one was used for close-range fighting, with the other a Mongol could shoot arrows some 350 metres. Since European knights fought with sword, battle-axe, or lance, this gave the Mongols a huge fighting advantage against the knights. Beyond their distance capabilities, the Mongol horsemen developed the ability to shoot in any direction, even to the rear. This made them dangerous, even in retreat.

Military Techniques

Under Chinese tutelage, the already formidable Mongol armies learned much more sophisticated military tactics. One they utilized effectively was the feigned retreat. Mongol armies were never large, by comparison with those they faced: the largest force the Mongols ever mounted was about 100,000. Most of the time, though, their armies were considerably smaller. They often managed, nevertheless, to manipulate the numerical discrepancy to their advantage by the strategem of a feigned retreat.

In this tactic, the front lines of the Mongol armies, having drawn near their opponents, would suddenly react as if disorganized by panic at the numbers they were facing. Their cavalry would feign confusion and fear, and soon they would wheel and bolt from the battlefield, in apparent disarray. Seeing this, their opponents would pursue, hoping to drive the Mongols headlong from the region. Along the way, some of the Mongols would peel off to one side or another, as if they were galloping off in a different direction to avoid capture or death. The European cavalry, chasing on heavy mounts, would eventually become more and more spread out—until the Mongols wheeled about and sent a hail of arrows raining down on their pursuers. From the sides, the supposedly fleeing Mongols would do the same, with the result that their opponents were surrounded on three or four sides. The Mongols used this tactic to devastating effect in their invasion of Eastern Europe.

Another tactic was to use a pincers movement. Mongols would divide their forces into two groups, which would attack their opponents from two sides. Of course, attacking from two sides made defense doubly difficult.

The Mongols had excellent communications. For this, they relied on the speed and durability of their horses. It was recorded that one warrior needed to carry a message back from his general to Genghis Khan in Mongolia. He could rely on replacing his pony frequently by stopping at Mongol camps. He covered the 1,200 miles in only seven days. Mongols could pass communication from one place to another in speeds that by European standards of the time were unimaginable.

Another aspect of Mongol communications was that they did not use trumpets or other sound-making instruments on the field of battle. Instead, they communicated by using various colored banners, signalling attack or withdrawal, or for moving in one direction or another. This was totally outside the experience or understanding of their European opponents—which served to confuse and disorient them.

All this enabled extraordinary coordination of the Mongol forces. To this day, the Mongol invasion of Eastern Europe is studied in military colleges. When they finally launched their invasion, they attacked on two fronts, separated by considerable geographical distance. Even so, they managed to coordinate their attacks on alternating days, so that their opponents could not offer reinforcements to other opponents attacked elsewhere. This all required careful planning and good communication.

Instilling Terror

The final strength of the Mongol armies was the terror they provoked. Life on the steppes had hardened them: they were callous to feelings, whether their own or others': they could endure pain without much reaction and inflict it without much conscience. Their cruelty was not heated and wild, like someone who flies into a rage. The Mongol army's cruelty was cool and methodical, with a definite purpose—to terrorize, so that the next target for conquest would not dare to oppose them.

In that regard, they faithfully followed Genghis Khan's advice. He had directed his troops that if any town fought against the Mongols, then every man, woman, child, and animal there should be put to death; if, though, a town did not withstand them but submitted, then most of the men, women, children, and animals would be spared. Because of this ruthless approach, terror spread before the Mongols; often, cities would capitulate and agree to pay tribute rather than trying to fight the Mongols. Much of their empire was added in this way: the terror they engendered served their purposes well.

Invading Eastern Europe

The Mongol Empire under Genghis Khan encompassed a vast territory. But it did not yet include Eastern Europe by the time of his death. The invasion of Eastern Europe was left to one of his successors, Batu Khan.[6]

---

6. "Khan" was a title, not a last name. It was used commonly among peoples of Asia for their leading rulers. The Mongols had a chief khan with responsibility for the whole empire and several lesser rulers (usually sons or favorites of the chief khan) who served as governors of the segments of the empire and who also carried the title "khan." The area ruled by a khan was called a "khanate."

The Leader: Batu Khan

Batu Khan was commonly acknowledged as the grandson of Genghis Khan. There was question about this, however, for the paternity of Batu's father was in some doubt. This hung in the air over Batu for his early life and put him in a somewhat awkward position with regard to the rest of the family. The way he was dealt with by Genghis as the latter lay dying officially removed the cloud and led to Batu being entrusted with the invasion of Eastern Europe.

The reason for the uncertainty about paternity was that Genghis Khan's wife, Batu's grandmother, had been captured by opponents shortly after her marriage to Genghis. She was forced to be a concubine to a noble of another tribe for a few months, after which Genghis received her back. Somewhere along the way she had become pregnant, but there was question whether by the noble of the other tribe or by Genghis. Consequently, a question lingered as to the paternity of the son who was born—who became Batu's father.

Genghis fathered several sons, among whom he accepted Batu's father as his own son—although almost everyone in the Mongol leadership recognized the uncertainty of that status. Batu's father died before Genghis—which would have made for an easy way of dealing with this uncertainty. At his death, Genghis would divide up his possessions among his sons; this meant that he would allocate portions of the empire to each of them to rule. He expected that they would cooperate: in this regard, the utter loyalty demanded by Genghis among the Mongols assured a good result of such division. When Genghis died, his will did thus segment the empire; what was striking in this was that he included Batu among those who inherited. Thus, Genghis Khan publicly indicated his acceptance of Batu and of his father as members of his line.

Batu's segment of the empire was the one furthest west. That gave him the readiest opportunity for significant military expansion, since Eastern Europe was just beyond the limits of his khanate. The loyalty demanded among the Mongols manifested itself in Batu's favor: knowing that he would need excellent forces to expand the empire into Eastern Europe, and further recognizing that Batu had the least territory and the most area to conquer, the other khans (all sons of Genghis) loaned Batu the best of their armies to assure success to Batu as he invaded Eastern Europe. With those forces, Batu embarked on that invasion.

The Destruction of Kievan Rus'

The largest state of Eastern Europe was Kievan Rus'.[7] It was also the one furthest east, directly in the path of Batu Khan. For the invasion to have any hope of success, the Mongols had to overwhelm and utterly destroy Kievan Rus', so that they would not face any danger to their rear as they proceeded further into Eastern Europe.

The Mongols were helped by what had been going on for about a century in Kievan Rus'. During that time, the various rulers in its leading cities failed to cooperate, and sometimes fought, with each other. All of them wanted to establish their freedom vis-à-vis the Grand Prince of Kiev and each other. As a result, Kievan Rus' had been decentralized by the time the Mongols moved against it.

The Mongols took advantage of that, and in the summer of 1240 they began to pick off one city after another. With the decentralization that had taken over Kievan Rus', a Mongol attack on one city did not automatically attract defenders from elsewhere in the state; each city stood—and fell—on its own. The Mongol forces took cities to the north and then to the south, gradually moving toward Kiev itself. They encamped outside Kiev just before December 1241; Kiev withstood them. Kiev had long been the richest city of all Kievan Rus'; by the time the Mongols attacked, it was the last major city left in the state. Before the end of December, the Mongols broke into Kiev, looted, sacked, and almost totally destroyed it. Of the four hundred churches, they burned all except St. Sophia, built in the eleventh century under Jaroslav the Wise; it was such a magnificent structure that the Mongols decided to let it stand, although they did knock down the columns in front of it. They slaughtered the entire population—men, women, and children alike, except for a few whom the Mongols allowed to escape westward, to spread terror. This worked effectively: the remaining cities capitulated one after the other to the Mongols, who faced no further opposition as they marched across what had been Kievan Rus'. Within three weeks after destroying Kiev, they stood at the border of Poland.

Thus the glorious state of Kievan Rus', the jewel of Eastern European civilization, came to an end. In 1245, the pope sent a representative to Mongol headquarters, to try to negotiate with their leaders. When he passed through Kiev, he noted that it was still littered with skulls and bones—four years after its conquest.[8] Almost no one had settled in the depopulated city; the bodies of the slaughtered had simply rotted where they fell.

---

7. See above, chapter 7.
8. This report is given in Carpini, *Story of the Mongols*, 68.

Further into Eastern Europe

With Kievan Rus' destroyed, the way into the rest of Eastern Europe lay open to the Mongols. But now they faced several different states. This presented the Mongols with a considerable problem: how should they proceed so as to subjugate all these states while not allowing any of them to mount a resolute defense or shore up the defenses of another state under Mongol attack? The Mongols needed to keep all the states of Eastern Europe "off balance" and complete their conquests in short order.

The question was rendered even more difficult by the size of the Mongol armies. Altogether, Batu had only some 70,000 cavalry at his disposal. By medieval standards, this was not a large army. Batu developed an audacious plan: he divided his forces in two, sending some 20,000 on a fast and furious onslaught against the northern nations of Eastern Europe and the other 50,000 on a similar tirade against the southern nations of the region. This meant that these two armies were spread out, eventually to a distance of some six hundred miles from each other. To succeed, the Mongols would have to coordinate their attacks with consummate precision and move with great speed—both of which were strengths of their armies.

The Goal: Hungary

The ultimate target of all this activity was Hungary. Batu wanted to incorporate all of Eastern Europe into his khanate, but if he did so, he would need a place from which to rule. Hungary suited his needs nicely: it was by now a wealthy state; it was geographically central to the whole of Eastern Europe and would serve well as a capital; further, it offered broad plains where Mongol horses could pasture, where Mongol forces could be trained, and from which they could readily be deployed. But in order to conquer Hungary, the Mongols recognized that they needed to deal powerfully and ruthlessly with its nearest neighbors.

Strategy

The northern force attacked Poland and conquered the major city of Krakow. In the battle, the Mongols used the feigned retreat tactic to perfection. Their horses neighed and reared, and the apparently disorganized and fearful Mongol force fled the scene. Their headlong flight covered some eleven miles—quite enough to assure that the Polish cavalry was well strung out by the time the Mongols turned and took the offensive. The Polish forces were cut down in a hail of arrows. Then the Mongols moved against Sandomierz and Lublin, treating them as ruthlessly as they had Kiev. Swift movement precluded support from elsewhere in Poland. Several smaller Polish cities capitulated, rather than face the wrath of the Mongols.

Afterwards, the Mongol forces peeled back and attacked cities in Lithuania, to eliminate possible dangers to their northeast. Then the Mongols swung through Moravia, bringing it quickly and brutally under their control. They did the same with the region of Silesia and the area known today as Slovakia.

The only northern state in Eastern Europe not attacked by the Mongols was Bohemia. The reason was two-fold: firstly, the Mongols did not need to subjugate Bohemia in order to reach their ultimate goal, Hungary; secondly, since Bohemia was part of the Holy Roman Empire,[9] attacking Bohemia would only invite retaliation from that empire. If they left Bohemia alone, the Mongols hoped, then the Holy Roman Empire would not march against them. Their desire was fulfilled. So, Bohemia escaped the Mongol terror—the only Eastern European nation to do so. In control of the north, the small Mongol force encamped near the Carpathian Mountains, ready to join its confreres to the south in an assault on Hungary.

The 50,000 who had gone south attacked and subjugated Moldavia, near the Mongols' previous encampment. Then they turned west, bringing the whole of Wallachia under their control. With these areas conquered, the Mongols turned against Transylvania, again defeating armies and conquering the cities that lay in their way. By these tactics, the Mongols eliminated dangers to their rear and kept moving in the direction of Hungary.

All this took only a few weeks. It had become clear to the King of Hungary, Béla IV, that his state was the ultimate Mongol goal. He tried to rally support from his nobles, but that ran against the grain of recent Hungarian history. For all its wealth and power, Hungary had been weakened by nobles who wanted to limit the power of the kings in order to maintain their own authority as much as possible. Thus, like Kievan Rus', Hungary had been decentralized. She was in grave danger from the Mongol forces.

The two segments of the Mongol army coordinated their attack on Hungary closely. Entering Hungarian territory from two points at considerable distance from each other, the Mongols precluded the Hungarians mounting a large single force anywhere to oppose the attack. Hungary was caught in a pincer movement, and several battles along the two fronts fell to the Mongols. The two Mongol armies then converged at the city of Pest, the main city of the state.

---

9. See the treatments in chapters 8 and 12.

The Hungarians massed their remaining forces—which by then outnumbered the combined Mongol army. As at Krakow, so at Pest, the Mongols employed the tactic of a feigned retreat. The results were similar: in this battle between 25,000 and 30,000 Hungarian cavalry were, like the Polish knights of Krakow, cut down in a hail of arrows. Hungary lay wide open to the Mongols.

The king of Hungary fled to Croatia. The Mongols pursued him, but he managed to elude them there. Frustrated, the Mongols ravaged Croatia. Béla escaped to Bosnia and then to Serbia, somehow managing to escape capture in either state. However, Bosnia and Serbia suffered the same treatment from the Mongols as had Croatia. Then he fled through the regions we know today as Albania and North Macedonia, with the same results, both for himself and for the two regions. The Mongols never did manage to capture him.

Reprieve

By this point, every state in Eastern Europe except Bohemia had been attacked and ravaged by the Mongols. The future of the whole region looked utterly grim. But suddenly, the Mongol forces stopped their assaults and withdrew from most of their conquests.

The reason for this sudden turn of events was that the chief khan in Mongolia had died. According to Mongol law, all the subordinate khans—including Batu—had to return to Mongolia for the selection of the chief khan's successor and to pledge loyalty to him. Thus, Batu had no choice but to bring his campaigns to a halt, no matter how successful they had been or how close to ultimate victory they were.

The Eastern Europeans had to fear that Batu and his formidable forces would return, and they began to do whatever they could to prepare for a second invasion. They could not have known that Batu had decided to give up on the idea of ruling Eastern Europe. He had come to recognize that the topography of Eastern Europe was not congenial to setting up a khanate. There was too much marshland, where Mongol horses could not effectively be deployed. As well, the various mountain ranges in Eastern Europe posed great danger for Mongol forces: they were unused to mountains; their methods of warfare demanded easy cavalry movements, impossible in mountainous terrain; and mountains were ideal haunts for guerrilla forces that could harry Mongol detachments. Beyond all this, he had discovered that, even though Hungary had quite a good plain, it would probably not be large enough to offer pasturage to the large numbers of horses needed by his Mongol armies. Batu would not be back; Eastern Europe would be spared.

However, Batu was not one to go lightly. To that point, Bulgaria had largely escaped Mongol depredations. As his forces left Hungary behind, they turned with a vengeance against Bulgaria and ravaged it, laying waste several cities. Indeed, while the Mongol forces would not proceed again with an invasion of all of Eastern Europe, they set up their state north of the Black Sea, with its capital at Serai on the Volga River. From there, the Mongols repeatedly attacked Bulgaria over the next century.

Aftermath of the Mongol Invasion

While the immediate threat of further Mongol invasions was eliminated by Mongol decision, that did not mean that they left Eastern Europe alone. The khanate established at Serai on the Volga came to known as "the Golden Horde." From there, Batu and his successors exacted tribute from the surviving cities of the former Kievan Rus'. When tribute moneys were not forthcoming, the khan would send Mongol forces to enforce the demand; brutalities against the would-be rebels followed.

Even so, the Mongols slowly changed from being a fierce invading force to becoming the rulers of a wide expanse of territory. Modifications in attitude and lifestyle inevitably followed, eventually undermining their previous power. In the late fourteenth century, the Mongols were defeated by a prince from the northern regions of the old Kievan Rus' state, Dmitri Donskoi. He would become a hero to a state that would emerge from the ruins of old Kievan Rus'—that state was Muscovy, which eventually expanded into the Russian Empire. Over the next decades after their defeat by Dmitri, Mongol control of the territory encompassed within the Golden Horde slipped; in due course, they were defeated and reduced to just another state along the Volga River.

As for Eastern Europe itself, it was devastated by the Mongol invasions. With the exception of Bohemia, every state in the region had been attacked and drastically weakened by the Mongol onslaughts. Major cities in all these states were destroyed and their inhabitants slaughtered. Significant proportions of their armies died on the field of battle. All these states were plundered.

It took every Eastern European state decades to rebuild from the devastation—if they managed to rebuild. Poland and Hungary needed more than half a century to recoup their strength, and even when they rebuilt, neither state was as strong as it had previously been. Bulgaria was so enfeebled by the Mongol depredations that it never fully recovered.

Until the Mongol invasion, Eastern European civilization's development had outstripped that of the nations of Western Europe. While Western Europe periodically suffered from internecine strife during the Middle Ages, it escaped the sort of devastation that Eastern Europe suffered in the mid-thirteenth century at the hands of the Mongols. As it turned out, the thirteenth century became the pinnacle of Western European civilization's medieval development; since the Mongols decided to stop their European ventures with their ravaging of Eastern Europe, Western Europe escaped the depredations that would certainly otherwise have drastically changed the course of her medieval development—and the subsequent history of the West. Although Eastern Europe had been in the lead of Europe's cultural and civilizational development until the mid-thirteenth century, with the Mongol invasions, the region experienced such utter devastation that it lost that leadership to the western half of the continent. However much Eastern Europe managed to recover, it was never again to recapture the preeminence it had known before the Mongol invasion.

In a less wide-sweeping regard, it should be noted that because of the Mongol invasion, the state of Kievan Rus' disappeared, never to return. This magnificent state, with all its cultural accomplishments, sophistication, broad expanse of territory, and influence throughout Europe, was destroyed and wiped off the map. It was not forgotten, though. Soon after its demise, two rival states claimed to be its successor, ready to carry on its tradition. One of them was Galicia-Volhynia, in the southwest of contemporary Ukraine, but incorporated in the mid-fourteenth century into Poland. The other was far to the northeast, at Vladimir-Suzdal, which was soon replaced as the dominant power in the region and as the claimant to the heritage of Kievan Rus' by Muscovy.

This rivalry in claims to the heritage of Kievan Rus' would lead to hostilities in the not distant future. Staking a claim as the successor of Kievan Rus' meant not only intending to continue its traditions, but espousing a right to its former territories. These rival claims thus paved the way for the conflict that eventually erupted between Poland and Muscovy—a conflict continued by the Russian Empire that grew out of Muscovy. This tension between Poland and Russia—exacerbated by subsequent historical developments, to be sure, and by the religious divergence between the two large Slavic states—has lasted down to the present day and has shaped much of the history of Eastern Europe. Without a doubt, the Mongol invasion of Eastern Europe in the 1240s was a turning point in the history of Eastern Europe.

CHAPTER 11

The Battle of Kosovo (1389)

"Kosovo is many diverse things to different living Serbs,
but they all have it in their blood."[1]

IN 1999, KOSOVO WAS in the news every day. Pictures of Albanian inhabitants fleeing from Serb paramilitaries and NATO jets bombing Serbian targets filled television screens. What transpired in 1999 arose, not just from events of 1998 or 1997, or even from the breakup of Yugoslavia in 1991. The backdrop to the calamity of Kosovo in 1999 reaches back more than six hundred years, to the Battle of Kosovo in 1389. One cannot understand Kosovo 1999 without understanding Kosovo 1389, because the fourteenth-century battle has shaped the Serbs' understanding of themselves, their neighbors—and, even more broadly, of history and destiny.

Even the significance of the Battle of Kosovo can only be appreciated against the history that preceded it. For seven centuries, the Serbs had lived in the area—invited to invade it, they eventually erected a strong kingdom that rivalled what remained of the Byzantine Empire itself. Devoted to Eastern Orthodoxy, they saw themselves in 1389 as the last line of defense against the Ottoman Turks' infidel hordes threatening Christendom. All this has shaped the Serbs' approach to the Battle of Kosovo itself, and the battle has had a more dramatic influence on their subsequent development than anything else in their history.

Invited to Invade

The Serbs ended up in the region they now inhabit by invitation. The territory had historically been part of the Byzantine patrimony, but the Byzantine emperor invited the Serbs to take it for themselves in the early 600s. Invitations of this sort are hardly common occurrences in imperial histories, of

1. Dragnich and Todorovich, *The Saga of Kosovo*, 4.

course. This one came because of the extraordinary circumstances in which the Byzantine Empire then found itself.

In the first decade of the seventh century, Byzantium was passing through the throes of one of her worst periods. Its emperor, Phocas, had come to the throne by way of revolution. However highly his soldiers may have thought of him as a military officer, Phocas was totally unsuited to the task of governing a large empire. Fearing that leaders in the capital might become possible usurpers like himself, he engaged in a campaign of terror against any and all supposed rivals. In the meanwhile, he neglected territorial defenses, economic concerns, and the other tasks of government. With these egregious failures as emperor, whatever laws he enacted were disregarded by the citizenry. To the east, the reinvigorated Persian Empire was making significant inroads into Byzantine territory in Asia Minor, and the Balkan region was being ransacked by invaders from Asia.

In these desperate straits, many Byzantine notables looked for help to a highly respected governor, Heraclius. Invited by them to assume the reins of power, Heraclius eventually acquiesced, sailed to Byzantium, and—with Phocas deposed—was welcomed to the imperial throne. As emperor, Heraclius (r. 611–41) managed the remarkable feat of dealing with all the problems that had arisen; his accomplishments breathed new life into the Byzantine Empire.

For one thing, the internal structure of the government of the empire was no longer working. Heraclius introduced a new organization to the especially endangered regions; it proved successful and, in due course, was spread over the rest of the empire, offering excellent government and protection for the next several centuries. The second formidable challenge was the Persian menace to the east. Heraclius took responsibility for campaigns against them himself. Over the course of about fifteen years, his careful military strategy, plus astute diplomatic initiatives as unusual opportunities arose, led to a remarkable outcome: not only did Heraclius manage to defeat the Persians and reclaim Byzantine territory from them, but his victory was so overwhelming that he was asked to become the guardian and protector of the Persian monarch (against internal divisions that had broken out in the Persian Empire).

But the third major problem was beyond Heraclius's reach. Since his forces were tied up with the Persian challenge in the east, he could not himself attend to the marauding forces that had lately been wreaking havoc in the western Balkans. The Avars were the most recent in a long line of invaders from the depths of Central Asia.[2] The Avars had earlier

---

2. See the treatment above in chapter 10.

defeated the Huns and driven them westward. In due course, beaten by yet another Central Asian power, the Avars had swept over the steppes of Russia, through the plains of Ukraine, and plunged down into Romania and Bulgaria. They forced the Slavic inhabitants of the areas into their military forces and, with these reinforcements, ransacked the eastern Balkans and Greece, even marching up to the gates of Constantinople, before settling into the western Balkans and continuing their marauding from there. In the early 600s, they were causing problems in this area, devastating, looting, killing, and otherwise ravaging Byzantine territory. Phocas had done nothing to limit their depredations, and the menace had only grown worse. The Byzantine Empire had to deal with them, but Heraclius needed outside help. He got it from the Serbs and the Croats.

The Serbs and Croats were distinct but neighboring Slavic peoples who spoke the same language. They were still living north of the Carpathian Mountains, in the Slavs' original homeland. Emperor Heraclius contacted them, asking them to come to fight against the Avars and expel them from Byzantine territory. Their reward for doing so would be the emperor's welcome to settle into the territory they would thus cleanse. (They were also to swear loyalty to Byzantium.) This was an extraordinary invitation, by any measure. Recognizing the necessity of dealing with the Avars, though, what prompted Emperor Heraclius to extend this offer to these distant peoples?

The answer is simple but significant. The Serbs and Croats had defeated the Central Asian people who had earlier defeated the Avars, when that people was itself driven westward by yet others who had conquered them. We do not know who these people were, because the Serbs and Croats defeated them soundly and drove them back into the steppes. The point of significance is that the Serbs and the Croats were obviously excellent, fearsome warriors—a pattern quite other than what the rest of the early Slavs were known to be.[3] Early historical sources give no other information about the Serbs and the Croats apart from that, but Heraclius knew that much about them—and, for his purposes, that was enough. While the various Slavic peoples in due course did develop consider military ability—as noted above, the Avars had already forced some Slavs into battle under Avar leadership—the first known reference to the Serbs and the Croats fixed upon their military prowess. From the early 600s onward, through their conflict with the Avars, and down through their history to the present day, both Croats and Serbs have prided themselves, among other traits, on their ferocity as warriors. They have often been used by powerful neighbors

---

3. See the discussion above in chapter 2.

as border troops, whose fighting prowess would at least seriously delay the advance of any invaders.[4] In any event, Heraclius had heard about them and their fighting prowess, and he invited them to repeat their feat with the Avars: they did, and they stayed.[5]

The Serbs and Croats were also noteworthy for their physical size. Statistical comparisons have shown that they have long been among the largest people living in the whole of Europe;[6] not every Serb or Croat is imposing in size, of course, but in general they are tall and sturdily built,[7] a characteristic that itself contributes to both their fearsomeness as warriors and the way their military opponents think of them.[8]

The Serbs and Croats accepted Heraclius' invitation. Together they fought against the Avars and managed to drive them northward and westward, beyond the territories Byzantium claimed. In the late eighth century, Charlemagne's powerful Frankish armies moved against the Avars and destroyed their power base; significantly, Charlemagne enlisted the aid of the Croats (who lived nearest his realm) for this venture. In accordance with the promise Heraclius made, the Serbs and Croats were allowed to settle in the lands that basically approximate where their respective descendants live now, with the Croats to the north and west, the Serbs to the south and east. The Croats and the Serbs swore an oath of loyalty to Byzantium, and things settled down in that region, as the two peoples turned to the farming and herding occupations, for which Slavs were noted. But both peoples defended their lands well against invaders.

---

4. An example of this is found in what transpired around 1700, soon after the Habsburg and Ottoman empires signed a truce to end their recent warfare. Both had been impressed with the warring capabilities of the Serbs, and both empires settled Serbs along their respective borders, to serve as a first line of defense against any invasion by the other empire. In this way, Serbs ended up living in the Krajina of Croatia and in much of Bosnia, down to the 1990s.

5. This story is recounted in the remarkable work written by the Byzantine Emperor, Constantine Porphyrogenitus, *De Administrando Imperio*, 143–61.

6. Merrill points out that the Montenegrins—who consider themselves a distinct people, but who others say are a subset of the Serbs—are "the tallest Europeans" (*Only the Nails Remain*, 188).

7. This can be recognized by considering what has long been true in basketball, a game in which tall players (if they have skill) have great advantage. Prior to the collapse of the Communist bloc, the three top teams in Olympic basketball were the USA, Russia, and Yugoslavia. To this day, in the National Basketball Association, the largest single contingent of non–North American players comes from the former Yugoslavia.

8. Hall reflects on his height as a North American in comparison with commonly much taller Yugoslavs in his *The Impossible Country*, 20.

THE BATTLE OF KOSOVO (1389)

Division in the Land

Croats and Serbs were distinct peoples, as they both recognized. While they spoke (and still speak) the same language, known as "Serbo-Croatian" by Serbs or "Croato-Serbian" by Croats, the differences amount to little more than minor dialectical variations. However, in Croatia the language is printed with Latin characters (the ones used in the West); whereas Serbian is printed with Cyrillic ones. In that comparison is packed much of the history of the two peoples; how did that divergence come about?

The histories of the Serbs and the Croats have always been intertwined, for as far back as there are any records at all. The places where they settled, respectively, were on different sides of the ancient dividing line drawn in the Roman Empire, to distinguish its western and eastern segments.[9] Roman emperors long before Constantine had found it wise thus to distinguish the two segments of their realm, but the impact of that line has been even greater historically than those early emperors could have imagined. This awkward line runs right through the country known during most of the twentieth century as Yugoslavia. The Croats had settled on the west side of that line, although they were unaware of that fact; the Serbs ended up on its east side.

Because of where each settled, the two peoples were drawn in different directions—the Croats westward, toward Rome, and the Serbs eastward, toward Byzantium. The rivalry that had developed between Rome and Byzantium fleshed itself out in the two centers' respective attempts to evangelize and civilize the European continent.[10] Both Western Christianity and Eastern Christianity wanted to draw the peoples of Europe into Christianity, and each labored in this regard as far as the line of demarcation that had long before been settled. But each of them exercised influence sometimes a little beyond the old dividing line. Despite the Croats' declaration of loyalty to Byzantium, Rome sought especially hard to bring the Croats into Western Christianity. The Byzantines expected to work among the Serbs and bring them into Eastern Christianity; the Byzantines also expected the Croats to live up to their oath. Even so, Rome was geographically much closer to both peoples, and Byzantium—distracted by the many other demands of its empire—did not end up influencing the Croats and Serbs as much as they had originally intended. The Byzantines were irritated that the Croats, despite their oath of allegiance, were actually being drawn in the other direction.

---

9. See the treatments above in chapters 6 and 9.
10. See the treatments above in chapters 6 and 9.

The consequences were significant for both peoples. Croats were drawn into Western/Roman Christianity, and to this day Croats are overwhelmingly Roman Catholic in their religious commitment. The Serbs were evangelized by the Byzantines and Bulgaria and were thus drawn into Eastern/Byzantine Christianity. To this day, most Serbs adhere to the Orthodox church.

As regards nation-building, the Croats managed to attain statehood and independence by 910. In 925, their ruler, Tomislav, received coronation under papal auspices.[11] The kingdom of Croatia flourished for nearly two centuries, until 1102. The Croatian ruling dynasty had already died off, and the Croats hoped to avoid civil war among noble families who aspired to the royal dignity. They sought this via affiliation with the powerful nation of Hungary to their north and east; in 1102 that affiliation was made binding and permanent.[12]

The nation of Serbia flourished later. The earlier Croatian kingdom had included a fair amount of territory later incorporated within the Serbian state, but by the time Serbia developed as a state, those territories were no longer under either Croatian or Hungarian control. The Serbian state did not develop a lasting presence until nearly seventy years after the Croatian kingdom had ceased to exist: Serbia emerged as a genuine polity in 1168. Her ruler was crowned in 1219. Like Croatia, the Serbian kingdom flourished for about two centuries, until 1389 (although a drastically weakened rump Serbia survived for another seventy years).

So Croats and Serbs, neighbors in both north-central Eastern Europe and in the Balkans, each developed significant, powerful states—but they existed at different times. In the 1990s, when Yugoslavia broke apart and Croatia declared its independence, Croat leaders sought to reclaim, as the Croats' rightful patrimony, all the territory that had once been in the Croatian kingdom; this meant that Croatia wanted, in addition to the territory already recognized as hers, a considerable portion of contemporary Bosnia. Similarly, the Serbs laid claim to all the territory within the former Yugoslavia that had once been in the Serbian kingdom—which would have required a large portion of contemporary Bosnia, plus some of Croatia. These opposed and irreconcilable claims were among the reasons for the warfare that savaged the peoples of the former Yugoslavia in the first half of the 1990s.

But that warfare was not just another manifestation of the alleged "ancient enmities" or of the supposedly continuous warfare that has ostensibly

---

11. An imposing equestrian statue erected in the primary city square in Zagreb, Croatia, is dedicated to King (Croatian, *Kralj*) Tomislav: see picture 17.

12. For a brief reflection on how Croatia and Hungary viewed this affiliation and its implications, see the treatment in chapter 8.

marked Balkan history (as has been claimed in some interpretations). To be sure, there had been tensions between Croats and Serbs for centuries: although the two peoples had been neighbors and had fought together against the Avars, they had been drawn into the rival orbits of Rome and Byzantium, with their contrasting versions of culture and Christianity. Periodically, fighting broke out in the region, with Croats on one side and Serbs on the other; however, this was usually an offshoot of tensions between the larger rival civilizations of Western and Eastern Europe. This happened only occasionally: they have not been fighting for centuries. But the tensions between their respective Western and Eastern mentors rarely abated, so the pressure was fairly constant. The West/East rivalry has often been played out between the Croats and Serbs down to the present day. It contributed significantly to the conflict in Bosnia in the early 1990s.

Serbia's Empire

So far, this chapter has looked at the Croats and Serbs together because of their common background and in view of the historiographical convention of considering them vis-à-vis each other. Now, though, it is necessary to focus attention on Serbia and the fateful Battle of Kosovo in 1389. For that, it is important to stress the significance of the Nemanjić dynasty.

The Nemanjić line was the great dynasty of the Serbian state. During the more than two hundred years that Serbia flourished, she was ruled by one or another member of this dynasty. It was founded by Stjepan [Stephen] Nemanja (r. 1168–96). Serbia had already been drawn into the Eastern Christian faith by missionaries from Byzantium and Bulgaria; so, Serbia was firmly in the Eastern Christian camp by the time government consolidated itself in Serbia under him. He established an independent Serbia at a time when Byzantium had been weakened.

The last member of the Nemanjić line was Stjepan Uroš (r. 1355–71). From Nemanja through Uroš, the Nemanjić line was firmly committed to Christianity: Stjepan Nemanja, the founder of the dynasty, abdicated the throne later in his life in order to become a monk; and several of his descendants lavished considerable expense on the erection and beautification of churches and monasteries throughout the Serbian realm. Whatever else might be said about aspects of their lives and their interactions with others, the Serbian rulers always sought to be benefactors of the church—not only Eastern Christian, but also Western Christian.[13] The Nemanjić line was

---

13. E.g., Stjepan "the First-Crowned" (r. 1196–1228) sponsored church and monastic edifices for both Eastern and Western Christianity.

the great dynasty of Serbia; to this day, Serbs look back with pride on the Nemanjić family as the most glorious period of Serbia's history.

The most significant expansion of Serbia took place under Stjepan Dušan (r. 1331–55). Military adventurism rankles sensibilities in the present day: we do not look with favor on nations engaging in territorial acquisition, conquest, or military empire-building as appropriate. However, during the Middle Ages that was the pattern followed by most states. The way to measure the greatness of a nation was by its size and military power. By those standards, Stjepan Dušan was an exceptional ruler: his reign is viewed as the most glorious time of the Serbian nation, because he expanded the state considerably and brought it good government.[14] By 1334, he had doubled Serbia's size to include, not only Serbia, but all of Albania, North Macedonia, the western third of contemporary Bulgaria, and most of mainland Greece except the Peloponnesian peninsula. By the time of his death in 1355, he had built Serbia into the largest state in the southern half of Eastern Europe—including Byzantium.[15]

Under his leadership, Serbs gave proof of their reputation as tough warriors, and by 1355 Serbia was unquestionably the most powerful state in the region—and the only Christian nation left there powerful enough to stand in the way of the Ottoman Turks. Several other Christian nations had earlier arisen—Byzantium, Bulgaria, and Croatia. By the mid-1300s, though, Byzantium had been weakened, Bulgarian power had faltered, and Croatia had been subsumed into Hungary. So the Serbian kingdom was the only one left strong enough to offer significant opposition to the Ottoman Turks. In 1371, Serbs and Ottoman Turks confronted each other in battle for the first time, near the Maritsa River in Thrace. This was to the east of Serbia's greatest strength, but Serbia felt compelled to fight the Turks there because of the danger they posed to Christian Europe.

Who were the Ottoman Turks? They were the new power in Asia Minor (known today as "Turkey," after them). A preceding Turkish people (the Seljuks) had earlier taken control of the Holy Land—a development that triggered the Crusades.[16] In the Mongol invasions, though, the Seljuk domination among the Turks had been brought to an end,[17] and several Turkish tribes fought to attain prominence; in due course, the followers of Osmanli

---

14. The original of a law promulgated and signed by Stjepan Dušan can be seen in the Serbian Orthodox church's museum in Belgrade.

15. This was about a century after the Byzantines had taken back their capital from the crusaders (in 1261), but Byzantium had been drastically weakened (see the treatment above in chapter 9) and had not recovered her former greatness.

16. See the treatment above in chapter 9.

17. See the treatment above in chapter 10.

prevailed. He consolidated his rule over other the others, and the Turks were hereafter known, after him, as "Ottoman" Turks. They became a significant military power themselves: they regularly fought with Byzantium, resulting in Ottoman gains and Byzantine losses in Asia Minor. Committed Muslims, the Ottoman Turks sought to extend the sway of Islam as far as possible. They wanted Byzantium—and Europe.

In 1371, the Ottoman Turks faced off against the Serbs at the Battle of the Maritsa. The Turks had already established a foothold in Europe. With Byzantium opposed to them, that would not have been easy; however, events within the Byzantine Empire itself had afforded them the opportunity they had long looked for. The Byzantines had reclaimed Constantinople from the Western Crusaders, but Byzantium was a weakened power, its treasury had been depleted, and there was considerable tension as to who ought to be emperor. In due course, a civil war broke out among the Byzantines during the 1350s over the question. Both sides needed fighting forces, but one of the claimants did not have a private army, so he sought to hire mercenaries. Some of the best available fighters were Ottoman Turks, and he secured their services. He allowed them to use a major fortress he controlled in Gallipoli, in northern Greece, as their base of operations. With their formidable help, he won the imperial throne. When the civil war was over, he urged them to give Gallipoli back to him, leave Europe, and return to Asia Minor; however, they declined to do so.

The Ottoman Turks kept Gallipoli as their initial base of operations for campaigns in Europe. The Byzantine ruler now was satisfied to be on the throne, but he and other Christian rulers recognized that they had a major problem, because the Turks started to move out from Gallipoli in campaigns into Eastern Europe. First they marched against Bulgaria, repeatedly defeating its forces. The southern half of Bulgaria fell under their control by the 1360s; by 1396, they would conquer all of Bulgaria.

As the Turkish strength in Eastern Europe grew, it became obvious that their only major opponent would be Serbia, the last major Christian power left in the Balkans. The Turks had already swept through and subjugated southern Bulgaria, and all the Balkans were endangered. So, in 1371 the Serbs marched east into Thrace into the territory near the heartland of what was Ottoman Europe at the time, to face the Turks in battle there.

The results of the 1371 battle shook Serbia to its foundations: its forces were defeated, and Stjepan Uroš was slain. His death brought an end to the Nemanjić dynasty, the only ruling line Serbia had ever known. Given the danger now facing the Serbs, a more devastating turn of events could hardly be imagined. The Ottoman Turks had won the battle, but at great cost. After a period to replenish their forces, they swept through the rest of Bulgaria, consolidating their control over the rest of that state. It required no great military insight to realize they were not going to stop their conquests with Bulgaria; Serbia would be their next major focus.

This all threw the Serbian kingdom into turmoil. It was perhaps not surprising that rivalry broke out among the nobles for leadership. To be sure, a distant relative of the Nemanjić line, Prince Lazar, received official recognition as the new leader of the country; however, the nobles were indifferent to his pleas to organize against the common foe. Instead, nobles jockeyed with each other for increasing areas of influence within the Serbian territories, basically ignoring the Ottoman threat.

Confusion and decentralization weakened the Serbian Empire from 1371 to 1389. While none of the nobles intended it, their rivalries and their undermining of Prince Lazar played into the Ottoman Turks' hands: after securing control over southern Bulgaria and so weakening the remaining Bulgarian state that it could cause no danger to them, the Ottoman Turks proceeded westward and overran one after another of the Serbian nobles' territories. The Turks marched through and took control of Greece, North Macedonia, and Albania. Finally, it became obvious to the remaining Serbs they would have to stand together and face the Turks again. That is what they did at the Battle of Kosovo in 1389.

June 28, 1389, and Its Aftermath

By the late 1380s, it had become obvious to most of the Serbian nobles that they ought to start listening to Prince Lazar's pleas to stand together. He urged them to unity, as the only way to save the Serbian nation and stop the advance of the Ottoman Turks. He appealed to a well-known declaration from the patron saint of the nation, St. Sava: "*Samo sloga Srbina spašava*"—"Only with unity will Serbs survive," a declaration that has echoed down the corridors of Serbian history. Lazar also appealed for help from other Christian powers in Bosnia, Hungary, and the Christian West, urging them to fight alongside the Serbian forces against the invading Muslims. Many Christians already saw the Ottoman Turks as the forces of Antichrist.[18] It seemed obvious to Lazar that Christian forces should

---

18. St. Paul had warned that in the future a great opponent to Christ and the church would arise (see 2 Thess 2:1–11, where this one is called "the Man of Lawlessness"), and St. John had warned about "antichrists" (see 1 John 2:18–19, 22; 4:3). Later Christians often saw these texts (and "the Beast" warned about in Rev 13:1–10) as referring to a figure whom they called "the Antichrist." Although St. John did not speak of a single great opponent of Christ and the church, he ended up providing the language that later Christians used to describe such a figure.

unitedly oppose the Ottoman Turks, who endangered not only Serbia but all of Christian Europe. The approaching battle would determine whether the Muslim forces would take over all of Southeastern Europe; if they did, the rest of Europe lay open to them. However, despite his earnest appeals, only a handful of other warriors came to fight alongside the Serbs; basically, the Serbs stood alone against the Ottoman Turks.

The battle broke out on June 28, 1389, on the field of Kosovo-Polje ("the field of blackbirds"). The battle lasted most of a hot day, under a blazing sun—the best forces of the Ottoman armies against the pride and flower of the Serbian military. The battle ebbed and flowed, with first one and then the other side achieving advantage; as the day wore on, though, the momentum of battle swung increasingly in favor of the Turks and against the Serbs. Determined to turn the tide of battle, Miloš Obilić, a relative of Prince Lazar, came up with a desperate plan. He passed himself off to Ottoman leaders as a turncoat who would advise the sultan, Murad I, how to defeat his countrymen, promising that he could deliver the rest of the Serbs into the sultan's hands. These Ottoman leaders took him to the sultan to confer with him in the sultan's tent. Obilić urged that he would have to speak with the sultan in absolute privacy; Murad acquiesced and dismissed everyone else. Alone in the tent with the sultan, Obilić pulled out a dagger he had secreted in his robes and killed the Ottoman ruler. Clearly, he had no hope of escape; however, he reckoned that the results of his desperate self-sacrifice might throw the Turkish forces into confusion and turn the tide of battle again in the Serbs' favor.

Once the assassination was discovered, though, the sultan's son Bayezid quickly and effectively took command of the Ottoman forces, and Miloš Obilić suffered a long and excruciating execution. Bayezid managed to rally the Turkish forces, who eventually won the battle of Kosovo. By its end, Serbia's forces had been defeated, most of her knights and warriors had been slain, and many of her leaders had been killed. In due course, the Ottoman Turks found the badly wounded Prince Lazar. He was brought before Bayezid and slowly put to death.

Reliquary with the remains of Prince Lazar, in the Serbian Orthodox church's museum in Belgrade. This reliquary was carried throughout Serbia for veneration in 1989, the six hundredth anniversary of the Battle of Kosovo.

The Battle of Kosovo ended with the defeat of the Serbs, but they had made the Turkish forces pay dearly for their victory: the battle cost the Ottoman Turks so many dead and wounded that they were unable to proceed further into Serbia, but had to retire to Bulgaria to recover from their losses and prepare for later campaigns. Even so, Serbia had been overwhelmed, and the Serbs lost their freedom. With the defeat of the Serbs, the Ottoman Turks were poised to roll over the rest of the Balkans and on into Europe, once they could regroup. In due course, they rebuilt their forces, and then conquered the rest of Bulgaria (1396), subjugated the rest of Serbia (by 1459), and absorbed Bosnia (1463) and Herzegovina (1466), as well. The Turks ruled over the southern half of Eastern Europe for several centuries; the Turkish Empire lasted until the twentieth century.

During that extended period of time, Serbs and other Christian peoples of the Balkans were subjected to brutal repression. The Turks tolerated no manifestation of national loyalty: no printing presses could produce Serbian or any other national literature; no ethnic dress could be worn; no schooling was allowed; no teaching of the language in written form was permitted; and no clubs or other organizations that might foment any kind of yearning for freedom from the Turkish yoke were permitted. Anything tending toward national awareness or longing for independence was ruthlessly repressed. This was, of course, not distinctive to the Ottoman Turks: other empires have also sought to squelch such longings. But the Turkish repression was especially restrictive. The only freedom accorded the Christians of the Balkans was the freedom to worship in their churches.

While the Ottoman Turks engaged in no religious proselytism, they nonetheless offered many blandishments to convert to Islam. If a Christian became a Muslim, his taxes were drastically reduced; moreover, conversion to Islam opened the possibility of improving one's social standing, a possibility not open to those who remained Christian. Further, Muslims were not subject to the *devsçhirme*—the "child tax," to which Serbs were especially exposed. The child tax involved Ottoman forces taking away young boys ten years of age or less, who would be impressed into the sultan's service in Constantinople. There was rarely any warning; this might not occur for several years but then happen in recurring years. Turkish forces would sweep into villages, pick the boys they wanted, and march them off to Constantinople. There they would be converted to Islam, raised as Muslims, and trained to be janissaries—ruthless fighters, the toughest forces in the sultan's army. The *devsçhirme* was never demanded of Muslims—only from Christians. With all these enticements, it is striking that, in nearly four centuries in Serbia (and throughout most of the rest of the Balkans, as well), few Christians converted to Islam.

The Epic of Kosovo

During the dark centuries of Ottoman oppression, the story of Kosovo was told and retold in Serbian families and among the Serbian people. Eventually, it was reduced to writing and became the Serbs' national epic. In addition to presenting the battle itself, the epic elaborated the significance of the battle.[19]

---

19. It is available in English translation in Velimirovich and Popovich, *The Mystery and Meaning*.

According to the presentation in the epic, on the night before the battle, Prince Lazar received a vision. A gray falcon came to him, bearing an offer from God. Prince Lazar could fight and would defeat the Ottoman Turks and Serbia would continue as a nation, with Lazar enjoying wide influence and power; the price would be, though, that both he and his people would fall under divine judgment. Alternatively, Prince Lazar and his forces could fight the Turks, but the Serbs would lose the battle: the Serbian nation would succumb to the Ottoman advance and be ruthlessly ruled by their conquerors; but both Lazar and his people would win a heavenly kingdom, given to those who are faithful to Christ. The epic declares that Prince Lazar chose the heavenly kingdom, that he advised his nobles of the vision and the plan, and that he encouraged them to fight bravely the next day, since they were fighting for the honor of Christ's name against the forces of Antichrist. Their suffering would be great, both in the battle and in coming generations; but their reward would be greater—a heavenly kingdom, and the promise that God himself would honor the Serbs in the future for remaining faithful.

This was the ultimate background for the battle, as the Serbs came to understand it. Through the Epic of Kosovo, the Serbs learned to view their defeat as ultimately a victory, offering themselves unreservedly to the cause of Christ. Like St. Paul, their strength would be perfected in weakness;[20] in the footsteps of Christ himself, their self-sacrifice would issue into resurrection to greater life. Even through the darkest hours of foreign oppression, Serbs could—and, via the Epic of Kosovo, did—retain hope for the future. The epic assured them that, whatever their oppressors might do, Serbia would be reborn and God himself would honor her. The Serbian people, down through multiple generations, have taken the Epic of Kosovo to heart.

How did this affect them? First of all, it kept the memory of the Serbian nation alive among them. The Turks allowed no manifestation of national longings or loyalty whatsoever, but while they could regulate what went on publicly, they could not control what went on at the hearth. The Epic of Kosovo was sung and sung again, memorized and passed down through the generations, and elaborated. It became the historical school of the Serbian people, teaching them how to understand who they were—and what the rest of the world was like. They learned their sense of history, their sense of themselves, and their sense of others largely from the Epic of Kosovo. It encouraged them to hang together through the long night of Turkish repression, confident that God would eventually honor them. God would resurrect the Serbian nation; someday the Battle of Kosovo would be overturned.

20. See 2 Cor 12:8–12.

With all this, secondly, Kosovo became to the Serbs a holy place, where their ancestors—and, as they understood the implications of the epic, they themselves—had sacrificed themselves and their nation for the sake of Christianity. As they learned from the Epic of Kosovo, they could have received an earthly kingdom but chose a heavenly one instead. The Serbs learned that their ancestors—and, again, they themselves—had heeded Christ's warning not to lose their soul by trying to gain the world.[21] All this was tied to Kosovo: for the Serbs, it was a consummately holy place, where their ancestors' blood was shed for the sake of Christ. Indeed, Kosovo became the holiest place of the Serbian nation.

This was only made more poignant when the Turks, sensing what Kosovo might come to mean to the Serbs, expelled Serbs from it and populated it with Albanians and others. While Albanians might settle in Kosovo, for the Serbs that could only be a temporary situation, another attempt by Antichrist's forces to thwart divine purposes for the Serbs. As the holiest place of the Serbian nation, the Serbs must take Kosovo back. From their perspective, developed over centuries by taking the Epic of Kosovo to heart, Serbs must make Kosovo the center of their nation again if they were to be faithful to God and to their ancestors. From that perspective, if Kosovo was where God had used them for his glory in 1389, Kosovo would be where God would honor them in the future. Collectively, the Serbs came to understand that they must not rest until Kosovo was again the center of their nation. So, when Slobodan Milošević proclaimed to Serb residents of Kosovo in 1987 that they would never again be beaten in Kosovo, that shrewd manipulator of public opinion played on the hopes and fears of the whole Serb nation.

Finally it is important to consider the significance for Serbian self-understanding of the declaration of St. Sava, repeated by Prince Lazar: "*Samo sloga Srbina spašava*"—"Only with unity will Serbs survive." The Battle of Kosovo had borne out the veracity of this ancient utterance, and from the Epic of Kosovo the declaration took deep root in Serb minds. That utterance shaped how Serbs learned over the centuries to view themselves and others in this broken world: it called Serbs to hang together and, conversely, it warned them against putting trust in others. The slogan was often used later on as a rallying cry for Serbian ventures in their nineteenth-century attempts to break free from Ottoman control, and in the challenges of the two world wars of the twentieth century, the declaration called Serbs to unity in whatever their nation faced. Conversely, it taught them not to expect help from others: Serbs had not received it from other ostensibly Christian

---

21. Matt 16:26.

nations at the Battle of Kosovo in 1389, and subsequent history had too often confirmed the truth of the declaration.[22]

But while that declaration—"Only with unity will Serbs survive"—could call Serbs to work with each other, the warning about others could become a call to turn from others. At times, *Samo sloga Srbina spašava* has come to mean, for some of them, "Serbs against the world." During the 1990s, in the tensions and fighting in the former Yugoslavia, the world had opportunity to see some of the effects of the Battle of Kosovo of 1389, as the Serbs sought to re-establish a "Greater Serbia" and to cleanse Kosovo of the Albanians who live there. Seemingly indifferent to world opinion, the Serbs pursued their goals—goals learned, in large part, from the Epic of Kosovo. The 1999 conflict in Kosovo has come to an end, but the future there is uncertain. Unquestionably, the Battle of Kosovo was a turning point in the history of Eastern Europe.

---

22. In the Serbian reading of their history, "the West" has repeatedly (about a dozen times) left Serbia "out to dry," rather than helping it or coming to its defense; thus, the slogan has become for the Serbs a historical maxim, as well.

— CHAPTER 12 —

The Battle of White Mountain (1620)

> "The battle of Bílá hora—the battle of White Mountain—on the outskirts of Prague on 8 November 1620 . . . settled the fate of the Kingdom of Bohemia for the next three centuries; it was without any doubt the most cataclysmic event in modern Czech history."[1]

To appreciate the significance of the Battle of White Mountain in 1620, it is necessary to consider the prior history of the Bohemians (with the Moravians, now known as Czechs) vis-à-vis their neighbors, the Germans. Of course, Eastern European nations are distinct entities in their own right, not just smaller-print footnotes to powerful nearby states. Even so, a smaller nation often ends up having its history profoundly influenced by its strong neighbors.

Bohemia and the Germans: A Constant Theme

That was the case for the early Slavic peoples: already in prehistoric times, they experienced contact with Germanic ones, who had a significant impact on the early Slavs.[2] In recorded history, that tension has continued often enough. How has it manifested itself in the relationships between the Germans and the Bohemians?

Scholars have minted the phrase, "*Drang nach Osten*" (German for "push to the east") to describe a consistent pattern: German rulers seeking to expand their territories in the only direction they could readily move, eastwards. Significantly, Bohemia was immediately east of their borders,

---

1. Sayer, *The Coasts of Bohemia*, 45.
2. See the treatment above in chapter 2.

and so was always the first in line in this regard, the Slavic nation most exposed to that drive toward the east.

This was already evident in the first recorded encounter between Germanic and Slavic peoples during Charlemagne's time. Due to the dispersion of the original Germanic inhabitants away from their original homeland, some Slavic peoples had been able to spread westward into the vacated territories.[3] Those who did so are called, collectively, West Slavs; the ones furthest to the West were the Bohemians, whose settlements reached all the way to the Elbe River. Across the river were Germanic peoples.

By subduing the Saxons, Charlemagne brought the entire territory from the Atlantic Ocean to the Elbe River under his control. If he had desired to continue to expand his realm, the next obvious target would have been Bohemian settlements across the river. However, with Charlemagne's practice of consolidating his rule over any conquered territory, he was in no rush to move against the Bohemians. Whatever may have been his intentions with regard to them, he did not cross the Elbe River.

At his death in 814, Charlemagne passed the large Frankish realm into the control of his son. An ineffectual ruler, at his death, he divided the realm among his three sons. The easternmost section was the only one with any possibility of expansion, and within a couple of decades, the ruler of that section crossed the Elbe River and forced the Bohemians into vassal status. Soon thereafter, the ruler—Louis the German—managed to push the nascent Moravian state into a similar relationship.[4] For our purposes, it is important to note that even before the Bohemians had the opportunity to coalesce into a state themselves, they had been brought under Germany's domination. In due course, though, Bohemians established their own state within the expanding German empire—a state that managed to attain significant status within that empire.

Bohemia's Success within the German Empire

In 906, the neighboring Slavic polity, Moravia, was destroyed. Subsequently, during the tenth century, Bohemia coalesced into a nation under Václav I. He became the founder of the Přemyslid dynasty, which ruled Bohemia for the next four hundred years. While Bohemia remained part of the German empire, under Václav and his successors Bohemia was able to rule itself to a significant degree while nonetheless remaining under the ultimate rule of the German emperor.

3. See the treatment in chapter 2.
4. See the treatment in chapter 6.

In 1085 a Přemyslid, Vratislav II, was crowned king. The Bohemian rulers had made the best of their situation within the empire and had remained loyal servants of the emperor. In 955, the Bohemian ruler had fought alongside the German emperor, Otto I, to defeat the marauding forces of the Magyars[5] (who eventually coalesced into the kingdom of Hungary). This brought an end to the Magyars' banditry in and terrorizing of Western Europe. Bohemian imperial loyalty had continued for another century and more; that faithfulness to the German emperor culminated in the Bohemian ruler standing beside Henry IV during his conflict with Pope Gregory VII in the Investiture Controversy.[6]

As sovereign of the Holy Roman Empire, Henry IV had an ongoing conflict during the 1070s and 1080s with Pope Gregory VII over who would control the appointments to the high-ranking church offices in the Holy Roman Empire. In that time, archbishops and bishops played a large role, not only in the church, but also in civil government. Henry IV wanted to control what was going on in his empire, and he adamantly believed that he should appoint these people because they had so much civic responsibility. The pope, of course, saw things differently: archbishops and bishops were, first of all and ultimately, hierarchs within the church, responsible for her well-being; so, it should be the church that appoints these people. Neither Henry IV nor Gregory VII would back down.

The ruler of Bohemia was in a difficult spot. The Bohemians had been drawn into the Western Christian orbit sometime during the ninth century, through the work of German missionaries. Consequently, the Bohemian ruler and his people were in the Roman obedience, but Bohemia was a state within the German empire, and Henry IV was the Bohemian ruler's sworn lord. Somehow, through all this, the Bohemian ruler managed to be loyal to the pope, but in civil matters to support Henry IV. In view of this loyalty, manifested in various ways during the controversy, Emperor Henry IV authorized Vratislav II to receive the royal dignity in 1085.

That was an extraordinary situation, but it was not quite a gratuitous reward for his loyal servant. In 1076, Pope Gregory VII had authorized crowning the Polish ruler, Bolesław II, for his staunch support for the pope and his opposition to Henry IV. The emperor took this as an affront, of course; he recognized that this papally sanctioned coronation of a Polish ruler put an awkward roadblock in the way of further German expansion eastward. But he could counter the papal move with one of his own if he authorized the coronation of the ruler of Bohemia, the state adjacent to

---

5. See the treatment in chapter 10.
6. See the treatment in chapter 8.

Poland. Henry IV's purpose was clear when he had Vratislav II crowned as "King of Bohemia *and Poland*": the title was an open invitation for the Bohemian king to march against the neighboring state. However, Vratislav II and all his successors never sought to establish their claim to the latter part of the title.

Even so, in the huge, ramshackle federation of the Holy Roman Empire (with more than 320 states, plus more than sixty-five free imperial cities) Bohemia thenceforth had a distinctive honor: apart from the emperor himself, the only crowned monarch was Bohemia's ruler.

The kings of Bohemia were crowned in St. Vitus Cathedral in the Hradčany Castle in Prague (seen here from across the Vltava River).

This made Bohemia the most exalted state in the entire federation: her king was second in dignity and status only to the emperor. So, in all the processionals and affairs of state concerning the empire, the Bohemian king always ranked just below the emperor. With her own crowned monarch, Bohemia held a dignity equal to that of Europe's other great nations. To be sure, Bohemia was part of the Holy Roman Empire, but her ruler was a king—just like the King of England, the King of France, and the Holy Roman Emperor.

During the fourteenth century, Bohemia's status was enhanced further when her king also became the Holy Roman Emperor. In that empire, the imperial dignity was not a dynastic right, passed on from father to son; rather, the emperor was elected. By the fourteenth century, the right of choosing the next emperor had devolved upon seven privileged states: their rulers constituted the electoral council that picked the next emperor. So, when an emperor died or abdicated, an election was held—sometimes the son of the former ruler would be elected, and sometimes someone else would be chosen. The latter happened in the mid-1300s.

In 1347, Charles I had become King of Bohemia, putting him second in status only to the emperor himself. The next year, in 1348, he was chosen Holy Roman Emperor, becoming Charles IV. With this elevation of her monarch, Bohemia—a Slavic nation within an overwhelmingly German empire—was extraordinarily privileged. In the face of longstanding German/Slav tensions, Bohemia became undeniably the leading state of the empire. Charles I/IV went on to make that unmistakably clear: he declared that, among the seven states whose rulers chose the emperor, Bohemia was the premier state—first in status and rank. At subsequent electoral meetings of this privileged council, the president of the council of electors would be the King of Bohemia.

Statue of King Charles I/IV in Prague.

So, by 1378, when Charles I/IV died, Slavic Bohemia was the leading state in the entire Holy Roman Empire, both in view of her ruler being a crowned king and because of Bohemia's status among the electors who would choose the next emperor. Even so, by this time, tensions had developed between German and Slavic inhabitants of Bohemia. Those tensions exploded in the fifteenth century.

Bohemian Tensions with Germans

While Bohemia had enjoyed remarkable status within the German empire, problems had been developing between Germans and Bohemians within the state. As time passed, the tensions grew in significance for the Bohemians.

During the twelfth century, some Bohemian kings, while recognizing the status their state enjoyed, also realized that the country was not as economically advanced as their neighbors to the west, the Germans. To overcome this disparity, Bohemian kings invited Germans to come and build up agricultural and production enterprises. The kings also saw that the Germans were more accomplished in their trade practices than the Bohemians, so the kings also invited other Germanic colonists to settle in Bohemia to improve that area of endeavor. The Bohemian rulers sought thus to kick-start their state's economy. While those invitations proved to be successful in economic regards, the results ended up with some unintended consequences, which the Bohemian citizenry came to resent intensely.

The upshot of these twelfth-century invitations was that, by the fourteenth century, Germans dominated Bohemia. In the economy, Germans superintended and controlled trade and production: Germans ran the big farms and the factories, and Bohemians worked for the numerically much smaller upper crust of Germans. Bohemians bristled that they were servants in their own land to people who—however long those Germans and their ancestors had lived in Bohemia—maintained a distinct status, kept to themselves, and spoke their own language. The Bohemians perceived the Germans as foreign interlopers.

Secondly, the Bohemians recognized that the Germans' economic importance gave them considerable influence on the government. While the state had Bohemian kings, their advisors naturally came from their successful subjects—and the people dominating the economy were Germans. It was not as if there were no Bohemian advisors, but—at least in widespread Bohemian estimation—a disproportionate number of them were Germans. To Bohemians, this seemed like foreigners ruling them, especially when governmental decisions favored those shaping the economy.

A further irritant was, in the third place, that along with the German influence on the economy and government, Germans also dominated the upper levels of the church's hierarchy in Bohemia. Archbishops, bishops, and the abbots of major monasteries were, almost without exception, men of German extraction. What typically happened during the Middle Ages throughout Western Europe was that leaders of the church were chosen from among noble families. In Bohemia, this meant, though, that virtually every abbot, bishop, and archbishop came from a German family. In Bohemian perspective, given other German/Bohemian irritants, this was especially onerous: even the church, God's house, was dominated by these "foreigners." The Bohemians were indignant that while Bohemia was a great state within the Holy Roman Empire, in reality the Bohemians were dominated by the Germans.

What made the church problem even worse was the life-style of the church's prelates. This was not a complaint exclusive to Bohemia; indeed, during the fourteenth and fifteenth centuries, Western Europe was deluged by a flood of anti-clerical sentiment focused especially on the hierarchy.[7] Much of the leadership of Western Christianity was not particularly noted for its piety and godliness. Most of the leaders were from noble families and, like their siblings, enjoyed falconry and hunting; many bishops focused more on typical noble pastimes than they did on their ecclesiastical duties.

Contributing to this development was the fact that, over the centuries, the church had been deeded an enormous amount of land. Repeatedly, wills included the church in the disbursement of estates. The church needed people to work all this land, of course; but the land and its produce belonged to her. Not surprisingly, the land donated to the church was of prime quality: after all, giving something less than the best to God's church on earth was hardly a way of impressing God with one's commitment, and such carelessness could have devastating consequences for one's afterlife.

The result of this ongoing practice was that, by the fourteenth century, the church owned one-third of all the arable land in the nations within Western Christianity. This entailed for the hierarchs responsibility for managing the land, its produce, and its workers—much like those prelates' brothers in the noble families. Not surprisingly, such focus of hierarchs' attention kept them distracted from the spiritual responsibilities that should have concerned them.

---

7. During the last four decades, scholarship of the late medieval and the Reformation periods has closely examined the widespread anti-clericalism that marked most of northern Europe. For a recent discussion, see Payton, *Getting the Reformation Wrong*, 41–43, 247–48.

This was a problem in every state. But in Bohemia resentment for these hierarchical failings was intensified by the German/Bohemian tensions. While corruption was rife in the church throughout Europe, in Bohemia it was even more resented because the church's prelates were German—another manifestation of the German domination over the Bohemians.

In the fifteenth century, this resentment all found its outlet in the rebellion that broke out in the wake of the Jan [John] Hus affair. Hus was a priest, but also a theology professor at St. Charles University in Prague. In due course, he was chosen to serve as university rector—a one-year position roughly equivalent to the post of principal or president of a university today. He also served as chaplain at the university.

A Bohemian himself, Hus knew the seething Bohemian/German tensions. As a priest and theologian, though, his primary concern was with the corruption of the church: he was not first of all concerned about German influence within Bohemia. From his perspective, as he read the Christian Scriptures and reflected on what the church should be teaching and doing, he found one flaw after another—a whole series of problems, from corruption and financial mismanagement, lack of spiritual concern, all the way to skewed doctrinal teaching and questionable liturgical practices. From a host of angles, he saw things that in his estimation needed to be changed. Priests and theologians elsewhere in Europe had recognized some of the same problems, but Hus began to speak out openly and to write about them; he ended up publishing a series of works examining and criticizing the contemporary church for her grievous failings.

While people in Bohemia largely agreed with him and saw the point he was making, his criticism—directed as it was against a church with a hierarchy dominated by Germans—became a catalyst for the general Bohemian resentment against Germans. The situation became so tense that a number of German professors and students left St. Charles University to found a German university in Leipzig during the early 1410s. Some German nobles and economic magnates thought it wise to leave Bohemia, as well.

In any event, Hus became not so much a spokesman against Germans himself, but he was the one around whom anti-German resentment coalesced. Bohemians appropriated his outspoken criticisms of the church as an outlet for their opposition to the Germans. The tensions in Bohemia, and especially the challenge to the church there, became well known throughout Europe and led to what happened in 1415.

Serious problems existed at that time in the Western church: beyond the obvious problem of having three rival popes, there was an almost universal clamor for reform from top to bottom of the church (the demand for *reformatio in capite et membris*). Ecclesiastical dilatoriness provoked civil authorities to call a general council of the church to deal with the problems: the Council of Constance met from 1415 to 1418. Constance tried to get the church back on track, by straightening out the papal morass and correcting some of the corruption that had so infuriated much of Western Christendom.

The Council of Constance also needed to deal with the problem of Jan Hus. While the council might have welcomed his vigorous criticism of some of the problems within the church, the stridency of his declarations raised concerns, and some of the positions he had propounded evoked suspicions. Furthermore, the situation in Bohemia had become more than just an issue of faith and practice, and the council fathers were concerned that criticism of the church not engender problems of other sorts. So, the council sent for Hus, summoning him to appear at the council to explain what he believed and answer questions about his vigorous criticism of the church. Hus and his followers hesitated for him to go until the Holy Roman Emperor, Sigismund, promised Hus a "safe conduct"—meaning that Hus could go to the council and respond to questions, but that whatever the decision about his views would be, he would be able to return to Bohemia in safety. That was the promise; that was not how things worked out.

Hus agreed to go to Constance, even though he and many of his followers still had reservations about the promise. In Constance, what was supposed to be a discussion of his views became a trial for heresy. Hus was not given a fair hearing, by any standards of justice. He was accused of saying things he probably had not said, and meanings were read into his statements by his accusers he certainly had not intended. At the end of the trial, he was summarily condemned as a heretic and sentenced to be burned at the stake. The council fathers knew that the emperor had sworn that Hus would be able to return to Bohemia safely, no matter the outcome of the interviews in Constance. However, the council fathers reasoned that Hus—who had sworn faithfulness to God at his ordination as a priest—had broken his word to God, so no one need keep a promise made to Hus. Thus, the council trumped the emperor's safe conduct. On July 6, 1415, Hus was executed, despite the emperor's promise.

When news of Hus' execution reached Bohemia, his followers became furious. To them this was not only a violation of a promise by the *German* emperor, but a trick foisted on Bohemia by a church council meeting at a *German* city. (Constance was then still part of the Holy Roman Empire.) A revolt broke out in Bohemia; the Hussite Revolt lasted for most of the next two decades, to the mid-1430s. Early on in the revolt, Emperor Sigismund sent his forces into Bohemia to quell it. However, the ragtag bands of Hussites defeated the imperial forces, not only in the first attempt, but repeatedly over the next twenty years. Even when other nations' forces were brought in to augment those of the emperor, the Hussites prevailed. In fact, they became so successful that they invaded surrounding territories and added them temporarily to Bohemia. From the perspective of the church and the emperor, the situation had gotten entirely out of hand.

The Church of Our Lady Before Týn, in Prague, which served as a major center of the Hussite Revolt.

Ultimately, the Hussites won the war and achieved a measure of independence in both church and state. In the mid-1430s, as a way of achieving Bohemia's reintegration into the Holy Roman Empire and the Western church, the empire allowed Bohemians a greater degree of self-government, and the church granted certain concessions in liturgical practices that were approved only for Bohemia. That satisfied the large majority of the Hussites, and the revolt came to an end.

So, during the fifteenth century, Bohemia knew great achievements.[8] The sixteenth century proved to be the beginning of the endgame, however. With the nailing of his ninety-five theses on the church door in Wittenberg, Martin Luther inaugurated the Protestant Reformation; soon enough, Bohemia was swept up into it. Although the Protestant Reformation initially had an unmistakable (and undeniably unwelcome) German tinge to it, the descendants of the Hussites soon recognized significant commonality between

---

8. The Czechs have always looked back to the period of the Hussite movement and rebellion as the greatest period in their history.

what Hus had taught and some of the things being urged by the Protestant Reformers. When, in due course, the Reformed (as distinguished from the Lutheran [and, thus, *German*]) wing of the Reformation developed, with its more international appeal,[9] it is perhaps not surprising that Bohemia embraced the Reformed version of the Protestant Reformation.[10]

The Bohemian nobles—the new ruling class, spawned from the Hussite Revolt and the 1430s settlement with the empire—especially turned to the Protestant Reformation; indeed, the overwhelming preponderance of them became Protestant. The conversion was no doubt genuine; commonality between Hus' teachings and those of the Protestant Reformers struck the Bohemians. The fact, though, that the Holy Roman Emperor, Charles V—both their sovereign and Luther's—opposed Luther and set himself forward as the champion of the Roman church made the choice for the Protestant Reformation even more attractive. The Bohemian nobles were again refusing to be dominated by Germans. In addition to typical Bohemian/German tension, a recent political development triggered this response.

In 1515, a "Family Compact" (also known as the "Treaty of Vienna") had been signed. This document was not a treaty to end a war, but an agreement between two ruling families. One was the family that ruled over both Bohemia and Hungary. (The two states had agreed to share a monarch; this sort of thing had happened before in Europe.)[11] Even though Bohemia and Hungary remained distinct states, they had the same king. The other family was the Habsburgs, who ruled the small neighboring principality of Austria.[12] The rulers recognized that if a ruler died childless, civil war sometimes ensued and neighboring countries might try to take advantage of weakness in a state. To forestall such an eventuality, the King of Bohemia and Hungary and the Prince of Austria agreed that if either of them (or their descendants) should die childless, then the sovereign from the other family would become the ruler of the state thus left without a leader.

---

9. This is demonstrated, inter alia, in the treatments in Graham, *Later Calvinism*, and McNeill, *History and Character*; however, the first of these includes no discussion of Bohemian or other Eastern European influence, and the latter devotes fewer than twenty-five pages to discussing the whole of Eastern Europe.

10. Two recent works offer fine studies on various facets of the Protestant Reformation's influence in Bohemia and other Eastern European nations: Maag, *Reformation in Eastern*; and Crăciun, Ghitta, and Murdock, *Confessional Identity*; see also Payton, "Calvin and Eastern Europe," 10–19.

11. This had become common among the nations of Eastern Europe; for additional examples of the practice, see below in chapter 13.

12. At the beginning of the sixteenth century, the Habsburgs were a noble family with small holdings; by 1521, though, they had come to control Spain and its far-flung holdings in the Americas, the Holy Roman Empire, Austria, Bohemia, and Hungary.

At the time, no murky conspiracy was underway; this was merely a way of guaranteeing safety for the states and avoiding civil war. It was nothing more than insurance against possible developments, which no one expected to see transpire—after all, the Austrian ruler and the King of Bohemia and Hungary both had sons ready to assume the thrones. However, within eleven years, this family compact would have enormous consequences. In 1526, the King of Bohemia and Hungary, Lajos II [Louis] (the son of the monarch who had signed the family compact) marched out with his forces to meet the invading armies of the Ottoman Turks. In pursuit of their plans to subdue the whole of Europe, the Turks had invaded Hungary. They had taken Constantinople in 1453 and had swept over the whole of Southeastern Europe—a control they would not relinquish over the region for more than four centuries. The Turks' intention was to spread the rule of Allah through all of Europe—and Hungary was the country directly in their path. In the Battle of Mohacs in 1526, the Ottoman forces were victorious, and Lajos was killed; the King of Bohemia and Hungary died childless.

Ferdinand, the son of the Austrian ruler who had signed the family compact, pressed his claim to the throne of Bohemia and Hungary. (The Austrian prince had not been involved in the Battle of Mohacs, since it was not his territory being invaded, and Lajos had not sought his help.) Given the tensions Bohemians had experienced in the past with Germanic domination, they might have been disinclined and somehow tried to find a way to evade the implications of the document. However, the Turks had swept on up through most of Hungary, and Bohemia was exposed to their onslaughts. The Bohemians could hardly afford an uncertain interregnum, and civil war would have been suicidal for the nation. So, whatever hesitations they may otherwise have had, they accepted the Germanic ruler of Austria as their monarch.

Through a piece of paper and some ink, the Habsburg Austrian prince became King of Bohemia—a region much richer and more highly developed than anywhere else in his domain. Because of the family compact, the Habsburgs—who were German in heritage—began to rule over Bohemia. Given that, the conversion of the Bohemian nobles to the Protestant Reformation is even more understandable, even if it was not merely a political movement on their part. Certainly, the embrace of Protestantism did not endear them to the Habsburgs, who were devoted champions of the Roman Catholic church. Even so, Bohemia existed without particular difficulty but uneasily within the Habsburg empire for the rest of the sixteenth century. That changed dramatically in the seventeenth century.

Battle at Bílá hora (1620)

The tensions occasioned by the Protestant Reformation within the Habsburg domains led their rulers to various efforts to establish or reimpose religious unity. The Habsburg-initiated War of Smalcald (1546–47) resulted in a Habsburg victory, followed by a surprising loss of imperial control of the situation, which issued into the Peace of Augsburg (1555). According to that treaty, both Roman Catholicism and Lutheranism could exist within the Holy Roman Empire. However, that did not quite satisfy the Habsburgs, who were convinced that religious unity was necessary for their holdings to coalesce into a more unified federation of states. Further, the Peace of Augsburg accorded no legitimacy to the Reformed version of Protestantism—the one embraced by most of the Bohemian nobility. The stage was set for further conflict. It broke out in Bohemia and issued into the Thirty Years' War (1618–48).

After the Peace of Augsburg, for most of the rest of the sixteenth century, the Habsburgs tried to entice or compel the peoples of their European holdings (including Bohemia) to embrace Roman Catholicism. However, the Protestant nobles of Bohemia held their religious ground. Beyond faith convictions that kept them from turning in this direction, they and their people had long endured too much German domination, and they were unwilling to accede to these pressures. Eventually, in 1609, the Austrian ruler, recognizing he had too many other problems to deal with in his realm, granted the Bohemian Protestants toleration, with wide concessions for freedom of worship. The Bohemians rejoiced in this concession; however, the Habsburgs reneged on the promises once they had dealt with other problems. Within less than a decade, the Habsburg ruler began to act in ways that undermined this 1609 declaration.

By 1618, the promised toleration had been clearly and repeatedly violated: that much was unmistakable when Habsburg forces marched into Bohemia, closed down two Protestant churches, and then demolished one of them. Pursuing further his determination to take tighter control of the religious situation, the Habsburg ruler, who obviously thought he was now in command of the situation, sent two ambassadors to Prague, the capital city of Bohemia. These representatives came not to negotiate with the Protestant nobles but to dictate to them the new religious terms on which the emperor would insist. From the Bohemian nobles' perspective, this was doubly irksome: it not only challenged their faith; it was another example of Germans reasserting themselves over Bohemians. This meeting took place on the top floor of Hradčany Castle in Prague. The meeting ended with what is called "the Defenestration of Prague"—the incensed Bohemian nobles threw the two ambassadors from the Habsburg emperor out a window. (A manure pile below the window broke their fall, and both survived.)

The windows in Hradčany Castle from which
the Habsburg representatives were thrown.

This act of obvious defiance indicated the Bohemians' breach with the Habsburg ruler—and was the beginning of the Thirty Years' War. Since the Habsburg emperor had broken his word to them, the Bohemian nobles asked another prince, the elector of Palatine—a German, to be sure, but someone who had also embraced the Reformed faith—to assume rule over them.

The Bohemians followed up on this political initiative with a military one: shortly after the Defenestration of Prague, their forces invaded Austria. They had quite a proud fighting heritage and would have been formidable foes for the imperial forces. However, Habsburg generals determined not to engage the Bohemians in Austria, but in Bohemia itself. So, Habsburg forces avoided the Bohemian armies and marched directly to Prague, to strike at Bohemia's heart. The Bohemians returned quickly to the defense of their capital city and engaged the Habsburg armies at a place called White Mountain (in Czech, *Bílá hora*) on November 8, 1620.

In the Battle of White Mountain, the imperial forces won a resounding victory. While the war itself would drag on for another desultory twenty-eight years, the Battle of White Mountain was decisive for Bohemia—not only then but for centuries afterwards. It has dramatically influenced and shaped the history of the Bohemians ever since. Five such influences can be noted.

In the first place, the Battle of White Mountain resulted in the destruction of their nobility. In the battle, a great proportion of the Protestant nobles of Bohemia died. The battle was brutal by any estimation, and the Habsburg forces were determined to eliminate Bohemian leadership. Nobles could be identified by their banners and armor; in their attacks, the Habsburg armies especially focused on the nobles, and wounded Bohemian nobles were finished off summarily. After the battle, many noble families fled Bohemia to escape possible further Habsburg vengeance, and with good reason: the imperial forces caught twenty-seven Protestant Bohemian nobles, executed them publicly in the square in Prague, and then mounted their heads on pikes in the city center, where they remained for several years. Further, the Habsburg emperor launched a reign of terror against nobles suspected of supporting Protestantism or opposing Austria; in this way, many nobles were forthwith thrown into jail. This led to further exile on the part of Bohemian nobles: by 1628, more than 36,000 noble families had fled the country. Among them were the cultural, economic, and political leaders of the people: Bohemia lost virtually all her noble class as a result of the Battle of White Mountain. It was clear, indeed, that the Habsburg emperor was ruthlessly asserting his control over the Bohemians. For them, this was another manifestation of the German domination they had come to loathe.

A second influence of the Battle of White Mountain was the way it affected land-ownership within Bohemia. Given the way society was structured at the time, until 1620 the Bohemian nobles had owned nearly three-fourths of the land. (As part of the 1430s arrangement between the Hussites and the empire and church, Bohemian leaders had been allowed to appropriate much of the church's former holdings.) With the nobles decimated, and because of their rebellion against him, the Austrian ruler confiscated their lands. He distributed them to the people who had fought for him—to Italians, Spaniards, other Germans, but not to Bohemians. In the aftermath of the Battle of White Mountain, three-fourths of the land of Bohemia was turned over to foreigners. The Bohemians were, indeed, dispossessed—strangers in their own land. This was a far worse subjugation to foreign rule than the Bohemians had ever known, and it was owing to the decision of this Germanic emperor.

In addition to these more immediate results, the Battle of White Mountain carried with it long-term effects for the Bohemians. The third major influence on subsequent Bohemian/Czech history was the fact that because of the Battle of White Mountain, Bohemia was reduced to a mere province in the Habsburg Empire. That was an extremely bitter pill for a people whose nation had played such a significant role in the past. Bohemia had been the highest-ranking state in the Holy Roman Empire, and her king had been second in status only to the emperor himself. In their recent Hussite past, the Bohemians had attained virtual independence, with significant control over even religious practices. After the Battle of White Mountain, Bohemia became just a province, exploited for the good of Vienna. From 1620 on, all Bohemian government was entirely placed in Vienna—and that remained the case until 1918. Bohemia was eliminated as a free and active member of the community of nations in Europe. The Bohemians recognized that this resulted from the Battle of White Mountain.

A fourth influence of that battle was the settled Bohemian/Czech resentment toward the Germans. This has not meant, of course, that all Bohemians carry the same resentment toward all Germans. However, the general pattern is this: the old German/Slav tensions—tracing all the way back to prehistoric times—which had surfaced at several points and in numerous ways in Bohemian history, were intensified for the Bohemians because of the Battle of White Mountain and its aftermath. All that Bohemia suffered fell upon them because of a German ruler; the result was a seething resentment toward Germans. That pattern remained for three centuries, until the end of World War I; it returned, after a brief interlude, with Nazi Germany's subjugation of Czechoslovakia in 1938.

The final effect of the Battle of White Mountain to be mentioned is the resultant resentment toward religion that arose among the Bohemians. Those who remained in the country after the elimination of the noble class were almost all Roman Catholic—and, thus, on the same religious side as the Habsburg ruler. However they may have initially felt about the religious question, though, Bohemians soon came to recognize that it was religion that had led to the demise of their nation. This soured many Bohemians on religion as a motive force within their society; in the aftermath of the Battle of White Mountain, most of them became indifferent toward religion. It had left a bitter taste in their mouths. Over the course of subsequent centuries,

Bohemians (later known, with Moravians, as Czechs) dealt with this tension by becoming generally indifferent toward religion.

Down to the present day, the Czech Republic is of all the nations of Eastern Europe—in which religion has otherwise continued to play a significant role—the most secular. After World War II, the Czechoslovakian Communist state was able to repress the Roman Catholic church (and, after 1968, the Protestants) far more vigorously than their counterparts in the Polish Communist government could, because Czech loyalty to the church was nowhere near as deep as it was among their Polish neighbors. Later, in the efforts that led to the end of Communist rule in the two states in 1989, the dissimilarity again manifested itself: whereas in Poland the Roman Catholic church played a significant role in the process, in Czechoslovakia the churches' influence was not decisive.[13]

The Battle of White Mountain of 1620 has had serious and long-term results for the Bohemians/Czechs. It was unquestionably a turning point in the history of Eastern Europe.

---

13. This contrast comes across dramatically in the PBS documentary "Faith under Fire."

CHAPTER 13

The Dismemberment of Poland (1772, 1793, 1795)

"The size and power of Poland repeatedly thrust it into a vital international role, but . . . only a century after the Battle of Vienna [1683] a declining Poland was neatly removed from the map of Europe by a coalition of Russia, Prussia and Austria. The civilised world was horrified. Here was surreptitious power-politics at its shameful worst. Three crowned heads aspiring to the name of enlightened monarchs had haggled greedily over the spoils before committing an act of cannibalism which cut across every concept of legality, morality and honour held at the time."[1]

DURING THE LAST QUARTER of the twentieth century and the first years of the twenty-first, probably the most influential, widely respected, and trusted individual in the world was a man from Poland, Karol Jan Wojtyła—Pope John Paul II.[2] People around the world also came to know Poland during the 1970s and 1980s through news coverage of the endeavors and accomplishments of the labor movement, Solidarity, and its vigorous leader, Lech Wałesa. But most people in the West will not know that Poland was the first country ever to have a written constitution, that it was the first European nation to exercise genuine religious toleration, and that for 140 years, Poland was the largest nation in all of Europe—or that, 226 years afterwards, Poland had disappeared from the map of Europe. How did that happen, and what events and patterns in Polish history led up to it?

---

1. Zamoyski, *The Polish Way*, 4.
2. John Paul II was the first non-Italian pope since 1523, when Adrian VI (from the Netherlands) died.

The Conversion of Poland

The year 966 is reckoned as the beginning of Poland as a nation, because by that date Poles had coalesced into a distinct nation under Mieszko I (r. 960–92), the founder of the Piast dynasty that ruled Poland until 1370. The Poles were the last of the West Slav peoples to attain statehood—but their state maintained its independence longer than the others.

An insightful ruler, Mieszko wanted to solidify the status of his realm among the commonwealth of European nations. Among the things requisite to that was regularizing its religious status; unquestionably, political considerations played a role in his turn to Christianity. The territories he ruled had already seen missionaries from the neighboring state of Bohemia. In addition, contacts between the Přemyslid dynasty in Bohemia and Mieszko enticed the Polish leader toward conversion. In 966, like the other West Slavs, he and his Polish nation converted to Western Christianity. Even so, the subsequent reign of Mieszko and the history of the Poles indicate that this conversion was not merely a political strategem but a genuine religious conversion: then and almost always since, the Piast dynasty that succeeded Mieszko and the history of Poland have manifested a resilient but steadfast devotion—with the exception of the period 1550–1600, to be considered below—to the Roman church and her pontiff.

The Challenge of Germany

Poland immediately faced the challenge of the German empire. In the tenth century, the empire was pursuing its *Drang nach Osten*.[3] Eager to expand its territory, the empire had already swallowed up Bohemia and Moravia—and Poland, the only free West Slavic state at the time, was immediately to the east of the empire. The Germans wanted to continue expanding their state, and Poland was next in line.

The Poles and the Germans were at that point, and throughout subsequent history, usually in tension. They were not continually at war, but there were almost always intrigues and contention between them. In the next century, during the 1070s, those tensions were compounded by the struggles between the Holy Roman emperor and the pope. The Investiture Controversy[4] reached its denouement in 1076 to 1078, with the conflict between two forceful personalities, Pope Gregory VII and Emperor Henry IV.

---

3. See the discussion of this above, in chapters 8 and 12.

4. See above, in chapter 12; the presentation of the Investiture Controversy in that chapter offers further detail relevant to the Polish situation.

The two leaders faced off over the question of who should control appointments to the higher realms of the ecclesiastical hierarchy, the church or the civil ruler. A resurgent papacy insisted that the church must make the final decision, and Gregory VII issued a papal bull to that effect. However, Henry IV intended to be in charge of what transpired in his far-flung realm, and so he ignored that bull; when the Archbishop of Milan died, Henry peremptorily appointed his successor. Gregory reacted with the threat of ecclesiastical discipline, but Henry ignored the threat until almost the last moment. The issue dragged on for months. During that time, the Piast leader faithfully supported the papal position.

Recognizing this, and the continued threat of German invasion of Poland, Gregory VII authorized the Polish prince to be crowned king. This would put a significant roadblock in the way of German expansion eastwards, since a move against Poland would amount to an attack on a papal-authorized kingdom. At the least, that would give the German empire pause—and being invested as king would certainly reward a prince who had stood forthrightly on the papal side during the controversy.

So, in 1076, the Polish ruler, Bolesław II (r. 1058–79), was crowned king. The pope authorized this at a point when it appeared that Henry IV had lost the struggle. As things turned out, though, the pope had not yet won. While eventually the papal position prevailed, the emperor managed to take the initiative not long after Bolesław's coronation and to forestall ecclesiastical censure through some surprising—and, with hindsight, unquestionably hypocritical—actions.[5] Even so, Bolesław had already been invested with the royal dignity. The emperor recognized that, and it only irritated him further with Poland. Henry IV saw Bolesław's coronation as a slap in the face; within a decade, the emperor authorized the ruler of Bohemia, Vratislav II, to be crowned as "King of Bohemia *and Poland*"—a title that carried an invitation to assert claim over Poland.[6] However, as we have seen, the Bohemian king declined to try to make good the latter portion of his title.

The tension between Germany and Poland persisted and has been an important factor in subsequent Polish history. This point needs to be made, not to demonize the Germans, but to point out how Poles understand a major

---

5. Henry IV intercepted Gregory VII at Canossa, where the pope had stopped in the winter on his way up to Germany to preside over a conclave that was supposed to dethrone Henry and select his replacement as emperor. However, Henry came barefoot and in sackcloth and ashes, the garb of a penitent. After three days' delay, Gregory VII granted Henry absolution and consequently lifted his excommunication and the threat of having his imperial dignity stripped from him.

6. See above, in chapter 12.

element that has shaped their nation's history. These tensions have reverberated down the corridors of following centuries: Poles were faced to their west by a powerful state that would have preferred to conquer them but was at least intent on subduing and controlling them. So, for centuries Poland was—or, at least, almost always felt herself to be—threatened by Germany.

Tensions within Poland

During this time, Poland not only had problems with Germany; she also faced tensions from within. Throughout her whole history, from the time of Mieszko I to the end of her monarchy in 1795, she suffered from rivalry between the nobles and the king. Prior to the 960s, certain families had attained prominence among the Poles and had been accepted as their nobles. Eventually, one of those nobles, Mieszko, consolidated authority over the rest of the Poles, and his family, the Piasts, emerged as the ruling dynasty. With his solid government of the nascent state, Mieszko undeniably deserved respect, but the development of dynastic pretensions irritated other noble families. They could remember when the Piasts were just another member of their group, but Mieszko had been in the right place at the right time. The other noble families resented the ascendancy of the Piasts; they also came to fear that the ruler—later, a king—would try to undermine their authority or usurp some of their power.

The result of such widespread fears among the Polish nobility was the early development of a group spirit intent on keeping the central authority as weak as it could, so as to protect the nobles' rights and privileges. Often and regularly throughout Polish history, the nobles worked together to oppose their king; in effect, they formed his "loyal opposition." While they wanted Poland to flourish, of course, they did not want it to do so as a unified state, in which the king wielded authority over and to the detriment of the nobles. However, this self-serving determination kept Poland from becoming as centralized and strong as many other nations would become over the centuries—nations that included Poland's neighbors. That ended up exposing Poland repeatedly to danger, and would eventually contribute to her disappearance from the map of Europe.

The Piast dynasty ended up being the focus of intrigue by the rest of the noble families. This was not distinctive to Poland, to be sure: the pattern obtained, as well, in Hungary and in Bohemia. By comparison with these other Eastern European nations, though, the nobles were far more successful in Poland—a "success" that contributed significantly to the weakening and eventual destruction of their country.

With the death of Kazimierz III [Casimir] (r. 1333–70), the Piast dynasty died out. Given the more than four hundred years of noble intrigues against the Piasts, it hardly seemed wise to seek a ruler from within Poland. Civil war would almost certainly ensue if one or another Polish noble family put one of its members forward to become the next ruler of the nation. Even should one of those families succeed in such an endeavor, the ruler would almost certainly be even more resented and tightly circumscribed by the other noble families than the Piasts had been.

Instead of seeking a Pole to become the next king, Poland followed the path taken by Hungary when her founding dynasty, the Árpáds, died out in 1301, and by Bohemia when hers, the Přemyslids, came to an end in 1306. Poland sought a ruler from another nation—someone with the "blue blood" of royalty. The notion had been widely accepted throughout Europe that birth in a royal family equipped one with special abilities for rule, and that these abilities were transferrable from one nation to another, inasmuch as they resided in the person; at least, that seems to have been the working assumption behind the choices made in Hungary, Bohemia, and Poland during the fourteenth century.

In 1370, the choice of the Polish court fell on the King of Hungary, Lajos I [Louis]. He continued to reign as the monarch of Hungary, but he also ruled Poland from 1370 to 1382. Like his Piast predecessors, he faced the intrigues of the Polish nobles, though, who remained determined to protect their historic rights against any and all royal encroachments on noble prerogatives.

Expansion of Poland

Whatever roadblocks the nobles put in the way of political centralization did not preclude Poland from expanding her borders. In the 1340s, under Kazimierz III, Poland added the formerly Kievan Rus' territory of Galicia, which had survived the destruction of Kievan Rus' by the Mongols in the 1240s[7] and for a century had maintained its own distinct existence. The small state was exposed, though, to the expansionist desires of its Polish neighbor. Poland sent in troops and brought it under control.

In so doing, Poland expropriated territory that had formerly been part of Kievan Rus'. At the point in time when she did so, that in itself carried no particular significance and implied no problem. However, that would change in the future, when Muscovy came to see itself as the heir of the former Kievan Rus', entitled to reclaim all the territories of that predecessor

---

7. See the treatment above, in chapter 10.

state—including Galicia. Furthermore, Muscovy took on the role of champion of Eastern Orthodoxy, and in conquering Galicia, Poland—a Western Christian state—came to rule over people who had embraced Eastern Orthodoxy. That would only further increase the tensions.

Another way Poland soon expanded was by merger. In 1386, Poland effected a union with Lithuania. The peoples who had coalesced into the state of Lithuania originally lived along the Baltic Sea in a loose collection of tribes. Eventually, they had been brought under the single rule of Mindaugas (r. c. 1240–63), under whom the Lithuanians had engaged in wide-ranging conquests. A large part of their territorial additions had come from the northern segments of the former Kievan Rus'—in contemporary Belarus. Furthermore, they swept to the south and east, swallowing up Volhynia and other remnants of the old Kievan Rus' state. By the early 1380s, Lithuania had become a very large state in Europe; however, it was still a pagan state, the only one on the continent.

The nobles of Poland had come to resent their ruler, Lajos; it seemed to them that his interests remained focused on Hungary. So, when he died in 1382, the Polish court opted out of the arrangement and was again in the market for a ruler, hoping to avoid civil war over the position. At the time, Lithuania also faced the prospect of internecine strife. The ruling courts of the neighboring nations hit upon a plan for dealing with their mutual problems: they decided to merge into a federation, with the Grand Duke of Lithuania accepted as ruler of both Lithuania and Poland. To legitimize this, though, he had to convert to Western Christianity and wed Jadwiga [Hedwig], one of the daughters of Lajos. In 1386, these arrangements were sealed when the Lithuanian Grand Duke, with his people, converted to the Western Christianity embraced by the Poles; he became Władysław V Jagiełło (r. 1386–1434).

Of the two constituent elements in the federation, Poland was the more sophisticated and tightly coordinated of the two, but Lithuania was the larger. Given the prior social and political development of Poland, Lithuania remained much the junior partner in the relationship. Through the merger, though, Poland-Lithuania became the largest state in all Europe—bigger even than the Holy Roman Empire. The resultant state was formidable, but much of its increased size had come by acquisition of formerly Kievan Rus' territories. To the Polish-Lithuanian federation's east, though, Muscovy intended to reunite all Kievan Rus' territories under its Eastern Orthodox banner.

With the conversion of Lithuania and the merger with Poland, the Jagiełłonians became the ruling dynasty of Poland. The other royal families and nations of Europe obviously accepted these recent converts from paganism, and over the course of the next century, the Jagiełłonians became one of the greatest of all the European ruling houses. Jagiełłonians intermarried with several other royal families throughout Europe, and by 1490, Jagiełłonians ruled all the nations in the northern tier of Eastern Europe—Bohemia, Hungary, and Poland.

Throughout Europe and in Poland, respect developed for the Jagiełłonians. Predictably, given the patterns of prior Polish history, the noble families reacted to this growing respect by opposing Jagiełłonian attempts to consolidate rule in Poland. Noble pressures led to the drafting in 1573 of the *Pacta Conventa*, which served as the constitution for the nation of Poland—the first such written constitution in human history. At the election of each new king, it was revised, to further assure the protection of noble privileges.

Over the centuries, the nobles had managed to win certain significant concessions from the kings of Poland. With other countries becoming more centralized under their monarchs, the nobles in Poland discerned a need to establish a bulwark against possible royal encroachments on their prerogatives. So, in due course, the nobles forced the king to recognize in writing, as law for the government of Poland, the rights they had as over against the kings.

So, Poland (as merged with Lithuania) was a large and apparently powerful state, but, whatever its kings may have wished, owing to the nobles' resistance to them, Poland was internally weaker than many smaller nations of Europe. Poland's size, though, ensured that she was viewed enviously by her neighbors—some of those smaller but more centralized and, consequently, more tightly controlled nations.

One such state was Prussia; it had developed out of Brandenburg, which had long played a significant role within the Holy Roman Empire. Now on its own, Prussia had become a military powerhouse, even though it did not control a large expanse of land. Because of that, though, the overwhelming size of her Polish neighbor made Prussia nervous: she felt potentially threatened by Poland. At the time, the Habsburg Empire, to the southwest of Poland, was already endangered by the Ottoman Empire; the Habsburgs came to view Poland similarly, as a possible threat. Across the Baltic and North Seas, the kingdom of Sweden had become a significant player on the European stage. Sweden feared the further expansion of Poland into Baltic territory and determined to oppose Poland. Finally, Poland faced opposition from another state to her northeast, a state that would become her most formidable foe, Muscovy. So Poland was surrounded by enemies who wanted to bring the large state down a few steps. In due course, those neighbors did much more than that: they eliminated Poland from the map of Europe.

Problems for Poland

No one enjoys a loss of power or influence, so one can appreciate the nobles' desire to keep the Polish king in check. But the sturdy determination to stay the course, no matter what came, was short-sighted. By the late fourteenth century, with neighboring nations centralizing and developing formidable military power, the Polish nobles' pattern kept the great state of Poland weak. That amounted almost to an invitation to nearby states to attack. To be sure, Poland could mount considerable force to defend herself, but it was always a scramble to do so—with nobles wringing concessions from a beleaguered king at the last moment as the price of their support. That was a major problem for Poland, a problem further compounded by what transpired in the country during the last half of the sixteenth century.

By the mid-sixteenth century, the Protestant Reformation began to make inroads in Poland. The movement had started in Germany and had already spread to various other countries, not only in Western Europe, but also in Eastern Europe—in contemporary Hungary, Croatia, Slovenia, the Czech Republic, Slovakia, Ukraine, and Poland.[8] Beginning around 1550, the Protestant Reformation exercised considerable influence within Poland, attracting a large number of nobles. The Polish king remained committed to the papacy, as his predecessors had been for centuries, so he supported the Roman Catholic church. Given the longstanding tension between king and nobles, though, it is not particularly surprising to discover that a significant portion of the nobles became Protestant. This does not require the conclusion that such conversion of religious commitment was only a superficial cover for opposition to the king—although for some that may have been the case. Prior Polish history had allowed and even encouraged the nobles to look at issues independently from the monarch's preferences, and a considerable percentage of the nobles did so in the controverted religious question within Western Christianity in the period, opting in due course to embrace some variety of the Protestant movement. This was not an insignificant movement among the nobles.

---

8. In a brief 2009 article, I expressed hope that study of how the Reformation took root and developed in Eastern Europe would become one area of growth for studies in the field (Payton, "The Reformations in Eastern Europe"); a fine recent contribution to this precise area is Wien and Grigore, *Exportgut Reformation*.

Since the Poles have long been recognized as among the most faithfully committed of Roman Catholics, this may initially be hard to appreciate, so some statistics may be helpful. In the early twenty-first century, as has been the case for centuries before, the Polish population is over 90 percent Roman Catholic. However, as of 1569, the Polish Parliament—which was composed only of the nobles—was 50 percent Protestant. As of 1591, one in every six parishes in Poland was Protestant.[9] Clearly, the Protestant Reformation had considerable impact during the last half of the sixteenth century in Poland. Two relevant questions are the following: How did the king of Poland respond to this? And how did this end up changing again in the direction of the current pattern?

By the late sixteenth century, the Poles already had a constitution that recognized and enshrined the rights of nobles. In the structures of Poland's government at the time, the parliament had overwhelming power: indeed, if only one Polish noble opposed some royal decision or proposed law, the decision or law could not be implemented. Unquestionably, the nobles had attained extraordinary power vis-à-vis the king—who doubtlessly abhorred the situation but could do almost nothing about it. Given that, even though the king was committed to Roman Catholicism, he could not realistically hope to impose his religious perspectives throughout his kingdom. So, rather than try to fight the Protestants, he put the best possible face on the situation and proclaimed toleration in religious matters—one wider than was accepted and practiced anywhere else in Europe at the time. According to the toleration practiced in Poland, Roman Catholics were accepted, but so were Lutherans, Calvinists, Anabaptists, Anti-Trinitarians, and Jews.

The king's declaration thus allowed people to worship as they chose. That tolerance seemed to work for a while. In the Counter-Reformation, though, spawned in Western Europe in the late 1540s, the Roman Catholic church finally began to deal seriously with the challenge posed by the Protestant Reformation and even earlier urged by many late medieval Christians.[10] By the late 1530s and on into the early 1540s, much of the Roman Catholic leadership was becoming committed to reform—in part, in response to the Protestants, but also to the criticisms of their own faithful, both in that generation and for several preceding ones. This movement seeking thorough reform of the Roman Catholic church found its marching orders in the Council of Trent, which met intermittently from 1545 to 1563.[11]

9. These statistics are taken from Małłek, "The Reformation," 189.

10. For further background on reform endeavors in the Roman Catholic church, see Payton, *Getting the Reformation Wrong*, 173–90.

11. For a related examination of these developments in Poland see Payton, "Influence of the Reformation."

The Council of Trent took vigorous control of and insisted on significant reform in the Roman Catholic church. One way it did so was by directly addressing Protestant teaching: the movement within the Roman Catholic church has come to be known as the "*Counter*-Reformation" primarily for this reason. The council's doctrinal declarations pointed out a variety of Protestant doctrines and emphases, evaluated them, denounced them, and set forth what Roman Catholics must believe in contrast. Unquestionably, the Council of Trent was vigorously anti-Protestant.

A second major component of the Counter-Reformation was a reforming papacy. Unlike some of the papal predecessors whose lifestyles and practices had called forth criticism, beginning with Paul III (r. 1534–49) a series of men committed to reforming the church and papal practice were chosen as popes. They occupied the See of St. Peter in the last few years before, during, and after the Council of Trent. They oversaw the development of the council and ensured the implementation of its decrees.

To do that, though, the popes relied extensively on the Jesuits—"the Society of Jesus," recently founded by Ignatius Loyola. The Jesuits had become a vigorous movement, committed to the well-being of the Roman Catholic church. Among the various areas in which they served with distinction, they excelled in setting up and running schools. In these schools, young people received education that met the highest standards of the time, but it was an education steeped in and oriented toward Roman Catholicism. In 1564, the Polish king welcomed the Jesuits to enter Poland to set up some of these this top-notch, first-rate schools. The Jesuit-run academies offered the best education available in the kingdom—and this is, pre-eminently, what won Poland back from its nobles' Protestant leanings to a committed Roman Catholic stance.

Nobles, of course, wanted their children to have the best education available; so, with whatever misgivings Protestant nobles may initially have had about the decision, most of them ended up sending their children to the Jesuit schools for their education. Perhaps the Protestant nobles received assurances that no attempts would be made to convert their children; perhaps those nobles were themselves not particularly insightful about the potential consequences of such an educational choice for their children; perhaps they were not as deeply committed to their Protestant faith as they claimed. Whatever the case, almost every one of those Protestant nobles' children who studied at a Jesuit academy came out of it a committed (and anti-Protestant) Roman Catholic. By 1600, Poland had returned almost entirely to the Roman Catholic church.

While this transformation put an end to the Protestant tensions within Poland, it did not end the tensions between nobles and kings. Those continued, and they weakened Poland by comparison with her neighbors. She had a particularly hostile neighbor to her northeast—the Muscovite state that was developing into the Russian Empire.

From 1550 onwards, fighting between Muscovy/Moscow and Poland was periodic, but hostility was constant. In the first two decades of the seventeenth century, Poland sought to benefit from the period later Russian historians called Moscow's "Time of Troubles." The extinction of the Rurik dynasty, with the death of Fyodor (r. 1584–98), issued into a period of nearly two decades of internal strife over which family would become the next royal line. The uncertainty weakened Moscow, and Poland took advantage of the situation. In 1605, Polish forces supported the claims of a Russian pretender who passed himself off as Dmitri, the younger brother (rumored to have been killed) of the deceased tsar; with their backing, Dmitri took the throne in Moscow. However, unlike other Eastern European nations, Muscovy was unwilling to accept a foreign ruler: whatever relationship he may have had to the Ruriks, since this supposed Dmitri had embraced Western Christianity by converting to Roman Catholicism (as a way of securing Polish support), Moscow would not begin to accept him; in the following year, he met a gruesome death at the hands of an enraged Muscovite populace. Again in 1610, Polish forces marched into Muscovite territory; this time they captured Moscow itself. In 1612, though, the Muscovites expelled them and attacked Polish holdings. Resentment against Poland for her incursions during the time of Moscow's weakness rankled Muscovy's leaders—and fired them with a determination to deal definitively with Poland.

Once it had passed through this time of troubles, Moscow regained its former strength. With that strength, the Muscovite state—the core and foundation of the emerging Russian Empire—pushed to rid herself of this dangerous, troublesome neighbor to her west. Russia had developed a settled antipathy for Poland. This resolute determination arose, not just as a reaction to recent Polish military adventurism, though; Russian hostility toward Poland was also rooted in religious difference. This requires some explanation.

Russia was vigorously committed to Eastern Orthodoxy—the faith that her predecessor state, Kievan Rus', had professed. In the 1240s, Kievan Rus' had been obliterated by the Mongols, but in 1380, at the Battle of Kulikovo, the Muscovites defeated the Mongols and re-established their independence. Moscow had remained committed to Eastern Orthodoxy; she believed that the reason she had risen as a state and been able to defeat the Mongols was divine blessing for standing without flinching for the true faith, Eastern Orthodoxy.

In the early thirteenth century, the long-developing differences and tensions between Western Christianity and Eastern Orthodoxy had borne their ugliest fruit with the Fourth Crusade.[12] That event had rendered trust between the two Christendoms virtually impossible, and the breach between Western Christianity and Eastern Orthodoxy unbridgeable. By the seventeenth century, the tension between Western Christianity and Eastern Orthodoxy had long been so intense that neither was willing to look on the other as a faithful version of Christianity: both of them viewed the other as apostates and rebels against God. True to this pattern, Russia saw Western Christianity as wrapped up in false teaching and practice, and as untrustworthy—a perversion of the Christian teaching and practice faithfully passed down through the ages in Eastern Orthodoxy.

Further influencing Russian perspectives was what had transpired in the mid-fifteenth century. In 1453, the Ottoman Turks had overrun Byzantium; the Russians interpreted this as divine judgment on the Byzantines for failing to stand unflinchingly for Eastern Orthodoxy.[13] Of all the Eastern Orthodox nations, as of 1453 only Russia was independent. She saw herself as responsible for the protection and, if possible, the advance of Eastern Christianity.

So, in Russian perspective, Western Christianity was an apostate pattern of religious practice that must be opposed, out of concern for divine truth—and Poland was firmly committed to Western Christianity. To the Muscovites, the Roman Catholic/Protestant tensions made little difference, but the recent return of Poland to an overwhelmingly Roman Catholic stance put them firmly in the papal camp—which Moscow found particularly objectionable. The fact that this nation, recently reunified religiously in what the Muscovites viewed as an apostate stance, had marched against Muscovy herself, the only free nation still committed to the one true faith, merited in the Russians' eyes the antipathy they felt toward their western neighbor. Compounded with the additional fact, though, that Poland (along with her junior partner, Lithuania) had subjugated the western portions of the former Kievan Rus'—which had embraced Eastern Orthodoxy—and was now ruling over these siblings in the true faith, Russia was utterly

---

12. See the treatment above, in chapter 9.

13. At the Council of Ferrara-Florence (1437–39), the Byzantine emperor and church representatives sought help from the Christian West against the imminent danger posed by the Ottoman Turks; ultimately, almost all the Byzantine representatives, under considerable pressure from the desperate Byzantine emperor, accepted the Western Christian doctrinal and administrative perspectives demanded as the price of reunion (and the expected military aid—which never materialized). This decision, however, was denounced by the Byzantine populace.

determined to destroy Poland. As the seventeenth century passed into the eighteenth, the Russian Empire only grew in power; Poland was under constantly increasing threat.

During much of the seventeenth century, Poland was at war with one or more of her neighbors. She fought with Prussia, Sweden, the Cossacks (from contemporary southern Ukraine), and Russia (allied with the Cossacks); in each of those conflicts, Poland lost. Weakened by noble intrigues, the kings were unable to obtain enough finances for their armies, as nobles desperately held on to their power. These wars resulted in Poland's neighbors demanding and receiving increasing segments of Polish territory. By the early 1700s, Poland was a pale shadow of her former self, considerably smaller than she had been.

Dividing up Poland

The rest of the eighteenth century offered no improvement to Poland; indeed, by the end of that century, Poland had ceased to exist. By the mid-eighteenth century, Poland—once the largest state in all Europe—had shrunk dramatically: a century of intermittent warfare had cost Poland various chunks of her border territories. Poland was still respectable in size, though, in 1770. However, as her neighboring states recognized, Poland was weak—a fruit ripe for the taking. In a series of three steps, taken in 1772, 1793, and 1795, those neighbor states helped themselves to Polish territory.

The Polish king was powerless himself to prevent this rapaciousness on the part of the nearby states, and the nobles—even though they had finally come to recognize the danger—were so firmly ensconced in their unwillingness to work with the king that they could not figure out how to protect Polish territories. So, in 1772, Russia, Prussia, and Austria simply decided how much Polish territory they wanted and then demanded it of the Polish king. In 1793, Russia and Prussia, without waiting for Austria to join them, demanded and received some more Polish land. Two years later, in 1795, Austria got back into the game, and the three neighboring states divided up the rest of Poland among themselves: in less than a quarter-century, Poland disappeared from the map of Europe—without even one sword being drawn against her. Of course, the territory she had occupied was still there in Europe, but it had been dispersed among her neighbors. The state of Poland disappeared; it would not reappear until 1918, after the end of World War I.

The significance of this was great, of course, for the Poles. For some five generations, the Polish people had no nation of their own. Recognizing the desire that surfaced in Eastern Europe in the 1990s (and sometimes led to bloodshed) among formerly subject peoples for their own state may enable the reader to sense some of the grief this loss of nation entailed for the Polish people.

But the dismemberment of Poland carried wider significance, too. Poland had been the last independent nation in Eastern Europe. The eastern half of the continent had known several leading, powerful states over the centuries—the Byzantine Empire, Moravia, Bulgaria, Croatia, Serbia, Bosnia, Kievan Rus', and Bohemia. Some of these had been in the vanguard of the sophisticated and accomplished cultures of their time. They had flourished in the period we in the West typically denominate the "Middle Ages"—the period between the ancient civilization and the "Early Modern" one (to use western historians' common designation), which have marked western civilization's heydays. But by then, the nations and sophisticated cultures of Eastern Europe had fallen prey to the depredations of emerging empires from outside Eastern Europe—Ottoman, Prussian, Habsburg, and Russian. By 1770, Poland was the only independent, self-governing nation left in Eastern Europe; and by 1795, Poland had ceased to exist.

The formerly brightly shining light of Eastern European accomplishment had been snuffed out. Not until the various oppressing empires were defeated and dismantled would Eastern European nations re-emerge. This period of darkness—123 years for Poland, but more than seven hundred for Croatia and over five hundred for Bulgaria—was undeniably significant for the history of Eastern Europe. The final signpost of this period of eclipse was the dismemberment of Poland in 1772, 1793, and 1795. That dismemberment was unquestionably a turning point in the history of Eastern Europe.

CHAPTER 14

The Aftermath of World War I (1918–22)

"Versailles Eastern Europe never reflected the Western ideal that each nation-state would truly represent the interests of its total population.... Even if the mapmakers had been objective in their determinations, ethnonational development in Eastern Europe made the drawing of truly national borders difficult, if not impossible."[1]

A LONG HISTORICAL VIEW is necessary for appreciating the aftermath of World War I, in the period from 1918 to 1922. The previous chapters have stressed that the peoples and nations of Eastern Europe have been profoundly shaped by their history—in ways that may seem unusual to us in the West, who are usually less aware of the influence exercised by our history on us. In turning to what ensued for Eastern Europe after the First World War, though, it becomes evident that the peoples and nations of Eastern Europe were then significantly shaped by *our* history in the West—specifically, by how we in the West had learned history for centuries, and by what we had *not* learned. This profoundly influenced Eastern European history in the aftermath of World War I.

Deep Historical Roots

For centuries, dating back to the renewal of education during the Renaissance, education in the West built on the writings of the ancient Greeks and Romans. During those two great civilizations—a golden age, in the estimation of Renaissance figures, by contrast to the medieval period they were escaping—civilization had attained its greatest heights. In the works of the Greek and Roman authors of antiquity, one could find the greatest

---

1. Hupchick and Cox, *A Concise Historical Atlas*, introduction to Map 42.

storehouses of wisdom available to humankind. Not surprisingly, Renaissance educators shaped the curricula they developed to focus especially on those ancient founts of wisdom. Antiquity came to be viewed as a standard for learning and culture. Ultimately, this attitude spawned the designation commonly used for the period: it came to be referred to as "*classical* history"—a designation that implied a standard of excellence, a norm for cultured civilization.

The Renaissance attitude prevailed in subsequent education: until well into the nineteenth century, students in the West received a "classical" education. Whatever else may have been added (in the sciences, social studies, etc.), students received a broad exposure to ancient Greece and Rome, their histories, and their authors. This was so certainly the case that entrance requirements for major universities in North America in the 1860s included reading ability in both Greek and Latin. The prominence of classical antiquity in educational curricula declined drastically during the twentieth century, pushed aside in favor of other emphases. With this, a "classical education" was no longer the common background of the educated. However one may view this development, it was a significant change from what had been a constant in education in the West for several centuries. As the twentieth century dawned, a classical education, dependent on Greek and Roman sources, was still the norm for an educated person—including the western leaders who decided the fate of Eastern Europe after the First World War.

This was important because of the limitations of the classical sources' information about the eastern half of the European continent. For both the Greeks and the Romans, the extent of their firsthand acquaintance with Eastern Europe stopped just south of the Carpathians. Consequently, neither the Greek nor the Roman authors wrote much about anything or anyone beyond those mountains. They had heard that a large group of peoples lived north of them, indeed, but the Greeks and the Romans did not encounter them and so could not offer much information about them.[2]

This is significant: as seen above,[3] the Carpathians were the southwestern limit of the original Slavic homeland until the sixth century—by which time, ancient Greek civilization had long passed from the scene and Roman civilization in the West had collapsed under the weight of Germanic invasions. The Slavic peoples ventured south, west, and east of the

---

2. The only exceptions to this were Herodotus, a notable Greek historian who may have lived in the Crimean peninsula for a while and who wrote about some peoples who lived north and west of there; and Tacitus, who wrote about peoples who lived to the east of the Germans. Neither of them gave much information about these peoples—who were, almost certainly, Slavs (see the discussion in chapter 2).

3. See chapter 2.

Carpathians and spread throughout Eastern Europe in the sixth through eighth centuries and have lived there ever since. Because of all this, although the Slavic peoples, who constitute the large preponderance of the population of contemporary Eastern Europe, have lived for centuries in the region, the classical sources from Greece and Rome offer virtually no information about them. With western education, from the Renaissance down to almost the present, using the classical sources as the cornerstone for educational curricula, people in the West learned virtually nothing about Eastern Europe's nations and peoples.

To be sure, from the sixth century onwards, the Byzantine Empire had much contact with those Slavic peoples, and so Byzantine authors ended up writing about them. But with the breakdown in communications between Byzantium and Western Europe, little of that material became available in the West until the Renaissance era. By then, Byzantium was reeling before the onslaughts of the Ottoman Turks, and so a number of Byzantine scholars fled Constantinople for Italy—where, with their facility in Greek and their mastery of ancient Greek literature, they contributed to the developing Renaissance.[4] However, their western hosts were not interested in Byzantine information; they wanted to learn about ancient Greek literature. The information these Byzantine scholars had about the peoples and the history of Eastern Europe was neither appreciated nor desired in the West. So, that reservoir of information was lost to Western Europe.

The result of all this was that for centuries people in the West have known very little about the peoples of Eastern Europe, even though they have lived right next door in the continent. Even intermittent warfare between Western European and Eastern European nations did not spawn appreciable interest in learning about Eastern Europeans. Proximity did not lead to significant intellectual curiosity.

Beginning with the eighteenth-century Enlightenment, a modicum of information (and misinformation) spread into Western Europe about the eastern half of the continent.[5] Subsequently, a few intrepid scholars began studying about the peoples and nations of Eastern Europe, but such scholars always remained a minuscule minority. It was not until after the end of World War II, in the wake of the Communist take-over of the region and because of fear of the Soviet empire, that the study of Eastern Europe even became a distinct historical field of scholarly specialization: until then, one could search university catalogues in vain for academic departments (or

---

4. See the interesting treatment in Geanakoplos, *Byzantine East and Latin West*, especially "Part II: Byzantium and the Renaissance" (112–93).

5. For a stimulating presentation of this, see Wolff, *Inventing Eastern Europe*.

even courses) focusing on Eastern Europe.⁶ Until Eastern Europe became a threat to its safety, the West developed no particular interest in learning about the history or peoples of the region.

Predictably, this led to ignorance in the West about Eastern Europe. That was the case from the average person to the statesman leading a country; and it became painfully obvious at the end of the First World War.

Nineteenth-Century Influences

In addition to the role played by the West's centuries-long ignorance about Eastern Europe, factors specific to the nineteenth century helped shape what happened in the aftermath of World War I. The first is that by the dawn of the nineteenth century, all the peoples and nations of Eastern Europe had been subsumed within one of four rival empires that together encompassed the entire region—the Ottoman Empire, the Prussian Empire, the Austrian (Habsburg) Empire, and the Russian Empire. There was not even one free and independent state in all of Eastern Europe, and (apart from Poland)⁷ there had not been one for a long time.⁸ Whatever aspirations for the independence of their own nation may have developed among the peoples of Eastern Europe, it was the empires—plus England and France, other major powers from Western Europe—that decided what would happen in Eastern Europe. Almost always, these decisions were taken with no concern for the hopes of the affected inhabitants of Eastern Europe; instead, the decisions served the purposes of the major European powers.⁹

---

6. See the discussion above in chapter 5.

7. Poland had been removed from the map in 1795: see chapter 11.

8. In the southern tier of Eastern Europe, Croatia had not known independence since 1102, Bulgaria since 1396, Bosnia since 1463, Herzegovina since 1466, Albania since 1468, Romania since 1475, and Moldova since 1512; in the northern tier, Bohemia had not known independence since 1526, Hungary also since 1526, Slovakia since 906 (if ninth-century Moravia is counted as its heritage—otherwise, the Slovaks had never previously had a state), and Poland since 1795.

9. The Treaty of Berlin in 1878 cavalierly rejected both the earlier Treaty of San Stefano and the aspirations of the Bulgarians (who, with Russian help, had defeated Ottoman Turkey) and dramatically reduced the resultant Bulgarian state, in addition to allowing it only partial independence, so as to maintain a balance of power between the Western European powers and Russia. Additionally, the Treaty of Berlin peremptorily wrested Bosnia-Herzegovina out of the control of Ottoman Turkey and handed its oversight to the Austro-Hungarian Empire, although the young Serbian state had pressed its claims to the region (where many Serbs lived and over which the earlier Serbian state had ruled); subsequently, in 1908, the Dual Monarchy simply annexed Bosnia-Herzegovina, again disregarding Serbia's claims to the region.

The second factor, which flew in the face of the first, was the spread of the ideology of nationalism into Eastern Europe. In the present day, most people in the West have a general sense of what nationalism is, even if the concept is not crisply defined in their thoughts: it is related to patriotism and positive feeling about one's own country, and it includes a sense of a nation's value in the world and of the privilege of being a citizen of that nation. Regardless of the specifics of that notion, though, those who live in the West already have a nation that serves as referent for them; the givenness of their nation, as shaped by its history, sets the contours for their perception of "nation." What many may not realize, though, is that the idea of nationalism is only a little more than two centuries old: spawned by the upheavals of the French Revolution in 1789, the ideology of nationalism spread throughout Europe—first in the western half of the continent and subsequently to the east. As it spread, it influenced developments in distinctive ways in the two segments of the continent.

How does one define "nation"? Prior to the casting aside of the *ancien regime* in France, any thoughts about "nation" would have focused largely on the ruler of the "nation" and the territory he or she controlled. A positive sense of being in that nation probably marked most segments of the aristocracy, who benefited from the structure of society in that nation; for those lower in the socio-economic ladder, though, a sense of belonging to the nation may have been more tenuous, probably linked to whatever benefits (e.g., protection in the courts, defence during war, etc.) one perceived in being within that body politic. In whichever case, the sense of "nation" revolved around the ruler and the realm he or she controlled.

With the revolution against royal domination in France, though, this concept of "nation" was no longer viable. The revolutionaries shared a sense of belonging to each other and saw themselves as serving the well-being of the common people of the "nation"—which only focused the question sharply: *what is* a "nation"? The ideology that developed focused no longer on the ruler and what people shared under that person's demesne but rather on what the people shared with each other—on their prior history, the land and language they shared, and the culture that had developed among them.[10]

10. This assessment has been well received among historians and is especially associated with Benedict Anderson's stimulating book, *Imagined Communities*. I have argued elsewhere that focusing on what a people shared as definitive of "nation" should lead to a much earlier exemplar than what happened in the wake of the French Revolution, for such a notion arose more than 335 years previously, stimulated by earlier historical developments and the influence of the Ottoman establishment of "millets" as a way to structure their empire in southeastern Europe: see Payton, "Orthodox 'Imagined Communities'"; I expanded on this assessment, with contemporary application, in Payton, "Ottoman Millet, Religious Nationalism."

This worked well enough for the French. It helped them "connect" within the geography that had already been demarked as the French king's territory, and it held together the people over whom the French monarchs had ruled. This variety of "nationalism" effectively dispensed with the royalty while managing to keep the French related, through what they shared with each other.

This ideology was perceived, predictably, as dangerous in much of the rest of Western Europe. The populist approach, leaving monarchies to the side as irrelevant, certainly did not commend it to ruling powers elsewhere, who perceived it as dangerous to what they held dear as the foundation of civilization itself, and of their own nations. Nevertheless—or, perhaps, consequently—this ideology of nationalism spread rapidly among the peoples of Western Europe. It spawned a series of attempts to cast off ruling oligarchies and establish "nations" framed around the various peoples themselves. In due course, the ideology was accepted widely enough that governments in several Western European nations were changed, either by force or by peaceful decision.

Even so, this sense of nationalism could succeed in Western Europe, in large part, because while the peoples affected may have previously identified with a nation in the former sense, they also had a shared history, land, language, and culture that connected them with each other. By and large, the various "nations" of Western Europe were homogeneous in cultural background and language (in the face of divergent dialects of the major language, to be sure). They all had a "nation" in place, ready to be identified according to the new definition.[11]

Problematic as the new ideology of nationalism was for rulers in Western Europe, it was utterly unwelcome to the empires that collectively dominated all of Eastern Europe. Virtually by definition, an empire is multinational: it would be the antithesis of the new ideology. If even defining a single nation in terms of its ruler was scandalous according to nineteenth-century nationalism, then surely an empire in which loyalty is supposedly fixed on the ruler would be even more reprehensible. That was how all four empires assessed the new ideology. It is perhaps not surprising, though, that the new sense of nationalism appealed to the various peoples of Eastern Europe.

In due course, some Eastern Europeans became acquainted with the ideology. Students from the region studying in Western European universities encountered it, and some intellectual leaders within the region who

---

11. This also offered support to the desires of Italians and Germans to have their own states; these aspirations were fulfilled, respectively, in 1870 and 1871.

kept contact with scholars and trends in the West also learned about it. This new sense of nationalism offered them hope for a rebirth of their long-suppressed Eastern European nations. Over the course of the nineteenth century, this new ideology captured the allegiance of leading cadres of the various peoples of the region. For some, it was a tantalizing ideal, but one they did not seek to achieve by organized protest or revolt.[12] Others, however, tried to attain the ideal;[13] each of these attempts was put down with the heavy forces of imperial power. Defeat did not entail, though, destruction of hope: the nineteenth-century ideology of nationalism continued to live among large sections of the inhabitants of Eastern Europe. Eventually, two nations—Serbia in 1830 and Romania in 1878—managed to attain virtual independence from their Ottoman Turkish overlords during the nineteenth century; the Bulgarians achieved this early in the twentieth, in 1908. Significantly, all three of these fledgling Eastern European nations urged that others of their nation lived outside the new national borders—and so their respective nations needed to be increased in size.

This shows a major potential problem for implementing the nineteenth-century version of nationalism in Eastern Europe. It was hardly possible to find a "nation" in Eastern Europe in which virtually everybody shared a common background in history, land, language, and culture. Over the preceding centuries, for a bewildering variety of reasons—colonization, conquest, invitation, emigration, fleeing from invaders, et al.—peoples had intermingled throughout Eastern Europe. Even in regions—as, for instance, among the Poles or the Czechs—where a large central core seemed homogeneous enough, in outlying regions the population was intermingled with peoples of dissimilar language, history, and culture; in that situation, where should national boundaries be drawn? Nevertheless, this nineteenth-century version of nationalism was in the air and was tremendously appealing to people longing for independence and the rebirth of their own nation. That dream had never died out for the peoples of Eastern Europe over the long night of imperial repression.

This significantly influenced what happened after World War I. As the twentieth century dawned, almost everyone in Eastern Europe was calling for independence for their nation. But for centuries, empires had been in control of the whole of Eastern Europe, and the nineteenth-century attempts to achieve independence had met ruthless repression. So, while

12. This was true of the Czechs, the Slovaks, the Slovenes, the Croats, and the Albanians.

13. The peoples who attempted to achieve independence by protest or revolt were the Serbs (in 1816 and 1830), the Poles (against the Russians, in 1832), the Hungarians (in 1848), the Romanians (in 1848 and 1878), and the Bulgarians (in the 1860s).

many clamored for independence for their nations, virtually no one expected it any time soon—and no one was prepared for it. Then the First World War came—and all the empires were defeated.

Dismantling the Empires

World War I began in Eastern Europe, with the assassination of Archduke Ferdinand in Sarajevo, Bosnia. In 1908, the Austro-Hungarian Empire had annexed Bosnia. As a region where numerous Serbs lived outside the boundaries of the Serbian nation, it was coveted by the young Serbian state. Long before, during Serbia's glory days under the Nemanjić dynasty, Sarajevo had been in Serbian territory. The transfer of Bosnia-Herzegovina from Ottoman to Austrian control rankled the Serbs, who hoped—in nineteenth-century nationalistic terms—that the region would become part of Serbia. Of all things, the heir to the Austrian throne determined to visit Sarajevo on the anniversary of the Battle of Kosovo[14]—about as insensitive a selection of dates as he could have chosen. Whether through ignorance of the significance of the date, indifference to Serbian desires, or imperial arrogance, Archduke Ferdinand and his wife rode through the streets of Sarajevo on June 28, 1914; a young, idealistic Serb, Gavrilo Princip, assassinated the Austrian heir. Austrian demands against Serbia exceeded what the Serbian nation believed were legitimate, and Austria declared war. With the various coalitions that had been established, this local melee escalated quickly into a conflict throughout much of the continent and, in due course, drew in participants from abroad; the First World War was on.

It lasted until November 11, 1918. The "Central Powers"—Germany, the Austro-Hungarian Empire, and the Ottoman Empire—ended up surrendering. The fourth empire that had dominated part of Eastern Europe, the Russian Empire, had already fallen apart, owing to the October Revolution of 1917. Thus, all the empires that had ruled over Eastern Europe met defeat, and the victorious allies—England, France, Italy, and the United States of America [USA]—were determined to make them pay the consequences. The allies wanted to assure that there would be no further such war; it became common to refer to the war of 1914–18 as "the war to end all wars." The allies were first of all determined to dismantle these empires, as a way of assuring that they would not have the wherewithal to initiate such a war again.

---

14. See the treatment above, in chapter 11.

If the allies were to do that, though, they would, secondly, have to erect nations throughout Eastern Europe. How were they to do that? They intended to follow the nineteenth-century ideology of nationalism.

Setting up States in Eastern Europe

During the nineteenth century, the western powers had pursued their own concerns in the arrangements in Eastern Europe, with little regard for the peoples of the region or their desires. With the possibilities opened up by the end of World War I, though, the allies could move in a different direction. As the victors, the allies wanted to impose their will on the empires that had lost the war, to be sure. But the allies also hoped to serve the aspirations of the various peoples of Eastern Europe in their negotiations at the end of the war. The allies thought they could blend the two: the treaties that would wrap up the end of the war could make sure the defeated powers were dismantled and thus unable to start another such conflagration, on the one hand; and the various peoples of Eastern Europe could be given the independence for which they had been clamoring, on the other.

This appeared relatively straightforward. However, as the peace negotiations showed, the two aspirations sometimes conflicted. As well, they manifested how much more complicated nineteenth-century nationalism was "on the ground" than it was "in the air."

With the two goals of taking apart the empires and establishing states in Eastern Europe both clearly in view, the allies set about the lengthy and complicated process of drawing up separate treaties with each of the defeated powers. While many people think of the Treaty of Versailles as the treaty that ended the war, that treaty dealt only with Germany. Actually, five distinct treaties were produced: Versailles (with Germany), Saint Germain-en-Laye (with Austria), Neuilly (with Bulgaria [which had joined the war on the side of Russia]), Lausanne (with the Ottoman Empire), and Trianon (with Hungary). Negotiations were intense and long-lasting: it took more than four years to get these all drafted and ratified, from early in 1919 to 1923. Each treaty sought to punish the defeated power and to establish independent nations in Eastern Europe out of the territories previously dominated by that empire.

The allies' determination to serve the aspirations of the peoples of Eastern Europe by living up to the noble ideals of nineteenth-century nationalism was unquestionably an improvement over the western powers' practice during the nineteenth century itself. Indeed, the allies were publicly committed to it by "The Fourteen Points," a document produced by Woodrow

Wilson, the president of the USA. In it, he had promised the peoples of Eastern Europe that after the war the allies would establish independent nations throughout the region—a promise made in the name of all the allied states. In the five treaties, the allies tried to keep that promise.

The leaders involved in this process were Georges Clemenceau, premier of France; Vittorio Orlando, premier of Italy; David Lloyd George, prime minister of Britain; and Woodrow Wilson, president of the USA. They had numerous advisors, but these four leaders made the decisions.[15] They received numerous delegations and spokespersons from many (but not all) of the peoples of Eastern Europe; these delegations and spokespersons argued the cases for their respective hopeful nations and offered strong advice about where and how borders should be drawn. Significantly, such advice often turned out to be in conflict with that vigorously proffered by delegations from other Eastern European peoples.

Some of those peoples had prepared for the possibility that "The Fourteen Points" would actually guide the peace negotiations and had coordinated presentations putting forward the claims of their people in the most positive light. Among them, the Poles made a compelling case; so too did a group representing the Czechs and Slovaks—who surmised that their two peoples, although never previously united in a state, stood a better chance of being established as a nation together than either would separately. Serbia also made a vigorous presentation. However, others among the peoples of Eastern Europe had no such delegation or spokesperson to plead their case before the allied leaders. Working with what they knew about Eastern Europe, plus what they learned from the representations made to them, and trying to juggle the disparate claims advanced for the respective would-be nations, the allies' leaders set about redrawing the map of Eastern Europe.

It turned out to be one thing to espouse nineteenth-century nationalism, but quite another to implement it in Eastern Europe. The rhetoric about a nation established in view of its shared history, geography, language, and culture ran aground on the *actual* history, geography, and inhabitation patterns throughout most of the region—as the competing claims of the delegations and spokespersons of various Eastern European peoples indicated. In order to draw up a new map of Eastern Europe, the allied leaders needed precisely what their excellent respective classical educations had not given them—namely, a good understanding of the history and development of Eastern Europe. Unquestionably, the leaders had good intentions, and they used as much advice and information as they could, but the borders were drawn up based on the knowledge that Clemenceau, Orlando, Lloyd

---

15. For an engaging presentation of the process, see MacMillan, *Paris 1919*.

George, and Wilson had of the region—which was, in keeping with their educational training, not a great deal.

Even given those limitations, though, the way the map of Eastern Europe was redrawn bordered on the comical: a large map of the region was spread on the floor and Clemenceau, Orlando, Lloyd George, and Wilson walked around on the map, trying to figure out where to put the borders. With pencils and erasers, they drew and redrew borders for the new Eastern Europe. The results fell far short of the ideals of nineteenth-century nationalism: three points show this clearly.

In the first place, even though nineteenth-century nationalism called for the national unity of people who shared the same territory, history, language, and culture, the Eastern European nation of Hungary lost 70 percent of her territory and almost half of that Magyar populace, which shared history, language, and culture. Hungary had been swallowed up into the Austrian Empire nearly four centuries previously,[16] but in 1867 the Austrian Kaiser had raised Hungary to a virtually equal status with Austria itself, as a way to placate the nationalistic aspirations of the Magyar people.[17] Consequently, Hungary was part of the Austro-Hungarian Empire defeated in World War I—and she had to pay the consequences. So, the allies stripped her of most of her territory, and in the process nearly half of the Magyar people were excluded from that nation with which they shared history, language, and culture.[18] Nationalism in the nineteenth-century sense was a noble goal, but twentieth-century punishment carried the day.

Secondly, it proved impossible for the allied leaders to incorporate the entirety of any of the Eastern European peoples within their own state. With the various peoples of the region having intermingled over the centuries, all over Eastern Europe pockets of people who shared history, language, and culture were separated from the dominant location of their nation; those pockets were like islands in the sea of a different people group who shared its own history, language, and culture. Consequently, the boundaries drawn for the new states of Eastern Europe included within each a sizeable minority population—often, several such minorities. The problem with that

---

16. This had transpired after the Battle of Mohacs in 1526, when her monarch, Lajos, had been killed; see the treatment in chapter 12.

17. This decision of the Habsburg ruler was not merely gratuitous benevolence: in 1848, the Hungarians had revolted and the Habsburg forces had only with difficulty managed to reassert control over them; this led the Kaiser to find a way to accommodate Hungarian aspirations within the structures of the empire; the result was the 1867 establishment of the Dual Monarchy.

18. As a result of the borders drawn up with Hungary, large numbers of Magyar peoples ended up within Romania, Yugoslavia, and southwestern Ukraine.

was that nineteenth-century nationalism had no room for minorities in its theoretical constructs.

In a third way, the allied leaders' decisions failed to live up to the ideology of nineteenth-century nationalism. To be sure, in dealing with Eastern Europe after World War I, the victorious allies tried to turn from their predecessors' pattern of manipulating the peoples of Eastern Europe for western powers' ends. They attempted to honor the Eastern European peoples' desires for national freedom: that was the professed goal. But a certain measure of paternalism evidenced itself in a requirement placed on those newly established Eastern European nations: each of them had to become like the victorious western allies in their government; that is, each of the newly-established Eastern European nations was required to become a constitutional democracy.

From the allies' perspective, this made good sense. Such a form of government avoided the kinds of tyranny from which each of those nations had just been delivered, and it offered each of the respective peoples the opportunity to govern themselves, rather than being governed by others (as had been the case for so long). Significantly, though, the victorious allies all governed themselves by some form of constitutional democracy. The newly established states of Eastern Europe were not consulted on this direction for government; it was simply made a requirement in the various treaties that established them as states, even though none of the Eastern European nations—except for Serbia, incorporated into the Kingdom of the Slovenes, Serbs, and Croats (in 1929, renamed "Yugoslavia")—had any experience of democratic self-government.

Evidently, even if the allies did not recognize it themselves, paternalism on their part toward Eastern Europe had not entirely died out. Well-meant paternalism—and is there any other kind?—is, after all explanation and excuse-making, still paternalism. None of the Eastern European nations was free to govern itself in whatever way it might choose; each of them was required to adopt a democratic form of government with a written constitution, like the allies—and each Eastern European state did so. Whatever might have been the preferences of the respective nations of Eastern Europe, each became a constitutional democracy after World War I. As will be seen below, though, democracy did not last long in the region; by 1939, all the nations of Eastern Europe had opted for some other form of government.

Problems

Four major problems developed for the Eastern European nations in the wake of these treaties. These problems made the transition into nationhood turbulent initially. Unresolved, they kept the region in constant turmoil in the aftermath of World War I.

One was that each of the Eastern European states ended up with disputed borders. Over the centuries, borders had often changed within Eastern Europe, both during the periods of independence for the various nations and also during the time of their domination by empires; consequently, no border was in some sense "sacrosanct" because of long acceptance or standing. Further, many of these Eastern European peoples had excitedly elaborated on the ideology of nineteenth-century nationalism to imply the reestablishment of their nation with all the land it had held at the zenith of its prominence in the region. Clearly, this could not have been implemented by the allied leaders, since the various Eastern European nations that had previously existed had flourished at different times, and the borders of nations in those different times had significantly overlapped. However, even those Eastern European peoples with less grandiose aspirations found themselves frustrated by the decisions after World War I about national borders. Meeting the conflicting hopes of all the Eastern European peoples would have been impossible; even so, the result of the allied leaders' decisions, not surprisingly, pleased few and left most disgruntled. Virtually all the peoples of the region were profoundly disappointed with the borders of their respective states.

A second problem was closely related—that of ethnic minorities. Every Eastern European state set up after World War I had one or more of them within its borders. Given the patterns of migration and resettlement over the centuries, almost every Eastern European people had long had some of its own living as virtual islands in the sea of a surrounding majority people of another background. When the borders were drawn up after World War I, these pockets of one ethnic background ended up as minorities within the state of another people; thus, there were concentrations of Czechs living in Poland, of Poles living in Russia, of Hungarians living in Ukraine and Romania, and so on.

The reason this is problematic is that nineteenth-century nationalism had no room for minorities. As an ideology, it affirmed the right of a people who shared, not only the same territory, but also the same history, language, and culture to be a nation. Consequently, anyone not fitting into that sameness had only a tenuous connection to the "nation" thus described—and, after World War I, established. It was almost unavoidable that such "outsiders" were regarded as "second-class" citizens.

So, no matter where borders might be drawn, each of the Eastern European states would have a significant minority or minorities within it. The allied leaders had foreseen this as they became more familiar with the region during the long process of negotiations after World War I. So, the treaties drawn up demanded that each Eastern European state's constitution include special provisions to ensure the fair treatment of its minorities—and each of those constitutions dutifully included such assurances. These provisions specifically included the right to have schools and court systems that would use the minority's language—provided there was a certain critical mass of the minority (determined by the size of its population in the area). Moreover, they were not to suffer discrimination in regard to employment or the political process. The constitutions promised that the minorities in each state would not endure oppression or ostracism.

Such promises proved easier to make, in the exuberant prospect of again having national independence, than they were to keep, in the complications of actually getting on with nation-building. In the tumultuous years between World War I and the outbreak of World War II, virtually no effort went into keeping those promises—not necessarily because of ill will toward the minorities (although, not surprisingly, that was how the minorities viewed the situation), but because of the multitude of other demands on national governments. As will be seen, economic and other problems for the majority people so taxed the fledgling democracies that minority rights and claims ended up being ignored. The governments of the various Eastern European states could excuse their failures toward the minorities because of the legitimate need to serve the overwhelming majority. Even so, minorities ended up being treated as second-class citizens, and they profoundly resented it. When their mistreatments became known in neighboring states—where the former nation's minority was the majority—tensions between states arose (and sometimes broke out into armed conflict).

A third problem in the aftermath of World War I was inexperience in self-government throughout Eastern Europe. While many had clamored for national independence in the nineteenth century and the early twentieth, nobody was expecting it, as noted above; when they nonetheless received it, none of the Eastern European nations established after World War I had any experience in actually governing themselves. Only a few of them had even known the privilege of being represented in the parliament in the empires of which they were part. Those who did had no actual power to govern: the most they could do was to delay passage of laws that they had no voice in framing.[19] Most of the Eastern European peoples, though, had not even enjoyed this much experience of government.

The novelty of self-government after World War I was nevertheless so enticing that it spawned scores of political parties in every nation. Post-World War I Poland had several competing peasant parties, various socialist parties, plus other special-interest parties; other states suffered a similar political prolixity. With so many scores of parties, though, government in the Eastern European states often ended up a fragile coalition of parties of different orientations, each of which had received only a small percentage of the popular vote in the latest election. In that awkward situation, it was difficult for a government to accomplish much; when the coalition broke down (as regularly happened), new elections had to be called. It was exceedingly difficult for even the best-intended national leaders to get much done.

Further in this regard, not only the people themselves, but their elected leaders were inexperienced in government. Almost no one anywhere in Eastern Europe who ended up leading any of the nations established after World War I had any experience in managing any major enterprise, governmental or otherwise. In the aftermath of the establishment of their states, often that inexperience showed. (One remarkable exception was Tomáš Masaryk, the first president of Czechoslovakia, who served with noteworthy distinction.)

---

19. The Croats had been allowed representation in the Habsburg Empire's parliament (after 1867, in the Hungarian parliament); however, their opportunities for influence were so strictly circumscribed that Croat representatives usually engaged only in delaying tactics—a style they carried over into their participation in the Kingdom of the Slovenes, Serbs, and Croats (later called Yugoslavia) and which infuriated their Serb counterparts.

Statue of Tomáš Masaryk, erected in his honor
in Hradčany Castle in Prague.

Appointees named to head up the respective bureaucracies requisite to a functioning government were similarly inexperienced. Virtually none of them had ever worked in management levels of a bureaucracy, so they had little appreciation of paper flow, precise understanding of chains of command, and what ought and ought not to be done to make the bureaucracy function well. Their subordinates in the respective bureaucracies were similarly inept at their respective levels of responsibility. In all this, even the best of intentions was no substitute for experience; chaos resulted in the bureaucracies of the Eastern European states. Where intentions were not the best, the possibilities for corruption proved enormous: frustrated individuals were too often willing to pay bribes to lubricate the machinery of government, and bureaucrats at all levels found this an attractive way of supplementing their meager salaries.

Not surprisingly, government did not work well in the nations of Eastern Europe in the aftermath of World War I. All these complications led to frustration with democracy throughout the region. Before the outbreak of World War II in 1939, all the states of Eastern Europe had foresworn democracy in favor of some more tightly controlled and efficient form of government.

Fourthly, all these Eastern European states faced huge economic challenges. None of them had a well-stocked treasury. Their former empires had set up no trust funds for their subject peoples to draw on in case of independence. These recently established nations only had what lay within their borders. So, all the Eastern European nations were starting virtually from ground level and trying to build an economy. That was a huge and risky undertaking.

Beyond that, each of these new states needed trading partners. Prior to World War I, whatever trade passed through any of the areas later designated states was for the benefit of the respective empires. So, for the independent nations of Eastern Europe, who wanted to do nothing to strengthen their former imperial lords, old trading patterns were not an option: they all had to find new trading partners. In other circumstances than those that obtained after World War I, neighboring nations would have been a likely option. However, every Eastern European state had border disputes with its neighbors, making them less desirable as potential trading partners. Further, complaints from neighboring nations of alleged mistreatment of its people, who were minorities, further decreased the possibility that an Eastern European state would establish trading relations with its neighbors. Trade was necessary, but setting it up proved extraordinarily difficult for each of the Eastern European nations.

In that awkward situation, they all looked to the West for help. Their hopes were largely disappointed, though, because western nations had gone into an isolationist/protectionist economic mode, figuring in part that if they were each not dependent on other nations, then they would less likely be drawn into another nation's war. So, while western nations doubtlessly wanted the Eastern European nations to thrive, the West was not particularly willing to involve itself in trade with them.

Even so, western nations were willing to offer extensive loans to the Eastern European states, to help them get their economies going. Interest rates were kept low, and each Eastern European nation—with the exception of Czechoslovakia, where the former Austro-Hungarian Empire had located significant factories, which allowed Czechoslovakia to prosper[20]—took out extensive loans with western creditors. All the states of Eastern Europe were in desperate need of funds, so they all took loans; the total amounts are staggering to contemplate. During the 1920s and 1930s, every nation in Eastern Europe (except Czechoslovakia) relied heavily on foreign loans—for between 50 and 70 percent of its entire budget! These loans, of course, would eventually have to be paid back, with interest. Even so, they offered hope—for a while. However, on "Black Monday" in 1929, the bottom fell out of worldwide economies and the Great Depression began—and the western creditors wanted their loans repaid.

Results

In summarizing the results of the allied leaders' decisions regarding Eastern Europe after World War I, it is important first of all to emphasize the significance of the establishment of free nations throughout the region. After centuries of repression under foreign empires, many of the peoples of Eastern Europe had their own nation. For some of these peoples, their state was a renewal of a bygone nation; for others, their state was a new creation. For all of them, independence meant new opportunities and challenges. In the way things fell out in the subsequent decades up to the Second World War, the challenges loomed large—and, much of the time, beyond mastering.

A second major result of the decisions regarding Eastern Europe in the post-World War I era, though, was tension among these newly-established states; this tension had various provocations that persisted throughout the decades after World War I. All these states had border disputes with their neighbors; sometimes, these disputes broke out into armed conflict. All these states had minorities who spoke out against perceived oppression and ostracism, pointing out failures of the government to live up to constitutional assurances to minorities; these complaints exacerbated relationships with neighboring states, at least one of which would commonly be dominated by the ethnic group that nearby was a minority. The ideals of nineteenth-century nationalism made these displaced minorities yearn for some way of being incorporated within the state where their ethnic kin were the majority. Equally, nineteenth-century nationalism predisposed those majority states at least to protect their ethnic kin in other states—and, even more, to desire their reincorporation into the majority nation. Often enough, this exacerbated the border disputes; sometimes it led to calls for forcible assimilation of the region in which

20. See the treatment below in chapter 15.

the separated ethnic kin lived. None of this made for peace in Eastern Europe in the aftermath of World War I.

A third major outcome of the decisions of the allied leaders regarding Eastern Europe was governmental confusion. Without experience in democratic self-government on the part of the peoples themselves, and with their leaders (whether elected or appointed) similarly inexperienced in leading governments and keeping bureaucracies functioning, the governments regularly fell into chaos and their officials into corruption. This was neither intended nor excused, of course; even so, the pattern recurred. The allied leaders' insistence that each of the Eastern European nations follow the western governmental pattern and become constitutional democracies not only failed to consult the nations themselves regarding their preferences regarding government; it also failed to consider what inexperience with democratic self-government would likely mean for the stability of these nations. The aftermath of World War I taught this lesson clearly to both the nations of Eastern Europe and to the West.

A fourth major consequence of the decisions regarding Eastern Europe after World War I was the overwhelming economic difficulty for all the nations of the region. Without viable trading partners, with little in the way of capital, and dependent on huge loans from western sources, the Eastern European states faced nearly insuperable problems in making their economies work. Eager hopes for their nations' flourishing gave way to profound disillusionment in the wake of soaring inflation, unemployment, and monetary devaluation.

In the aftermath of World War I, the debilitating problems faced by the nations of Eastern Europe exhausted and frustrated them. The initial joy at independence could not sustain itself in the turbulence of the overwhelming challenges each nation faced. No one in the region seemed ready to give up on independence, to be sure; but many had serious second thoughts about how their nation had been set up by the allied leaders. This led to the fifth major result of the allied leaders' decisions: before 1939, all the states of Eastern Europe had jettisoned constitutional democracy in favor of another form of government, one that promised to eliminate governmental chaos, strengthen the economy, and protect both borders and ethnic kin.

As a sixth point, it should be noted that all these Eastern European states were desperately looking for outside help during the 1930s, in the wake of their own prior problems, the effects of the Great Depression, and the unwillingness of western sources to offer further loans. They all ended up finding help from another nation, on which they ended up becoming economically dependent. This nation had also suffered from the results of World War I and, like the nations of Eastern Europe, could not count on western trade or loans. Nevertheless, it had managed to recover significantly from its economic difficulties, to eliminate governmental chaos and achieve strong government, and had learned how to negotiate effectively regarding its borders and its ethnic kin outside those borders. This nation worked out special trading arrangements with each of the Eastern European states that enabled those nations to survive the 1930s, and they became economically dependent on that nation. In this way, though, the nations of Eastern Europe were drawn into the orbit of that other nation—so much so that they found it necessary to side with it in the initiatives it undertook at the end of the 1930s. The nation was Nazi Germany. This too was, in its own intricate way, a result of the decisions made at the end of the First World War.

Unquestionably, the aftermath of World War I was a significant turning point in the history of Eastern Europe.

CHAPTER 15

The Coming of Communism (1945–48)

> "[The] implementation [of people's democracies] in East Central Europe required methods that were so harsh and so transparently dictated by Moscow as . . . to provoke deep resentment among the subject peoples . . . ."[1]

THOSE WHO GREW UP during the post-World War II period remember well the tensions and fears of the Cold War, when the Union of Soviet Socialist Republics [USSR], the leading state of the Communist world, and the United States of America [USA], the most powerful state in the free world, along with their respective allies, faced off over a mountain of intercontinental ballistic missiles. Nuclear proliferation mushroomed to the point where the USSR and the USA each had enough nuclear firepower to destroy the entire population of the world at least twelve (some military experts calculated as much as fifteen) times. Each side wanted "first-strike" capabilities sufficient to "win" a nuclear war—whatever that might mean. Both also wanted enough capacity to assure that even if the other side attacked first, they would have too much nuclear weaponry to obliterate in a first assault and so would be able to launch a counter-assault. That was the nuclear nightmare with which peoples throughout the world lived for nearly four decades, during the 1950s, 1960s, 1970s, and well into the 1980s.

By the twenty-first century, though, university students have no memory of the Cold War their parents and grandparents lived through: that frightening period had already ended before these young people were even born—both in "the free world" and throughout the old Communist bloc. The world has changed dramatically—in ways that have allowed for better knowledge about, free travel in, and new possibilities for the nations of Eastern Europe, members of the former Communist bloc.

---

1. Rothschild, *Return to Diversity*, 78.

THE COMING OF COMMUNISM (1945-48)   235

Communist Moscow's hegemony dictated what took place throughout Eastern Europe for four decades. It also shaped world history during the lengthy chill of the Cold War. Western scholarship did not turn its attention significantly to Eastern Europe until Communism raised threats to the West, but when it did, that scholarship focused almost entirely on the period of Communist domination.[2] As this volume has tried to show, the history of Eastern Europe that deserves to be studied is much longer than the four decades of Communist dominance over the region. Even so, the coming of Communism throughout Eastern Europe after World War II was undeniably a major turning point in Eastern European history.

Eastern Europe between the World Wars

To understand how Communism could sweep over all of Eastern Europe in the post-World War II period, it is necessary to overview the preceding half-century's developments in the region. Just prior to World War I, almost all of Eastern Europe was ruled by an empire located outside the region—Russian, Austro-Hungarian, German, or Ottoman. The only exceptions were Serbia, Romania, and Bulgaria—all recently wrenched out of the grip of "the sick man of Europe," the Ottoman Empire. The Russian Empire dissolved during the war, because of the revolution that swept through it; the other empires were on the losing side of the war and were dismantled in the peace negotiations held between 1919 and 1923. From the rubble of those empires, states were formed throughout Eastern Europe—some fledgling ones that had never before existed and others as reincarnations of a former polity, but all without recent experience of independence or its responsibility side, self-government. As seen above, this resulted in significant challenges and problems for those Eastern European states in the two decades leading up to World War II. Each state faced a number of significant issues: border disputes, minority rights, inexperience (by the people in self-government and by the officials in leading states and directing bureaucracies), and economic problems.[3]

The situation in which Eastern Europe found itself can be more readily appreciated by considering a specific problem in one of those main issues, as a way of gauging the depth of the challenges offered. That should help readers sense the multitude of other problems in that particular issue—and, from that, the tangle of difficulties engendered by all the big issues together, a complexity pervasive throughout the region and yet also distinctive in its

2. See the discussion above in chapter 5.
3. See the treatment above, in chapter 14.

manifestations within each state. The issue to be treated is the economy, with a major problem—namely, the transportation of goods.

If the economies in these Eastern European nations were going to work, each nation would need to transport goods from one area to the other within the state, on the one hand, and outside the state, to its trading partners, on the other. How were they to do that, though?

Transport by air was then only a wild dream. Trucks were not built large and sturdy enough at the time to haul significant loads, and road systems were neither extensive nor well-built enough to support heavy trucking. Some shipping could be done up the Danube River, but it was the sole navigable major river in the entire region.

So the only way for these Eastern European nations to ship goods was by train. Railroads had already been set up throughout the region, of course, but they had all been built by the empires that formerly dominated Eastern Europe. Those empires built the railroad systems to serve imperial interests. Consequently, the tracks ran to the capital cities or other major cities of the respective empires.

Because of that, for the purposes of the newly independent Eastern European states, the trains ran to the wrong destinations. None of those nations wanted to aid their former masters, fearful as the fledgling nations were that those powers might rise again. The Eastern European states all needed other destinations than the railroad systems within their nations now offered them. Consequently, to enable transport of goods, so essential to a viable economy, each of the states in Eastern Europe had to devote much attention to the time-consuming, labor-intensive, and expensive task of laying new track.

To complicate this challenge, the various states of Eastern Europe also had to deal with the problem that (as of the early 1920s) there was no universally accepted track gauge for railroads. This is a major issue in building a railroad system. The track gauge determines the distance between the two rails on which train cars ride. Any dissonance between track and rail car would result in derailments: train cars ride atop heavy wheel-and-axle units that have no flexibility for expansion or contraction. Uniformity would be needed in all the rail cars and in the entire railroad system in order for the system to work safely. Further, uniformity was needed in the weight of rail used for each line of track;[4] the strength of rail needed to be consistent on each of the main lines of the rail system.

---

4. During my undergraduate years (in the late 1960s), I worked in the summers in a major rail interchange in Galesburg, Illinois, on the "section gang"—which had responsibility for repair and replacement of track. One of the things we had to be careful about was that rail came in various "weights" (per yard of length); these had differing degrees of strength to support rail traffic.

The problem with this was two-fold, one related to the past and the other specific to the post-World War I situation in Eastern Europe. In the past, the various empires had adopted a track gauge for the railroads they had set up throughout their dominions. However, each of the empires had chosen its own track gauge. Consequently, the empires already found it difficult to ship from one empire to another by train, since rail cars could not simply cross an imperial border. For empires, this was not as great a challenge as it would become for the successor states throughout Eastern Europe, since the empires largely sought to be self-sustaining. After the first World War, the various Eastern European states had inherited from their imperial predecessors whatever railroads those empires had previously built and, consequently, the track gauge used for those railroads; for the states that had been cobbled out of more than one empire's holdings, the challenge was to decide which gauge to adopt and what to do with the other rail lines. For all the nations of Eastern Europe, though, the situation demanded that they find ways to ship goods across borders to other Eastern European states—which were probably using the track gauge inherited from their own former imperial masters.

Beyond these formidable challenges, all the nations of Eastern Europe—except one, to be discussed below—depended heavily on foreign investments to sustain their economies; while the precise amount varied, it fell between 50 and 70 percent of the entire economy. Even with low interest rates, that was prohibitively expensive; the nations of Eastern Europe, now independent of their former empires, depended on the West for these loans. So, when the Great Depression broke loose in 1929 and creditors in the West demanded repayment, the nations of Eastern Europe were all hit thunderously. As noted above, this precipitated them into the arms of Nazi Germany as their economic savior.[5]

The only exception to this scenario was Czechoslovakia. She had been unusually privileged during the last half of the nineteenth century in the Austro-Hungarian Empire, since her imperial masters set up a number of factories in the regions that, after World War I, became the state of Czechoslovakia. Among those notable and modern factories were the Krupp Arms Works, which grew to become one of Europe's major producers of armaments. The reason the Austro-Hungarian Empire invested so heavily in the Czech lands was not altruism toward a long-subject people, however; it was a way of mollifying them because of a particular disappointment.

After the Hungarian Revolution of 1848 had been put down—an arduous, long, and costly affair for the Habsburg Empire—the Kaiser determined

5. See above, chapter 14.

to find a way of meeting enough of the Hungarian desire for independence to keep them quiescent within the empire. In due course, he transformed his state into a Dual Empire, with Hungary as an equal partner to Austria. While each of the two would have its own parliament and court system, the two states would have one foreign policy, one military, and one imperial ruler. The Magyars accepted this, and in 1867 the old Habsburg Empire became the Austro-Hungarian Empire.

This development encouraged the next largest subject people in the empire, the Czechs, to seek a similar arrangement. They argued that their loyalty to the Habsburg Empire during the upheavals of the mid-nineteenth century deserved reward, and their large numbers merited special consideration. While the emperor was open to this suggestion, the Hungarians vetoed it: they reasoned that any such arrangement would dilute their own power within a resultant imperial triad, and they did not want to have to reckon with a Slavic entity that could use its authority within the realm to speak out against mistreatment of Slavs within the Hungarian part of the empire. The emperor, recognizing the frustration of the Czechs, wanted to placate their disappointment. To do this, he decided that a large number of the major factories that the Dual Monarchy was erecting would be located within Czech lands. Those factories brought a good measure of prosperity; after the dissolution of the Austro-Hungarian Empire and the establishment of the nation of Czechoslovakia in the wake of World War I, those factories assured Czechoslovakia of an economic strength unique among the peoples of Eastern Europe in the interwar period.

Nevertheless, this all had an unwelcome result: the Dual Monarchy's earlier beneficence toward the Czechs ended up inviting the special attentions of Nazi Germany in the late 1930s. As Adolf Hitler moved inexorably through a military build-up toward the outbreak of hostilities, he cast a covetous eye on the Krupp Arms Works in Czechoslovakia. His war machine needed their capabilities, and possessing them would assure that other nations could not purchase military hardware from them. So he set about appropriating Czechoslovakia to his German realm, legitimizing his claims by alleging the mistreatment of the large numbers of Germans living in the Sudetenland, within the state of Czechoslovakia. He demanded the separation of the Czechoslovak state into a Slovak protectorate and a Czech section dominated by Germany. In 1938, at Munich, "peace in our time" was supposedly purchased, in the stunning brokerage description of the British prime minister Neville Chamberlain, at the low cost of "a far away country [inhabited by] people of whom we know nothing."[6] The Austro-Hungarian

---

6. Cited from Sayer, *The Coasts of Bohemia*, 22.

Empire had bought the favor of the Czechs at an awful cost, paid sooner by the Czechs, but ultimately by the other nations of Europe (and elsewhere) in World War II. By the time of the Munich Peace Conference in 1938, all the other nations of Eastern Europe had already been drawn into Nazi Germany's sphere of influence. In the following year, when World War II broke out, they had little choice but to work with Nazi Germany.

Eastern Europe and World War II

Dependent economically on Nazi Germany as the Eastern European nations had become during the 1930s, there was no easy way for them to dissociate themselves from Germany's path to warfare in 1939. While some Eastern European states managed a less supportive role vis-à-vis Germany than did others, the Nazis demanded loyalty and support from their former trade partners. Bulgaria was the most successful in standing her ground: it was able both to escape Nazi occupation and to offer only minimal cooperation to Hitler's forces throughout the war.

Until March 1941, Yugoslavia remained neutral, but then the Nazis forced the Yugoslav leadership to a decision. When, in the face of widespread disagreement, the government acquiesced to their demands, Serb patriots led a sudden putsch (on March 26, 1941); the government established out of it declined to cooperate with the Nazis. Furious at this, Hitler ordered the *Luftwaffe* to bomb Yugoslavia and sent the *Wehrmacht* into the country. In only a few weeks, the Yugoslav army was overwhelmed. Yugoslavia was dismembered, and a fascist group of Croats, the Ustashe (led by the notorious Ante Pavelić), were given control of Croatia and Bosnia-Herzegovina. They inaugurated a wave of terror, intimidation, and ethnic cleansing directed against non-Croats; Ustashe brutality in this venture was gross enough that Italy's Fascist leaders, co-belligerents with the Nazis, expressed horror at the atrocities perpetrated.[7]

Romanian fascists only too readily acquiesced to Nazi directives regarding Jews; indeed, Romania won the ignoble distinction of being the most complaisant Eastern European nation in the holocaust. The treatment meted out to the Jews by Romanian fascist forces was grotesque enough that even Adolf Eichmann expressed his revulsion.[8] By contrast, Bulgaria refused to comply with Nazi directives about Jews; King Boris III himself orchestrated this thwarting of Nazi purposes in the country.[9]

7. This was reported in Walters, *The Other Europe*, 292.
8. As reported in Kaplan, *Balkan Ghosts*, 128.
9. Kaplan, *Balkan Ghosts*, 204.

By 1941, Nazi Germany had brought all of Eastern Europe except the Russian-held parts of Poland under its control. The Ribbentrop-Molotov Pact of 1939 between Nazi Germany and Communist Russia had divided Poland between them and had promised a non-aggression stance between the two powers. By June 1941, though, Hitler had had enough of non-aggression, and he turned his forces against Russian-held territories. Quickly, the Nazis overran the rest of Poland, marched through and took possession of Ukraine, and invaded Russia herself. This fateful decision on Hitler's part turned Communist Russia into a foe.

The western forces arrayed against Nazi Germany were only too happy to welcome Russia as an ally in their determination to drive the Nazi forces back into Germany and reduce the German state to impotence. In the decades since the 1917 October Revolution in Russia, the western powers—the USA, Canada, England, and France—had often expressed fear of and opposition to the Communism that Russia embodied. In the exigencies of the Second World War, though, they gratefully acknowledged the contribution Russia could make to the collective opposition to Nazi Germany. Indeed, if the Nazis were to be defeated, some power would have to drive back German forces in Eastern Europe, and Russia was the only one positioned to do so. Whatever misgivings or apprehensions the allies from the West might have had regarding Communist Russia gave way to the practical realities of waging war. So, Communist Russia joined the USA, Canada, England, and France as the allies who opposed Nazi Germany.

The realities of the situation led to decisions about how the allies would fight. France, England, Canada, and the USA would attack from the west and south, the Soviet Union from the northeast and east. Basically, the allies would fight their way across Nazi-occupied Europe, through Germany herself, and meet at the German capital city, Berlin. But that meant that the Soviet Union was to liberate Eastern Europe.

The allies put pressure on Nazi Germany (and its ally, Fascist Italy) from numerous directions. Campaigns in North Africa cleared the way for the invasion of Italy, and intense planning led to the June 6, 1944, invasion of Normandy; these endeavors from west and south were led by the western allies—the USA, Canada, England, and France. At the same time, the forces of Communist Russia were rolling back the Nazi armies from Russia herself, and then out of Ukraine, Poland, Hungary, Romania, and Czechoslovakia. With the exception of Bulgaria, from which the minimal German forces withdrew on their own, and of Yugoslavia, where Josip Broz's Partisans expelled the Nazis, the rest of Eastern Europe was liberated by Russian force (aided, to be sure, by insurgent guerilla forces in several of the Nazi-occupied states). The Russian contribution to the defeat of Germany was absolutely necessary, since Nazi forces had to be driven out of their eastern conquests, and the western allies had no other way than the Russians to achieve that goal. For the Russians, though, the war was exceedingly costly: more than 22,000,000 citizens of the USSR lost their lives during it. But they liberated Eastern Europe from the Nazis.

Communist Russia and Eastern Europe

The allies recognized that they would need to do more than just defeat Nazi Germany: the war had devastated much of Europe, and it would need to be rebuilt—not only buildings, roads, and bridges, but also stable governments and working economies. The allies pledged themselves to this noble task. To achieve it, though, they would have to divide Europe up into spheres of influence.

The war was progressing well for the allies, and as of early 1945, it was obvious that Nazi Germany was "on the ropes"; it was only a matter of time before the knockout punch was delivered. So in February 1945 the allied leaders—Winston Churchill, prime minister of Britain; Franklin D. Roosevelt, president of the USA; and Josef Stalin, premier of the Soviet Union—met in Yalta, in the Crimea, to set up the respective spheres of influence for the allies after the war. At that meeting, it was agreed that the USSR would have the whole of Eastern Europe as its responsibility and sphere of influence.

In one sense, this was entirely understandable: the Russian military was forcing its way against stiff German resistance throughout the whole of Eastern Europe. Given the immense sacrifices Russia was making in her contribution to Nazi Germany's defeat, it was appropriate that her area of influence would also be considerable. The western allies were recapturing Western Europe and appropriately took responsibility for it. But by the Yalta decision, neither Roosevelt nor Churchill intended for Stalin and the Soviet Union to transform Eastern Europe into a group of Communist states or satellites. The Russians were supposed to help these nations get back on their feet, protect them against civil war, and facilitate their self-governance.

What was the original intention of the Soviet Union, though, as it marched into Germany and took responsibility for the Eastern European states after World War II? It is not at all clear that Stalin intended to force all the states to become Communist. Admittedly, that was his intention for Poland and Czechoslovakia; he wanted to assure that with both nations, so they could serve as buffer states between the USSR and Germany (whatever might happen with her). But the available data indicate that Stalin was at least ambivalent in 1945 about forcing Hungary, Romania, and Bulgaria into a Communist mold. He certainly intended to set up Communist parties in each of the countries, and the USSR would unquestionably offer those parties every financial assistance and other help necessary to come to power in the various Eastern European countries. But in the immediate aftermath of World War II, the respective Communists were only one party among many in the Eastern European states.

With the end of the war, though, tensions flared up between the western allies and the USSR. The other allies did not want Communism to spread beyond its Russian borders. The idealism expressed for a better collective future after World War II inspired some Western Europeans to look with favor on Communism as an option; the allies, openly wary again of Communism, spoke out about its dangers. With what was being said and the attitudes expressed about the Soviet Union and Communism, Stalin had second thoughts about his plans regarding Eastern Europe—or perhaps his thoughts came into greater focus. For centuries, Russia had entertained suspicions about the West's purposes with regard to her; the post-World War II comments from her erstwhile allies raised those suspicions to the surface again—this time focused especially on the Communist ideology that now shaped her existence.

From the Soviet Union's perspective, it appeared the western allies were ganging up to criticize her and to undermine Communism. If they would do this in the flush of victory, what might happen subsequently? So the USSR determined to protect itself against possible dangers from the West, in part by establishing Communist governments everywhere in Eastern Europe. In each country, the Soviet Union manipulated its protector status there and saw to it that the Communist Party became the leading party, the elected government, and in due course the sole legitimate party in each nation. The USSR's overwhelming power, manifest in her continuing military presence throughout the region, assured that each Eastern European nation followed the path of Communist development authorized by Moscow.

The USSR hoped to achieve two major purposes by this. Firstly, the Eastern European nations would serve as a significant buffer against any possible aggression from the West. To move against Communist Russia would require traversing and subduing a considerable portion of the region. With that, Russia would have ample time to prepare for the impending invasion, and her aggressors would sustain significant casualties in the process. Secondly, the Russian leadership was committed to the ideology of Communism. From their perspective, they were benefiting the Eastern European nations thus and were accelerating the coming eschaton of Communist fulfillment. According to Communist theory, history was inexorably moving toward an age of international proletarian brotherhood marked by shared ownership of the means of production and the disappearance of the state (since paradisiacal conditions would arise). By forcing the Eastern European nations to become Communist, the USSR was only speeding up the process for them and thus assuring their benefit sooner. So the USSR saw to it that all the nations of Eastern Europe became Communist states.

The Communist Bloc

In so doing, the USSR set up what came to be known as the Communist bloc. The increasing hostility of the verbal war between the former allies led each side to seek protection against the other. The West consolidated its defensive possibilities with the establishment of the North Atlantic Treaty Organization [NATO], a defensive affiliation according to which all the member states would unitedly come to the defense of any member state that came under attack. The greatest threat, in the estimation of the NATO signatories, came from Communist Russia and its satellites. For its part, the Communist bloc responded with a defensive organization of its own, which came to be known (from the Polish city in which it was signed) as the "Warsaw Pact." Its provisions made for the same kind of united defense of any signatory that came under attack. For the members of the Warsaw Pact, the danger to be defended against was aggression from the West. In due course, as nuclear capabilities developed on both sides, each of the major participants in the two defensive alliances—the USA for NATO and the USSR for the Warsaw Pact—developed first-strike capacities sufficient to cripple its alternate number. This was an unusual stance to take for powers focused, allegedly, only on defense; perhaps both sides heeded the old adage that the best defense is a good offense. In any event, with all this, the Cold War had broken out. Much of it was thus spent rattling sabres, producing nuclear weapons, and generating statements about peace that were coded warnings about conflict.

Fearful of the West and its intrigues against Communism, and suspicious of Eastern European commitment toward its Communist future, Russia sought to control the Eastern European countries closely. In those nations, no deviations from the Moscow-approved line of development toward the Communist golden age were to be tolerated; it was one thing to welcome these states along for the trip, but they must not arrogate to themselves the assumption that they should help describe the course—that was Moscow's exclusive prerogative. Indeed, from the USSR's perspective, and according to its practice for four decades, the Eastern European nations had no future except that envisioned for them by the leadership of the USSR. These satellites revolved around the Soviet Union. Their only approved purpose was to serve the needs of the mother state of Communism.

The leaders of the USSR were determined to coordinate the further development of Communism. Rather than just letting it develop on its own and proceed at a leisurely historical pace, the leaders of the Soviet Union decided to speed up the process and direct it. To achieve this, they needed and for nearly four decades required absolute obedience from the USSR's satellites in Eastern Europe. When Yugoslavia decided to take its own path into the Communist future in 1948, Stalin was furious but ultimately could not enforce his will there. Later, in the early 1960s, Romania set out on its own course, somewhat distinct from Moscow's intentions; the Soviet leadership barely tolerated the willfulness. When Albania subsequently denounced the USSR for going soft on Communism, Moscow was bemused but let its distant satellite go its own way. For the rest of Eastern Europe's states, though—the ones closest to the USSR and on which her security depended—there could be no deviation.

To facilitate the development of Communism in Eastern Europe, Moscow adopted central planning for the economies of the respective member states of the Communist bloc. Muscovite leaders determined which kinds of products would become the specializations of the Eastern European nations—Ukraine was to produce the heavy agricultural machinery for the bloc, for example, while Hungary would produce the pharmaceuticals. Beyond that, the Soviet Union engaged in central planning for the Communist bloc's armed forces, to assure maximum coordination. No deviations were to be tolerated from Moscow's line, whether in economic or military matters or in any other regard. The governments of Eastern Europe were free, but free only to do Moscow's will.

Eventually, Soviet leadership styles backed away from and, under Nikita Krushchev, denounced the rigidities and excesses of Stalin. The Communist period of Eastern European history was not one long, monotonous, monochrome blur.[10] In some of the Communist states in Eastern Europe, various modifications did take place that showed a measure of independence vis-à-vis Moscow. Nevertheless, the USSR managed to impose a commonality of experience over the entire region during the four decades following the coming of Communism between 1945 and 1948.

In the midst of all the developments that Eastern European peoples have subsequently been free to decry as objectionable, it should be acknowledged that the period of domination by the USSR instituted some

---

10. See the treatment below, in chapter 16.

significant changes throughout Eastern Europe, changes that had both positive impact and negative repercussions on the entire region. For all the upheaval caused by Moscow's rigid direction of developments, it nonetheless achieved significant transformation. Prior to World War II, the nations of Eastern Europe were overwhelmingly rural and agricultural. The Soviet Union forced on each of them a radical sociological and economic transformation: within a relatively short space of time—much shorter than in any of the countries of the West—each Eastern European nation became an industrialized state with a significant urban population base. That was a brutal change for most of the people who endured it: forced off their farms into cities and ensconced as laborers in factories, many Eastern Europeans found themselves dislocated from the familiar. Even so, in short order, the Communist hegemony from Moscow managed to achieve a drastic change of society throughout Eastern Europe. But this had its shadow side, as well: in addition to the psychological and sociological devastation visited upon the peoples of the region, the pell-mell rush to industrialize left scant room to be concerned with environmental repercussions. The fixation on industrial achievement led to ecological devastation throughout much of Eastern Europe: air quality suffered, and rivers were polluted with industrial waste. This, too, is a legacy of the Communist period of Eastern European history. Its effects will take a long time to correct.

Eastern Europe under Communism

More could be written about Communism's impact on Eastern Europe; indeed, the overwhelming majority of books about the region have focused on the period of the Cold War, so there are abundant resources for readers interested in exploring that period. Not so much, though, has been written about a significant question: how did Eastern Europeans react to Communism? The answer is as simple as it is telling: they reacted to Communist Russia as they had to the region's previous imperial masters.

In the first place, the Eastern European peoples soon came to look on Communism and its enforcer, the USSR, as just another form of repression. Not long before, all these peoples had emerged from multiplied centuries of rule by foreign empires bent on enforcing their will on their subjects. While some people sought to capitalize on the possibilities opened up by the coming of Communism, many Eastern Europeans just slipped back into the familiar mold of enduring repression; this was not a distant memory for the peoples of the region.

Secondly, they managed to reclaim the ability, developed over long centuries of imperial rule, to be complaisant with whatever was foisted on them, but without being convinced. During the long period of foreign overlordship, Eastern Europeans had learned to go along, to live through whatever they were facing. During the four decades of Communist dominance, only a small percentage of the populace in any Eastern European state ever became members of the Communist Party. Given the blandishments of possible personal advancement that would have been opened up by such membership, the low numbers of party members manifest Eastern European readiness to endure what had come over them without endorsing it or taking advantage of it.

Thirdly, these responses led to simply accommodating to survive, as they had before, under their previous imperial masters. This meant offering one face in public, where one's position might depend on saying what was expected of a person committed to Communist ideology, and putting on another at home, where one could be utterly honest. Of course, living in such a manner has consequences for personal integrity: as a respected Roman Catholic priest from Poland pointed out after the collapse of Communism, this pattern of dissimulation produced double lives, a legacy of the Communist period that will haunt people for many years and keep them from the internal freedom and integrity that they need.[11] The stimulus to this pattern of deception was the determination, common throughout Eastern Europe during the Communist period, to exist during and possibly outlive the situation.

In addition to these individual coping strategies, some Communist governments in Eastern Europe tried to achieve modifications in the Communist system. These were attempts to make Communism work better within their countries. Both Hungary, with its "goulash socialism" (in 1956), and Czechoslovakia, with its "socialism with a human face" (in 1968), found out, though, that Moscow expected compliance, not creativity.

The ruthless repression of these endeavors by Russian intervention, despite the obvious support of the Hungarian and Czechoslovakian populace, led many Eastern Europeans to a "This too shall pass" attitude. They recognized that the renewal endeavors in both Hungary and Czechoslovakia had been supported by students and workers—the two groups touted in Communist ideology as the hope of the future. Many people throughout Eastern Europe discerned that, in brutally crushing both these movements, the Soviet Union had squelched and denigrated the aspirations of the people they supposedly favored. Through this, Communism was widely

---

11. This assessment was offered by Fr. Michal Czajkowski in "Faith Under Fire."

discredited throughout the region. Many people in Eastern Europe came to the assessment that, whatever the rhetoric might be from Moscow or from their own Communist functionaries, Communism did not really serve the democratic longings of its subjects.

Many came to the conclusion after 1968 that Communism had failed and could only survive by force. For them, Communism was a defeated, defunct ideology. They believed it would eventually "wither away and die" (to appropriate the Communist mantra regarding the state). As 1989 showed, that is precisely what happened.

Even so, the coming of Communism between 1945 and 1948 was a significant turning point in the history of Eastern Europe.

CHAPTER 16

The Overthrow of Communism (1989)

*"Communism was overthrown by life,
by thought, by human dignity."*[1]

FOR THOSE LIVING IN the West—called "the free world" during the Cold War—the collapse of Communism throughout Eastern Europe in 1989[2] came like a bolt out of the blue. Tensions between the Communist bloc and the West had periodically abated somewhat over the course of the Cold War, only to be heightened again in one way or another. Whatever happened in these regards, though, Communist control of Eastern Europe remained solid. Communism had given no indication that it sensed its days in the region were numbered—at least, not by any signals picked up in the West.[3] For all the sophisticated political analysis of the Communist world by the West's most gifted and insightful experts, and despite the immense quantities of information assiduously gathered by the impressive espionage networks surreptitiously run by western governments, *no one in the West* saw that collapse coming—and certainly not the way it happened. Transforming the entire political landscape and inaugurating wide new possibilities for all the nations of the region, the overthrow of Communism throughout Eastern Europe in 1989 was unquestionably a major turning point in Eastern European history.

---

1. Havel, *Summer Meditations*, 5.

2. In the USSR, Communism survived until 1991; by then, the Communist bloc had ceased to exist, owing to the 1989 events in Eastern Europe.

3. In the years since 1989, some western scholars and pundits have suggested that they saw the collapse of Communism coming soon; however, the only published work that offered anything even remotely close to such a prognostication was Brzezinski, *Out of Control*, in which he urged that Communism would probably come to an end by 2000; significantly, when the work was published, this claim was scornfully derided.

Outside Influences

A few outside influences contributed to the overthrow of Communism in Eastern Europe in 1989. It should be stressed that these influences did not themselves cause the dramatic sea change in the region; for that, one must examine what transpired within Eastern Europe itself. Before turning to those intra-regional considerations, though, it is important to acknowledge three external factors that contributed to what happened in 1989.

The first of these was the USA's "Star Wars" defense initiative. Over the course of the Cold War, both the USA and the USSR had expended enormous sums arming themselves against possible warfare with the other. Research on and development of increasingly sophisticated nuclear capacities pushed each of the superpowers to match and then try to surpass the other's formidable latest developments, but this required the ongoing allocation of overwhelming amounts of funds. By the early 1980s, when the USA, under President Ronald Reagan, indicated that its newest defense initiative would be the mounting of nuclear weapons on satellites in space, from which they could be launched in the face of any aggression, the USSR's leadership had come to recognize that it could no longer afford the extravagant demands on its budget necessitated by the arms race. The Star Wars initiative thus brought on a crisis for the USSR, the dominant nation of the Communist bloc. The changes instituted to deal with that crisis helped precipitate the 1989 events.

The second contributing factor to the events of 1989 was the package of changes instituted by the Soviet general secretary, Mikhail Gorbachev, in the mid-1980s. When he attained that post in 1985, he inherited a financially crippled Soviet Union. Early in the Cold War, the USSR had outstripped the West in developing nuclear military capabilities, but the USA and its allies had long since caught up. By the late 1970s, the ongoing nuclear arms race demanded so much financial commitment that the necessities of life for the peoples of the USSR received little governmental attention; frankly put, the peoples of the Soviet Union (and of the Communist bloc more generally) were beginning to wonder rather openly when the workers' paradise promised by Communism was going to come. Missiles were no substitute for well-stocked market shelves or such foundational necessities as fruit, meat, and basic toiletries. Gorbachev recognized that the arms race had contributed significantly to the financial stress of the USSR, and that his country could no longer afford to keep pace with the proposed American deployment of missiles in space.

To deal with the challenges occasioned by this concern (and many others), Gorbachev set out on a new course. He startled his colleagues in the

Soviet Union and people around the world by insisting on *"Perestroika"*—"economic restructuring." This entailed a significant change in Communist Russia's views on economics and its practice. *"Perestroika"* was no turn toward the West's free market capitalism, but it was a significant shift away from the central planning that had dominated both the USSR's internal economic practice and its dealings with its Eastern European satellites.[4] The economic determinism associated with Communist ideology would have to force its way in the world on its own, rather than being directed by and implemented out of Moscow.

"Perestroika" entailed a profound adjustment of Communist practice, especially when tied to the other innovation Gorbachev introduced, *"Glasnost"*—"openness." This *"Glasnost"* offered political openness—inviting people to speak their minds, a loosening of the limits on free speech, even allowing the possibility that some might publicly disagree with the Communist political leadership. *"Glasnost"* was not absolutely without limits, but it offered opportunities for discussion and thus invited people to assess how well their Communist state was serving them (as well as moving toward the goal of Communist ideology).

As general secretary of the Soviet Union, Gorbachev was also the unquestioned leader of the Communist bloc. He startled the USSR's Eastern European satellites by indicating that he expected the governments throughout the region to follow the Soviet Union's lead in this economic restructuring and openness. This was unsettling for them: Gorbachev was indicating that they were on their own as far as carrying forward the Communist movement in their respective nations; changes would be allowed in the USSR and were to be allowed in the states of the Communist bloc that were simply unthinkable only months beforehand.[5] A startling corollary to all this was Gorbachev's broad intimation that the Soviet Union would not be sending in the tanks to quell developments that in Moscow's estimation had gotten out of line, as had periodically happened in the decades since World War II.[6] The Soviet premier indicated that thenceforward the member nations of the Communist bloc would work together as a federation of like-minded states, but would no longer be dictated to by the Soviet Union. Utterly unanticipated throughout Eastern Europe, this monumental transition in Moscow contributed to developments throughout the region that culminated in the events of 1989.

---

4. See above, chapter 15.
5. See the discussion of this in Bailey, *The Spring of Nations*, 58.
6. See the treatment below in this chapter.

The third outside influence was the election of a Polish cardinal, Karol Jan Wojtyła, as pope on October 16, 1978; he took the name John Paul II. It is significant that, as an Eastern European religious figure, he had long been recognized and respected as a leader of the Christian opposition to Communism.

Soon after his election, Pope John Paul II told the Polish Communist government—not "asked," but *told* them—that he was coming for a visit, and that he would advise (not "consult with") them when that would be. John Paul II knew, as did the Communist leaders of his homeland, that over 90 percent of the Poles were Roman Catholic. The pope recognized the attractiveness he would have and the authority he would wield by his presence among the Polish people, and he played the situation masterfully. He came to visit Poland June 2–10, 1979; four years later, he returned to Poland June 16–23, 1983.

When he arrived both times, he was greeted enthusiastically by hundreds of thousands of people, who filled the streets, no matter where he went. This became known throughout Eastern Europe. Prior to the pope's visit, over the more than thirty years of Communist experience in Poland, for any mass demonstration, the Communist government had to roust people out into the streets to produce a crowd dutifully cheering whatever foreign Communist dignitary came to visit. Of course, the Polish Communist government had no interest in thus encouraging its subjects for a religious leader, but no matter: the Polish people poured into the streets on their own. The Poles' excitement was obvious and spontaneous.[7] The other peoples of Eastern Europe recognized both sides of this scenario, as well. Eastern Europe was watching—and listening.

John Paul II spoke openly and vigorously about human dignity, freedom, human rights, and the need for all—including governments—to serve others and not just themselves. He spoke; the Polish people listened and cheered thunderously. The other peoples of Eastern Europe listened—and found hope. The Polish Communist government quailed;[8] it dared not do or say much about the pope's visit or his words. The visits by John Paul II had

---

7. In the years after John Paul II's first visit, I spoke with several Poles who were living in Poland when he came to Poland; they always indicate their own excitement and that of their fellow citizens at the Polish pontiff's visit and recall it with warm and joyful memories.

8. Kazimierz Kakol, the Communist Minister of Religious Affairs in Poland (1974–80), said, "Twenty minutes after the Pope was elected, I said that the Pope was going to come to Poland when he wanted to, and that's what happened. Generally, my feelings were complicated. On the one hand, satisfaction that . . . a Pole is the Pope, but on the other hand, we were scared of what's going to happen"; the interview in which Kakol made this statement is included in "Faith Under Fire."

a profoundly galvanizing effect on Polish aspirations for freedom, dignity, and a different future. The peoples of Eastern Europe watched carefully: they had seen an Eastern European stand up to a Communist government and make it back down. A seed had been sown among them; it would grow and bear surprising fruit in 1989.

Statues dot Eastern European countries that Pope John Paul II, as outspoken opponent of Communism, visited; here, the statue commemorating his visit in Djakovo, Croatia.

Background

In turning now to consider what transpired within Eastern Europe itself that led to the startling overthrow of Communism in 1989, it is necessary to acknowledge that this brief treatment can give only a cursory overview of a few significant developments that took place throughout the region. On almost all of these, much more extensive analyses are available, which offer painstaking consideration of developments and attention to specific detail. Even so, an overview is valuable in drawing together disparate evidence of what was going on throughout the region—especially if that overview is based on what people from within Eastern Europe itself have written about the developments leading up to 1989. Too often in the years since then, we in the West have listened only to the assessments of western analysts detailing what, in their estimation, led up to and transpired in 1989. The picture comes out somewhat differently if Eastern Europeans approach the canvas. The rest of this presentation will draw on what authors and scholars from the region have had to say, to show how Eastern Europeans themselves viewed what led to the overthrow of Communism in Eastern Europe in 1989.

In this regard, it is important to recognize, first of all, that the Communist experience was not monolithic. Often, the impression people in the West generally had was that the Communist period was a long, gray, unchanging, monotonous blur, always the same thing all those years. That was emphatically *not* how the peoples of Eastern Europe and the leaders of the Communist states experienced the four decades of Communism, however. Since things changed from time to time and from one region to another, the peoples of Eastern Europe had the opportunity to assess what was happening around them and to evaluate Communism and its practice among them, with consequences that contributed to what transpired in 1989. This presentation will note only the most dramatic of these changes.

By 1948, Marshal Tito (Josip Broz), the Communist leader of Yugoslavia, had made it clear that he intended to develop a distinctively Yugoslavian form of Communism, even though Josef Stalin wanted a more international movement, directed by Moscow. The Yugoslav leader respected the USSR as a great Communist state, but the Partisans he had led during World War II had not depended on the Soviet Union to liberate their nation; alone of all the Eastern European nations, the Yugoslavs had expelled the Nazi forces without Soviet help. Tito consequently did not feel beholden to Stalin.

The Soviet leader was furious with the Yugoslav upstart, but Tito stood his ground against the Soviet leader's fulminations. Much to his chagrin, Stalin was unable to impose his will on far-away Yugoslavia. But the USSR's leader was in more solid control of the rest of Eastern Europe, and he insisted that each of the governments in the Communist states put on trial all those who were guilty, like Tito, of seeking a national rather than an international form of Communism. Further, Stalin dictated to each of the satellite countries' Communist governments the percentage of Communist Party members who must be found guilty. This travesty of proletarian justice led to the infamous show trials of the early 1950s when, dutifully enough, throughout

Eastern Europe the Communist governments judged the requisite numbers guilty and either executed them or sent them to prison. Rigid, unquestioning obedience was expected and given by each of the Eastern European Communist satellite national governments.

In 1953, Stalin died. His eventual successor, Nikita Krushchev, startled the USSR and the Communist bloc in 1956 at the Twentieth Party Congress in the Soviet Union when he condemned Stalin's errors and excesses. Krushchev denounced the show trials of only a few years before, declared them irredeemably flawed, and called the Communist states of Eastern Europe to revisit those trials and exonerate those who were not really guilty. This was no minor adjustment in Communist practice for the Eastern European governments. Some of them (like Poland) welcomed the opportunity to clear the air,[9] but others (like Czechoslovakia) were stunned and hesitant. Many of the leaders in these Communist governments owed their positions to those trials, when others had been bumped out because of their alleged crimes against international Communism. If those people now were to be exonerated, what would happen to current rulers? Further, what if Moscow changed its mind again?

Each of the Eastern European Communist governments handled Krushchev's invitation its own way. Some, like Poland, vigorously set about the re-examination of the trials; others, like Czechoslovakia, temporized and basically did nothing. All of them could appeal to problems or difficulties, and the resultant process was far from uniform throughout Eastern Europe.

This was the first instance of a sudden transformation within Communist experience, occasioned by a dramatic shift in Moscow. As Eastern European nations would learn later in that year, though, and subsequently, the USSR was not opening the gates to initiatives for change spawned outside the Kremlin. Changes could be dictated by the USSR, but its satellites were not supposed to arrogate to themselves the authority to institute them on their own.

The Communist satellites had learned that a national path to Communism, such as Yugoslavia had openly adopted, was repugnant to the Soviet leadership. Even so, some Communist governments in Eastern Europe tried to effect modifications in what was expected in this internationalist Communism: they found that they needed to make accommodations to their people's background and predilections if they were to have any hope of imposing Communism successfully.

9. As a result of the re-evaluation of the earlier trials, Władysław Gomułka (earlier leader of the Communist government in Poland) was rehabilitated; eventually, he rose to lead the Polish Communist government again.

One example was in regard to religion in Poland. Marxism-Leninism was ideologically atheistic; its Muscovite interpreters were determined to root out religious faith and practice and had carried on a vigorous campaign to reduce the churches and other religious organizations in the USSR to impotence.[10] The Polish Communist leaders soon found that the Poles did not look on Communism as a viable substitute for their long-standing religious commitment: throughout the entire Communist period, 90 percent or more of the Polish people remained members of the Roman Catholic church. The Polish Communist leaders came to recognize that Communism needed to find some way of living with the Roman Catholic church in their nation if Communism were to take root there. They urged Moscow to acknowledge that what had worked in the USSR could not be implemented in Poland in the same way. This did not entail for them any doubt about the Marxist-Leninist expectation that religion would be eliminated; it would just have to be overcome in a lengthier, different way than had been pursued in the USSR. The Polish Communist leadership managed successfully to impress on Moscow that they would need to deal with the peculiarities of the Polish people in a way other than what had worked so ruthlessly and efficiently in the USSR. Moscow reluctantly acquiesced.

Further, Hungary's Communist leadership tried to get Moscow to appreciate that the distinctive Magyar culture needed to be accommodated in the attempt to impose Communism. A non-Slavic island in a sea of Slavs, Magyars had long prided themselves on their differences from their neighbors culturally (in everything from cuisine to scientific accomplishment, with all the arts interspersed between). This attitude, over nine centuries in the making, meant that too rigid a doctrine of internationalism would strike the Hungarians as an attack on all that they had held dear and would be virtually impossible to "sell" in Hungary. The Hungarian leadership pleaded for a bit of forbearance in their assimilation of Communism to Hungarian distinctiveness. Moscow granted it; however, as the events of 1956 demonstrated, there were limits to the USSR's willingness to bend in this direction.

The Soviet Union had opposed such accommodations in the immediate post–World War II years, but by the mid-1950s it was becoming obvious that certain adjustments needed to be made for the various nations of Eastern Europe. The sheer inertia of distinctive cultures, together with the undeniable difference among the nations of Eastern Europe, forced on

---

10. All the Christian churches in the USSR, but especially the largest one, the Russian Orthodox church, suffered terribly under harsh Communist repression; it has been estimated that Russian Orthodoxy had more martyrs in the twentieth century alone than the entire ancient church had suffered in the centuries before the Edict of Milan in 313 AD.

Moscow something for which she was not ready in Stalin's time. Instead of a Communist International in which every state was in lock-step and identical in practice, the USSR found it necessary to allow some variations; even so, as developments showed, until Gorbachev such divergences were strictly limited to what Moscow would approve.

This led to uncertainties and dangers for the Communist governments of Eastern Europe, which had to walk a tightrope between pleasing Moscow and keeping peace at home. There was an ongoing and complicated uncertainty about what the USSR would and would not allow, and so between what local Communist authorities might get away with and might not. Not surprisingly, the peoples of Eastern Europe, and certainly their leaders, were somewhat uneasy with the Communist status quo, because it could and periodically did change. One of the contributing factors to the overthrow of Communism in 1989 was the shifting sands on which Communism seemed to be built.

A second contributing factor to the overthrow of Communism in 1989 was what the Eastern Europeans recognized were Russian violations of Communist ideology. Radio and television broadcasts, newspaper reports and journal articles, public speeches and pronouncements, all worked together with what was taught in the school systems to ensure that, by the mid-1950s, everyone in Eastern Europe had been indoctrinated to some degree in Communist ideology. As a result, the peoples of Eastern Europe knew what was supposed to be true and what would supposedly happen in history according to that ideology. Consequently, they were equipped to evaluate on their own what transpired in Hungary in 1956 and in Czechoslovakia in 1968. In the estimation of many people in Eastern Europe, the result of such evaluation was that Communist ideology "had been weighed in the balances, and found wanting."[11]

The movements in Hungary in the mid-1950s and in Czechoslovakia in the later 1960s were not attempts to destroy Communism: both were attempts to help it work better as a form of government. The Communist promise was, after all, that Communism served the people; the peoples in Hungary and in Czechoslovakia urged some improvements. They found out, though, that the advertising for Communism was not necessarily what Moscow actually intended to provide.

During 1956, Hungary managed to develop a distinctive style of Communism, dubbed "goulash socialism." It reflected and responded to unique emphases of Magyar culture. For centuries, Magyars had recognized their

---

11. Cf. Daniel 5:27.

differences from neighboring peoples.¹² The people of Hungary endorsed the Communist emphasis that all ought to be cared for by all, and they appreciated the idea that everyone should have a job and contribute to the welfare of everyone else; with their "goulash socialism," they tried to find ways to modify the practice of Communism so that its supposed strengths would be more evident within a Hungarian perspective, and so that all the people would benefit and work together better, given Hungarian predilections.

The Communist leaders of Hungary were not involved in the discussions: they passively acquiesced, looking for what might come out of them. Students from the universities started holding strikes or protests to talk about things that needed to be changed in education and government practice. As their views became known, large numbers of workers also offered suggestions about what needed to be changed in work practices and government. So, students and workers—the two favored groups in Communist ideology, since they were the harbingers of the future, according to Communist expectations—got involved in assessing Communist practices and accomplishments, criticizing failures, and proposing strategies for improvement. The Hungarian Communist government was not leading; it was listening and, in due course, began to implement some of the suggestions made. Radio broadcasts in Hungary and newspapers there allowed open criticism of Communist practice and urged ways of improving Communist society in Hungary.

In Moscow's estimation, the Hungarian government had let this go on rather too long and too freely. Earlier in 1956, Krushchev had denounced Stalin's excesses in handling the supposed problem of national paths to Communism, but that did not mean that any and all such national paths to Communism were suddenly welcome. Krushchev made his displeasure known and instructed the Hungarian leadership to tighten things up immediately. When, nevertheless, things continued in the same vein in Hungary, Moscow sent in the tanks. The Russian forces stationed in Hungary marched into Budapest and other main cities to restore proper Communist order.

However, the Hungarian army regiments sided with their countrymen, rather than with the forces of their Muscovite lords. Fighting broke out; the Hungarian movement became a revolution. In short order, though, the Russian forces prevailed, and the Hungarian Revolution was quashed. Moscow's

---

12. Magyars speak a language unrelated to those of any of their neighbors; they had originally come from far out in eastern Asia, from deep in Siberia, and had settled in the middle of Eastern Europe; for almost 1,000 years their history and culture had developed as distinct from those of their neighbors. Even within the internationalism demanded by Communism, the Magyars instinctively expected that their distinctiveness would somehow certainly be manifested.

reprisals were severe: the entire leadership of the Hungarian Communist government was sacked and replaced with Communist functionaries who appeared to be more ready to do the USSR's bidding.

The Soviet Union had brought the Hungarian movement to a bloody end. Not surprisingly, many people in Eastern Europe reflected on what had just transpired. Out of supposed devotion to Communism, the Russians had destroyed a movement generated by the two favored groups of Communist ideology, the students and the workers, who had shown the effrontery to suggest better ways for government and society. Was this in the service of Communism, or of Russian hegemony?

An uneasy disquiet prevailed among the peoples of Eastern Europe for the next dozen years. Then in 1968, the Czechoslovakian Communist leadership moved toward some changes in practice in their country. This time, rather than bubbling up from below, where the people might be less committed to or knowledgeable in the technicalities of Communist ideology and expectation, the movement for renewal issued from those entrusted by Moscow with the direction of the Czechoslovak state. Alexander Dubček, the first secretary of the Communist party, and his colleagues sought what they called "socialism with a human face"—a kinder, gentler Communism that would meet the needs of its people better, encourage them to involve themselves vigorously in Communist society, and be open to them, rather than repressive of them.

Again, the students and the workers welcomed this move, as did the large majority of the people. With the government's encouragement and blessing, Czechoslovaks began openly calling for and seeking means to implement freedom of speech, the end of censorship, and open debate about public policy. Dubček and his colleagues wanted to have the citizens of their country discuss what the leadership proposed, to see if those proposals could be improved or replaced with even better ones. They thus hoped the people would come to own Communism for themselves. Arguing that Communism sought to carry out the will of the people, the Czechoslovak leaders tried to help Communism live up to its billing.

The movement—dubbed "the Prague Spring"—lasted a few months longer than its Hungarian predecessor, but it ended the same way. Without warning, Russian tanks rolled into the streets of Prague on August 21, 1968. Crowds assembled in protest, but water cannons were used against them, washing away their newfound liberty. Again, the USSR cut off a renewal movement, since the Soviet leadership feared what might develop in this (from its perspective) renegade approach to Communism.

The Czechoslovaks were profoundly traumatized and disheartened by the Soviet Union's response to their hopeful initiatives to reform

Communism. However, they did not respond with the force tried by the Hungarians a few years previously; instead, they engaged in acts that would frustrate their would-be Soviet repressors. A striking example of this was what transpired shortly after the Soviet tanks rumbled into Prague and took control of the government. The Russian forces intended to round up the various ringleaders of the Prague Spring from throughout the city, but by the morning after this intention was made known, almost all the street signs in Prague had mysteriously disappeared. Because of this, and the confusion about directions that the citizens of the city feigned without street signs to help them, the Russians could not find many of those they intended to arrest. By the time the Russians had produced enough maps for their henchmen to get to the addresses, most of the erstwhile leaders of the Prague Spring had escaped into the countryside, where they were not found. Even so, the USSR took ruthless control of the situation, and the Prague Spring came to an abrupt end.

What was the Eastern European reaction to this renewal of repression? How did the Eastern Europeans—not all of them, of course, but the reflective among them—look on this freezing of the Prague Spring? From some of what they wrote and distributed surreptitiously then and subsequently in the *samizdat*, it is clear that a number of Eastern Europeans interpreted the USSR's response as an indication that Communism was a dead ideology, one that had to be perpetuated by force since it could not stand on its own merits. These Eastern Europeans interpreted the Soviet Union's actions as a violation of what Communism supposedly taught and expected. They exegeted the USSR's reaction as a public confession of the bankruptcy of Communism as an ideology. To these Eastern Europeans, Communism was a spent force, kept in place only by brute power.

Moreover, the *samizdat* made clear that, from their perspective, Communism was only the latest in a long line of repressors—and that, like all the rest, Communism must surely at some point in the not too distant future come to an end. The USSR had pummelled them into submission. Many Eastern Europeans discerned that, whatever the propaganda claims, Communism certainly did not serve the democratic longings of the people; it only survived by the USSR's repressive power—which, like other powers before it, would in due course suffer its own demise. With that general sense, Eastern European attitudes generally shifted into the response their forebears had taken toward repressive empires: by 1968, many people in Eastern Europe were hanging on, waiting for what they were sure would come—the overthrow of Communism. The West was taken unawares by what transpired in 1989, but many Eastern Europeans were not.

The Beginning of the End

Certain developments throughout Eastern Europe more directly anticipated the events of 1989. The first such was the remarkable career of the Hungarian Communist leader János Kádár (r. 1956–88). He was the man set up by the USSR as Hungary's ruler after the abortive 1956 Hungarian Revolution; clearly, the Soviet leadership felt they could trust him, and they expected that he would countenance no further manifestations of the kinds of departures from approved paths that Hungary so recently had taken. Not surprisingly, the majority of the Hungarians despised Kádár for this.

Even so, he managed to stay in power in Hungary for more than three decades—a remarkable achievement in any form of government, and certainly so when one's leadership is subject to the whim of a great power that has strictly circumscribed limits of toleration. He began as a "yes-man" to Moscow, and throughout his long tenure as Hungarian leader, Kádár always managed to stay within the good graces of the Soviet politburo. But along the way the Hungarians came to respect their leader, because he managed—slowly, quietly, subtly, but surely—to adjust Communism's practice in Hungary to align with much of what the Hungarians had sought in 1956. He carefully conducted his leadership so that his innovations, introduced cautiously, without fanfare or public demonstrations, did not raise hackles in Moscow. The Hungarians generally recognized what he was doing and respected his shrewd leadership. Not surprisingly, the events that opened the floodgates in 1989 began in Hungary.

Better known in the West as a directly contributing factor to the events of 1989 was the role played by Solidarity (in Polish, *Solidarnosç*), the Polish labor union. The very fact of its existence was itself an indictment of the Communist system as it had been worked out in Poland. Even the designation itself was a stinging critique of Communism.

According to Marxist-Leninist ideology, eventually a brotherhood of workers would be recognized around the world, a brotherhood that would surpass all lesser loyalties. According to Communist doctrine, that international brotherhood of the proletariat would be a *Solidarity* that could not be broken. However, by the late 1970s, a large number of Polish workers had become profoundly frustrated with their employment and the economic situation in the country, especially in the face of the empty rhetoric about progress under the Communist system. As a way of reaction, they decided to establish a labor union to represent their interests, since the Polish Communist government offered no amelioration of conditions for them and seemed to have no prospects to improve the bad economy. To indicate their united purpose, and subtly to declare their frustration with their experience under Communism, they chose the ideologically sacrosanct name "Solidarity" for their labor union.

In 1980, Solidarity showed its strength when a large number of workers in the docks at Gdansk called a strike against their employer—which was, ultimately, the Polish Communist government. Never before had a group of workers in a Communist nation engaged in a strike. Such actions were understandable, from a Communist ideological perspective, in a repressive capitalist system. However, Communism had crowned itself as the ultimate state for the proletariat; according to Marxist-Leninist expectations, workers would only flourish under Communism. It was unthinkable that workers in a Communist state would ever strike. Whatever the ideological expectations, though, in 1980 workers in a Communist state did strike.

For any Communist government, this would have been a horrendous embarrassment; that was certainly the way the Polish government took it. There could be no sending in of tanks here, though: these were proletarians clamoring for precisely what Communism promised them but had failed to deliver. After weeks of tension, the strike ended, but only when the Polish government accepted Solidarity as a legal union and promised to deal with its demands. The electrician Lech Wałesa, leader of Solidarity, had the heady opportunity to negotiate with the Polish Communist government.

Late in the following year, 1981, the widespread disenchantment with the government's performance was exposed by an opinion poll that revealed that, with regard to national institutions, 95 percent trusted Solidarity, 93 percent the Roman Catholic church, but only 7 percent the Communist Party.[13] With its overwhelming support, Solidarity's leaders and publicity organs openly criticized the practices and failures of the Communist government and demanded reforms for the good of the Polish people. Solidarity called on the Polish government to live up to what Communism was supposedly all about: Communism was being hoist on its own petard.

The initiative had passed from the hands of the Polish government into the hands of Solidarity's leaders. Moscow eventually had enough and called on the Polish government to crack down. Duly obedient, in December 1981 it declared martial law and outlawed Solidarity. For the reflective in Poland (and elsewhere in Eastern Europe), the irony was all too thick: a trade union had been declared an enemy of Communism. Wałesa and many other leaders of Solidarity, as well as thousands of ordinary members, were arrested and imprisoned for a few months. Things in Poland quieted down during that time, but the economy went from bad to worse.

---

13. These data are reported in Crampton, *Eastern Europe*, 374.

The economic situation in Poland continued to deteriorate. The Polish people had not wavered in their support for Solidarity, and in April of 1989 the Polish government eventually found it necessary to legalize Solidarity and try to find ways to work with the trade union. Solidarity played an important role over the next months as it became the voice to express the frustrations of the people and give some advice to the Polish leaders. This time, owing to Gorbachev's attitude toward the USSR's Eastern European satellites, Moscow did not intervene to dictate how the Polish government must respond to this striking manifestation of the people of a Communist state calling for *Perestroika* and engaging in *Glasnost* with their Communist leaders. Only a few weeks later, in 1989, the Communist government and Solidarity's leaders sat down at a round table to talk about reforming the economic and political systems. Those discussions had some startling results.

A third significant development in Eastern Europe that anticipated the events of 1989 was "Charter 77" in Czechoslovakia. Except for the brief window of the Prague Spring, the Czechoslovakian Communist government had been the most repressive of all the Eastern European regimes; it had stood firm, never re-examining the show trials of the early 1950s and priding itself on its repressive reputation among the Communist satellites. Even so, in 1975, along with a host of other countries, Czechoslovakia had signed "the Helsinki Accords"—statements adopted in Helsinki, Finland, regarding human rights. The Soviet Union and its Eastern European satellites had signed similar pronouncements before and had nonetheless failed to live up to them. This governmental hypocrisy had rankled many Eastern Europeans in years past; within a few months of the signing of the Helsinki Accords, a group of Czech dissidents determined not to allow their government to get away with such dissimulation any longer.

These people put together a statement detailing the ways in which the Czechoslovak Communist government regularly violated specific provisions of the Helsinki Accords. They called this statement a "charter"; they published it surreptitiously and anonymously on January 1, 1977—hence the designation "Charter 77." The charter immediately caught the attention of the entire nation; not surprisingly, the Communist government was furious. It soon rounded up the ringleaders of the group and imprisoned several of them; among them was the dissident playwright Václav Havel. He and others were sentenced to prison terms; however, Charter 77 would not go away. The Czechoslovakian government was embarrassed before the world and shown to be in ongoing violation of the accords it had ratified only a few months earlier. The Czechoslovak populace supported Charter 77, in the face of their Communist government's hostile opposition to it.

Each of the signers of Charter 77 stood firm. All were harassed, and some were thrown into prison, but these Chartrists proved steadfast through all the harassment they faced from the government and its secret police. For that, and for their brave exposé of the Communist government's violations of human rights in Czechoslovakia, the people respected the Chartrists. Eventually, Havel and others were freed from prison. Charter 77 kept the pressure on the Czechoslovakian Communist government for a dozen years.

The final significant anticipation of the events of 1989 was the death of Marshall Tito of Yugoslavia in 1980. He had stood up to Stalin and had forged a distinctive way for Communism in Yugoslavia. Unlike any other Communist regime in Eastern Europe, Yugoslavia under Tito allowed its people freely to travel throughout the world: they could go to and work in the West and return as they willed. The greater freedoms enjoyed by the Yugoslavs allowed them to develop a sense of their distinctiveness among the Communist peoples of Eastern Europe—a deliberate ploy on Tito's part to entice them toward a Yugoslavian brotherhood, and away from the rivalries that down through history had bedevilled the diverse ethno-religious groups in the country.[14] In this regard, Tito was remarkably successful: many people in the country, especially the young who had grown up during his rule, thought of themselves as Yugoslavs (rather than as Serbs or Croats or Slovenes). However, when Tito died in 1980, there was no one who could carry on his approach with the endorsement of the various republics within the country. Short-sighted leaders saw resurrecting nationalist antagonisms as a way of securing their own political power; with that, Tito's accomplishments began to unravel. As elsewhere in Eastern Europe, things were not ending up as envisioned by Communist teaching (in this case, the distinctive Yugoslav variety). Communism had failed to deliver on its various hopes and promises. The stage was set for 1989.

1989: *Annus Mirabilis*

A Latin phrase that well captures the significance of 1989 is *annus mirabilis*—"miracle year." A number of books have been written recounting and analyzing what took place in that remarkable span of a few months.

---

14. It is historically necessary to avoid the simplistic "ancient enmities" approach sometimes offered as the key to understanding inter-ethnic relationships in the former Yugoslavia; even so, the peoples of the region have known ongoing and longstanding tensions, arising from their divergent cultural backgrounds and religious commitments, and conflicts have occasionally arisen among them (with some undeniable barbarities bring perpetrated).

This presentation can only offer an overview of major events that ended up making 1989 so significant for Eastern Europe and for the rest of the world. It is not possible here to cover what happened in all the countries of Eastern Europe; instead, the focus will be, in chronological order, on the dramatic events that took place in Hungary, Poland, Czechoslovakia, and Romania, as a way to appreciate the significance of what was happening and the momentum it generated throughout the region. Again, special attention is paid to what Eastern Europeans themselves have had to say about the events of that remarkable year.

The opening gambit in the overthrow of Communism in 1989 took place in Hungary, where the government in February embraced a multi-party system and abandoned the demand that the Communist Party must lead. In late June of that year, the Hungarian government opened its border with Austria (a non-aligned country, but with borders open to the West). This allowed Hungarians to cross without hindrance into Austria—but not only Hungarians. Since Hungary's borders were open with her Communist neighbors, in the tradition of Communism's vaunted international brotherhood of workers, the peoples of neighboring Communist states could get to the West via Hungary as well. Television footage showed hundreds from East Germany using Hungary as a corridor for escape to the West. This was no momentary lapse by unwitting Hungarian authorities; it was a deliberate decision to offer hope to peoples of Communist Eastern Europe and to force change in the region. It is doubtful, though, that Hungary's leadership foresaw just how drastic the changes would turn out to be.

In June of 1989, Poland held a free election. By then, the Communist government and Solidarity had been regularly holding round-table discussions about the country's economic and political situation. The government finally acquiesced to a consistent demand from Solidarity for an election. This election, however, was to be different from the ones that had been held throughout the Communist bloc over the past four decades, in that the Communist Party would not be alone in fielding nominees; other parties would be welcome to do so. Solidarity did.

The results of the election were astounding: Solidarity won ninety-nine out of a hundred seats in the upper house of parliament, and all 161 seats in the lower house. The Polish Communist government had expected to be re-elected, at least with a substantial majority. However, it had been *resoundingly* voted out of power by its own people. The government was shocked; Moscow must have been profoundly disappointed, but Gorbachev had declared a "hands-off" policy vis-à-vis its Eastern European satellites. So, the election results stood, and Poland ceased to be a Communist state. Its people cast Communism out via a free election.

Bordering both Hungary and Poland was Czechoslovakia, where the overthrow of Communism occurred somewhat later in the year. In the face of the repressive reputation of Czechoslovakia's Communist government, the toppling of Communism took place via a "Velvet Revolution." On November 17, a peaceful student protest called attention to continuing problems with the Czechoslovakian Communist government and to the greater freedoms allowed in nearby countries in recent months. In short order, the state's police presence turned from containment to force, and several students were brutally beaten. A brave newspaper reporter filmed the melee and managed to get the footage on public television. The people of Czechoslovakia, recalling the crushing of the Prague Spring two decades previously, and aware of the changes happening in neighboring states, reacted with outrage. No violence ensued from the people in response, but they soon had an outlet to express their pent-up frustration—the theater.

In Czechoslovakia, drama had enjoyed a long and distinguished role as a shaper of popular attitudes and an expression of contemporary opinion. This had been the case before the coming of Communism and had continued (with some limitations, of course) during the Communist period, as well.[15] So, when in response to the beating of the students, the drama theaters in Prague declared a strike, the Czechoslovakian people and government both took notice. Not only did theaters cancel performances, though: they opened up for public discussions of what had just happened with the students, specifically, and of the situation in Czechoslovakia and what needed to be done to correct it, more generally.

The most significant of these meetings led to the "Civic Forum," which drafted statements for release to the media. Many of the leaders of the Civic Forum had been signers of Charter 77 who had suffered ill treatment from the Communist government over the preceding dozen years. The Civic Forum demanded that the government repudiate the brutality visited upon the students—and declared openly that the Czechoslovakian Communist government had failed to live up to the name of the country: "the *People's Democracy* of Czechoslovakia." The Civic Forum called on the Czechoslovakian government to listen to the desires of its people—and went on to spell out some of those desires, all of which called for greater openness and

15. Commenting about the role played by authors in Czechoslovakia, Václav Havel said, "The idea that a writer is the conscience of his nation has its own logic and its own tradition here. For years, writers have stood in for politicians: they were renewers of the national community, maintainers of the national language, awakeners of the national conscience, interpreters of the national will. This tradition has continued under totalitarian conditions, where it gains its own special coloring: the written word seems to have acquired a kind of heightened radioactivity—otherwise they wouldn't lock us up for it!" (*Disturbing the Peace*, 72).

freedom. Much of this was reported in the media, which was slipping out of the control of the Communist authorities. Television, radio, and newspaper boldly carried reports of the latest developments; beyond such formal means, word of mouth spread information quickly.

The Civic Forum called for a mass meeting at St. Wenceslas Square in Prague on November 21, so that the people collectively could express their views to the Communist leadership. On that day, more than a million Czechoslovaks turned out for the meeting. There the collected people thundered their vocal approval of the Civic Forum, expressed their gratitude to the signers of Charter 77, applauded their former leader Alexander Dubček (who appeared at the meeting), and celebrated the efforts of Václav Havel, the playwright who had led the dissident movement for years and had suffered so greatly for it. When Havel, in describing what the Civic Forum wanted from the government, said, "In democracy, the state governs according to the suggestions and wishes of its citizens. That is exactly what we want!" the crowd expressed its approval via noisy acclaim.[16]

The overwhelming support offered by the Czechoslovak people caused a crisis for their Communist leaders. Intense discussions ensued in the government. Within a few days, it resigned, and a new government was appointed, in which non-Communists predominated. On December 28, 1989, the former leader of the Prague Spring, Alexander Dubček, was honored: he was chosen to serve as the speaker of the federal parliament; one day later, the *coup de grace* came when the federal assembly unanimously elected Václav Havel president of Czechoslovakia.[17]

To the southeast of Hungary lay Romania. Throughout the first eleven months of 1989, the Romanian Communist government remained under the tight control of Nicolae Ceaușescu. Even so, spurred on by reports of what was happening elsewhere in Eastern Europe, citizens of Romania openly expressed their yearning for improvement in the way their government led them and the country.

An outspoken Hungarian Reformed pastor in Timișoara, in the north of the country, had come to the attention of the authorities in far-off Bucharest, the capital. Since he was from the Hungarian minority, the government may have thought it could act on his case with impunity; they badly misjudged the situation, however. In mid-December, the government ordered the pastor to depart his charge, but he refused. When the Communist authorities sent in forces to execute its decision, the people in the region

---

16. As can be seen and heard in video clips from the November 21, 1989, meeting at Wenceslas Square which have been included in "Faith Under Fire."

17. Fawn, *The Czech Republic*, 27.

arose to defend the pastor. Not only ethnic Hungarians but Romanians also refused to knuckle under: people from the city and the surrounding countryside set up a human ring around his house and refused to allow police to enter. Although police tried to break through and struggles broke out, the protective ring was not breached.

Citizens of Romania elsewhere in the country became aware of what was transpiring in Timișoara. In numerous places, protests against the government erupted, police tried to quash them, and conflict ensued between the government's forces and the citizenry. Long pent-up frustrations were vented in the widespread reactions against the Communist government, and even the efforts of the dreaded Romanian secret police (the *Securitate*) could not quell the disturbances. The *Securitate* began using lethal force against the protesters, shooting into the crowds, but they soon found themselves facing lethal force in response: the Romanian army rose in defense of their fellow citizens and began fighting back. It was not the Romanian people who took up arms, but the army—which was, after all, supposed to protect the people. For the first time in its existence, the *Securitate* was not having its way in Romania. Soon, members of the *Securitate* began throwing down their weapons, casting off their uniforms, and trying to blend into the crowds. The situation had gotten out of hand for the Communist government.

In this situation, Nicolae Ceaușescu and his wife Elena, fearful of what might happen, decided to get out of Bucharest. Ostensibly leaving on vacation, they were actually trying to escape Romania with their lives. However, they were caught. Within only a few hours, they were tried and executed on December 25. All this brought an end to Communism in Romania.

These dramatic events that transpired in 1989 in Hungary, Poland, Czechoslovakia, and Romania manifest the overthrow of Communism. The other Eastern European Communist nations—Bulgaria, Albania, and Yugoslavia—each saw the end of Communism in the year, as well.[18] The *annus mirabilis* led to the ousting of Communist governments in all the countries of Eastern Europe.

This could be seen, literally, in the widespread removal of the symbols of Communism's presence throughout the region. On November 9, 1989, the Berlin Wall was broken down. It had served as a symbolic barrier between Communist Eastern Europe and Western Europe for almost four decades. Furthermore, throughout Eastern Europe, oversized statues of Lenin had been ubiquitous. Television footage from the various Eastern

18. For concise summaries of the pattern of events in each of these three states, see Rothschild, *Return to Diversity*: for Bulgaria, 250–53; for Albania, 253–57; and for Yugoslavia, 257–62.

European countries often showed the toppling of the statues, accompanied by cheering crowds. There could be no more graphic symbols of the overthrow of Communism.

The Surprise of 1989

The collapse of Communism in 1989 caught everyone in the West by surprise. No one saw it coming. Given the overwhelming power of and repression practiced by Communist states throughout Eastern Europe, no one in the West expected Communism to come to an end any time soon. And certainly, no one foresaw the way it would take.

In the face of the dizzying nuclear arms race that had preoccupied the superpowers of the Cold War and the military force available to Communist states, there is a delightful irony in the fact that Communism in Eastern Europe was overthrown without a single shot being fired by its opponents. This was not, despite the rhetoric and propaganda issued by some western spokespersons trying to take advantage of the remarkable events of 1989, a victory of the free West over the Communist East. The West did not cause it; indeed, the West had little to do with it. Moreover, the West did not even see it coming. Rather, it was a victory of the peoples of Eastern Europe over another oppressive foreign empire. They finally said, not with bullets but with their common will, "We're not taking it anymore," and they brought Communism to an end—in the words of Václav Havel, "Communism was overthrown by life, by thought, by human dignity."[19] The downfall of Communism in Eastern Europe in 1989 came from the people of the region refusing to tolerate oppression any more.

Unquestionably, the overthrow of Communism in 1989 changed the course of Eastern European history.

---

19. Havel, *Summer Meditations*, 5.

Part Three
Epilogue

Since 1989

"All nations must go through a phase of national self-awareness and, related to that, a phase of struggle for a state of their own, and they must experience national sovereignty before they can mature to the point of realizing that membership in supranational bodies does not suppress their national identity and sovereignty, but in a sense extends it, strengthens it, and nurtures it."[1]

HISTORY DID NOT END for Eastern Europe, of course, with the collapse of Communism in 1989. Indeed, from the perspective of many Eastern Europeans, history was only beginning for them. As it unfolds, there will doubtlessly be additional turning points in that history.

Events

It would be unwise to attempt to specify any such turning points that have transpired in the few years since 1989, though. We do not yet have enough historical perspective to be able to assess which of them might end up carrying lasting impact for the region. Some events have taken place that could eventually prove to be such turning points.

Much has happened in the region that has demanded international attention—and, sometimes, invited international intervention. In the immediacy of those events, television reportage and documentaries presented events in living color; articles in newspapers, magazines, and scholarly journals on those developments were regularly churned out; and book publishers met a ravenous appetite among a reading public for coverage of the latest events. Among those events were the peaceful separation of the Czech Republic

---

1. Havel, *Summer Meditations*, 29.

and Slovakia, as well as the anything but peaceful dissolution of the former Yugoslavia; the emergence of strident, exclusive nationalisms within several nations in the region; the attempts of Eastern European nations to win their way into NATO and the European Union; warfare in Slovenia, Croatia, and Bosnia; the attempts to resolve that conflict with the eventual adoption of the Dayton Peace Accords; the tensions in Kosovo, which led to ethnic cleansing by Serb paramilitaries and NATO's bombardment of Serbia; and the arrests of Slobodan Milošević, Radovan Karazić, and Miloš Radić for war crimes and their subsequent trials in the Hague.

Others could doubtlessly be added to this list. On each of them, interest in the West was intense for a while, and media and print coverage met that interest. However, with the resolution of the situation (or, at least, the quieting of the problem), the western audience's attention turned elsewhere. Among these events may be one or more that, with hindsight, will eventually be seen as another turning point in Eastern European history, worthy of being ranked with those considered in this book.

Other events in Eastern Europe have also been significant for peoples in one nation or another in the region but have largely been passed over by international media. Among them were the tensions between the Hungarian minority and the Romanian majority in northern Romania; the successful intervention in North Macedonia by United Nations peacekeeping forces in the endeavor to prevent civil war and to secure the nation's safety against invasion;[2] and the tensions between Bulgaria and her neighbor, Turkey, over treatment of ethnic Turks living in Bulgaria. One of these (or other similarly unreported events elsewhere in the region) may in due course require recognition as epochal for Eastern Europe.

At this relatively early point in the twenty-first century, though, it is impossible to assess which (if any) of the events in the brief period since the overthrow of Communism might qualify to be recognized in this fashion. In drawing this treatment to a close, it would be enlightening to consider how Eastern Europeans themselves have understood what happened in 1989, and then to point out a few of the challenges they recognize they are facing in its aftermath. The way the peoples of the region interpret what transpired in 1989 and assess their challenges since then may well lead them to developments in one or more of the nations that would eventually come to be recognized as additional turning points in Eastern European history.

---

2. This is described in Williams, *Preventing War*.

What Happened in 1989?

The events of 1989 unquestionably introduced overwhelming changes for all the peoples of the region. A question that ineluctably arises is, how did they interpret what transpired in that remarkable year? Again, it is well to listen to Eastern Europeans in this regard, rather than the sometimes triumphalistic pronouncements of western spokespersons.

While Eastern Europe has shown interest in western products in the intervening period, Eastern Europeans themselves did not view the events of 1989 as a victory of free-market capitalism over Communist economics. Specifically, numerous Eastern European leaders pointed to serious problems with capitalism as practiced in the West. One main concern is that western capitalism accepts an unemployment rate of up to 5 percent or so as necessary to allow the economy to function well. For Eastern Europeans, who have historically embraced a much less individualistic approach to life than is common in the West, such casual acceptance by the group of something that humiliates and excludes 5 percent of the workforce is reprehensible. This is no hangover from Communism, in which everyone had a job of some sort; it arises from the more communal experience and instinctive predilections of virtually all the peoples of Eastern Europe.

Furthermore, Eastern Europeans have not interpreted the overthrow of Communism in 1989 as necessarily an endorsement of the liberal democracy practiced in the West. For them, the rejection of Communism was another turning away from an oppressive foreign empire toward freedom, but the contents of "freedom" do not necessarily coincide with what the West assumes is involved in the term. Since 1989, Eastern European nations have all been wrestling, in several ways, with what freedom means for the dominant people group in each land, for the minority groups each finds within its borders, and for their economies. It is anything but a foregone conclusion that they will eventually opt for all that the West has come to denote with "freedom"—even though entrance into NATO and the European Union entails adopting at least some of that western understanding.

Moreover, as has been seen above, Eastern Europe's history and its various cultures are different in significant ways from the history and cultures of the West. They do not expect, and the West should not demand, that Eastern Europe become only a pale eastern version of what the West has become.[3]

---

3. The theme paper for the twelfth assembly of the Conference of European Churches [CEC], held in Trondheim, Norway (June 23–July 2, 2003), expressed concern that enlargements of the European Union to include nations from Eastern Europe should not come with the requirement of conformity to Western European patterns, noting that CEC had sent a letter to its 126 member churches in November 2002 encouraging

Several Eastern European leaders in the political or religious realms have urged, in the years since 1989, that they must seek a third way, economically and politically, between Communism and the West. A significant challenge for each of the nations of Eastern Europe in the post-Communist period is to find such a way, one that will honor its own historical and cultural heritage and allow it to function well in the twenty-first century.

Challenges

Among the specific challenges that the nations of Eastern Europe recognize they are facing since 1989, one that demands attention is the attempt to overcome the *environmental* legacy left over from the Communist period. The post-World War II Communist rush to transform the region into an industrial powerhouse left no room for concern with how the new heavy industries might affect air and water quality, on the one hand, or the health of either the workers or the peoples living in the areas near the new factories, on the other. As is now well known, environmental disaster ended up befalling much of Eastern Europe in the wake of this neglect. Correcting this damage demands much attention by Eastern European governments[4]—in the midst of the ongoing struggle to get the economies productive and competitive on the world stage.

Perhaps even more complex than this, though, is the attempt to overcome the *social* legacy of Communism. Trust was badly broken among the peoples themselves. In the situation that prevailed under earlier empires, Eastern Europeans had almost always been dominated by foreigners. Under Communism, though, while the orders came from Moscow, their own people were the leaders of government. Interpersonal trust suffered because of this: one could not instinctively count on one's own countrymen, the way previous generations had largely been able to do.[5] In this way, the

---

churches to use "every opportunity in public to remind people that the enlargement of the EU [European Union] should not be seen as simply the 'East' adjusting to the 'West'" (*Jesus Christ Heals and Reconciles*, 2.2.3, §44 [31]); cf. the same perspective expressed in *From Graz to Trondheim*, 53; a similar concern is set forth in *Charta Oecumenica*, "Part III: Our Common Responsibility in Europe," Section 7 (9).

4. In January 1990, shortly after his appointment as president of Czechoslovakia, in his first major public address, Václav Havel said, "Our obsolete economy is wasting the little energy we have available. . . . We have polluted our soil, our rivers and forests, bequeathed to us by our ancestors, and we have today the most contaminated environment in Europe" (*Open Letters*, 390). While Havel was speaking specifically of Czechoslovakia, his words described the situation throughout Eastern Europe.

5. In his January 1990 "New Year's Address," Havel lamented what had resulted from this in Czechoslovakia (and elsewhere in Eastern Europe): "We learned not to

communal ethos that had shaped so much of the heritage of the Eastern European peoples was damaged. It will be a major challenge for them to find ways to re-establish the common trust that had enabled their communities to flourish and offer mutual support.[6]

Essential to this endeavor will be the difficult challenge to overcome the *personal* legacy of life under Communist tyranny. Religious and political leaders have commented on the serious moral crisis afflicting the peoples of Eastern Europe in the wake of the Communist period. These leaders point out that people throughout the region learned to have two different faces—one in the workplace (where Communist expectations had to be met, at least hypocritically) and another at home (where one could usually express one's views without particular fear of reprisal). This double-mindedness introduced a terrible lack of integrity as a necessity to survive during the Communist period.[7] Overcoming that pattern and reintroducing the value of integral living, both for individuals and for society in general, will be a difficult task.[8] Difficult as it may be, though, it is essential for personal and social wholeness.[9]

---

believe in anything, to ignore each other, to care only about ourselves. Concepts such as love, friendship, compassion, humility, or forgiveness lost their depth and dimensions" (*Open Letters*, 391).

6. "Our main enemy today is our own bad traits: indifference to the common good; vanity; personal ambition; selfishness; and rivalry. The main struggle will have to be fought on this field" (Havel, *Open Letters*, 395).

7. As President of Czechoslovakia, Václav Havel described the "contaminated moral environment" left behind after the collapse of Communism by noting, "We fell morally ill because we became used to saying something different from what we thought" (*Open Letters*, 391).

8. Speaking of the situation after 1989, Fr. Michal Czajkowski, a Roman Catholic priest from Poland, said, "Our country is finally free, thank God, but we are not, still not entirely free. We have to fight for our internal freedom. This legacy of the Communists will be important for many years, I'm afraid. This legacy, for example, that you have a double life. You are one person in your home, with your family, with your friends, or in your church, and you are another person in your work, in public office. It was, if I can say so, a 'double truth': one truth for my personal life, and another truth for my boss, for the party, and so on" (cited [with minor stylistic improvements] from an interview that became part of "Faith Under Fire").

9. In 1991, Havel wrote, "I see the only way forward in that old, familiar injunction: 'live in truth'" (*Summer Meditations*, 8). The injunction, "live in truth," was one Havel had regularly urged and commented on during the Communist period; a January 1983 letter he penned offers a striking background for what he later urged as president of Czechoslovakia: "When a person chooses to take a certain stand, when he breathes some meaning into his life, it gives him perspective, hope, purpose. When he arrives at a certain truth and decides to 'live in it,' it is his act and his alone; it is an existential, moral, and ultimately a metaphysical act, growing from the depths of his heart and aimed at filling his own being" (*Open Letters*, 231).

A fourth major challenge for Eastern Europeans will be to learn to *live in freedom*. For all of them, after four hundred years or more (in Poland's case, significantly less), each of the Eastern European nations experienced a brief window of independence between the two world wars. As shown above,[10] that period was marked by all sorts of tensions and problems. Soon after World War II, they entered the four-decade night of Communist repression, in which freedom was a propaganda term without much content. In the aftermath of 1989, they have to deal with the uncertainty that Václav Havel, president of Czechoslovakia, recognized from his own earlier experience after being freed from prison:

> Freedom made them [the peoples of Eastern Europe after 1989] feel uncertain. Suddenly they felt like a prisoner who after many years of jail is released to freedom. He feels uncertain walking the ground. I experienced it several times myself. And sometimes you even have this perverted feeling, that "I would like to return to jail, to the place where there is this strict routine, because suddenly I have to make all the decisions for myself and nobody makes the decisions for me."[11]

As he thus indicated, Eastern Europeans have been finding out in the years since 1989 that living in freedom presents a complex challenge to those who have not known it.[12] As president of the Czech Republic, he noted that his people—and, by implication, all the peoples of Eastern Europe—have to learn what it means to live responsibly in their freedom.[13]

The period since 1989 has seen some genuine, outstanding successes in this regard. We in the West should offer our support in any way possible as the peoples of Eastern Europe continue on this journey. As they travel it, they will certainly come to further significant turning points in the history of Eastern Europe.

---

10. See the treatments above in chapter 14 and in chapter 15.

11. Quoted (with slight stylistic improvements) from Havel's statements near the end of "Faith Under Fire."

12. "Independence is not just a state of being. It is a task. And fresh independence, such as ours, is a particularly complex task" (Havel, *Summer Meditations*, 82).

13. In 1991, Havel wrote, "In all the post-totalitarian and post-Communist states, democracy is fragile, unstable, and untried. At the same time, these countries have to struggle with large problems that most stable western democracies are not at all familiar with: the revival of nationalism, the transition to a market economy, and the search for international standing as newly independent countries that are extricating themselves from their former satellite status. Simultaneously the threat of chaos in these countries is awakening the dangerous idea of 'iron-handed rule'" (*Summer Meditations*, 50).

Bibliography of Works Cited

Anderson, Benedict. *Imagined Communities: Reflections on the Origin and Spread of Nationalism*. Rev. ed. New York: Verso,1991.
Arseniev, Nicholas. *Russian Piety*. Translated by Asheleigh Moorhouse. The Library of Orthodox Theology and Spirituality 3. Crestwood, NY: St. Vladimir's Seminary Press, 1964.
Augustinos, Gerasimos. *The National Idea in Eastern Europe: The Politics of Ethnic and Civic Community*. Lexington, MA: Heath, 1996.
Bailey, J. Martin. *The Spring of Nations: Churches in the Rebirth of Central and Eastern Europe*. New York: Friendship,1991.
Barford, P. M. *The Early Slavs: Culture and Society in Early Medieval Eastern Europe*. Ithaca, NY: Cornell University Press, 2001.
Berresford, Peter. *Celtic Inheritance*. New York: Dorset, 1992.
Bideleux, Robert, and Ian Jeffries. *A History of Eastern Europe: Crisis and Change*. London: Routledge, 1998.
Browning, Robert. *The Byzantine Empire*. Rev. ed. Washington, DC: Catholic University of America Press, 1992.
Brzezinski, Zbigniew. *Out of Control: Global Turmoil on the Eve of the Twenty-First Century*. New York: Scribner, 1983.
Carpini, Friar Giovanni DiPlano. *The Story of the Mongols Whom We Call the Tartars: Friar Giovanni DiPlano Carpini's Account of His Embassy to the Court of the Mongol Khan*. Translated by Erik Hildinger. Boston: Branden, 1996.
Chambers, James. *The Devil's Horsemen: The Mongol Invasion of Europe*. New York: Atheneum, 1985.
Charta Oecumenica: Guidelines for the Growing Cooperation among the Churches in Europe. St. Gallen and Geneva: Council of European (Roman Catholic) Bishops' Conferences and Council of European Churches, 2002.
Čiževskij, Dmitrij. *Comparative History of Slavic Literatures*. Translated by Richard Noel Porter and Martin P. Rice. Nashville, TN: Vanderbilt University Press, 1971.
Cohen, Lenard. *Broken Bonds: The Disintegration of Yugoslavia*. Boulder, CO: Westview, 1993.
―――. *Broken Bonds: Yugoslavia's Disintegration and Balkan Politics in Transition*. Boulder, CO: Westview, 1995.

Constantelos, Demetrios J. *Byzantine Philanthropy and Social Welfare*. 2nd rev. ed. Studies in the Social and Religious History of the Medieval Greek World 1. New Rochelle, NY: Caratzas, 1991.

———. *Poverty, Society and Philanthropy in the Late Medieval Greek World*. Studies in the Social and Religious History of the Medieval Greek World 2. New Rochelle, NY: Caratzas, 1991.

Constantine Porphyrogenitus. *De Administrando Imperio*. 2nd rev. ed. Translated by R. J. H. Jenkins. Washington, DC: Dumbarton Oaks, 2009.

Crăciun, Maria, Ovidiu Ghitta, and Graeme Murdock, eds. *Confessional Identity in East-Central Europe*. Aldershot, UK: Ashgate, 2002.

Crampton, R. J. *A Concise History of Bulgaria*. New York: Cambridge University Press, 1997.

———. *Eastern Europe in the Twentieth Century*. London: Routledge, 1994.

Cross, Samuel Hazzard, trans. *The Russian Primary Chronicle*. Cambridge: Harvard University Press, 1930.

———. *Slavic Civilization through the Ages*. New York: Russell & Russell, 1963.

Dolukhanov, Pavel M. *The Early Slavs: Eastern Europe from the Initial Settlement to the Kievan Rus*. New York: Longman, 1996.

Drachkovitch, Milorad M., ed. *East Central Europe: Yesterday, Today, Tomorrow*. Stanford, CA: Hoover Institution, 1982.

Dragnich, Alex N. *Serbs and Croats: The Struggle in Yugoslavia*. New York: Harcourt Brace, 1992.

Dragnich, Alex N., and Slavko Todorovich. *The Saga of Kosovo: Focus on Serbian-Albanian Relations*. Eastern European Monographs 170. New York: Columbia University Press, 1984.

Drakulić, Slavenka. *Café Europa: Life after Communism*. London: Abacus, 1996.

Dvornik, Francis. *The Slavs in European History and Civilization*. New Brunswick, NJ: Rutgers University Press, 1962.

———. *The Slavs: Their Early History and Civilization*. Boston: American Academy, 1959.

Evdokimov, Paul. *The Art of the Icon: A Theology of Beauty*. Translated by Steven Bigham. Redondo Beach, CA: Oakwood, 1990.

"Faith under Fire: The PBS Documentary on the Democratic Revolutions in Poland and Czechoslovakia." Greenwich, CT: Sage, 1993.

Fawn, Rick. *The Czech Republic: A Nation of Velvet*. Postcommunist States and Nations Series. Amsterdam: Harwood Academic, 2000.

Ferguson, Niall. *Civilization: The West and the Rest*. New York: Penguin, 2011.

From Graz to Trondheim: Report to the Assembly on the Work and Decisions of the Presidium and Central Committee between the 11th and 12th Assemblies. Geneva: Council of European Churches General Secretariat, 2003.

Gazi, Stephen. *A History of Croatia*. New York: Philosophical Library, 1973.

Geanakoplos, Deno J. *Byzantine East and Latin West: Two Worlds of Christendom in the Middle Ages and Renaissance*. New York: Harper, 1966.

Gojda, Martin. *The Ancient Slavs: Settlement and Society*. Edinburgh: Edinburgh University Press, 1991.

Graham, W. Fred, ed. *Later Calvinism: International Perspectives*. Sixteenth Century Essays and Studies 22. Kirksville, MO: Sixteenth Century Journal, 1994.

Hall, Brian. *The Impossible Country: A Journey through the Last Days of Yugoslavia.* New York: Penguin, 1994.
Harcave, Sidney. *Russia: A History.* 5th ed. Philadelphia: Lippincott, 1964.
Havel, Václav. *Disturbing the Peace: A Conversation with Karel Hvíždala.* Translated by Paul Wilson. Toronto: Vintage, 1990.
———. *Open Letters: Selected Writings 1965–1990.* Edited by Paul Wilson. New York: Knopf, 1991.
———. *Summer Meditations.* Translated by Paul Wilson. Toronto: Vintage, 1992.
Held, Joseph, ed. *The Columbia History of Eastern Europe in the Twentieth Century.* New York: Columbia University Press, 1992.
Herm, Gerhard. *The Celts: The People Who Came Out of Darkness.* New York: St. Martin's, 1975.
Heymann, Frederick G. *Poland and Czechoslovakia.* Englewood Cliffs, NJ: Prentice-Hall, 1966.
Hoffman, Eva. *Exit into History: A Journey through the New Eastern Europe.* New York: Penguin, 1993.
Hupchick, Dennis. *The Bulgarians in the Seventeenth Century: Slavic Orthodox Society and Culture under Ottoman Rule.* Jefferson, NC: McFarland, 1993.
———. *Conflict and Chaos in Eastern Europe.* New York: St. Martin's, 1995.
———. *Culture and History in Eastern Europe.* New York: St. Martin's, 1994.
Hupchick, Dennis, and Harold E. Cox. *A Concise Historical Atlas of Eastern Europe.* New York: St. Martin's, 1996.
Hussey, J. M. *The Orthodox Church in the Byzantine Empire.* New York: Clarendon, 1986.
Jesus Christ Heals and Reconciles: Our Witness in Europe. Geneva: Council of European Churches General Secretariat, 2003.
Kaplan, Robert D. *Balkan Ghosts: A Journey through History.* Toronto: Vintage, 1994.
Krleza, Miroslav. *The Return of Philip Latinovicz.* Translated by Zora Depolo. London: Lincolns-Prager, 1959.
Leithart, Peter. *Defending Constantine.* Downers Grove, IL: IVP Academic, 2010.
Longworth, Philip. *The Making of Eastern Europe.* 2nd rev. ed. New York: St. Martin's, 1997.
Maag, Karin, ed. *The Reformation in Eastern and Central Europe.* Aldershot, UK: Ashgate, 1997.
MacMillan, Margaret. *Paris 1919: Six Months That Changed the World.* New York: Random House, 2003.
Magocsi, Paul Robert. *Historical Atlas of East Central Europe.* Toronto: University of Toronto Press, 1993.
———. *A History of Ukraine: The Land and Its Peoples.* 2nd ed. Toronto: University of Toronto Press, 2010.
Malcolm, Noel. *Bosnia: A Short History.* New York: New York University Press, 1994.
Małłek, Janusz. "The Reformation in Poland and Prussia in the Sixteenth Century: Similarities and Differences." In *The Reformation in Eastern and Central Europe*, edited by Karin Maag, 182–91. Aldershot, UK: Ashgate, 1997.
Mallory, J. P. *In Search of the Indo-Europeans: Language, Archaeology, and Myth.* London: Thames and Hudson, 1989.
McNeill, John T. *The History and Character of Calvinism.* New York: Oxford University Press, 1954.

Merrill, Christopher. *Only the Nails Remain: Scenes from the Balkan Wars*. New York: Rowman & Littlefield, 1999.
Meyendorff, John. *St. Gregory Palamas and Orthodox Spirituality*. Crestwood, NY: St. Vladimir's Seminary Press, 1974.
———. *A Study of Gregory Palamas*. 2nd ed. Crestwood, NY: St. Vladimir's Seminary Press, 1974.
Michener, James A. *Poland*. New York: Random House, 1983.
Mojzes, Paul. *Yugoslavian Inferno: Ethnoreligious Warfare in the Balkans*. New York: Continuum, 1994.
Norwich, John Julius. *A Short History of Byzantium*. New York: Knopf, 1997.
Obolensky, Dimitri. *The Byzantine Commonwealth: Eastern Europe, 500–1453*. London: Phoenix, 2000.
———. *Byzantium and the Slavs*. Crestwood, NY: St. Vladimir's Seminary Press, 1994.
Ostrogorsky, George. *History of the Byzantine State*. Rev. ed. Translated by Joan Hussey. New Brunswick, NJ: Rutgers University Press, 1969.
Ouspensky, Leonid, and Vladimir Lossky. *The Meaning of Icons*. Translated by G. E. H. Palmer and E. Kadloubovsky. Crestwood, NY: St. Vladimir's Seminary Press, 1983.
The Oxford Dictionary of Quotations. New York: Oxford University Press, 1992.
Ozment, Steven. *Protestants: The Birth of a Revolution*. New York: Doubleday, 1992.
Papadakis, Aristeides. *Crisis in Byzantium: The Filioque Controversy in the Patriarchate of Gregory II of Cyprus (1283–1289)*. New York: Fordham University Press, 1983.
Pascal, Pierre. *The Religion of the Russian People*. Translated by Rowan Williams. Crestwood, NY: St. Vladimir's Seminary Press, 1976.
Payton, James R. Jr. "Bypassing the History of Eastern Europe: A Failure of Twentieth Century Christian Scholarship." *Christian Scholar's Review* 29 (2000) 713–30.
———. "Calvin and Eastern Europe: What Happened?" *Religion in Eastern Europe* 30.2 (2010) 10–19.
———. *Getting the Reformation Wrong: Correcting Some Misunderstandings*. Downers Grove, IL: IVP Academic, 2010.
———. "The Influence of the Reformation on the History of Ukraine." *Journal of Ukrainian Studies* 28 (2003) 105–17.
———. *Light from the Christian East: An Introduction to the Orthodox Tradition*. Downers Grove, IL: IVP Academic, 2007.
———. "Orthodox Imagined Communities in the Ottoman Balkans." *Occasional Papers on Religion in Eastern Europe* 35.3 (2015) 1–17. http:digitalcommons.georgefox.edu/ree/vol35/iss3/2.
———. "Ottoman Millet, Religious Nationalism, and Civil Society: Focus on Kosovo." *Religion in Eastern Europe* 26.1 (2006) 11–23.
———. "The Reformations in Eastern Europe." *The Sixteenth Century Journal* 40 (2009) 268–70.
———. "Religion, Nationalism, and National Identities." In *Quo Vadis Eastern Europe? Religion, State and Society after Communism*, edited by Ines Murzaku, 49–60. Europe and the Balkans: A Series of Balkan and East-European Studies 30. Ravenna, Italy: Longo Editore, 2009.
———. "Revisioning the Historiography of Eastern Europe." *Fides et Historia* 31 (1999) 81–89.
Petkov, Kiril. *Infidels, Turks, and Women: The South Slavs in the German Mind, ca. 1400–1600*. New York: Lang, 1997.

Reed, Fred A. *Salonica Terminus: Travels into the Balkan Nightmare*. Vancouver, BC: Talonbooks, 1996.
Rothschild, Joseph. *Return to Diversity: A Political History of East Central Europe Since World War II*. 2nd ed. New York: Oxford University Press, 1993.
Runciman, Steven. *Byzantine Civilization*. New York: Barnes & Noble, 1933.
———. *Byzantine Style and Civilization*. New York: Penguin, 1975.
———. *The Eastern Schism: A Study of the Papacy and the Eastern Churches during the Eleventh and Twelfth Centuries*. Oxford: Clarendon, 1955.
Sayer, Derek. *The Coasts of Bohemia: A Czech History*. Princeton, NJ: Princeton University Press, 1998.
Simons, Thomas W. Jr. *Eastern Europe in the Postwar World*. 2nd ed. New York: St. Martin's, 1993.
Subtelny, Orest. *Ukraine: A History*. 2nd ed. Toronto: University of Toronto Press, 1994.
Sugar, Peter F., and Donald W. Treadgold, eds. *A History of East Central Europe*. Toronto: University of Toronto Press, 1993-.
Sugar, Peter F., Péter Hanák, and Tibor Frank, eds. *A History of Hungary*. Indianapolis, IN: Indiana University Press, 1990.
Swain, Geoffrey, and Nigel Swain. *Eastern Europe since 1945*. New York: St. Martin's, 1993.
Tachiaos, Anthony-Emil N. *Cyril and Methodius of Thessalonica: The Acculturation of the Slavs*. Crestwood, NY: St. Vladimir's Seminary Press, 2001.
Toumanoff, Cyril. "Moscow the Third Rome: Genesis and Significance of a Politico-Religious Idea." *The Catholic Historical Review* 40 (1955) 411–47.
Treadgold, Warren. *A Concise History of Byzantium*. New York: Palgrave Macmillan, 2002.
Velimirovich, Bishop Nikolai, and Archimandrite Justin Popovich. *The Mystery and Meaning of the Battle of Kosovo*. Translated by Todor Mika and Steven Scott. A Treasury of Serbian Orthodox Spirituality 3. Grayslake, IL: The Free Serbian Orthodox Diocese of America and Canada, 1989.
Walters, E. Garrison. *The Other Europe: Eastern Europe to 1945*. Syracuse, NY: Syracuse University Press, 1988.
Wandycz, Piotr S. *The Price of Freedom: A History of East Central Europe from the Middle Ages to the Present*. London: Routledge, 1992.
Wien, Ulrich A., and Mihai D. Grigore, eds. *Exportgut Reformation: Ihr Transfer in Kontaktzonen des 16. Jahrhunderts und die Gegenwart evangelischer Kirchen in Europa*. Veröffentlichungen des Instituts für Europäische Geschichte Mainz 113. Göttingen: Vandenhoeck & Ruprecht, 2017.
Williams, Abiodun. *Preventing War: The United Nations and Macedonia*. New York: Rowman & Littlefield, 2000.
Wolff, Larry. *Inventing Eastern Europe: The Map of Civilization on the Mind of the Enlightenment*. Stanford, CA: Stanford University Press, 1994.
Wolfram, Herwig. *History of the Goths*. New ed. Translated by Thomas J. Dunlap. Berkeley, CA: University of California Press, 1988.
Zamoyski, Adam. *The Polish Way: A Thousand-Year History of the Poles and Their Culture*. New York: Hippocrene, 1994.

For Further Reading

Atlases

Hupchick, Dennis P., and Harold E. Cox. *A Concise Historical Atlas of Eastern Europe.* New York: St. Martin's, 1996.
———. *The Palgrave Concise Historical Atlas of the Balkans.* New York: Palgrave, 2001.
Magocsi, Paul Robert. *Historical Atlas of East Central Europe.* A History of East Central Europe 1. Toronto: University of Toronto Press, 1993.
———. *Ukraine: A Historical Atlas.* Toronto: University of Toronto Press, 1987.

General Overviews

Augustinos, Gerasimos. *The National Idea in Eastern Europe: The Politics of Ethnic and Civic Community.* Lexington, MA: Heath, 1996.
Beck, Paul, Edward Mast, and Perry Tapper. *The History of Eastern Europe for Beginners.* New York: Writers and Readers, 1997.
Bideleux, Robert, and Ian Jeffries. *A History of Eastern Europe: Crisis and Change.* London: Routledge, 1998.
Bogdan, Henry. *From Warsaw to Sofia: A History of Eastern Europe.* Edited by Istvan Fehervary. Santa Fe, NM: Pro Libertate, 1989.
Drachkovitch, Milorad M., ed. *East Central Europe: Yesterday, Today, Tomorrow.* Stanford, CA: Hoover Institution, 1982.
Fischer-Galati, Stephen, ed. *Man, State, and Society in East European History.* New York: Praeger, 1970.
Hupchick, Dennis P. *Conflict and Chaos in Eastern Europe.* New York: St. Martin's, 1995.
———. *Culture and History in Eastern Europe.* New York: St. Martin's, 1994.
Johnson, Lonnie R. *Central Europe: Enemies, Neighbors, Friends.* 3rd ed. New York: Oxford University Press, 2011.
Longworth, Philip. *The Making of Eastern Europe: From Prehistory to Postcommunism.* 2nd ed. New York: St. Martin's, 1997.
Wolff, Larry. *Inventing Eastern Europe: The Map of Civilization on the Mind of the Enlightenment.* Stanford, CA: Stanford University Press, 1994.

Series

A History of East Central Europe

Edited by Peter F. Sugar and Donald W. Treadgold.
Toronto: University of Toronto Press, 1993-.

Jelavich, Charles, and Barbara Jelavich. *The Establishment of the Balkan National States, 1804–1920*. Vol. 8. 1993.
Kann, Robert A., and Zdeněk V. David. *The Peoples of the Eastern Habsburg Lands, 1526–1918*. Vol. 6. 1984.
Magocsi, Paul Robert. *Historical Atlas of East Central Europe*. Vol. 1. 1993.
Rothschild, Joseph. *East Central Europe between the Two World Wars*. Vol. 9. 1992.
Sedlar, Jean W. *East Central Europe in the Middle Ages, 1000–1500*. Vol. 3. 1994.
Sugar, Peter F. *Southeastern Europe under Ottoman Rule, 1354–1804*. Vol. 5. 1996.
Wandycz, Piotr S. *The Lands of Partitioned Poland, 1795–1918*. Vol. 7. 1996.

Eastern European Monographs

Boulder, CO. Distributed by Columbia University Press, New York.

Bradley, John F. N. *Czech Nationalism in the Nineteenth Century*. No. 157. 1984.
Castellan, Georges. *History of the Balkans: From Mohammed the Conqueror to Stalin*. Translated by Nicholas Bradley. No. 325. 1992.
———. *A History of the Romanians*. Translated by Nicholas Bradley. No. 257. 1989.
Ciesla-Korytowska, Maria. *The Slavs in the Eyes of the Occident, The Occident in the Eyes of the Slavs*. No. 355. 1992.
Clucas, Lowell. *The Byzantine Legacy in Eastern Europe*. No. 230. 1988.
Dragnich, Alex N., and Slavko Todorovich. *The Saga of Kosovo: Focus on Serbian-Albanian Relations*. No. 170. 1984.
Fischer-Galati, Stephen. *Eastern Europe and the Cold War: Perceptions and Perspectives*. No. 400. 1994.
Király, Béla, and Dimitrije Djordjević, eds. *East Central European Society and the Balkan Wars*. No. 215. 1987.
Lange-Akhund, Nadine. *The Macedonian Question, 1893–1908: From Western Sources*. No. 486. 1998.
Pekar, Athanasius B., OSBM. *The History of the Church in Carpathian Rus'*. Translated by Marta Skorupsky. No. 322. 1992.
Péter, László, ed. *Historians and the History of Transylvania*. No. 332. 1992.
Zlatar, Zdenko. *Our Kingdom Come: The Counter-Reformation, the Republic of Dubrovnik, and the Liberation of the Balkan Slavs*. No. 342. 1992.

Byzantium and Its Influence on Eastern Europe

Browning, Robert. *The Byzantine Empire*. Rev. ed. Catholic University of America Press, 1992.

Constantelos, Demetrios J. *Byzantine Philanthropy and Social Welfare*. 2nd rev. ed. Studies in the Social and Religious History of the Medieval Greek World 1. New Rochelle, NY: Caratzas, 1991.

———. *Poverty, Society and Philanthropy in the Late Medieval Greek World*. Studies in the Social and Religious History of the Medieval Greek World 2. New Rochelle, NY: Caratzas, 1991.

Evdokimov, Paul. *The Art of the Icon: A Theology of Beauty*. Translated by Steven Bigham. Redondo Beach, CA: Oakwood, 1990.

Herrin, Judith. *Byzantium: The Surprising Life of a Medieval Empire*. Princeton, NJ: Princeton University Press, 2007.

Norwich, John Julius. *A Short History of Byzantium*. New York: Knopf, 1997.

Obolensky, Dimitri. *The Byzantine Commonwealth: Eastern Europe, 500–1453*. London: Phoenix, 2000.

———. *Byzantium and the Slavs*. Crestwood, NY: St. Vladimir's Seminary Press, 1994.

Ostrogorsky, George. *History of the Byzantine State*. Rev. ed. Translated by Joan Hussey. New Brunswick, NJ: Rutgers University Press, 1969.

Ouspensky, Leonid, and Vladimir Lossky, *The Meaning of Icons*. Translated by G. E. H. Palmer and E. Kadloubovsky. Crestwood, NY: St. Vladimir's Seminary Press, 1983.

Runciman, Steven. *Byzantine Civilization*. New York: Barnes & Noble, 1933.

———. *Byzantine Style and Civilization*. New York: Penguin, 1975.

Treadgold, Warren. *A Concise History of Byzantium*. New York: Palgrave, 2002.

Early Slavs/Eastern Europe

Barford, P. M. *The Early Slavs: Culture and Society in Early Medieval Eastern Europe*. Ithaca, NY: Cornell University Press, 2001.

Cross, Samuel Hazzard. *Slavic Civilization through the Ages*. New York: Russell & Russell, 1963.

Dolukhanov, Pavel M. *The Early Slavs: Eastern Europe from the Initial Settlement to the Kievan Rus*. New York: Longman, 1996.

Dvornik, Francis. *The Slavs in European History and Civilization*. New Brunswick, NJ: Rutgers University Press, 1962.

———. *The Slavs: Their Early History and Civilization*. Boston: American Academy, 1956.

Gojda, Martin. *The Ancient Slavs: Settlement and Society*. Edinburgh: Edinburgh University Press, 1991.

Tachiaos, Anthony-Emil N. *Cyril and Methodius of Thessalonica: The Acculturation of the Slavs*. Crestwood, NY: St. Vladimir's Seminary Press, 2001.

General Histories of Eastern Europe

The Twentieth Century

Crampton, R. J. *Eastern Europe in the Twentieth Century*. London: Routledge, 1994.

Ference, Gregory C., ed. *Chronology of 20th-Century Eastern European History*. Washington, DC: Gale Research, 1994.

Held, Joseph, ed. *The Columbia History of Eastern Europe in the Twentieth Century.* New York: Columbia University Press, 1992.

Before the Coming of Communism

Armour, Ian D. *A History of Eastern Europe: 1740–1918.* New York: Bloomsbury Academic, 2010.
Berend, Ivan T. *Decades of Crisis: Central and Eastern Europe Before World War II.* Los Angeles: University of California Press, 1998.
Crankshaw, Edward. *The Fall of the House of Habsburg.* New York: Penguin, 1963.
MacMillan, Margaret. *Paris 1919: Six Months That Changed the World.* New York: Random House, 2003.
Walters, E. Garrison. *The Other Europe: Eastern Europe to 1945.* Syracuse, NY: Syracuse University Press, 1988.
Wolff, Larry. *Inventing Eastern Europe: The Map of Civilization on the Mind of the Enlightenment.* Stanford, CA: Stanford University Press, 1994.

Under Communism

Brzezinski, Zbigniew. *Out of Control: Global Turmoil on the Eve of the Twenty-first Century.* New York: Scribner, 1983.
Ludlow, Hope T. *The Soviet Union and Eastern Europe.* New York: Scholastic, 1973.
Pittaway, Mark. *Eastern Europe 1939–2000.* Brief Histories Series. London: Arnold, 2004.
Rothschild, Joseph. *Return to Diversity: A Political History of East Central Europe since World War II.* 2nd ed. New York: Oxford University Press, 1993.
Simons, Thomas W. Jr. *Eastern Europe in the Postwar World.* 2nd ed. New York: St. Martin's, 1993.
Swain, Geoffrey, and Nigel Swain. *Eastern Europe since 1945.* New York: St. Martin's, 1993.

The Overthrow of Communism

Ash, Timothy Garton. *The Magic Lantern: The Revolution of '89 Witnessed in Warsaw, Budapest, Berlin and Prague.* New York: Vintage, 1993.
Bailey, J. Martin. *The Spring of Nations: Churches in the Rebirth of Central and Eastern Europe.* New York: Friendship, 1991.
Brown, J. F. *Surge to Freedom: The End of Communist Rule in Eastern Europe.* Durham, NC: Duke University Press, 1991.
Bultman, Bud. *Revolution by Candlelight: The Real Story Behind the Changes in Eastern Europe.* Portland, OR: Multnomah, 1991.
McDermott, Kevin, and Matthew Stibbe, eds. *Revolution and Resistance in Eastern Europe: Challenges to Communist Rule.* New York: Berg, 2006.
Stokes, Gale. *The Walls Came Tumbling Down: Collapse and Rebirth in Eastern Europe.* 2nd ed. New York: Oxford University Press, 2012.

After Communism

Augustinus, Gerasimos. *The National Idea in Eastern Europe: The Politics of Ethnic and Civic Community*. Problems in European Civilization Series. Toronto: D.C. Heath, 1996.
Drakulić, Slavenka. *Café Europa: Life After Communism*. London: Abacus, 1996.
———. *How We Survived Communism and Even Laughed*. New York: Harper, 1991.
Hoffman, Eva. *Exit into History: A Journey through the New Eastern Europe*. New York: Penguin, 1993.
McBride, William L. *Philosophical Reflections on the Changes in Eastern Europe*. New York: Rowman & Littlefield, 1999.
Pond, Elizabeth. *Endgame in the Balkans: Regime Change, European Style*. Washington, DC: Brookings Institution, 2006.
Wedel, Janine R. *Collision and Collusion: The Strange Case of Western Aid to Eastern Europe*. New York: Palgrave, 2001.

Religion in Eastern Europe

Arseniev, Nicholas. *Russian Piety*. Translated by Asheleigh Moorhouse. The Library of Orthodox Theology and Spirituality 3. Crestwood, NY: St. Vladimir's Seminary Press, 1964.
Berglund, Bruce R., and Brian Porter-Szűcs, eds. *Christianity and Modernity in Eastern Europe*. Budapest: Central University Press, 2010.
Bremer, Thomas, ed. *Religion and the Conceptual Boundary in Central and Eastern Europe: Encounters of Faith*. New York: Palgrave MacMillan, 2008.
Crăciun, Maria, Ovidiu Ghitta, and Graeme Murdock, eds. *Confessional Identity in East-Central Europe*. Aldershot, UK: Ashgate, 2002.
Maag, Karin, ed. *The Reformation in Eastern and Central Europe*. Aldershot, UK: Ashgate, 1997.
Mojzes, Paul, Leonard Swidler, and Heinz-Gerhard Justenhoven, eds. *Interreligious Dialogue toward Reconciliation in Macedonia and Bosnia*. Philadelphia: Ecumenical, 2003.
Murzaku, Ines Angeli, ed. *Monasticism in Eastern Europe and the Former Soviet Republics*. London: Routledge, 2016.
———. *Quo Vadis Eastern Europe? Religion, State and Society after Communism*. Europe and the Balkans: A Series of Balkan and East-European Studies 30. Ravenna: Longo Editore, 2009.
Pascal, Pierre. *The Religion of the Russian People*. Translated by Rowan Williams. Crestwood, NY: St. Vladimir's Seminary Press, 1976.
Wien, Ulrich A., and Mihai D. Grigore, eds. *Exportgut Reformation: Ihr Transfer in Kontaktzonen des 16. Jahrhunderts und die Gegenwart evangelischer Kirchen in Europa*. Veröffentlichungen des Instituts für Europäische Geschichte Mainz 113. Göttingen: Vandenhoeck & Ruprecht, 2017.

History of Region: Hungary, Czechoslovakia, Poland

Dmitrieva, Marina, and Karen Lambrecht. *Krakau, Prag und Wien: Funktionen von Metropolen im frühmodernen Staat*. Forschungen zur Geschichte und Kultur des östlichen Mitteleuropa 10. Stuttgart: Franz Steiner, 2000.

"Faith under Fire: The PBS Documentary on the Democratic Revolutions in Poland and Czechoslovakia." Greenwich, CT: Sage, 1993.

Heymann, Frederick G. *Poland and Czechoslovakia*. Englewood Cliffs, NJ: Prentice-Hall, 1966.

Wandycz, Piotr S. *The Price of Freedom: A History of East Central Europe from the Middle Ages to the Present*. London: Routledge, 1993.

Hungary

Donaghy, Gregory, ed. *Canadian Diplomacy and the Hungarian Revolution 1956-1957*. Ottawa, ON: Historical Section, Foreign Affairs Canada, 1957.

Gabori, George. *When Evils Were Most Free*. Translated by Eric Johnson and George Faludy. Toronto: Deneau, 1981.

Mindszenty, József Cardinal. *Memoirs*. Translated by Richard and Clara Winston. New York: Macmillan, 1974.

Osterhaven, M. Eugene. *Kollegium: The Story of Sarospatak*. Zeeland, MI: Holland Litho, 1980.

Porter, Anna. *The Storyteller: A Memoir of Secrets, Magic and Lies*. Toronto: Douglas & McIntyre, 2006.

Sugar, Peter F., Péter Hanák, and Tibor Frank, eds. *A History of Hungary*. Bloomington, IN: Indiana University Press, 1994.

Czechoslovakia (including Czech Republic and Slovakia)

Agnew, Hugh. *The Czechs and the Lands of the Bohemian Crown*. Studies of Nationalities Series. Stanford, CA: Hoover Institution, 2004.

Demetz, Peter. *Prague in Black and Gold: Scenes from the Life of a European City*. New York: Hill and Wang, 1997.

Dery, Dominika. *The Twelve Little Cakes: Memoir of a Prague Childhood*. New York: Riverhead, 2004.

Fawn, Rick. *The Czech Republic: A Nation of Velvet*. Postcommunist States and Nations Series. Amsterdam: Harwood Academic, 2000.

Havel, Václav. *Disturbing the Peace: A Conversation with Karel Hvížďala*. Translated by Paul Wilson. Toronto: Vintage, 1990.

———. *Open Letters: Selected Writings 1965-1990*. Edited by Paul Wilson. New York: Knopf, 1991.

———. *Summer Meditations*. Translated by Paul Wilson. Toronto: Vintage, 1993.

———. *To the Castle and Back*. Translated by Paul Wilson. Toronto: Vintage, 2008.

Kirschbaum, Stanislav J. *A History of Slovakia: The Struggle for Survival*. 2nd ed. New York: Palgrave Macmillan, 1995.

Kovaly, Heda Margolius. *Under a Cruel Star: A Life in Prague 1941–1968*. New York: Holmes & Meier, 1986.
Lau, J. M. *Prague: Then and Now*. San Diego: Thunder Bay, 2007.
Sayer, Derek. *The Coasts of Bohemia: A Czech History*. Princeton, NJ: Princeton University Press, 1998.
Sire, James W. *Václav Havel, The Intellectual Conscience of International Politics: An Introduction, Appreciation & Critique*. Downers Grove, IL: InterVarsity, 2001.
Wright, Cornelia B., ed. *A Thousand Years of Czech Culture: Riches from the National Museum in Prague*. Winston-Salem, NC: distributed by University of Washington Press, 1996.

Poland

Halecki, O. *A History of Poland*. New ed. New York: Barnes & Noble, 1993.
Michener, James A. *Poland*. New York: Random House, 1983.
Zamoyski, Adam. *The Polish Way: A Thousand-Year History of the Poles and Their Culture*. New York: Hippocrene, 1994.

History of Region: The Balkans

Bailey, Douglass W. *Balkan Prehistory: Exclusion, Incorporation and Identity*. London: Routledge, 2000.
Clark, Victoria. *Why Angels Fall: A Journey through Orthodox Europe from Byzantium to Kosovo*. New York: St. Martin's, 2000.
Crampton, R. J. *The Balkans since the Second World War*. New York: Longman, 2002.
Fine, John V. A. Jr. *The Early Medieval Balkans: A Critical Survey from the Sixth to the Late Twelfth Century*. Ann Arbor, MI: University of Michigan Press, 1991.
———. *The Late Medieval Balkans: A Critical Survey from the Late Twelfth Century to the Ottoman Conquest*. Ann Arbor, MI: University of Michigan Press, 1994.
Gerolymatos, André. *The Balkan Wars: Conquest, Revolution and Retribution from the Ottoman Era to the Twentieth Century and Beyond*. New York: Basic, 2002.
Hupchick, Dennis P. *The Balkans: From Constantinople to Communism*. New York: Palgrave, 2002.
Jelavich, Barbara. *History of the Balkans: Eighteenth and Nineteenth Centuries*, Vol. 1. New York: Cambridge University Press, 1983.
Kaplan, Robert D. *Balkan Ghosts: A Journey through History*. New ed. New York: Picador, 2005.
Madgearu, Alexandru. *The Wars of the Balkan Peninsula: Their Medieval Origins*. Toronto: Scarecrow, 2008.
Mazower, Mark. *The Balkans: A Short History*. New York: Modern Library, 2000.
Mojzes, Paul. *Balkan Genocides: Holocaust and Ethnic Cleansing in the Twentieth Century*. New York: Rowman & Littlefield, 2011.
Pavlowitch, Stevan K. *A History of the Balkans, 1804–1945*. New York: Longman, 1999.
Petkov, Kiril. *Infidels, Turks and Women: The South Slavs in the German Mind, ca. 1400–1600*. New York: Lang, 1997.

Reed, Fred A. *Salonica Terminus: Travels into the Balkan Nightmare.* Vancouver, BC: Talonbooks, 1996.
Schevill, Ferdinand. *A History of the Balkans: From the Earliest Times to the Present Day.* New York: Dorset, 1991.
Stavrianos, L. S. *The Balkans since 1453.* New York: Holt, Rinehart and Winston, 1961.
Todorova, Maria, ed. *Balkan Identities: Nation and Memory.* New York: New York University Press, 2004.
———. *Imagining the Balkans.* New York: Oxford University Press, 1997.
Wachtel, Andrew Baruch. *The Balkans in World History.* New York: Oxford University Press, 2008.
White, George W. *Nationalism and Territory: Constructing Group Identity in Southeastern Europe.* New York: Rowman & Littlefield, 2000.

Bulgaria

Crampton, R. J. *A Concise History of Bulgaria.* New York: Cambridge University Press, 1997.
Hupchick, Dennis P. *The Bulgarians in the Seventeenth Century: Slavic Orthodox Society and Culture under Ottoman Rule.* Jefferson, NC: McFarland, 1993.

Romania

Boia, Lucian. *History and Myth in Romanian Consciousness.* Budapest: Central European University Press, 2001.
Bria, Ion. *Romania: Orthodox Identity at a Crossroads of Europe.* Gospel and Cultures Series 3. Geneva: WCC, 1995.
Florescu, Radu R., and Raymond T. McNally. *Dracula, Prince of Many Faces: His Life and His Times.* Toronto: Little, Brown, 1989.
Galloway, George, and Bob Wylie. *Downfall: The Ceausescus and the Romanian Revolution.* London: Futura, 1991.
Hitchins, Keith. *Rumania 1866-1947.* The Oxford History of Modern Europe Series. Oxford: Clarendon, 1994.
Pacera, Ion Mihai. *Red Horizons: The True Story of Nicolae and Elena Ceausescus' Crimes, Lifestyle, and Corruption.* Washington, DC: Regnery Gateway, 1987.

Yugoslavia

Dragnich, Alex N. *Serbs and Croats: The Struggle in Yugoslavia.* New York: Harcourt Brace, 1992.
Hall, Brian. *The Impossible Country: A Journey through the Last Days of Yugoslavia.* New York: Penguin, 1994.
Jelavich, Charles. *South Slav Nationalisms: Textbooks and Yugoslav Union before 1914.* Columbus, OH: Ohio State University Press, 1990.

Ognjenović, Gorana, and Jasna Jozelić, eds. *Tito's Yugoslavia, Stories Untold, Vol. 1: Revolutionary Totalitarianism, Pragmatic Socialism, Transition.* New York: Palgrave Macmillan, 2016.

———, eds. *Tito's Yugoslavia, Stories Untold, Vol. 2: Titoism, Self-Determination, Nationalism, Cultural Memory.* New York: Palgrave Macmillan, 2016.

Perica, Vjekoslav. *Balkan Idols: Religion and Nationalism in Yugoslav States.* Religion and Global Politics Series. New York: Oxford University Press, 2002.

Sörensen, Jens Stilhoff. *State Collapse and Reconstruction in the Periphery: Political Economy, Ethnicity and Development in Yugoslavia, Serbia and Kosovo.* New York: Bergbahn, 2009.

West, Rebecca. *Black Lamb and Grey Falcon: A Journey through Yugoslavia.* New York: Penguin, 1969.

War in the former Yugoslavia

Antonić, Zdravko, ed. *Jasenovac: Proceeedings of 3rd International Conference on Jasenovac.* Translated by Svetlana Mitić. Banja Luka, RS: Svetozar Ćerketa, 2007.

———. *Jasenovac: Proceeedings of 4th International Conference on Jasenovac.* Translated by Svetlana Mitić and Blanka Blagojević. Banja Luka, RS: Svetozar Ćerketa, 2007.

———. *Jasenovac: Proceeedings of Speeches of the 4th International Conference on Jasenovac.* Translated by Svetlana Mitić. Banja Luka, RS: Svetozar Ćerketa, 2008.

Bursać, Dušan. *Angels in Hell.* Banja Luka, RS: Association of World War II former concentration camp Prisoners and their descendants, 2006.

Cohen, Lenard J. *Broken Bonds: The Disintegration of Yugoslavia.* Boulder, CO: Westview, 1993.

———. *Broken Bonds: Yugoslavia's Disintegration and Balkan Politics in Transition.* Boulder, CO: Westview, 1995.

Denitch, Bogdan. *Ethnic Nationalism: The Tragic Death of Yugoslavia.* Rev. ed. Minneapolis: University of Minnesota Press, 1996.

Drakulić, Slavenka. *The Balkan Express: Fragments from the Other Side of War.* New York: Harper, 1993.

———. *They Would Never Hurt a Fly: War Criminals on Trial in the Hague.* New York: Viking, 2004.

Filipović, Zlata. *Zlata's Diary: A Child's Life in Sarajevo.* Translated by Christina Pribichevich-Zorić. New York: Penguin, 1995.

Gjelten, Tom. *Sarajevo Daily: A City and Its Newspaper under Siege.* New York: Harper, 1995.

Job, Cvijeto. *Yugoslavia's Ruin: The Bloody Lessons of Nationalism, a Patriot's Warning.* New York: Rowman & Littlefield, 2002.

Kurspahic, Kemal. *Prime Time Crime: Balkan Media in War and Peace.* Washington, DC: United States Institute of Peace, 2003.

Lukić, Vladimir, ed. *Šušnjar 1941: Proceedings—Papers, Testimonies and Documents.* Translated by Svetlana Mitić and Dragana Ratković. Oštra Luka, RS: "Slovo" Banja Luka, 2008.

Maass, Peter. *Love Thy Neighbor: A Story of War.* New York: Vintage, 1997.

Merrill, Christopher. *Only the Nails Remain: Scenes from the Balkan Wars.* New York: Rowman & Littlefield, 2001.

Mojzes, Paul. *Yugoslavian Inferno: Ethnoreligious Warfare in the Balkans*. New York: Continuum, 1994.
Ramet, Sabrina Petra. *Balkan Babel: The Disintegration of Yugoslavia from the Death of Tito to Ethnic War*. Boulder, CO: Westview, 1996.
Softić, Elma. *Sarajevo Days, Sarajevo Nights*. Translated by Nada Conić. Toronto: Key Porter, 1995.
Sudetic, Chuck. *Blood and Vengeance: One Family's Story of the War in Bosnia*. New York: Penguin, 1999.
Winchester, Simon. *The Fracture Zone: My Return to the Balkans*. New York: Perennial, 1999.

Croatia

Gazi, Stephen. *A History of Croatia*. New York: Barnes and Noble, 1993.
Goldstein, Ivo. *Croatia: A History*. London: McGill-Queen's University Press, 1999.
Gunjević, Lidija, and Boris Gunjević. *Evangelici a ne anđeli: Prepičano stvaranje zajedništva*. Vinkovci, HR: ECRH, 2008.
Tanner, Marcus. *Croatia: A Nation Forged in War*. New Haven, CT: Yale University Press, 1997.
Travirka, Anton. *Dubrovnik: History, Culture, Art Heritage*. Translated by Vjekoslav Suzanić and Stipe Grgas. Kranj, SI: Gorenjski Tisk, 2007.

Bosnia-Herzegovina

Andrić, Ivo. *The Bridge on the Drina*. Translated by Lovett F. Edwards. Chicago: University of Chicago Press, 1977.
Bringa, Tone. *Being Muslim the Bosnian Way: Identity and Community in a Central Bosnian Village*. Princeton, NJ: Princeton University Press, 1995.
Cousens, Elizabeth M., and Charles K. Cater. *Toward Peace in Bosnia: Implementing the Dayton Accords*. International Peace Academy Occasional Paper Series. Boulder, CO: Lynne Rienner, 2001.
Demick, Barbara. *Logavina Street: Life and Death in a Sarajevo Neighborhood*. New York: Spiegel & Grau, 2012.
Donia, Robert J. *Sarajevo: A Biography*. Ann Arbor, MI: The University of Michigan Press, 2006.
Donia, Robert J., and John V. A. Fine Jr. *Bosnia and Herzegovina: A Tradition Betrayed*. New York: Columbia University Press, 1994.
Heleta, Savo. *Not My Turn to Die: Memoirs of a Broken Childhood in Bosnia*. New York: American Management, 2008.
Hunt, Swanee. *This Was Not Our War: Bosnian Women Reclaiming the Peace*. Durham, NC: Duke University Press, 2004.
Malcolm, Noel. *Bosnia: A Short History*. Washington Square, NY: New York University Press, 1994.
Markowitz, Fran. *Sarajevo: A Bosnian Kaleidoscope*. Urbana, IL: University of Illinois Press, 2010.
Mojzes, Paul, ed. *Religion and the War in Bosnia*. Atlanta: Scholars, 1998.

Mousavizadeh, Nader, ed. *The Black Book of Bosnia: The Consequences of Appeasement*. New York: Basic, 1996.
Pinson, Mark, ed. *The Muslims of Bosnia-Herzegovina: Their Historical Development from the Middle Ages to the Dissolution of Yugoslavia*. Cambridge, MA: Harvard University Press, 1996.
Rieff, David. *Bosnia and the Failure of the West*. New York: Touchstone, 1995.
Shatzmiller, Maya, ed. *Islam and Bosnia: Conflict Resolution and Foreign Policy in Multi-Ethnic States*. Kingston, ON: McGill-Queen's University Press, 2002.
Trevinčević, Kenan, and Susan Shapiro. *The Bosnia List: A Memoir of War, Exile, and Return*. New York: Penguin, 2014.

Serbia

Anzulovic, Branimir. *Heavenly Serbia: From Myth to Genocide*. New York: New York University Press, 1999.
Ćirković, Sima M. *The Serbs*. Translated by Vuk Tošić. Malden, MA: Blackwell, 2004.
Doder, Dusko, and Louise Branson. *Milosevic: Portrait of a Tyrant*. New York: Free Press, 1999.
Dragnich, Alex N., and Slavko Todorovich. *The Saga of Kosovo: Focus on Serbian-Albanian Relations*. Eastern European Monographs 170. New York: Columbia University Press, 1984.
Judah, Tim. *The Serbs: History, Myth and the Destruction of Yugoslavia*. New Haven, CT: Yale University Press, 1997.
Laffan, R. G. D. *The Serbs: The Guardians of the Gate*. New York: Dorset, 1989.
Matthias, John, and Vladeta Vučković, translators. *The Battle of Kosovo*. Athens, OH: Ohio University Press, 1987.
Taylor, Scott. *Inat: Images of Serbia & the Kosovo Conflict*. Ottawa, ON: Esprit de Corps, 2000.
Velimirovich, Nicholai. *The Faith of Chosen People*. Translated by Theodore Mika and Steven Scott. A Treasury of Serbian Orthodox Spirituality 2. Grayslake, IL: The Free Serbian Orthodox Diocese of America and Canada, 1988.
———. *The Life of St. Sava*. Translated by Veselin Kesich. Crestwood, NY: St. Vladimir's Seminary Press, 1989.
———. *The Mystery and Meaning of the Battle of Kosovo*. Translated by Theodore Mika and Steven Scott. A Treasury of Serbian Orthodox Spirituality 3. Grayslake, IL: The Free Serbian Orthodox Diocese of America and Canada, 1989.
———. *The Serbian People as a Servant of God*. Translated by Theodore Mika and Steven Scott. A Treasury of Serbian Orthodox Spirituality 1. Grayslake, IL: The Free Serbian Orthodox Diocese of America and Canada, 1988.

Kosovo

Buckley, William Joseph, ed. *Kosovo: Contending Voices in Balkan Interventions*. Grand Rapids: Eerdmans, 2000.
Campbell, Greg. *The Road to Kosovo: A Balkan Diary*. Boulder, CO: Westview, 2000.

Huntley, Paula. *The Hemingway Book Club of Kosovo.* New York: Tarcher/Penguin, 2004.
Judah, Tim. *Kosovo: War and Revenge.* 2nd ed. New Haven, CT: Yale University Press, 2002.
———. *Kosovo: What Everyone Needs to Know.* New York: Oxford University Press, 2008.
King, Iain, and Whit Mason. *Peace at Any Price: How the World Failed Kosovo.* Ithaca, NY: Cornell University Press, 2006.
Malcolm, Noel. *Kosovo: A Short History.* London: Macmillan, 1998.
Mertus, Julie A. *Kosovo: How Myths and Truths Started a War.* Berkeley, CA: University of California Press, 1999.
O'Neill, William G. *Kosovo: An Unfinished Peace.* International Peace Academy Occasional Paper Series. Boulder, CO: Lynne Rienner, 2002.
Schwartz, Stephen. *Kosovo: Background to a War.* London: Anthem, 2000.
Vickers, Miranda. *Between Serb and Albanian: A History of Kosovo.* New York: Columbia University Press, 1998.

North Macedonia

Pavlovski, Jovan and Michel Pavlovski, eds. *Macedonia: Yesterday and Today.* Translated by Zaharija Pavlovska. Skopje: Mi-An, 1998.
Pettifer, James, ed. *The New Macedonian Question.* New York: Palgrave, 2001.
Poulton, Hugh. *Who Are the Macedonians?* 2nd ed. Bloomington, IN: Indiana University Press, 2000.
Williams, Abiodun. *Preventing War: The United Nations and Macedonia.* New York: Rowman & Littlefield, 2000.

Albania

Forest, Jim. *The Resurrection of the Church in Albania: Voices of Orthodox Christians.* Geneva: WCC. 2002.
Murzaku, Ines Angeli. *Returning Home to Rome: The Basilian Monks of Grottaferrrata in Albania.* Rome: Grottaferrata, 2009.
Veronis, Luke. *Go Forth: Stories of Mission and Resurrection in Albania.* Ben Lomond, CA: Conciliar, 2009.

History of Region: Ukraine, Belarus, Russia

Carpini, Friar Giovanni DiPlano. *The Story of the Mongols Whom We Call the Tartars.* Translated by Erik Hildinger. Boston: Branden, 1996.
Chadwick, N. K. *The Beginnings of Russian History: An Enquiry into Sources.* New York: Cambridge University Press, 1966.
Chambers, James. *The Devil's Horsemen: The Mongol Invasion of Europe.* New York: Atheneum, 1985.

Cross, Samuel Hazzard, trans. *The Russian Primary Chronicle*. Cambridge, MA: Harvard University Press, 1930.
Dimnik, Martin. *Mikhail, Prince of Chernigov and Grand Prince of Kiev 1224-1246*. Studies and Texts 52. Toronto: Pontifical Institute of Mediaeval Studies, 1981.
Dmytryshyn, Basil, ed. *Medieval Russia: A Source Book, 850-1700*. 3rd ed. New York: Holt, Rinehart, 1991.
Fedotov, George P. *The Russian Religious Mind (I): Kievan Christianity, The 10th to the 13th Centuries*. The Collected Works of George P. Fedotov, 3. Belmont, MA: Nordland, 1975.
———. *The Russian Religious Mind (II): The Middle Ages, The 13th to the 15th Centuries*. The Collected Works of George P. Fedotov, 4. Belmont, MA: Nordland, 1975.
Plokhy, Serhii. *The Origins of the Slavic Nations: Premodern Identities in Russia, Ukraine, and Belarus*. New York: Cambridge University Press, 2010.
Zenkovsky, Serge A., ed. *Medieval Russia's Epics, Chronicles, and Tales*. New York: Meridian, 1974.

Ukraine

Bociurkiw, Bohdan R. *Ukrainian Churches under Soviet Rule: Two Case Studies*. The Millennium of Christianity in Rus'-Ukraine Series. Boston: Harvard Ukrainian Studies, 1984.
Czumer, William A. *Recollections about the Life of the First Ukrainian Settlers in Canada*. Translated by Louis T. Laychuk. Edmonton, AB: Canadian Institute of Ukrainian Studies, 1981.
Fedoriw, George. *History of the Church in Ukraine*. Translated by Petro Krawchuk. Toronto: "St. Sophia" Religious Association, 1983.
Garnett, Sherman W. *Keystone in the Arch: Ukraine in the Emerging Security Environment of Central and Eastern Europe*. Washington, DC: Carnegie Endowment, 1997.
Goa, David J., ed. *The Ukrainian Religious Experience: Tradition and the Canadian Cultural Context*. Edmonton, AB: Canadian Institute of Ukrainian Studies, 1989.
Gogol, Nikolai Vasilevich. *Village Evenings near Dikanka and Mirgorod*. Translated by Christopher English. New York: Oxford University Press, 1994.
Gregorovich, Andrew. *Chronology of Ukrainian Canadian History*. Toronto: Ukrainian Canadian Committee, 1974.
Gudziak, Boris A. *Crisis and Reform: The Kyivan Metropolitanate, the Patriarchate of Constantinople, and the Genesis of the Union of Brest*. Harvard Series in Ukrainian Studies. Cambridge, MA: Harvard University Press, 1998.
Hosking, Geoffrey A., ed. *Church, Nation and State in Russia and Ukraine*. Edmonton, AB: Canadian Institute of Ukrainian Studies, 1990.
Kappeler, Andreas. *Kleine Geschichte der Ukraine*. Munich: Beck, 1994.
Kappeler, Andreas, Zenon E. Kohut, Frank E. Sysyn, and Mark von Hagen, eds. *Culture, Nation, and Identity: The Ukrainian-Russian Encounter (1600-1945)*. Edmonton, AB: Canadian Institute of Ukrainian Studies, 2003.
Kardash, Peter. *Ukraine and Ukrainians*. Edited by Brett Lockwood. Melbourne: Fortuna, 1988.
Krushelnycky, Askold. *An Orange Revolution: A Personal Journey through Ukrainian History*. London: Harvill Secker, 2006.

Lindheim, Ralph, and George S. N. Luckyj, eds. *Towards an Intellectual History of Ukraine: An Anthology of Ukrainian Thought from 1710 to 1995*. Toronto: University of Toronto Press, 1996.

Luckyj, George S. N. *Ukrainian Literature in the Twentieth Century: A Reader's Guide*. Toronto: University of Toronto Press, 1992.

Magocsi, Paul Robert. *A History of Ukraine: The Land and Its Peoples*. 2nd ed. Toronto: University of Toronto Press, 2010.

———. *Ukraine: An Illustrated History*. Toronto: University of Toronto Press, 2007.

Martynowych, Orest. *Ukrainians in Canada: The Formative Years, 1891–1924*. Edmonton, AB: Canadian Institute of Ukrainian Studies, 1991.

Metropolitan Ilarion. *The Ukrainian Church*. Translated by Orysia Ferbey. Edited by Stephan Jarmus. Winnipeg, MB: Ukrainian Orthodox Church, 1986.

Mykula, W. *The Gun and the Faith: Religion and Church in Ukraine under the Communist Russian Rule*. London: Ukrainian Information, 1969.

Pavlychko, Solomea. *Letters from Kiev*. Translated by Myrna Kostash. Edmonton, AB: Canadian Institute of Ukrainian Studies, 1992.

Pelikan, Jaroslav. *Confessor between East and West: A Portrait of Ukrainian Cardinal Josyf Slipyj*. Grand Rapids: Eerdmans, 1990.

Plokhy, Serhii, and Frank E. Sysyn. *Religion and Nation in Modern Ukraine*. Edmonton, AB: Canadian Institute of Ukrainian Studies, 2003.

Popivchak, Ronald Peter. "Peter Mohila, Metropolitan of Kiev (1633–47): Translation and Evaluation of His 'Orthodox Confession of Faith' (1640)." STD diss., Catholic University of America, 1975.

Potichnyj, Peter J., ed. *Poland and Ukraine: Past and Present*. Edmonton, AB: Canadian Institute of Ukrainian Studies, 1980.

Potichnyj, Peter J., Marc Raeff, Jaroslaw Pelenski, and Gleb N. Žekulin, eds. *Ukraine and Russia in Their Historical Encounter*. Edmonton, AB: Canadian Institute of Ukrainian Studies, 1992.

Potichnyj, Peter J., and Howard Aster, eds. *Ukrainian-Jewish Relations in Historical Perspective*. Edmonton, AB: Canadian Institute of Ukrainian Studies, 1990.

Reid, Anna. *Borderland: A Journey through the History of Ukraine*. Boulder, CO: Westview, 2000.

Rudnytsky, Ivan L. *Essays in Modern Ukrainian History*. Edmonton, AB: Canadian Institute of Ukrainian Studies, 1987.

———, ed. *Rethinking Ukrainian History*. Edmonton, AB: Canadian Institute of Ukrainian Studies, 1981.

Saunders, David. *The Ukrainian Impact on Russian Culture 1750–1850*. Edmonton, AB: Canadian Institute of Ukrainian Studies, 1985.

Ševčenko, Ihor. *The Many Worlds of Peter Mohyla*. The Millennium of Christianity in Rus'-Ukraine Series. Boston: Harvard Ukrainian Studies, 1985.

———. *Ukraine between East and West: Essays on Cultural History to the Early Eighteenth Century*. Edmonton, AB: Canadian Institute of Ukrainian Studies, 1996.

Smal-Stocki, Roman. *Shevchenko Meets America*. Milwaukee: Marquette University Slavic Institute, 1964.

Sorokowski, Andrew. *Ukrainian Catholics and Orthodox in Poland and Czechoslovakia*. The Millennium of Christianity in Rus'-Ukraine Series. Boston: Harvard Ukrainian Studies, 1988.

Subtelny, Orest. *Ukraine; A History*. 2nd ed. Toronto: University of Toronto Press, 1998.
Sysyn, Frank E. *The Ukrainian Orthodox Question in the USSR*. The Millennium of Christianity in Rus'-Ukraine Series. Boston: Harvard Ukrainian Studies, 1987.
Torke, Hans-Joachim, and John-Paul Himka, eds. *German-Ukrainian Relations in Historical Perspective*. Edmonton, AB: Canadian Institute of Ukrainian Studies, 1994.
Velychenko, Stephen. *National History as Cultural Process: A Survey of the Interpretations of Ukraine's Past in Polish, Russian, and Ukrainian Historical Writing from the Earliest Times to 1914*. Edmonton, AB: Canadian Institute of Ukrainian Studies, 1992.
Verba, Lesya, and Bohdan Yasen, eds. *The Human Rights Movement in Ukraine: Documents of the Ukrainian Helsinki Group, 1976–1980*. Baltimore: Smoloskyp, 1980.
Wilson, Andrew. *Ukraine's Orange Revolution*. New Haven, CT: Yale University Press, 2005.
———. *The Ukrainians: Unexpected Nation*. 2nd ed. New Haven, CT: Yale University Press, 2002.
Yekelchyk, Serhy. *The Conflict in Ukraine: What Everyone Needs to Know*. New York: Oxford University Press, 2015.
———. *Ukraine: Birth of a Modern Nation*. New York: Oxford University Press, 2007.

Belarus

Garnett, Sherman W., and Robert Legvold, eds. *Belarus at the Crossroads*. Washington, DC: Carnegie Endowment for International Peace, 1999.

Russia

Adamsky, Dmitry. *Russian Nuclear Orthodoxy: Religion, Politics, and Strategy*. Stanford, CA: Stanford University Press, 2019.
Berdjajew, Nikolai. *Wahrheit und Lüge des Kommunismus*. Translated by J. Schor. Baden-Baden, DE: Holle, 1957.
Berlin, Isaiah. *Russian Thinkers*. New York: Penguin, 1953.
Billington, James H. *The Icon and the Axe: An Interpretive History of Russian Culture*. New York: Vintage, 1970.
DeHaan, Heather D. *Stalinist City Planning: Professionals, Performance, and Power*. Toronto: University of Toronto Press, 2013.
Dziewanowski, M. K. *A History of Soviet Russia and Its Aftermath*. 5th ed. Upper Saddle River, NJ: Prentice Hall, 1997.
Edie, James M., James P. Scanlan, and Mary-Barbara Zeldin, eds. *Russian Philosophy, Vol. 1: The Beginnings of Russian Philosophy—The Slavophiles, The Westernizers*. Chicago: Quadrangle, 1965.
Fedotov, George P., ed. *A Treasury of Russian Spirituality*. The Collected Works of George P. Fedotov, 2. Belmont, MA: Büchervertriebsanstalt, 1988.
Freeze, Gregory L. *The Russian Levites: Parish Clergy in the Eighteenth Century*. Cambridge, MA: Harvard University Press, 1977.

Grey, Ian. *Boris Godunov: The Tragic Tsar.* Newton Abbot, UK: Readers Union, 1974.
Harcave, Sidney. *Russia: A History.* 5th ed. Philadelphia: Lippincott, 1964.
Kohn, Hans, ed. *The Mind of Modern Russia: Historical and Political Thought of Russia's Great Age.* New York: Harper, 1955.
Kovalevsky, Pierre. *Saint Sergius and Russian Spirituality.* Translated by W. Elias Jones. Crestwood, NY: St. Vladimir's Seminary Press, 1976.
Kuvakin, Valery A., ed. *A History of Russian Philosophy: From the Tenth through the Twentieth Century.* 2 vols. Buffalo, NY: Promotheus, 1994.
Lossky, N. O. *History of Russian Philosophy.* London: Allen and Unwin, 1952.
Raeff, Marc, ed. *Peter the Great Changes Russia.* 2nd ed. Problems in European Civilization series. Lexington, MA: Heath, 1972.
———, ed. *Russian Intellectual History: An Anthology.* The Harbrace Series in Russian Area Studies. New York: Harcourt, Brace, 1966.
Riasanovsky, Nicholas V. *Russia and the West in the Teaching of the Slavophiles: A Study of Romantic Ideology.* Gloucester, MA: Smith, 1965.
Schmemann, Alexander, ed. *Ultimate Questions: An Anthology of Modern Russian Religious Thought.* Crestwood, NY: St. Vladimir's Seminary Press, 1977.
Terras, Victor. *A History of Russian Literature.* New Haven, CT: Yale University Press, 1991.
Valliere, Paul. *Modern Russian Theology: Bukharev, Soloviev, Bulgakov—Orthodox Theology in a New Key.* Grand Rapids: Eerdmans, 2000.
Zernov, Nicolas. *The Russian Religious Renaissance of the Twentieth Century.* New York: Harper & Row, 1963.

www.ingramcontent.com/pod-product-compliance
Lightning Source LLC
Chambersburg PA
CBHW021345300426
44114CB00012B/1090

The Unknown Europe